THE UNCHOSEN ONES

THE UNCHOSEN ONES

Diaspora, Nation, and Migration in Israel and Germany

JANNIS PANAGIOTIDIS

INDIANA UNIVERSITY PRESS

This book is a publication of

Indiana University Press
Office of Scholarly Publishing
Herman B Wells Library 350
1320 East 10th Street
Bloomington, Indiana 47405 USA

iupress.indiana.edu

Manufactured in the United States of America

Cataloging information is available from the Library of Congress.

ISBN 978-0-253-04361-0 (hardback)
ISBN 978-0-253-04362-7 (paperback)
ISBN 978-0-253-04364-1 (ebook)

1 2 3 4 5 23 22 21 20 19

For Greta, Felix, Milan, and Sara
And Γιαγιά

CONTENTS

ACKNOWLEDGMENTS

THIS BOOK IS THE OUTCOME of a project that has been with me for more than a decade. The topic of co-ethnic migration first tickled my interest while I was studying Eastern European history at Tübingen University. For my MA thesis, which I completed in 2007 under the supervision of Dietrich Beyrau and Jan Plamper, I studied the historical-legal foundation of Pontian Greek migration from the former Soviet Union to Greece. While writing the thesis, I simultaneously applied for a PhD scholarship at the European University Institute (EUI) in Florence, boldly claiming in my research proposal to turn this single case study into a three-way comparison of Greece, Germany, and Israel. As the reader of this book will realize, Greece somehow got lost on the way to the final product. There were practical reasons for this—not the least of which was the unavailability of archival sources. But there were also conceptual considerations: only in the German-Israeli constellation was it possible to write the kind of comparative, transnational, and entangled history that has become this book.

There is no better place to learn about the merits and challenges of these approaches to history than the EUI, which accepted me as a PhD student in 2007. My project has benefited greatly from the unique international environment of this school and the input I received from distinguished academics with an impressive variety of intellectual and national backgrounds. First and foremost, my thanks go to my thesis supervisor, Philipp Ther, who shaped this work from day one, giving me much-appreciated freedom to pursue my research as I saw fit while providing me with equally appreciated input and guidance when needed. Sebastian Conrad was my second reader for the first three years; Dirk Moses capably replaced him for the final draft. All of them have been helpful ever since. Christian Joppke and Leo Lucassen were external members of my thesis committee and provided valuable advice from which I greatly benefited while turning the thesis into a book. Additional thanks go to Tony Molho, Kiran Patel, Antonella Romano, and Steve Smith, who hosted me in the stimulating intellectual environment of their thesis writing seminars.

The Israeli part of this project could not have been completed without my ten-month research stay at the Bucerius Institute for Research of Contemporary German History and Society at the University of Haifa in the 2010/2011 academic year. In Israel, too, I owe gratitude to many people. Sandy Kedar agreed to supervise me and thus gave me the opportunity to come to the Bucerius Institute in the first place. I also benefited from the input and ideas of Angel Chorapchiev, Yolande Cohen, Sagit Mor, Amos Morris-Reich, Iris Nachum, Dalia Ofer, Ilan Saban, and Yfaat Weiss. Special mention needs to be made of my Hebrew teachers Chava Sommer and Mina Ben Meir of the Haifa University Ulpan, as well as Carmit Horev at the Jewish community in Florence, whose amazing teaching abilities enabled me to learn sufficient Hebrew to study primary sources and secondary literature. This list would be incomplete without thanking Lea Dror-Batalion for keeping the Bucerius Institute up and running.

The Institute for Migration Research and Intercultural Studies (IMIS) at Osnabrück University, where I took the position in 2014 of Junior Professor of Migration and Integration of Germans from Russia, has been the perfect place to further develop this book as a work of not only comparative and transnational history but also of migration history and interdisciplinary migration studies. Among many able and inspiring colleagues that I have been privileged to work with for the past years, I would like to single out Marcel Berlinghoff, Sebastian Musch, Jochen Oltmer, Andreas Pott, Christoph Rass, and Frank Wolff. This book has become much better thanks to their input.

My work would have been much harder without capable archivists directing me to the right kind of material. While they deserve a collective thank you, I would like to single out Albrecht Ernst and Hermann Schäffner at the Hauptstaatsarchiv Stuttgart, who allowed me to use classified materials up to the year 1990. Among the archivists who assisted me in Israel I would like to make particular mention of Galia Weissman at the Israel State Archives in Jerusalem. Diane Afoumado of the ITS Research Branch at the United States Holocaust Memorial Museum in Washington, DC, first introduced me to the treasure trove that is the International Tracing Service (ITS) Digital Archive, which made many of the cases discussed in chapter 3 come to life. Henning Borggräfe of the ITS in Bad Arolsen was helpful with some last-minute data research.

My work would have been impossible without generous institutional funding. The German Academic Exchange Service (DAAD) provided me with a long-term PhD fellowship at the EUI as well as a return fellowship after completion. The EUI provided a write-up grant for the final year as well as financial support for research missions. The ZEIT Stiftung Ebelin und Gerd Bucerius funded my ten-month research stay in Haifa. In Osnabrück, I benefit from funding provided by the Bundesbeauftragte für Kultur und Medien (BKM) and the University of Osnabrück. I am grateful to all of them.

Over the years, I have talked about my work to many people in many different conferences and workshops, making it hard to pinpoint the contribution each one has made to the final outcome. I would like to highlight the history *Kroužeks* at the University of California, Berkeley, in 2008 and 2011, which I attended upon invitation from Mark Keck-Szajbel; the 2011 workshop at Cambridge University on "Migration, Mobility and Movement in Modern German History," organized by Richard J. Evans, Victoria Harris, Barbara Koenczoel, and David Motadel; the 2011 German Studies Association (GSA) panel on "Yugoslavs in Germany" at the GSA annual conference, where Rita Chin commented on what was to become the German part of chapter 2; the 2014 workshop on "Medical Selection Examinations during the Recruitment of Work-Related Migrants in Europe between 1950 and 1990," organized by Sascha Topp and Volker Roelcke at the University of Giessen, which taught me a lot about "medical borders"; and the 2016 German-Israeli Frontiers of Humanities (GISFOH) Symposium "Witnessing and Knowing: Challenging Re/Sources of Knowledge" in Potsdam, where I could put my ideas to the test in front of a critical Israeli and German audience. Special thanks are due to Maike Lehmann for inviting me to this particularly inspiring forum.

Significant parts of chapter 2 have previously been published as "Sifting Germans from Yugoslavs: Co-Ethnic Selection, Danube Swabian Migrants, and the Contestation of Aussiedler Immigration in West Germany in the 1950s and 1960s," in *Migrations in the German Lands, 1500–2000*, edited by Jason Coy, Jared C. Poley, and Alexander Schunka (New York: Berghahn, 2016), 209–226. Portions of chapters 3 and 5 have appeared in "'The Oberkreisdirektor Decides Who Is a German': Jewish Immigration, German Bureaucracy, and the Negotiation of National Belonging (1953–1990)," *Geschichte und Gesellschaft* 38, no. 3 (July–September 2012): 503–533. This book has also benefited from input I received from the editors and reviewers of these individual pieces.

This manuscript has undergone several rounds of editing and linguistic revision at different stages. For their efforts I would like to thank Kim Friedlander, Mark Jones, and Charlotte Adèle Murphy. The creation of the maps in chapter 3 was in the able hands of Lukas Hennies, my former research assistant in Osnabrück and one of the few people I know who is good with computers *and* history. Grete Binder, Judith Bucher, Joscha Hollmann, Micha Keiten, and Lars Kravagna also contributed as research assistants. Ferenc Laczó kindly helped procure the rights for the Floris chocolate factory poster from the Hungarian Museum of Trade and Tourism that is reproduced in chapter 3. I also thank Gesine Wallem for providing the image of the Friedland administrative archive reproduced in chapter 1 and Gerald Volkmer of the Bundesinstitut für Kultur und Geschichte der Deutschen im Östlichen Europa (BKGE) in Oldenburg for the uncomplicated granting of reproduction rights.

I was very happy to see my book accepted into the perfectly suitable forum of the Indiana University Press German Jewish Cultures series. I am most grateful to series co-editor Iris Idelson-Shein for making this happen. At IUP, I was lucky to collaborate on the production of the book with Dee Mortensen, Darja Malcolm-Clarke, Paige Rasmussen, David Hulsey, and Rhonda Van der Dussen. I particularly appreciated Dee's inspired choice of title, which elegantly captures the essence of this book. Michael Taber ably produced the index.

While personal thanks are better delivered in person than on paper, it is also true that the outcome of this years-long project would have been very different without the contribution—academic and otherwise—of many friends and colleagues at various times in many different places. Always at the risk of unfairly leaving someone out, I would like to mention in particular and in alphabetical order: Alex Breuer, Thomas Cauvin, Jozefien de Bock, Emmanuel Deonna, Stefan Ferrari, Luma Gatejel, Pablo del Hierro, Manuel Honisch, Mats Ingulstad, Mark Keck-Szajbel and family, Isabell Kmen, Joris Larik, Lucas Lixinski, Enrico Lucca, Giovanni Mazzoni, Martin Müller, Max Mutschler, Aga Oleszak, Alanna O'Malley, Marco Panchetti, Michael Panzram, Tobias Rupprecht, Annica Starke, Susanne Stein, Costy Vaiani Lisi, Antoine Vandemoortele, and Misha Velizhev.

Finally, it should be said that transnational research works best with a transnational family in the background. I am immensely grateful for everything to my parents, Margarete and Kostas Panagiotidis in Korbach, Germany, and to my sister Elena Panagiotidis and my brother-in-law Stefan Kube in Zurich, Switzerland. And while this book was in the making, I have also made a family of my own. The biggest *gracias* goes to Eva Garcia Moran and Greta Panagiotidis Garcia, who make all of this worthwhile.

NOTE ON FOREIGN TERMS, TRANSLATION, AND TRANSLITERATION

THIS BOOK INCLUDES QUITE A few foreign-language terms in both Hebrew and German. Frequently used words like *Aliyah, Olim, Klitah, Aussiedler, Aussiedlung,* and *Landsmannschaft* are only italicized at their first mention and subsequently appear in roman type. I do, however, consistently italicize legal terms such as *Volkszugehörigkeit, Volkstum, Bekenntnis,* and *Leom*. Both Hebrew and German terms included in the English text are generally capitalized.

When quoting Hebrew terms in their original, for the sake of readability I have generally opted for phonetic transcription instead of a standardized transliteration. I do not distinguish between characters that represent the same sound in Modern Hebrew but would have to be distinguished in an accurate transliteration (e.g., *tet* and *tav, kaf* and *kuf*). Similarly, I do not distinguish between the silent consonants *alef* and *ayin* but simply transcribe them according to the vowel sound that they assume. I do, however, write the silent *he* at the end of a word (e.g., *Aliyah*), unless there is an accepted spelling without it (e.g., *halacha* rather than *Halachah*). The letter *het* is generally represented as *ch* (as in Scottish *loch*) rather than *ḥ* or *h*, except in terms or names with a commonly accepted transcription (e.g., *Herut, Yitzhak,* but *chisul, chalutzim, mizrach*). In general, I have tried to use accepted and easily recognizable transcriptions of personal names. Definite articles and prepositions are distinguished from the word of reference by means of a hyphen (e.g., *chok ha-shvut, mosad la-teum*). Translations of quotes are my own unless otherwise noted. If there was an official English translation available (e.g., of laws), then I have used it. Monographs and articles are cited with their bibliographically valid parallel English title, omitting the Hebrew original. In case no such title was given, the translation is also my own. Sources from Israeli archives are generally in Hebrew and from German archives in German unless otherwise noted.

LIST OF ABBREVIATIONS

AA	Auswärtiges Amt (German Foreign Office)
AAG	Aussiedleraufnahmegesetz (Law for the Reception of Aussiedler)
Argeflü	Arbeitsgemeinschaft der Landesflüchtlingsverwaltungen (Committee of Refugee Administrations of the Federal States)
BAA	Bundesausgleichsamt (Federal Office for the Implementation of the Equalization of Burdens Act)
BdV	Bund der Vertriebenen (Federation of Expellees)
BEG	Bundesentschädigungsgesetz (Federal Restitution Law)
BKA	Bundeskanzleramt (Federal Chancellery)
BMGF	Bundesministerium für Gesamtdeutsche Fragen (Federal Ministry for All-German Questions)
BMI	Bundesministerium des Innern/Bundesinnenministerium (Federal Interior Ministry)
BMVt	Bundesministerium für Vertriebene, Flüchtlinge und Kriegsgeschädigte/Bundesvertriebenenministerium (Federal Expellee Ministry)
BSASF	Bayerisches Staatsministerium für Arbeit und Soziale Fürsorge (Bavarian Ministry for Labor and Social Welfare)
BSMI	Bayerisches Staatsministerium des Innern (Bavarian Interior Ministry)
BSVA	Bundesstelle für Verwaltungsangelegenheiten (Federal Office for Administrative Matters)

BVA	Bundesverwaltungsamt (Federal Administration Office)
BVerfG	Bundesverfassungsgericht (Federal Constitutional Court)
BVerwG	Bundesverwaltungsgericht (Federal Administrative Court)
BVFG	Bundesvertriebenengesetz (Federal Expellee Law)
BW	Baden-Württemberg
CC	Coordination Committee
CDU	Christlich-Demokratische Union (Christian Democratic Union)
CIS	Commonwealth of Independent States
CSCE	Conference for Security and Cooperation in Europe
DRK	Deutsches Rotes Kreuz (German Red Cross)
DVL	Deutsche Volksliste
FDP	Freie Demokratische Partei (Free Democratic Party)
FRG	Federal Republic of Germany
Gahal	Gush cherut-liberalim (Freedom-Liberals Bloc)
GDR	German Democratic Republic
GG	Grundgesetz (Basic Law)
GK	Generalkonsulat (Consulate General)
Hadash	Ha-chazit ha-demokratit le-shalom u-le-shivion (The Democratic Front for Peace and Equality)
HASt	Heimatauskunftstelle
HIAS	Hebrew Immigrant Aid Society
HOK	Heimatortskartei
IM	Innenministerium (Interior Ministry)
ITS	International Tracing Service
JAE	Jewish Agency Executive
KfbG	Kriegsfolgenbereinigungsgesetz (Law for the Settlement of War Consequences)
LAG	Lastenausgleichsgesetz (Equalization of Burdens Act)
MAGS	Ministerium für Arbeit, Gesundheit und Soziales (Ministry for Labor, Health, and Social Affairs)
Maki	Miflegah kommunistit israelit (Israeli Communist Party)
Mapai	Mifleget poalei eretz yisrael (Workers' Party of the Land of Israel)
Mapam	Mifleget ha-poalim ha-meuchedet (United Workers Party)
MVFK BW	Ministerium für Vertriebene, Flüchtlinge und Kriegsgeschädigte Baden-Württemberg (Expellee Ministry of Baden-Württemberg)
NRP	National Religious Party

NRW	Nordrhein-Westfalen (North Rhine-Westphalia)
ORT	Obshchestvo remeslennogo i zemledel'cheskogo truda (Society for Handicrafts and Agricultural Work)
Rakach	Reshimah kommunistit chadashah (New Communist List)
RP	Regierungspräsidium (Regional Council)
Shas	Shomrei-torah sfaradim (Sephardic Torah Guardians)
SMV	Schutzmachtvertretung (Interests Section)
SPD	Sozialdemokratische Partei Deutschlands (Social Democratic Party of Germany)
TPO	Travel Permit Office
UN	United Nations
VDA	Verein für das Deutschtum im Ausland (Association for Germans Abroad)

THE UNCHOSEN ONES

INTRODUCTION

The Importance of the Unchosen Ones

CHOCOLATE MANUFACTURER JOSEF FLORIS ARRIVED in West Germany in 1958. A survivor of Mauthausen concentration camp, he was born into a Jewish family in Budapest in 1905 but converted to Catholicism in 1943 while performing forced labor in one of Hungary's "labor battalions." Floris and his wife, Elisabeth, married soon after he had been liberated and had returned to Budapest. In 1957 the couple left their native Hungary for Israel, where Elisabeth's mother lived, and later they moved to West Germany. There Josef applied for ethnic German *Aussiedler* status, which would secure him German citizenship and certain integration benefits. His application was rejected by the administration and courts at several levels of jurisdiction. Although the judges acknowledged that Floris and his family spoke German and partook in German culture, they ruled that he had not publicly declared himself German back in Hungary and therefore lacked the *Bekenntnis* (literally "avowal" or "confession") necessary to be considered German. Floris did not receive the desired recognition until October 1968, more than ten years after filing his first application.[1]

Around the same time, Barbara K. (born in 1914) and her family from the Croatian town of Komletinci were refused admission to West Germany twice, in 1963 and 1968. Even though the authorities acknowledged that both Barbara and her husband, Marko, were of German descent on the maternal side, it was ruled that they were Croatian, not German, because they spoke Croatian with their four children.[2]

In a different country and context, Oswald Rufeisen, who was also known by his monastic name Brother Daniel, wanted to obtain Israeli citizenship under the Law of Return—that is, based on his ancestral right as a Jew. Yet despite his birth to Jewish parents, his Zionist upbringing in interwar Poland, and his self-declared belonging to the Jewish people, the Israeli Supreme Court refused to grant Rufeisen citizenship in 1962, because he had converted to Christianity while in hiding during the war and had become a monk.[3] Rufeisen eventually became an Israeli citizen through regular naturalization for foreigners, without, however, being recognized as a Jew.[4]

Some years earlier, in 1948, Misa Giulia B., a young Jewish woman from Tripoli, Libya, tried to make her way through Italy to newly independent Israel, where her husband, Giulio, already lived. Although no one questioned her Jewish identity, she was initially disqualified for immigration because she was suffering from tuberculosis. After three years of treatment in different Jewish facilities near Florence and Rome and receiving professional training as a dressmaker, Misa was finally cleared for immigration to Israel in August 1951 and left Italy soon after to join her husband.[5]

These individual cases, which we will encounter again and discuss in more detail in subsequent chapters, represent a type of migration characteristic of the twentieth century: co-ethnic migration. Coming from a diasporic situation abroad, co-ethnic migrants seek admission to a country and/or its citizenship on the basis of their purported ethnicity—understood as ethno-national, ethno-religious, or otherwise ethno-cultural identifications beyond political citizenship—which is identical to that of the titular nation in the country of destination.[6] Israel is the most famous case of a country granting immigration privileges on such grounds. The state was founded in 1948 with the express purpose of "ingathering the exiles" and thus of "returning" a whole people to its "historical homeland." This notion found expression in the 1950 Law of Return (*chok ha-shvut*), which famously postulated that "every Jew has the right to immigrate to this country."[7]

Although Israel's open invitation to a global diaspora to migrate to its homeland is certainly unique, the phenomenon of co-ethnic immigration is not. A remarkable parallel situation can be found in the Federal Republic of Germany. Both countries were hallmark cases of states granting co-ethnic immigration privileges during the postwar decades. From independence in 1948 until the end of the Cold War in the late 1980s, Israel received about two million immigrants from all continents. About half of the immigrants to Israel were from Europe (both East and West), and the other half hailed from Arab states in Asia and Africa and from the Americas.[8] During the same period, about two million ethnic Germans relocated to West Germany. By the Cold War–inspired political definition, they came exclusively from the Communist states of Central, Eastern, and Southeastern Europe.[9] As part of the mass exodus of ethnic minorities from the disintegrating Eastern Bloc and the Soviet Union in the late

1980s and early 1990s, Germany (by then reunited) and Israel accommodated, respectively, two million and one million co-ethnic immigrants.[10]

But co-ethnic immigration to Israel and West Germany has more in common than the geographic origin of many of the migrants. Both of these countries use a distinctive terminology to speak about co-ethnic migration: it is not simply immigration, but *Aliyah* ("ascent") in Israel and *Aussiedlung* (resettlement) in Germany. It is also subject to particular legal arrangements providing access to national citizenship for diasporic co-ethnics, called respectively *Olim* ("those going up"; singular *Oleh*) and *Aussiedler* ("out-settlers" or resettlers). These "laws of return" provide precise definitions of who qualifies as a co-ethnic. In Germany, an ethnic German (*deutscher Volkszugehöriger*) is someone "who has identified in his country of origin as belonging to the German *Volkstum* (*wer sich in seiner Heimat zum deutschen Volkstum bekannt hat*), provided that this self-identification is backed up by certain characteristics like descent, language, upbringing, culture."[11] The Israeli Law of Return in its original 1950 version simply extended the right of immigration to "every Jew," without specifying how this term was to be understood. The traditional halachic definition of a Jew as "a person who was born of a Jewish mother or has become converted to Judaism and who is not a member of another religion" was not added until 1970.[12] Whatever the exact definition, these rules were subject to interpretation by various specialized state bureaucracies. When doubts arose, the legal system made the final determination. These institutions thus had the power to accept or reject applicants for co-ethnic status.

Surprisingly, all four applicants described earlier were rejected by state authorities, at least initially. This contrasts with the Israeli Law of Return's promise of legally guaranteed immigration for every Jew. Their rejection also confounds the notion in the literature that the German co-ethnic immigration regime was "an open-door policy for anyone from Eastern Europe and the Soviet Union who could claim, however remotely, German origin."[13] These four migrants were rejected from co-ethnic status despite their suitable cultural traits (in Josef Floris's case), their descent (in Barbara K.'s case), or their descent *and* self-identification (Brother Daniel). In Misa Giulia B.'s case, even undisputed Jewishness could not outweigh her poor health. The doors were clearly not unconditionally open. Some had to force them open; for others, they remained closed.

To be sure, none of these four cases are typical in the sense that their experience would match that of the majority of co-ethnic migrants to either country. Most Aussiedler to Germany and Olim to Israel did not encounter comparable troubles in gaining recognition, and their applications did not cause major complications in either the administration or the courts. This book concerns those whose applications did. I argue that it is precisely such marginal cases that allow us to detect the limits of each country's co-ethnic commitment and question its boundaries of belonging. These cases forced the nations' respective gatekeepers to explicitly spell out why someone was or was not admitted, thereby drawing boundaries around the nations while giving sharper contours to their respective cores. By deciding who did not belong, it also became clearer who did as a matter of course. It was the unchosen ones who defined the chosen ones.

THE TRANSNATIONAL PRAXEOLOGY OF MIGRATION REGIMES

Co-ethnic immigration involves a process of definition and identification. If every Jew has the right to immigrate to Israel, the question inevitably arises: Who is a Jew? And how can one recognize a Jew? Analogously, if Germany accepts ethnically German immigrants, it faces the problem of establishing who could be a German. Rogers Brubaker and Jaeeun Kim have described the collective constitution of co-ethnic transborder populations by states as a "contingent, contested, variable, and revocable" politics of identification.[14] When it comes to managing co-ethnic migration, the theoretical issue of defining ethnic belonging on an aggregate group level turns into the practical challenge of identifying a prospective individual immigrant as someone of a particular ethnicity. Therefore, if a state wants to know whether a person seeking entry is eligible as a German, as a Jew, or whatever the case may be, it needs gatekeeping institutions to enter the "murky terrain of examining individual 'identity' claims" and conduct the screening.[15] If we think of nation-states as exclusive clubs, these institutions are the bouncers conducting checks at the entrance. Yet rather than screening for adequate shoes and attire, they are interested in the ethnic affiliation of the people queuing outside. How these bouncers allowed entry to or turned people away from the club—in other words, "unchose" them—is the central issue analyzed in this book.

But of course ethnic screening by state institutions is not the work of muscular men wearing sunglasses and suits. In the cases under examination here, the bouncers were mainly administrators and judges, sometimes also expellee activists, doctors, and rabbis. Their screening was part of a bureaucratic and jurisdictional process that brings the workings of the migration regime into focus. The migration regime can be understood "as a model to describe and to understand a complex and decentralized power formation," an "arena" or "power-based contact zone" in which state representatives, experts, civil society actors, and the migrants themselves negotiate migration.[16] The way individual cases such as the ones outlined above were treated serves as a focal point to analyze the production of ethnicity within this setting.

This analysis requires transcending the letter of the law defining belonging and delving deeper into how migration control and management work on the ground, in offices and courts, and in the direct encounters between state representatives and migrants.[17] In short, it requires breaking open the black box that is the "politics of identification" involved in co-ethnic migrant recognition. Conceptualized in this agency-based way, this politics is not simply a one-way street of state institutions unilaterally exercising their "power to name, identify, define, and demarcate; to classify and categorize; to specify authoritatively who is who, and what is what."[18] Rather, identification as co-ethnic is the outcome of the interplay between the actions of individuals—bureaucrats, lawyers, and experts but also, and crucially, migrants—who act within the institutional structures of the migration regime. In a circular process of reflexive structuration, these structures—including immigration law, bureaucracy, and the courts—shape individual actions, while these very actions simultaneously reproduce and alter the structures of the regime, including the definitions and meaning of ethnicity and nationhood.[19] Through this process, different, potentially competing visions of belonging embraced by different actors come to interact. Based on this praxeology of the migration regime, this book explains how German and Israeli citizenship and nationhood were produced through migration regime practices.

In methodological terms, the way this study is set up calls for a simultaneous comparative and transnational approach.[20] The comparison is based on the observation of a common phenomenon, the ethnicity-based admission of immigrants in both Germany and Israel. Germany is analyzed against the Israeli "model case," as it were, of an ideological project of diaspora return to its historical homeland. In cross-case synchronic perspective, the comparison allows us to identify the similarities and differences in the respective policies and practices of admitting immigrants and defining national membership. In addition, the analysis involves an element of intracase diachronic comparison of how the cases evolved over time.

Yet, crucially, these regime practices of delineating nations must also be understood as a transnational process. Because they deal with a border-transcending phenomenon, migration regime practices are transnational by definition.[21] In the context of co-ethnic migration, the movement of people across borders brings the "regimes of ethnicity" in the countries of origin and the receiving countries into dialogue.[22] The definition of membership in one place—say, Russia—becomes relevant in the receiving countries as gatekeeping institutions are forced to decide whether someone who counted as German or Jewish there should also count as such in Germany or Israel. The receiving country may choose to reject, ignore, or incorporate such third-party definitions of belonging. Moreover, migrants like Josef Floris, who claimed membership in both Israel as a Jew and in Germany as a German, brought the two receiving countries into direct contact. The historical entanglement between the two nations is thus an additional factor that drives the dynamic of the comparison, because they mutually shaped each other's recognition practices.

Analyzing co-ethnic migration from this agency-based regime perspective implies a shift from literature that, following Rogers Brubaker's seminal *Citizenship and Nationhood in France and Germany,* sees co-ethnic migration policies as the result of preexisting "ethno-cultural" conceptions of nationhood and citizenship.[23] Rather than asking what kind of understanding of nationhood co-ethnic migration expresses, the issue at stake here is how practices of recognizing co-ethnic migrants shape conceptions of ethnicity, ethno-national belonging, and state citizenship. This approach also makes it possible to deconstruct the notions of ethno-cultural nationhood that scholars have used to describe German and Israeli and, more recently, in fact any kind of European conceptions of the nation.[24] Pieter Judson, for instance, claims that "wherever we encounter it in mid-twentieth-century Europe, nationalism rested on the idea of a prior national community defined by shared culture if not ethnicity."[25] This quote already hints at the prevalent uncertainty about the exact nature of the components that make up these national communities. While Judson appears to distinguish culture and ethnicity, other authors lump them together under the label "ethno-cultural." One publication, for instance, defines "ethno-cultural citizenship" as "driven by conceptions or understandings of membership that celebrate ethnic descent and shared ethno-cultural identity."[26]

In this book, I attempt to take apart this package, which appears to include more exclusive (ethnic) and—potentially—more inclusive (cultural) criteria. Moreover, as the cases described above indicate, there are additional components to be considered. Josef Floris was culturally German but was initially excluded from recognition because he lacked a statement of self-avowal (*Bekenntnis*) as German—essentially a "civic" criterion alluding to Ernest Renan's famous notion of the nation as a "daily plebiscite."[27] Barbara K. had German ancestors and could thus be considered a member of the ethnic community of descent, but she did not speak German. Brother Daniel had Jewish ancestors and identified as Jewish but had changed religion. Descent, self-identification, culture, language, and religion—civic as well as ethnic and cultural criteria—were thus all part of the equation whose solution promised to yield national belonging. Misa Giulia B.'s case further indicates that non-ethnic criteria such as health and fitness—and, on a related note, class—could also become part of this equation. In cases like hers, being Jewish turned into a necessary but not sufficient condition for becoming Israeli.

Rather than postulating that ideal types of civic, ethnic, or ethno-cultural conceptions of nationhood translate into citizenship practices, I ask in this study how historical actors combined different markers of belonging to produce co-ethnics. Based on a transnational and agency-based analysis of ethnic screening practices, I propose an understanding of ethnicity not simply as a unilateral act of definition imposed by the state but as a relational category produced by the interplay of state gatekeepers, civil society actors, migrants, and the migrants' countries of origin—each of which embraced a competing vision of ethnic and national belonging. Different actors within the migration regime had at their disposal varying degrees of agency and power to define, which were subject to constant renegotiation. In the end, the answer to the questions Who is a Jew? and Who is a German? depended on who got to define who was a Jew and who was a German.

(TRANS)NATIONAL HISTORIES FROM THE MARGINS

Studying the entangled history of German and Jewish co-ethnic migration contributes to a broader historiographical trend toward decentralizing and transnationalizing national and nation-state-centered historiographies. Rather than treating nation-states as given, self-contained units, this book focuses on the ways they grappled with the ongoing fuzziness of national boundaries. This approach entails approaching national histories from their respective margins, which in both cases lay beyond the confines of postwar borders. Such an approach complements existing studies on diasporic Israeli nation building among Jewish Displaced Persons in postwar Europe as well as work on making an Israeli nation out of "veterans" and "newcomers."[28] A comparable transnational perspective on the German nation—and on postwar Germany in particular—is still less common.[29] While the complicated relationship between the "two Germanies" is a well-studied topic, postwar German history is still explicitly or implicitly confined to the two states west of the Oder-Neisse line. With this geographic focus, the Central, Eastern, and Southeastern European dimension of German history—which is not just the history of the German nation-state—disappears from view. This book brings these "marginal" dimensions to the center of nation-state-centered historiographies.

The fuzziness of national boundaries in each case was a function of the different ways in which historically contested, undetermined, and deeply entangled national entities such as "the Jews" and "the Germans" (re)consolidated into territorial nationhood after the Second World War. This implied that there were uncertainties about the borders of the respective national territories, the boundaries of the corresponding transterritorial ethno-nations, and the relationship between nation-states and diasporas. The foundation of the State of Israel in 1948 marked the first time in modern history that the traditionally stateless, ethno-religiously defined diaspora nation of the Jews acquired a state to call its own. Although its exact territorial boundaries were and still are contested, Israel's foremost task was to define its relationship to the Jewish diaspora. Through its Law of Return, Israel turned every Jew in the world into a potential dual national. At the same time, the very term *Jew*—with its multiple religious, ethnic, and ethno-religious meanings, none of which were explicitly spelled out in the original law—introduced an important element of ambiguity about the target group of Israel's co-ethnic commitment.

Germany, in turn, had become a nation-state in 1871. However, this "Lesser German" (*kleindeutsch*) state never encompassed all Germans (or rather, all speakers of German).[30] Nazi plans to institute a "Greater German" (*großdeutsch*) empire had failed. After the Second World War, Germany's territorial shape was more precarious than ever, because the country had lost significant parts of its territory in the east and was divided into a western and an eastern part. Of the two postwar German states, only the Federal Republic claimed direct succession to the previous form of statehood. Part of this claim to continuity was offering membership to German citizens and ethnic Germans beyond the new borders—though not on a global scale, but only in the Central, Eastern, and Southeastern European territories where Nazi empire building had given way to Soviet hegemony. The German Democratic Republic, by contrast, was intent on stressing discontinuity with previous forms of statehood, striving to become a new "socialist nation."[31] Though not completely disinterested in ethnic German populations beyond its borders, East Germany never instituted a formal co-ethnic policy and remained a marginal player in this migratory scenario, receiving no more than 150,000 Germans from other socialist states in Eastern Europe during the 40 years of its existence.[32] Part of the claim to discontinuity was also the German Democratic Republic's early renunciation of the territories east of the Oder-Neisse-line in the 1950 Treaty of Görlitz. The Federal Republic of Germany, by contrast, kept the issue of the Eastern

Territories open until the Two Plus Four Agreement in 1990—a fact that would significantly shape its co-ethnic policy during the postwar period.

Beyond these specific histories of each case, the renegotiation of Jewish and German nationhood after the Second World War was an intertwined process, despite the preceding violent separation through genocide. It sat at the juncture of two interrelated, long-term developments that affected both Jews and Germans and joined them in a common historical macrocontext. The first was the formation of modern national identities, which had been going on since the early nineteenth century and had by no means come to an end by the middle of the twentieth century. Jews and Germans (as well as other nations) were tied to each other in this process as "problematic others," within nation-states as well as within the multiethnic settings of Central and Eastern Europe.

The second, related development was the "unmixing of populations" concomitant with the demise and/or nationalization of multiethnic empires and the ensuing national reordering of imperial spaces beginning in the late nineteenth century. This process started with the European continental empires of the Ottomans, the Habsburgs, and the Romanovs; continued with the European overseas empires in North Africa and the Middle East; and ended with the dissolution of the last multiethnic empire of the twentieth century, the Soviet Union. Postwar co-ethnic migration was in many ways a continuation of this migratory unmixing. As Jews and Germans from the nationalizing postimperial states moved to "their" nation-states, the multiethnic frontiers of Central and Eastern Europe and of the European colonial empires became inscribed in the definitions of nationhood and belonging at work in postwar Germany and Israel. At the same time, the often uncertain lines dividing Germans and Jews in these settings remained relevant well into the postwar period, as Eastern European Jews chose to migrate to Germany rather than to Israel (or often migrated to Germany via Israel) and thus defied the clear assignment to "their" national homeland. The shared history of Germans and Jews within and beyond the borders of the German state did not come to an end with the Shoah.

THE LONG SHADOW OF "OLD HISTORY"

In many ways, postwar West Germany and Israel were heirs to the "old history" of Germans and Jews, to their once allegedly symbiotic and subsequently genocidal entanglement.[33] Shared history thus implies not only a vision of peaceful coexistence or even symbiosis but also, and crucially, hostility and division (both these dimensions are captured in the German notion of *geteilte*

Geschichte as both "shared" and "divided"). Within and beyond the boundaries of the German Empire, the formation of modern Jewish and German national identities was an interwoven process spanning more than a century, ever since nationalism started to hold sway over European collective imaginations and self-conceptions and emancipation unsettled the traditional ethno-religious identity of Jewish communities. From early on, thinkers of German nationalism saw the Jews as an important and problematic "other" against whom to define their "own."[34] At the same time, the progressive loss of Jewish ethno-religious autonomy and the requirements of a new national society raised the issue of a modernized Jewish identity—as a religious denomination, like Catholicism or Protestantism, or as an ethnicity.[35]

As a consequence of these transformations, the compatibility of Germanness and Jewishness, *Deutschtum* and *Judentum*, was contentious for decades and was discussed at length by Jewish and non-Jewish intellectuals.[36] For each side, the question at stake was: Can a Jew be a German? Initially, German nationalists might have been inclined to say yes, provided that Jews stopped being Jewish.[37] Many Jews would also answer in the affirmative, though the necessary degree of assimilation was contested.[38] For a "German citizen of the Jewish faith" (*Deutscher Staatsbürger jüdischen Glaubens*), the solution was cultural assimilation while relegating Jewishness to the sphere of religion.[39] In the denominationally heterogeneous German society, this was not an unreasonable strategy.[40] A complementary approach that developed over the course of the nineteenth century conceived of Jewishness as a tribal identity under the common roof of the German nation—again, not unreasonable given the contemporary discourse on the German nation being composed of different "tribes" (as they were still called in the Weimar constitution) such as Bavarians and Saxons.[41] Racial anti-Semitism, by contrast, which gained a strong foothold in German society from the last quarter of the nineteenth century, denied any kind of compatibility and even precluded assimilation by conversion.[42] At that point, anti-Semitic nationalists in different European countries came to imagine the Jews as the irreconcilable opposite of any nationally defined community.[43] The 1935 Nuremberg Laws; racial laws in other countries produced in their wake; and eventually the deportation, ghettoization, and murder of Jews from many European countries in the Shoah were the most radical consequence of this thinking.

Outside the borders of the German Empire, debates on the compatibility of Germanness and Jewishness throughout the long nineteenth century and during the interwar period were shaped by the fact that Jews and Germans were important and conspicuous minorities with a long shared history across the multiethnic lands of Central and Eastern Europe.[44] In regions such as Prussian Posen, Russian Courland, Hungarian Croatia, and the Austrian provinces of Bohemia, Bukovina, and Galicia, Jews were representatives of German language and culture. Famous German-language writers of Jewish origin from these regions—Paul Celan, Rose Ausländer, Joseph Roth, and Franz Kafka—are the most prominent testimony to this heritage. With the advent of modern nationalism and the spread of anti-Semitism, the belonging of these people became contentious. For radical German nationalists, who were looking to construct a cross-border German *Volk* extending throughout Central and Eastern Europe, German-speaking Jews were not Germans, even if this meant numerically weakening the nation.[45] Such activists increasingly substituted imperial notions of German as a universal language of culture and civilization and embraced a provincialized view of German culture as the authentic expression of the identity of an exclusively defined German *Volksgruppe*.[46] Even so, identifying as German remained a viable option for Jews even after the creation of nation-states in the region after the First World War, despite the simultaneous recognition of separate Jewish national minorities in some of these states.[47]

The negotiation of co-ethnic migration cases such as Josef Floris's carried the question of whether a Jew could be ethnically German into the decades after the Second World War. Unlike Jews from the German Empire, who after the war did not need to prove any kind of ethnic Germanness to reclaim the German citizenship they had been stripped of during their flight from Nazism, these Central European Jews had no such firm legal ground to stand on.[48] They needed to stake a claim to fulfilling the criteria of German *Volkszugehörigkeit*—a claim that, as we will see, was always strongly contested, not least because the power of definition rested in part with German expellee activists who thought in exclusive interwar categories. By the same token, the contentious nature of these Jewish cases also helped to normalize the identity of non-Jewish Aussiedler, the vast majority of co-ethnic immigrants to Germany.

Central and Eastern Europe was also the birthplace of the most forceful response to the conundrum of modern Jewish identity and the increasingly exclusive position of different European nationalisms toward the Jews: Zionism.[49] Simultaneously including and transcending coetaneous West and East European notions of tribal, ethnic, or "folkist" Jewishness, Zionism postulated Jewish peoplehood in terms of modern nationalism. As Theodor Herzl wrote in *Der Judenstaat* (in German, the lingua franca of early Zionism), "the Jewish question is no more a social than a religious one, notwithstanding that it sometimes takes these and other forms. It is a national question," before famously postulating that "We are a people—one people."[50]

Yet exactly what defined this people was complicated. Though secular by origin and in outlook, Zionism could not sidestep the question of religion for belonging to the Jewish collective. For Herzl, who envisioned a Jewish state as a secular utopia, "adherence to Judaism was a prerequisite of membership" in the Zionist movement, thus disqualifying converts to Christianity.[51] Russian-born Zionist Yosef Chaim Brenner, by contrast, defined Jewish peoplehood in terms of ethnic affinity and subjective identification, regardless of religious affiliation.[52] According to this latter logic, a convert to Christianity like Brother Daniel, who identified with the Jewish people in a national sense, could indeed have been a Jew. During the early decades of Zionism, then, "there arose a variety of possible ways to define Jewish national identity, from absolute adherence to religious definitions and all the way to ideas concerning the establishment of an entirely new civic-secular-territorial nationality. However, until the establishment of the state, the practical implications of this debate were negligible; they became practical and the subject of fierce political debate only as of 1948."[53] This book engages with some of those debates over how to define a Jew in the Jewish state, both in theoretical terms and with a view to their practical implications and applications. As we will see, co-ethnic recognition practices went a long way to bring about the Israeli "ethnic-civic" nationhood that Israeli scholars Netanel Fisher and Avi Shilon postulate, accepting many "non-Jewish Jews" into the Israeli nation while never being able to completely sideline the religious definitions of belonging that the rabbinic gatekeepers of the nation held dear.[54]

MIGRATIONS OF "UNMIXING" IN EUROPE AND BEYOND

Postwar co-ethnic migration also represented the continuation of postimperial—or, as historian Philipp Ther would call them, "nation-state induced"—migrations of "unmixing," which had been a salient feature of the European migration landscape since the last quarter of the nineteenth century.[55] Such migrations were the by-product of ordering supranational imperial spaces along national lines, assigning particular nationalities to particular territories. In this process, some national groups became "owners" of their states, while other inhabitants of these territories became minorities disturbing the projected homogeneity of the nation-states in the making. In Southeastern Europe, this reordering of space resulted in a dynamic of "ethnic cleansing," which sometimes was the outcome of direct violence and expulsion, sometimes the result of more subtle forms of discrimination and pressure.[56] These movements of populations began with the departure of Muslims from the new Christian nation-states of the Balkans, following the gradual retreat of the Ottoman Empire.[57] The unmixing intensified numerically and in terms of violence during the period between 1912 and 1923. In the context of war, minorities were suspected of disloyalty, resulting, for instance, in the large-scale forced removal of Germans and Jews from the frontline districts by the Russian authorities as well as the genocidal deportation of Armenians in the Ottoman Empire.[58] The preliminary climax of these forced migrations of homogenization was the compulsory population exchange between Greece and Turkey following the Lausanne Convention of January 1923.[59]

In post-Habsburg Central Europe, no Lausanne-style "clean sweep" of minorities was implemented as yet. The postimperial nation-states formed in the suburbs of Paris in 1919 all contained sizable national minorities. Two minorities in particular were common to most states of the region: Germans and Jews. Although the identification of these heterogeneous linguistic and religious groups as "national" minorities was by no means self-evident, the Wilsonian logic of the "self-determination of peoples," the resulting minority protection system of the League of Nations providing rights to national collectives, the dialectic nationalization of minorities against the state-bearing national majorities in their respective countries, and the actions of "external homelands" (like Germany) or transterritorial national movements (like Zionism) claiming minority members as their own kin created a framework that favored nationalizing processes.[60] The Soviet Union, which kept the territory of the defunct Russian Empire largely intact, followed its own Leninist version of the principle of national self-determination and also reorganized people and space along national lines, even fostering national cultures where there had previously been none.[61] Both the Central European and the Soviet contexts of the interwar period would have important long-term consequences for the process of co-ethnic migration and ethnic classification in Germany and Israel long after the Second World War, shaping migration and citizenship possibilities into the late twentieth century.

While the breakup of multinational empires into national units was already a complicated process on a macroscale, research has shed light on the complications it created on the societal level. These complications reverberated in migration cases predicated on ethnic belonging, because the way individuals had negotiated these conditions in the past became important for ethnic recognition decades later. In the post-Habsburg lands in particular, "national indifference" was still a salient phenomenon throughout the interwar period.[62] For many individuals, it was anything but clear (or important) which national group—if any—they belonged to. As, for instance, the Floris case demonstrates, there was no clear dividing line between different national collectives-in-the-making, because one could easily speak both Hungarian and German and be of the Jewish faith—characteristics that could each imply belonging to one or the other national group.[63] Bi- or multilingualism and the ambiguous position of the Jews as both a religious denomination and an emerging national group thus created a host of identity options for nationally undefined individuals.[64] As nationalism spread and radicalized, people were increasingly constrained to choose sides, if they were able to choose at all.[65] This was especially true during the Second World War, when the question of belonging often turned into a matter of life or death.

Nazi policies of building a racial empire in Central and Eastern Europe before and during the Second World War brought additional—and more violent—ethnic and racial classification of the region's population. These classifications were the precondition for the deportation, extermination, and resettlement of large population groups.[66] Here, too, Jews and Germans were the center of attention, though in diametrically opposed ways and locked into a fateful dialectic.[67] Jews, defined by the Nazis as a separate "race" irrespective of previous belonging, national self-identification, or even religious creed, were segregated, deported, and murdered by German armed forces and in death camps.[68] Before the war, racial persecution had already pushed German Jews out of Germany, with many finding shelter in the Zionist community (*Yishuv*) in Mandate Palestine.[69] The German minorities in Central and Eastern Europe, by contrast, were embraced by the Nazis to promote empire building.[70] In Czechoslovakia and Poland, their alleged oppression served as a pretext for Nazi aggression and territorial expansion.[71] "Splinter" groups living within the Italian and Soviet spheres of influence were resettled *Heim ins Reich*, with the goal of turning them into vanguard settlers in annexed Poland.[72] Crucially for the context of this study, in parts of annexed Poland (as well as in Ukraine and Slovenia) the nationally ambiguous local population was classified in the so-called *Deutsche Volksliste*, which divided people into four categories depending on their degree of "Germanness" and political reliability.[73] As Doris L. Bergen has noted, the Nazis' search for *Volksdeutsche* in the territories they annexed and occupied in fact contributed to the exacerbation of anti-Semitism and to the local persecution of the Jews, because people could "prove" their often doubtful objective Germanness by participating in anti-Jewish violence while also benefiting from looted Jewish property earmarked for *Volksdeutsche*.[74] Despite this bloody legacy, these classification schemes and legal facts created by the expanding German Reich were to have a lasting impact on the development of German co-ethnic migration in subsequent decades.

In the wake of the German retreat and eventual defeat, these different groups of ethnic German populations, as well as German citizens from the Eastern Territories of the Reich, were in turn subjected to forced migration in what Winston Churchill in December 1944 affirmatively termed the "disentanglement of populations."[75] This took the shape of spontaneous flight from the advancing Red Army, evacuation by the retreating Wehrmacht, and internment and forced expulsion by the Soviets or by local or national authorities that had been reestablished.[76] By that time, both the victorious Allies and the reestablished nation-states of Central and Eastern Europe considered the forced resettlement of troublesome minorities in "their" nation-states a prophylactic against a repetition of the national strife of the interwar period.[77] At the 1945 Potsdam Conference, the Allies thus decided on the organized transfer of Germans from Poland (including the former German territories that were to become part of westward-shifted Poland), Czechoslovakia, and Hungary. These and other forced population transfers continued throughout the immediate postwar years, a period that Peter Gatrell has aptly termed the "violent peacetime."[78] By 1950, more than twelve million German citizens and *Volksdeutsche* from Central, Eastern, and Southeastern Europe had fled or been expelled to Germany west of the Oder-Neisse line.[79] About eight million of them settled in the western occupation zones.[80] Another approximately one million expellees who had initially been resettled in the Soviet occupation zone relocated to West Germany by 1961.[81]

As postwar Europe was rebuilt along national lines, the Jewish survivors of the Nazi genocide found themselves in search of a home.[82] Especially Jews originating from Eastern Europe were often left without a homeland to be repatriated to, as the Shoah had wiped out Jewish life and communities on a grand scale. They formed part of the Displaced Persons population, which was mainly concentrated in occupied Germany.[83] Emigration to Palestine was the preferred option for many, but due to the immigration restrictions of the British Mandate authorities dating back to the 1939 White Paper, it was not possible in large numbers.[84] Underground organizations such as Brichah ("flight") organized their illegal immigration.[85] It was only with the establishment of the State of Israel in May 1948 that unrestricted immigration became possible. Some 300,000 Eastern European Jews left Europe for Israel over the next three years.[86]

Through the emigration of Holocaust survivors to Palestine/Israel, the Middle East became an integral part of the postwar system of European migrations of "disentanglement."[87] The unmixing of populations also proved contagious, as the European principle of drawing ethnic borders and the concomitant assignment of ethnic groups to one particular homeland was introduced into the region around the same time.[88] With the United Nations Partition Plan of November 1947, Israeli Independence on May 14, 1948, and the subsequent Israeli-Arab War, partition and ethnic unmixing became reality. Some 700,000 Palestinian Arabs lost their homes in what had become the State of Israel and ended up in neighboring Arab states, most of which refused to grant the Palestinians citizenship and permanently integrate them.[89] In the postwar order of ethnically defined nation-states, they were nobody's co-ethnic, with the partial exception of Jordan.

The young state of Israel also became the destination of postimperial migrations from Arab countries such as Iraq, Yemen, Libya, Morocco, Tunisia, Algeria, and Egypt, which during the postwar period shed the dominance of British, Italian, French, and Spanish colonialisms. Some 600,000 Jews from Arab countries moved to Israel during the first 25 years of statehood. They were part of a larger emigration movement from the newly independent former colonies, which mostly involved European settlers and officials leaving for the metropole or other colonies.[90]

These postcolonial migrations from outside Europe are usually considered separately from the postimperial migrations and expulsions on the European continent.[91] But even where these two contexts are considered together, Jews only appear insofar as they (r)emigrated to the colonial metropole—for instance, from Algeria to France.[92] Jews who emigrated from the former colonies to their newly designated homeland of Israel usually fell off the radar. Yet their migrations are particularly interesting because they represent a liminal case between the ideal types of postcolonial migration and ethnic unmixing or even ethnic cleansing. Jewish migrants from Arab states were clearly postcolonial migrants as they left newly independent former colonies. But given the coetaneous flight and expulsion of Palestinian Arabs from Israel, they were also part of an extended process of population exchange between Israel and the Arab world, which, after centuries of European and Ottoman dominance, emerged from decolonization reorganized into independent nation-states.[93]

The exchange of Arab Jews for Palestinian Arabs acquired a tangible dimension when the immigrants moved into the abandoned homes of Palestinian refugees, such as the Wadi Salib neighborhood of Haifa, which later became the site of a much publicized riot by marginalized Moroccan immigrants.[94] The simultaneous resettlement of Oriental and European Jews in confiscated Arab properties, the European-inspired exchange of populations between Middle Eastern states, and the legacy of European colonialism make "Oriental" immigration to Israel a European story and place it in the same historical context as the East–West migration of Eastern European Jews and Germans.

ETHNICALLY CODED FAMILY REUNIFICATION DURING THE COLD WAR

After the end of the massive and forced migrations of the "violent peacetime," Central and Eastern European Germans and Jews, and, by extension, Germany and Israel, became locked in the same migration context of—now restricted instead of forced—East–West migration during the Cold War. Despite the near total expulsions of Germans from countries such as Poland and Czechoslovakia, the killing of over five million Eastern European Jews in the Shoah, and the subsequent exodus of many survivors, there remained sizable groups of (potential) Germans and Jews in the countries of what was now the Eastern Bloc. These groups were heterogeneous even within the different states, had different minority statuses, and were more or less clearly defined as German and Jewish. The German groups included traditionally ambiguous borderland populations such as the Upper Silesians, many of whom had been registered in the *Volksliste* as Germans before being "rehabilitated" as "autochthonous" Poles after the war; officially recognized German minorities such as the Swabians and Saxons in Romania; and initially persecuted and disenfranchised and then slowly reintegrated diaspora minorities such as the Danube Swabians in Yugoslavia and the Germans of the Soviet Union, who had both suffered wartime and postwar deportation and internment.[95] Jewish groups were the remnants of the once numerous communities in Poland, Hungary, and Romania, many of whom had lived through persecution and concentration camps, as well as the Jewish diaspora in the Soviet Union, where some 2.8 million Jews had survived in the unoccupied parts of the vast country, many of them fighting in the Red Army.[96]

The intermittent emigration of these minorities from the early 1950s onward was the most important exception to the generally valid "non-exit" policy that all socialist states other than Yugoslavia embraced.[97] As minorities disturbing the ethnic homogenization projects of postwar nation-states, the emigration of both Jews and Germans could be construed as beneficial from an ethno-demographic point of view and could hence be tolerated on occasion by states otherwise intent on keeping an available workforce inside the country.[98] However, belonging to a minority was not a sufficient condition in itself for becoming eligible for emigration. In most instances for most of the Cold War, prospective emigrants also needed something else: an invitation from a relative abroad to qualify for family reunification. German and Jewish Cold War migration thus represented the merging of two distinct principles of postwar population management—the ethnic unmixing of homogenizing nation-states and the reconstruction of divided families—into what I refer to in this book as ethnically coded family reunification.

As Tara Zahra explains, the family and the nation were the two central units for European reconstruction.[99] Reconstructing European families torn apart by the war was one of the priorities of the international relief community. The newfound centrality of family unity also found expression in the 1951 United Nations Convention and Protocol Relating to the Status of Refugees, which declared family unity to be "an essential right of the refugee."[100] Yet while Zahra has argued that "an overriding concern with crafting homogenous nation-states ultimately undercut the humanitarian rhetoric of family reunification, particularly in the case of transnational families,"[101] in the case of co-ethnic migration these two principles in fact complemented each other, as families were supposed to be reunited in their externally assigned homelands. The merger between these humanitarian and national principles went so far that when Poland temporarily opened its emigration gates in 1956, aspiring Jewish emigrants from Poland did not even need relatives in Israel to be granted "family reunification."[102]

In the ethnically coded segment of the Cold War East–West migration system, West Germany and Israel thus fulfilled similar functions as homelands, where members of their "kin minorities" were able to unite with family members. However, I argue in this book that these objective positions in the international order did not correspond to identical subjective positions of the receiving states. The countries' subjective stance, as it is conceptualized here, simultaneously includes and transcends Rogers Brubaker's notion of the "homeland stance" that certain states assume once "cultural or political elites construe certain residents and citizens of other states as co-nationals . . . and when they assert that this shared nationhood makes the state responsible, in some sense, not only for its own citizens but also for ethnic co-nationals who live in other states and possess other citizenships."[103] This "transborder membership politics," to use another term Brubaker coined, is an important part of the story.[104] As the Weimar Republic's lukewarm attitude toward Germans from the Soviet Union demonstrates, assuming responsibility for people who at other times were construed as co-ethnics was not self-evident in the 1920s.[105] Nor was it self-evident after the Second World War, as can be seen from the limited interest the German Democratic Republic displayed in (potentially) German populations beyond its borders. Yet the fact that states engage in transborder membership politics does not necessarily mean they do so for the same reason, with the same purpose, and in the same way. We need to ask instead about the underlying motivation and rationale of the respective ethnic migration regimes, which need to be understood in the historical context in which they emerged.

DIFFERENT PURPOSES OF CO-ETHNIC MIGRATION

Chapter 1 explains that an important difference between the Israeli and German homeland stances was their different diasporic ideologies. On the one side was Zionism, which had celebrated its greatest triumph thus far with the creation of the independent State of Israel in May 1948. Zionism had never been expansionist, but instead pursued the clear objective of "ingathering the exiles" in the national center. Instituting the Law of Return put this objective on a firm legal footing and gave expression to the idea that diasporic Jews were supposed to return home to Israel after 2,000 years of absence. On the other side was defeated expansionist German nationalism, which had not aimed at bringing the diaspora back to Germany, but to extend Germany to where the diaspora was and use it as a tool of empire building. This expansionism came crashing down with the violent flight and expulsion of Germans from Eastern Europe as well as the dramatic loss of territory imposed by the Allies. West Germany's denial of this loss and the resulting at least latent territorial revisionism placed significant constraints on the ability of the West German government to embrace an active return ideology and policy akin to Zionism, as the continued presence of a German minority in these territories could serve to justify territorial claims. With regard to the Aussiedler whom the Federal Republic of Germany did take in on ethno-humanitarian grounds, the government could not even speak of return or repatriation, because this would have denied both the territorial claims of the state and the "right to the *Heimat*" that the expellee associations held dear.[106] In Zionist terms, *Heimat* had to be in Israel. In the German case, the rightful *Heimat* of the expellees and Aussiedler was in the East. This latter position only began to change slowly in the 1970s, when Germany began to trade "land for people" with Poland in the context of the new *Ostpolitik* and increasing numbers of Aussiedler came from Romania and the Soviet Union and thus from territories beyond the former German borders.[107]

A second important difference discussed in chapter 1 concerns the divergent overarching purposes of taking in co-ethnic immigrants in Germany and Israel, and the corresponding legal and bureaucratic institutions designed to organize their reception. Neither state created the original institutions with the sole intention of accepting immigrants simply on account of their ethnicity and with the objective of gathering the diaspora in the national territory. Instead, these institutional setups emerged under specific circumstances for specific purposes, which differed greatly between the two cases. Whereas Germany passively received German refugees after the war and created an inward-looking domestic framework for their integration, the nascent State of Israel actively reached out and pursued the immigration of Jews who had the "working and fighting hands" that the country needed for its survival and to build a new nation.[108] The resulting institutions of the German and Israeli co-ethnic migration regimes were notably different because they served different original purposes: the reception of co-ethnic refugees into an ethno-humanitarian welfare state in Germany and the recruitment and resettlement of diaspora members for a pioneering state-building project in Israel. This difference was captured succinctly in 1954 by then Israeli prime minister Moshe Sharett, who, in a meeting of government and Jewish Agency representatives, rejected the acceptance of chronically and mentally ill immigrants on the grounds that "the State of Israel is not a charitable institution, it is a building enterprise."[109] Israel tackled the dilemma of reconciling the pledge of every Jew having the right to immigrate to Israel under the Law of Return with the needs of the fledgling state by means of an elaborate selective Aliyah policy that employed a host of medical and social selection criteria in addition to the underlying ethnic code. This utilitarian logic had no equivalent in the West German ethnic refugee state, which conceived of co-ethnic immigrants as clients to be supported rather than as additional labor.

CHOOSING AND UNCHOOSING

The institutional practices of choosing and unchoosing potential co-ethnics are the subject of chapters 2 and 3. The screening and selection were done in several steps and by different actors. Both systems involved two consecutive doors or gateways: one external, regulating access to state territory, and one internal, controlling access to citizenship and hence the nation. Under certain conditions, each of these gates could turn into the site of both ethnic and non-ethnic selection. They were guarded by different state institutions, which were in turn subject to the formal or informal influence of specific groups that claimed the power to define who would be admitted—expellee associations in Germany and the medical establishment and religious sector in the political system in Israel. The struggles over the question of who had the right to assert the power of definition are a recurrent issue throughout the book.

As discussed in chapter 2, the divergent institutional setups and logics resulted in very different selection practices at the external gateway when the states were able to choose freely among potential immigrants. Given the precarious nature of emigration from both socialist and Arab states, this was not often the case. Important exceptions were the emigration of Germans from nonaligned Yugoslavia and of Jews from colonial Morocco before 1956. In the absence of emigration restrictions, immigration control turned out to be much stricter than usual, and immigration bureaucrats can be observed exercising discretion. Embracing the approach of identifying the "chosen ones" by looking at the "unchosen ones," we can pinpoint the radically different characteristics of the ideal co-ethnic in each state model. An ideal Aussiedler was an endogamous, German-speaking victim of communism with no specific age and no predetermined social features. An ideal Oleh to Israel, by contrast, was—apart from Jewish, of course—healthy, young, and able to work, or alternatively at least economically well-to-do.

The discussion in chapter 2 also reveals that the cumulative effect of contesting many individual cases in the absence of external pressure was a more general contestation of co-ethnic migration. By studying the multidimensional screening of co-ethnic immigrants according to ethnic, political, and utilitarian criteria as well as what I call the normalization-contestation nexus, this book contributes to literature on citizenship, migration control, medical borders, and nation building through immigration.[110]

Chapter 3 zooms in on the production of co-ethnicity at the internal gate, where co-ethnic citizenship was granted or refused to people already inside the country. Here, too, ambiguous borderline cases are the center of attention: Jewish immigrants from Eastern Europe in Germany, and Jewish converts to Christianity in Israel. The mismatch between different categories and classifications of ethnic belonging in the country of origin, the immigration country, and sometimes also a transit country challenged the existing categories and forced the gatekeepers to make explicit criteria for recognition that were often implicit. This discussion highlights the relational nature of co-ethnicity and its construction against "problematic others." The in-depth analysis of the resulting court cases provides a close-up view of ethnic recognition techniques that sharpens the contours of the two countries' respective notions of ethnicity and nationhood. Ethnicity emerges as a complex notion that cannot be reduced to ethnic descent or ethno-cultural identity but can be better described in terms of its production through declaration and/or performance (of a credible identity by the migrant), intuition (of the respective defining gatekeeper regarding the credibility of migrant declarations and performances), and consensus (between ethnic categorizations in the country of origin and—possibly competing—categorizations in the country of destination).

CONVERGENCE AND DIVERGENCE

Remarkably, given the originally fundamentally different approaches to co-ethnic immigration in each country, by the time the Soviet Union definitively opened its gates during perestroika, Germany's and Israel's regimes came to resemble each other so much that they ended up absorbing most of their (post-) Soviet diaspora within a few years after the fall of the Iron Curtain. Chapters 4 and 5 trace the convergence of the initially divergent pathways of the co-ethnic immigration regimes in both states from the mid-1960s onward. Chapter 4 describes a transformation period that lasted slightly longer than a decade and constituted a watershed, when both Germany and Israel extended the scope of their co-ethnic immigration regimes beyond the initial core of potential migrants to include groups of people who had not been the target of the respective original conceptions of Aussiedlung and Aliyah. Both countries thus embraced broader approaches to co-ethnic immigration that bore greater resemblance to each other. At the same time, significant differences persisted in the degree of extension. In the long run, these extensions provided the foundation for the mass immigrations of the late 1980s. The transformation was driven by the conjunction of two independent developments: generational change and international détente. The passing of time created a new generation of people who descended from ethnic Germans or Jews but were not covered by the existing laws. At the same time, *Ostpolitik* and Cold War détente raised the expectation of ongoing and extended migration through an increasingly porous Iron Curtain. These developments, combined with domestic challenges, triggered changes to the legal and administrative immigration arrangements in each case. The generational and conceptual extensions triggered changes to the migration regimes' definitions of ethnicity—changes that were strongly contested in both nations.

The convergence of the national cases under the impact of international developments related to the Cold War and the process of détente are explored further in chapter 5. The creation of the Conference for Security and Cooperation in Europe (CSCE) and its human rights framework in the 1975 Helsinki Accords provided a common point of reference for West Germany, Israel, German and Jewish minority activists in the Eastern Bloc, and their transnational civil society supporters in the West. The emigration of both Germans and Jews could hence be understood in similar terms of "freedom of movement." The book thus also contributes to the growing body of literature about the transformations in Europe that took place in the context of the CSCE process as well as about the emergence of a human rights regime on a global scale.[111]

German and Jewish migrations came to resemble each other due to the common international context in which they occurred. As mentioned earlier, the outcome—mass migration after the gates opened in 1987—was even more strikingly similar.

These apparent similarities notwithstanding, the last chapter returns to one of the central observations made here: that the similar objective positions and outcomes do not necessarily imply that similar policies brought them about. Analyzing the practices of each state on the levels of policy, institutional gatekeeper struggles, and conceptual and legal reactions to the mass exodus, the last chapter reveals that, while the factors that led to convergence ultimately operated on the international level, the reasons for the eventual redivergence after 1987 need to be sought among the long-term trends on the national level. This redivergence manifested itself in the different positions that each country displayed regarding the new prospect of mass co-ethnic migration. While West Germany soon began to try to reduce the number of newcomers through administrative and legal changes, Israel sent emissaries to increase the number of Soviet Jewish immigrants to the country. Returning to the club metaphor used earlier, one might say that Germany instructed its bouncers to be stricter than before given the ever longer queue at the door, while Israel distributed leaflets and offered free drinks to anyone who would enter.[112]

As a consequence of these divergent positions, the German Aussiedlung regime underwent a process of gradual demise throughout the 1990s, while the Israeli framework for Aliyah remained firmly in place.[113] Paradoxically though, the demise of German co-ethnic immigration was coupled with the ethnicization of its concepts—that is, with tightening the selection criteria to let in only the most "authentic" Germans. This triggered the creation of a new ethnic immigration category, the Jewish "quota refugee" (*Kontingentflüchtling*), to accommodate Jewish immigrants from the Soviet Union who would no longer be subsumed under the category of ethnic German. The resilience of Israeli co-ethnic immigration, in turn, was achieved through "de-ethnicization"—the loosening of requirements of ethnic authenticity. Only in this way could the thoroughly secularized and exogamous Soviet Jewish diaspora be made part of the Israeli people, pushing the boundaries of belonging to hitherto unknown places.

This book is based on a broad range of mostly official archival and published sources that can be roughly classified into two types: materials that allowed me to reconstruct the making of policy and laws (in particular from ministries and parliaments) and materials that provide insights into the practical dimension of consular, bureaucratic, and judicial ethnic screening, such as official guidelines, administrative decisions, and court rulings. The latter type of sources also make it possible to touch on the human aspect of the migrations under examination here, as the screening process involved the interaction of officials and migrants and the evaluation of significant amounts of biographical data. We are thus able to follow individuals from their origins in the multiethnic settings of the interwar period along their migration trajectories within the ethnically coded migration regime of the postwar period. The origins of the legal and institutional systems that made up this regime and sustained these migrations over subsequent decades can be traced back to the extensive population movements that took place during decade that followed the end of the Second World War. It is to this task that the first chapter will now turn.

NOTES

1. BVerwG VIII C 30.64, April 26, 1967, *Entscheidungen des Bundesverwaltungsgerichts* (BVerwGE) 26, 344. Full documentation of the case can be found in Bundesarchiv (BArch), B 139/2105.

2. Hauptstaatsarchiv Stuttgart (HStAS) EA 12/201, Az. 2257, No. 286.

3. *State of Israel, the Supreme Court, Judgment: High Court Application of Oswald Rufeisen v. The Minister of the Interior,* Jerusalem, 1963.

4. Tec, *In the Lion's Den,* 231.

5. Central Zionist Archives (CZA), L16-588/1.

6. For this broad conception of ethnicity encompassing group identification based on national, religious, cultural, or other criteria, see Brubaker, "Religion and Nationalism," 5.

7. The Law of Return, July 5, 1950, in Rabinovich and Reinharz, *Israel in the Middle East,* 102–103.

8. DellaPergola, "Global Context."

9. For a brief overview, see Dietz, "*Aussiedler/Spätaussiedler.*"

10. Thränhardt, "European Migrations," 228. Other, numerically smaller groups of co-ethnic migrants included Pontian Greeks, Inkari Finns, Poles, and Koreans. About Pontian Greeks, see, for instance, Voutira, "*Right to Return*"; about Poles, see Iglicka, "Are They Fellow Countrymen"; about Koreans, see Brubaker and Kim, "Transborder Membership Politics."

11. "Deutscher Volkszugehöriger im Sinne dieses Gesetzes ist, wer sich in seiner Heimat zum deutschen Volkstum bekannt hat, sofern dieses Bekenntnis durch bestimmte Merkmale wie Abstammung, Sprache, Erziehung, Kultur bestätigt wird." Bundesgesetzblatt, Teil I, No. 22, May 22, 1953, http://www.bgbl.de/xaver/bgbl/start.xav?startbk=Bundesanzeiger_BGBl&jumpTo=bgbl153022.pdf.

12. Law of Return 5710-1950, July 5, 1950, http://www.mfa.gov.il/mfa/mfa-archive/1950-1959/pages/law%20of%20return%205710-1950.aspx.

13. Joppke, *Selecting by Origin*, 174.

14. Brubaker and Kim, "Transborder Membership Politics," 24.

15. Joppke and Rosenhek, "Contesting Ethnic Immigration," 303.

16. Rass and Wolff, "What Is in a Migration Regime?" 44–45, 52. For the notion of arena, see Oltmer, "Einführung," 12–19. See also Oltmer, "Einleitung," and Hoerder, Lucassen, and Lucassen, "Terminologies and Concepts of Migration Research."

17. Fahrmeir, "Law and Practice."

18. Brubaker and Kim, "Transborder Membership Politics," 24.

19. Rass and Wolff, "What Is in a Migration Regime," 51. About the use of sociologist Anthony Giddens's concept of structuration in historiography, see Welskopp, "Dualität von Struktur und Handeln." See also Reichhardt, "Praxeologische Geschichtswissenschaft."

20. This is in line with a common call in the theoretical literature on comparative history to extend the classic comparison of separate national cases. See Kocka and Haupt, "Comparison and Beyond," 21; Kaelble, "Interdisziplinäre Debatten," 478.

21. Rass and Wolff, "What Is in a Migration Regime," 47; Berlinghoff, "Transnationale, Internationale."

22. On regimes of ethnicity, see Aktürk, *Regimes of Ethnicity and Nationhood*.

23. Brubaker, *Citizenship and Nationhood*; Levy and Weiss, *Challenging Ethnic Citizenship*.

24. Brubaker, *Citizenship and Nationhood*; Levy, "Introduction."

25. Judson, "Nationalism," 520.

26. Dumbrava, *Nationality, Citizenship*, 13. Especially with regard to German citizenship, some authors have used historically more charged terms such as *blood-right*, *völkisch*, and *racial*. See, for instance, Fulbrook, "Germany for the Germans," 89; Hogwood, "Citizenship Controversies," 127, 132–133.

27. Renan, "What Is a Nation," 53. On the civic nation as a *Willens- und Bekenntnisprodukt*, see Salzborn, *Ethnisierung der Politik*, chap. 4. Salzborn contrasts this with the ethnic (*völkisch*) criteria of descent, language, and culture. For the disavowal of this dichotomy by an erstwhile proponent, see Brubaker, "Manichean Myth." For a recent discussion of its persisting relevance, see Liebich and Bauböck, "Is There (Still) an East-West Divide."

28. Patt, "Stateless Citizens of Israel"; Patt, *Finding Home and Homeland*; Hacohen, *Immigrants in Turmoil*; Segev, *1949*; Helman, *Becoming Israeli*; Rozin, *Home for All Jews*.

29. Examples of such historiography include the contributions to O'Donnell, Bridenthal, and Reagin, *Heimat Abroad*; Gregor, Roemer, and Roseman, *German History from the Margins*.

30. About the diaspora politics of this first German state, see Manz, *Constructing a German Diaspora.*

31. A comprehensive treatment of the evolution of East German conceptions of nationhood as part of an entangled German-German history is provided by Wolff, *Mauergesellschaft.*

32. Panagiotidis, "What Is the Germans Fatherland."

33. For the notion of "old history," see Walser Smith, *Continuities of German History,* 212.

34. Alter, Bärsch, and Berghoff, *Konstruktion der Nation;* Best, "Juden und Judenbilder"; Volkov, *Antisemitismus als kultureller Code.*

35. Lenhard, *Volk oder Religion.*

36. See, for instance, the texts assembled in Schulte, *Deutschtum und Judentum.*

37. Walser Smith, *Continuities of German History,* 220–221.

38. See, for instance, Schulin, "Doppel-Nationalität."

39. Barkai, *"Wehr Dich!"*

40. For the religious heterogeneity of modern German society, see, for instance, Walser Smith, *German Nationalism and Religious Conflict;* Walser Smith, *Protestants, Catholics and Jews.*

41. Brenner, "Religion, Nation oder Stamm"; van Rahden, "Germans of the Jewish *Stamm.*"

42. A classic study on the pervasiveness of anti-Semitism in German society of the Kaiserreich is Volkov, *Antisemitismus als kultureller Code.*

43. Holz, *Nationaler Antisemitismus.*

44. Grill, *Jews and Germans.*

45. Judson, "Nationalism."

46. Zahra, *Kidnapped Souls,* chap. 5; Judson, "When Is a Diaspora Not a Diaspora?"

47. Čapková, *Czechs, Germans, Jews.*

48. The history of the restitution of German citizenship to denaturalized Jews remains to be written. On return migration and its implications for Israeli nation building, see Panagiotidis, "Policy for the Future." See also Mendel, "Policy for the Past."

49. For a classic synthesis of the history of Zionism, see Laqueur, *History of Zionism.*

50. Theodor Herzl, *The Jewish State* (1896), http://www.jewishvirtuallibrary.org/quot-the-jewish-state-quot-theodor-herzl.

51. Fisher and Shilon, "Integrating Non-Jewish Immigrants," 168.

52. Ibid.

53. Ibid., 169.

54. Fisher and Shilon, "Integrating Non-Jewish Immigrants."

55. Bloxham, "Great Unweaving"; Brubaker, *Nationalism Reframed*, chap. 6. On "nation-state induced" migrations, see Ther, *Dunkle Seite der Nationalstaaten*, 45.

56. On forced ethnic cleansing, see Ther, *Dunkle Seite der Nationalstaaten*; Naimark, *Fires of Hatred*. An example of more complex emigration motifs among Muslims from Greece is provided by Immig, *Zwischen Partizipation und Emigration*.

57. Toumarkine, *Migrations*.

58. Lohr, *Nationalizing the Russian Empire*; Eisfeld, Hausmann, and Neutatz, *Besetzt, interniert, deportiert*; Akcam, *A Shameful Act*.

59. About the Greek-Turkish population exchange, see, for instance, Clark, *Twice a Stranger*; Hirschon, *Crossing the Aegean*.

60. On self-determination, see most recently Weitz, "Self-Determination." On minority protection, see Mazower, "Minorities and the League of Nations." On the "triadic nexus" between external homelands, national minorities, and nationalizing states, see Brubaker, *Nationalism Reframed*, chaps. 3, 5. About the dual nation building of the titular nation and national minorities, see Ther, *Dunkle Seite der Nationalstaaten*, 34.

61. Martin, *Affirmative Action Empire*; Hirsch, *Empire of Nations*; Jeremy Smith, *Red Nations*.

62. Zahra, *Kidnapped Souls*; Zahra, "Imagined Non-Communities."

63. For the fluid boundaries between the German, Jewish, and Hungarian minorities in interwar Romania, see Glass, *Zerbrochene Nachbarschaft*, 151–170.

64. A recent study on the identity options of Bohemian Jews is Čapková, *Czechs, Germans, Jews*.

65. Chad Bryant has explored this national dichotomization for the Czech lands in his essay "Either German or Czech." About national ascription, see Zahra, *Kidnapped Souls*, chap. 7. About the increasing objectivization of national belonging and the resultant loss of individual agency, see Ther, *Dunkle Seite der Nationalstaaten*, 52–56.

66. For an overview, see Ahonen et al., *People on the Move*, chap. 2.

67. A classic study of the nexus between the resettlement of ethnic Germans and the extermination of Jews in Eastern Europe by the Nazis is Aly, *"Endlösung."*

68. Literature on the Holocaust is too vast to list here. For a seminal classic, see Hilberg, *Destruction of the European Jews*.

69. Strauss, "Jewish Emigration from Germany." For the policies of the Yishuv, see also Edelheit, *Yishuv in the Shadow of the Holocaust*.

70. Lumans, *Himmler's Auxiliaries*; Heinemann, *"Rasse, Siedlung, deutsches Blut."*

71. See Kochanowski and Sach, *"Volksdeutschen."*

72. This affected Germans from South Tyrol, the Soviet-annexed Baltic States, Volhynia, Bukovina, and Bessarabia as well as those from the Slovenian

Gottschee and Bosnia. See Benz, "Zweifache Opfer." For the racist selection practices of the institutions in charge of the resettlement of ethnic Germans, see Strippel, *NS-Volkstumspolitik*.

73. Wolf, *Ideologie und Herrschaftsrationalität*; Heinemann, *"Rasse, Siedlung, deutsches Blut,"* 260–282; Fleischhauer, *Das Dritte Reich und die Deutschen in der Sowjetunion*, 185–192; Wörsdörfer, "Transnationale Aspekte."

74. Bergen, "Nazi Concept of 'Volksdeutsche'." About the nexus of the Holocaust and Nazi Germanization policies, see also Steinhart, *Holocaust and the Germanization of Ukraine*.

75. Reinisch, "Introduction," xviii.

76. Beer, *Flucht und Vertreibung*, 174–196.

77. Frank, "Reconstructing the Nation-State," 28. See also the contributions to Ther and Siljak, *Redrawing Nations*.

78. For an overview of these population movements, see, for instance, Ahonen et al., *People on the Move*, chap. 4; Ther, *Dunkle Seite der Nationalstaaten*, chaps. 3.2, 3.3; and the contributions to Reinisch and White, *Disentanglement of Populations*. For the notion of "violent peacetime," see Gatrell, "Trajectories of Population Displacement," 6.

79. Beer, *Flucht und Vertreibung*, 85.

80. Ibid., 102.

81. Ibid., 120.

82. Zahra, *Lost Children*, 243–244; Bankier, *Jews Are Coming Back*.

83. About Displaced Persons in general (including Jews), see Gerard Cohen, *In War's Wake*; on Jewish Displaced Persons in particular, see Grossmann, *Jews, Germans, and Allies*.

84. About Displaced Person Zionism, see Patt, "Stateless Citizens of Israel." About their migration options and strategies, see Veidlinger, "One Doesn't Make Out Much."

85. See the classic study by Yehuda Bauer, *Flight and Rescue*.

86. Hacohen, *Immigrants in Turmoil*, 267.

87. Gatrell, *Making of the Modern Refugee*, chap. 4.

88. Ther, *Dunkle Seite der Nationalstaaten*, 224–233. There had been previous attempts: in 1937, the Peel Commission, which had been appointed the year before to investigate Arab-Jewish violence, had already suggested the partition of Mandate Palestine into a Jewish and an Arab state and an exchange of populations to create clear ethnic majorities. About this and earlier British plans for partition, see Sinanoglou, "British Plans."

89. The creation of the Palestinian refugee problem (also known as the Nakba) is still a controversial topic that cannot be adequately addressed in this book. A by now classic account by an Israeli "new historian" is Morris, *Birth of the Palestinian Refugee Problem*. See also his subsequent *Birth of the Palestinian Refugee Problem*

Revisited, and *1948*. While Morris sees the mass uprooting of the Palestinian population as the result of military action combined with the subsequent prohibition of return, Ilan Pappé offers a more radical reading of the events as intentional ethnic cleansing by the Zionist leadership. See Pappé, *Ethnic Cleansing*. Pappé in many ways follows the interpretation of Palestinian historian Walid Khalidi, which he first developed in "Plan Dalet: The Zionist Master Plan for the Conquest of Palestine." For the radically opposed view of the Nakba as the Palestinians' "self-inflicted catastrophe," see Karsh, *Palestine Betrayed*. Seven hundred thousand refugees is a rough estimate based on Benny Morris's discussion of different available contemporary statistics and estimates, none of which can claim to be conclusive, however. See Morris, *Birth of the Palestinian Refugee Problem Revisited*, appendix 1, 602–604.

90. Andrea Smith, *Europe's Invisible Migrants*.

91. An early exception was Peach, "Postwar Migration to Europe." A more recent attempt at comparative treatment is Borutta and Janssen, *Vertriebene und Pieds Noirs*.

92. Shepard, *Invention of Decolonization*, chap. 6.

93. The argument to treat the expulsion of the Palestinians from Israel and the Jews from Arab states as a "dual Middle East refugee problem" is advanced by, among others, Martin Gilbert, *In Ishmael's House*, chap. 21. As Tom Segev has shown, this notion can be traced back to the Israeli newspaper discourse on the Palestinian exodus at the time. Segev, *1949*, 90–91.

94. On the complex memory of the Arab-Jewish history of Wadi Salib, see Yfaat Weiss, *Confiscated Memory*.

95. About Upper Silesians and their "rehabilitation," see Service, *Germans to Poles*. About Romanian Germans, see Weber et al., *Emigration der Siebenbürger Sachsen*, and Sebaux, *(Post)colonisation—(Post)migration*. On the wartime fate of Germans in Yugoslavia, see Janjetovic, *Between Hitler and Tito*. On Germans in the Soviet Union, see Mukhina, *Germans of the Soviet Union*.

96. About the Holocaust in Hungary, see Braham, *Politics of Genocide*. On Romania, see Ancel, *History of the Holocaust in Romania*. On Poland and the Soviet Union, see Polonsky, *Jews in Poland and Russia*. See also Arad, *Holocaust in the Soviet Union*. About the evacuation of Soviet citizens (including Jews) to the unoccupied parts of the country, see Manley, *To the Tashkent Station*.

97. On the anti-emigration stance of socialist states in Central and Eastern Europe and its roots in prewar demographic concerns, see Zahra, *Great Departure*. For the notion of "non-exit state," see Stola, "Opening a Non-exit State."

98. For the interplay of homogenizing efforts in the sending and receiving countries, see Silber, "Foreigners or Co-nationals?" About utilitarian and ethnodemographic considerations in postwar cross-bloc migrations, see Panagiotidis, "Utilitaristische und ethnodemographische Überlegungen."

99. Zahra, *Lost Children*.

100. Ibid., 236.
101. Ibid., 243.
102. Stola, *Kraj bez wyjścia*, 136.
103. Brubaker, *Nationalism Reframed*, 5.
104. Brubaker and Kim, "Transborder Membership Politics."
105. Oltmer, *Migration und Politik*, chap. 3.
106. For claims of Germany embracing "return" and "repatriation" discourses regarding co-ethnic immigrants see Münz and Ohliger, "Diasporas and Ethnic Migrants," and De Tinguy and Hadjiisky, "Repatriation of Persons." About the right to the *Heimat* see Demshuk, "What Was the 'Right to the Heimat'?"
107. For the notion of "land for people" as a variation of the Israeli-Arab "land for peace" theme, see Stola, *Kraj bez wyjścia*, 233.
108. For the notion of "working and fighting hands," see Segev, *1949*, chap. 5.
109. Coordination Committee Minutes, June 28, 1954, Israel State Archives (ISA) 43.0.6.2089 (=5383/16-ג).
110. On citizenship in comparative German-Israeli perspective, see Joppke, *Selecting by Origin*; Levy and Weiss, *Challenging Ethnic Citizenship*. Specifically on Germany, see Eley and Palmowski, *Citizenship and National Identity*; Klusmeyer and Papademetriou, *Immigration Policy*; Nathans, *Politics of Citizenship*; Sammartino, "After Brubaker." On Israel, see Rozin, *Home for All Jews*; Picard, *Cut to Measure*. On "medical borders," see Davidovitch and Zalashik, "Medical Borders." On migration and nation building in the United States, see Zolberg, *Nation by Design*.
111. Bange and Niedhardt, *Helsinki 1975*; Thomas, *Helsinki Effect*; Hakkarainen, *State of Peace*; von Saal, *KSZE-Prozess*; Moyn, *Last Utopia*, chap. 4.
112. I thank Marcel Berlinghoff for suggesting this fitting extension of the club metaphor.
113. Joppke, *Selecting by Origin*, chap. 4.

ONE

ORIGINATING DIFFERENCES

DR. STEPHAN BRAUN CAME TO Germany in 1946.[1] He was born in 1894 in the city of Kassa (German: Kaschau; Slovak: Košice) in what was then the Hungarian half of the Habsburg Empire. When Braun was two years old, his parents moved to Budapest, where he later attended school and the university. From late 1918, Braun was a state official working in the Hungarian police. When the Soviets came to Hungary in 1945, he fled to Vienna, Austria, and then to Germany, claiming to be an ethnic German (*Volksdeutscher*) from Hungary. In the Kislau refugee transit camp near Bruchsal in Baden—a former concentration camp and present-day jail—Braun received an identification card for German refugees (*Vertriebenenausweis*) in June 1946. Soon after, he moved to the nearby town of Leimen. Beginning in December 1951, he received retirement benefits according to Article 131 of the Basic Law, which accommodated former state officials who had lost their positions after the war, including ethnic Germans who had served other states and had been expelled because of their "German ethnicity" (*deutsche Volkszugehörigkeit*).[2] In July 1952, the Association of Germans from Hungary (*Ungarndeutsche Landsmannschaft*) complained to the Federal Interior Ministry about these payments. Its representatives argued that Braun had fled from communist Hungary because of his work as a state official under the previous regime, not because of his alleged German ethnicity, and that he had registered as a German refugee in Austria only to avoid repatriation to Hungary as a Hungarian Displaced Person. Therefore, he should not be entitled to benefits reserved for ethnic German refugees.[3] To address this complaint, the authorities proceeded to check Braun's *Volkszugehörigkeit* to determine the validity of his German status. After an inconclusive investigation, which took an entire year and involved as many as 19 witnesses, the regional council (*Regierungspräsidium*) concluded that there was little support for Braun's claim to being German, but even less evidence against it. He should therefore be considered an ethnic German refugee.[4]

Around the same time, but in a different place, Misa Giulia B., a young woman from Tripoli, Libya, tried to make her way to Israel to join her husband, Giulio.[5] Misa was born in 1927 or 1928 into a large family with eight children. Her father owned a textile business. Because Misa had to help care for her siblings, she never went to school or worked outside the home. In 1945, she married Giulio P., a construction worker who subsequently emigrated from Libya to Palestine/Israel, as did Misa's entire family, except one brother. While she was still in Tripoli, Misa was diagnosed with tuberculosis. When she tried to travel to Israel via Italy in 1948, she was hospitalized in Florence because of her medical condition. In June 1950, she was transferred to Grottaferrata near Rome, where the American Joint Distribution Committee—the largest transnational Jewish relief organization, which was also dedicated to preparing Jews for agricultural settlement—ran a rehabilitation center for tuberculosis patients.[6] There Misa's treatment continued while she also trained to become a dressmaker in the center's trade school. The school was operated by another transnational Jewish charitable and vocational organization, ORT, the Society for Handicrafts and Agricultural Work (originally *Obshchestvo remeslennogo i zemledel'cheskogo truda*). After over a year of treatment and rehabilitation, Misa finally received the green light for immigration to Israel in late August 1951, and she departed from Italy soon after.

These two cases succinctly illustrate the different workings and logics of the inward-looking German ethno-humanitarian refugee state and the institutions of the outward-looking Israeli diasporic nation-building project. Both were institutional responses of these states and their nonindependent predecessors to the postwar migration streams of their German and Jewish co-ethnics from Eastern Europe and, in the case of Israel, also from the decolonizing Mediterranean and Middle East. Yet while this common context of postwar population movements has been identified as one of the "originating similarities" between West Germany and Israel as destinations for co-ethnic immigration, it is here, in fact, where one finds fundamental "originating differences" between the resulting migration regimes.[7]

The crucial difference between German and Zionist-Israeli responses to the postwar movements of Germans and Jews is found on the level of intention and agency. With the Allied decision at Potsdam to remove the German population from Poland, Czechoslovakia, and Hungary and resettle them in what would be left of Germany, the country became the destination of German refugees.

After the breakdown of the National Socialist resettlement machinery, which had moved hundreds of thousands of ethnic Germans through Eastern Europe during the war to resettle them in what was supposed to become the Greater German Empire, the initially nonsovereign and subsequently divided country remained a passive recipient of German refugees, whom it was obliged to accommodate.[8]

In contrast, before 1948, the equally nonsovereign Zionist Jewish Yishuv in Palestine actively fought to bring Jews from Europe into Palestine despite the immigration ban imposed by the British Mandate authorities under the provisions of the 1939 White Paper. After the new state gained independence, it opened its gates to Jewish immigration from anywhere in the world and worked among Jewish Displaced Persons and Jewish communities to encourage Aliyah. Put simply, the nonsovereign authorities of occupied postwar Germany did not want the German expellees and refugees to come. Applying a quite different approach, the Zionist Yishuv struggled to bring Jews from Europe into Palestine against all odds.

As the cases of Stephan Braun and Misa Giulia B. show, these dissimilar intentions and degrees of agency corresponded to institutions with fundamentally different purposes and rationales. The inward-oriented welfare institutions of the German ethno-humanitarian refugee state provided access to welfare and integration benefits for people identified as German "refugees" (*Flüchtlinge*) or "expellees" (*Vertriebene*).[9] Access to this system was doubly coded: a German refugee was entitled to these benefits by virtue of being German by citizenship or ethnicity *and* being a refugee. According to a contemporary observer, this conditional eligibility for aid was partly modeled on the interwar and postwar international refugee aid programs of the League of Nations and the United Nations, the main difference being that the international criterion of "statelessness" to define a refugee was replaced by the criterion of German citizenship or ethnicity.[10] Reception in Germany as a German refugee could thus be defined as co-ethnic asylum.[11] The refugee state did not actively seek the immigration of Germans to what remained of Germany. Its institutions, the so-called refugee administration (*Flüchtlingsverwaltung*), worked instead to accommodate those who had ended up in the territories west of the Oder-Neisse line. In addition, it tried to reduce the number of refugees by promoting the emigration of certain parts of this population, especially farmers who had little chance of being resettled successfully.[12] In such an institutional framework, someone like Stephan Braun was seen first and foremost as a benefit seeker whose ethnicity-based entitlement to receiving these benefits had to be scrutinized.

The Israeli diasporic nation-building project, by contrast, actively sought the immigration of Jews from the diaspora with the aim of settling the land of Israel with Jews and building a new nation. The open border postulate of the 1948 Declaration of Independence and the 1950 Law of Return represented one pillar of this endeavor. In addition to promising diaspora Jews access to the country, the new state reached out to meet them in their countries of origin or in liminal spaces of transit. Its main organ for this purpose was the Jewish Agency for Palestine (after 1948, the Jewish Agency for Israel), whose emissaries (*shlichim*) operated in all the countries that tolerated their efforts to seek out potential immigrants. Having been the official representative of the Yishuv under the British Mandate since 1929, the agency was officially assigned the task of organizing Aliyah and the preliminary absorption of the immigrants after independence.[13] In its simultaneous efforts of ingathering and resettlement, Israel also relied on transnational Jewish institutions such as the American Joint Distribution Committee and ORT.[14] As Misa Giulia B.'s story illustrates, this active engagement with the diaspora combined elements of restriction, care, and education. While initially barring her immigration for health reasons, the transnational Jewish organizations that were active in Italy did not leave her to her fate but rather treated and trained her. To be sure, the training was not necessarily in line with Israeli interests. While the agricultural training (*hachshara*) provided in Grottaferrata was clearly oriented toward immigration to Palestine, the skills provided by ORT could also serve to restore its clients' livelihood in the diaspora. What all these efforts had in common, though, was the desire to "remake" the Jews and their occupational structure.[15] Once "productivized" in this way, someone like Misa Giulia B. was supposed to be transformed from a potential burden and health risk into an asset for the state once she had the opportunity to immigrate.

The German and Israeli institutions dealing with the postwar migrations of "disentanglement" and the concomitant influx of co-ethnic migrants were thus marked by the distinction between inward-looking ethno-humanitarianism on the one hand and outward-reaching nation-building on the other hand. This distinction is institutional and refers to the way the states conceptualized co-ethnic immigration; it does not tell us anything about the migrants themselves. In fact, though not immigrating to a "refugee state" according to the definition used here, most of the Jewish immigrants to Israel during the early years of statehood were undoubtedly refugees—people who could not return home for fear of persecution. Yet for the institutions of the migration regime, they were primarily an important demographic factor, in terms of both their ethno-demography—after all, the Jewish state needed Jewish inhabitants—and their utility as workers, soldiers, and agricultural settlers. In keeping with the terminology of the day, they were "human material" of value for the project of building the state.[16] German expellees were also a significant source of labor for the subsequent "economic miracle," though the refugee state conceptualized them mainly as clients to support.

Despite their different intentions and institutional setups, both of these migration regimes came to shape subsequent decades of German and Jewish migration with their respective laws and institutions. This might appear self-evident for Israel, with its unequivocal focus on making the diaspora move to the Jewish state, but it is much less true for Germany, which did not originally seek the immigration of ethnic Germans. The reasons for this unintended similar outcome should be sought in the geographic and temporal extension of the West German regime regulating the presence and integration of German expellees and refugees, which developed transborder effects and thereby evolved into a co-ethnic migration regime that made provisions for the admission of additional German co-ethnics. In this, it resembled the international refugee regime codified by the 1951 Geneva Convention on refugees, which was originally meant to accommodate people who became refugees due to events before January 1, 1951, but subsequently became permanent due to temporal and geographic extension.[17] In Germany, the extension implied legal, institutional, and political-ideological issues that will be addressed in the following sections.

In terms of ideology, the Israeli case shows that transborder co-ethnic commitment could be based on a profound commitment to returning a diaspora back to its purported original homeland. Did the Federal Republic of Germany embrace an ideology of diaspora return akin to Zionism, as some authors have suggested?[18] As will be demonstrated in this chapter, the issue of territorial claims—specifically to the German "Eastern Territories," whose loss the Federal Republic would not accept—placed significant constraints on any type of ingathering logic, because contemporary political actors thought the removal of co-ethnics from these regions would imply the renunciation of parts of the supposedly still undivided German state.

While untroubled by comparable fears of surrendering territory by removing co-ethnics, the Israeli commitment to the Jewish diaspora was complicated by the precarious situation of the young state and the resulting imperatives of nation building under conditions of significant material shortages and war. As Misa Giulia B.'s case reveals, despite the country's professed openness to every Jew in the world, the acceptance of Jewish immigrants in the Jewish state was not necessarily unconditional if an applicant's physical condition did not match the needs and capabilities of the young state. This approach implied the migration regime's focus on health and economic usefulness, which could place significant constraints on the open border policy. The paradigm of "selective Aliyah" that will be introduced in this chapter highlights the limits to the otherwise generous call of the Declaration of Independence and the Law of Return for Jews to return to their homeland—a call that was heeded by almost 700,000 individuals between 1948 and 1951 alone.[19]

Despite their significant differences in terms of rationale and scope, the West German and Israeli co-ethnic immigration regimes shared one important feature, which provides the major comparative theme for this book: access to citizenship in the respective countries was conditional on ethnic belonging. As the protracted and ultimately inconclusive investigation of the Braun case suggests, assessing ethnicity in practice could be anything but a simple task. This chapter therefore introduces the ethnic codes that were used in each case as well as the gatekeeping institutions that applied them in multitier procedures at the external and internal gates structuring immigration to both countries. The answer to the question of how the "bouncers" of each migration regime decided on the belonging of purported co-ethnic immigrants will thus receive its first contours, which will then be sharpened in later chapters.

GERMANY: TRANSBORDER EFFECTS OF AN INWARD-LOOKING MIGRATION REGIME

Unlike Israel, West Germany did not possess one comprehensive "law of return" that gave co-ethnics access to the country and its citizenship. Instead, a series of laws were created in the immediate postwar years to promote the social and political integration of the millions of expellees and refugees living on West German territory. It was these laws and the institutions built to implement them that constituted the ethnic refugee state.[20] Although their original primary focus was the expellee population inside the German borders, the laws contained certain provisions that intentionally or unintentionally affected people outside these borders either by entitling them to German citizenship upon resettlement in the FRG or by validating the German citizenship the Nazi authorities had granted them before or during the war. These provisions could thus be used for the continuous reception of German citizens and ethnic Germans from abroad and hence constitute a co-ethnic immigration regime.

The Basic Law's political integration provisions for ethnic German refugees were fundamental for the extension of this inward-looking regime across state borders and into the future. Its Article 116, paragraph 1 defined a German in a way that included not just German citizens but also ethnic German refugees and expellees of foreign or unclear citizenship. A German could thus be a person holding a citizenship other than German, which already implied the article's possible cross-border relevance. Even so, it was intended as an inland-oriented provision, given that only about 60 percent of the 7,825,000 expellees registered in West Germany in 1950 were undisputedly German citizens from the severed territories east of the Oder-Neisse line.[21] The creators of the Basic Law were hesitant to introduce a definition of the term *German* into the text that would somehow affect the already existing citizenship law, because they operated on the premises that the German Reich and its citizenship continued to exist and that there was only one unitary German citizenship.[22]

Yet leaving the citizenship status of those expellees with no or uncertain German citizenship unresolved would have meant disenfranchising a substantial part of the population. Article 116 offered a solution that equalized the status of German citizens and ethnic German refugees without granting citizenship to the latter for the time being, postponing the definitive solution of this problem until later. The exact wording read: "A German according to this Basic Law is—subject to the provisions of other laws—whoever possesses German citizenship or who has been admitted to the territory of the German Reich within its borders of December 31, 1937, as a refugee or expellee of German ethnicity (*Flüchtling oder Vertriebener deutscher Volkszugehörigkeit*) or as the spouse or descendant of such person."[23]

Despite the use of the perfect tense, the written report of the Parliamentary Council about the draft law explicitly stated that this definition also covered ethnic German refugees who would settle in Germany in the future.[24] They, too, would be treated as Germans. In retrospect, this created the constitutional basis for the subsequent immigration of more than 4.5 million Aussiedler, though this was hardly the intention in late 1948 when the law was drafted. As the minutes of the Parliamentary Council show, the immediate concern was with Germans from Czechoslovakia who had been held back and were not allowed to leave after the end of the mass expulsions.[25] The transborder opening thus originally targeted a precise group of people still living abroad who often had relatives who had been expelled to Germany. Although this does not indicate a time-transcending vision of perpetually enabling ethnic priority immigration to Germany, the explicit opening of the article toward the future did lay the basis for the transformation of the provisional, inland-oriented Article 116 of the Basic Law into the foundation of continued access to German citizenship for co-ethnics abroad.

The "other laws" the article referred to came into being in the 1950s and are known as the three Laws for the Settlement of Citizenship Issues

(*Staatsangehörigkeitsregelungsgesetze*). Section 6 of the first of these laws, which went into force in 1955, gave "status Germans" according to the Basic Law the right to automatically become German citizens. Moreover, section 1 of the law entitled German citizenship to all ethnic Germans who had been naturalized collectively or individually by Nazi laws and administrative regulations, unless they had explicitly rejected it or had assumed a different citizenship. This affected Sudeten Germans, Germans from Lithuania, Germans from Poland who had been naturalized through the *Deutsche Volksliste*, and Germans from Nazi-occupied parts of Slovenia as well as Germans from Ukraine.[26] Thus, the remaining 40 percent of the expellees living in West Germany had their legal status definitively resolved.

Like Article 116 of the Basic Law, the inland-oriented citizenship settlement law developed cross-border and future-oriented effects as it also recognized the German citizenship of ethnic Germans who had not fled or had not been expelled. The legality of this position was questionable: The West German state normally legitimized its recognition of the Third Reich's unilateral naturalizations through the legal construct that the expellees' countries of origin had forfeited their claim to their citizens the moment they expelled them.[27] Yet this argument was hardly plausible regarding those who had not been expelled or who, in the case of Ukraine Germans, had been forcibly repatriated to their country of origin.[28] In any case, the West German state institutions did not attach great significance to this creation of transborder citizens at the time. A contemporary commentator of the law merely referred to a "relatively small part" of Germans from the formerly annexed territories who had not been expelled and who would likely resettle in Germany in the future.[29]

Just how big or small this population of "claimed co-ethnics" was no one knew for sure.[30] In the process of drafting the law, the Federal Expellee Ministry only calculated how many people living in the FRG would be affected by its regulations but made no such projection about the people still living in Eastern Europe who were granted German citizenship in their absence.[31] While indicating a lack of awareness for the issue, this omission was arguably also due to the fact that the government considered the *Volksliste* files lost at the time.[32] The ministry did know about the more than one million inhabitants of the former German Eastern Territories—in particular, Western Upper Silesia and Masuria—who had been "verified" as Polish after the war but remained German citizens according to the West German viewpoint, which did not recognize the loss of these territories and hence did not accept any change to their inhabitants' citizenship.[33] The ministry seemed to have no clear idea that there were also hundreds of thousands of "rehabilitated" *Volksliste* members who were defined as potential German citizens in their absence.[34] Both of these groups were bound to grow, since German citizenship, according to the 1913 citizenship law, was inheritable qua jus sanguinis without generational restriction. In effect this meant that all the people in Eastern Europe who had been German citizens before the war or had received German citizenship in one of the collective naturalization campaigns for *Volksdeutsche* would pass their German citizenship on to all their descendants, who would, when the time came, be entitled to enter the Federal Republic of Germany as German citizens if they decided to respond the FRG's claim of co-ethnicity. This is precisely what happened to Germans from Upper Silesia, who made up a large part of Aussiedler until 1990.

In parallel to the provisions of the Basic Law and the citizenship settlement law, the 1953 Federal Expellee Law (*Bundesvertriebenengesetz*, or BVFG) provided a definition of the term *expellee* that transcended state borders and the immediate context of the postwar period by explicitly including people who came after the end of the actual expulsions. According to the basic definition of section 1, expellees were those German citizens or ethnic Germans who had lived in the Eastern Territories of the Reich or outside the Reich, as defined by its borders on December 31, 1937, and had lost their home "in the context of the events of the Second World War as a consequence of expulsion." The same status was conferred on German citizens or ethnic Germans who had left these territories after the Nazis' rise to power on January 30, 1933, for fear of persecution (*Fiktivvertriebene*); on people who had been resettled during the war because of bilateral treaties or unilateral German resettlement campaigns (*Umsiedler*); and, crucially, Aussiedler, defined as people who had left or would leave the communist countries of Eastern Europe—the so-called expulsion area (*Vertreibungsgebiete*)—after the end of the "general expulsion measures" (*allgemeine Vertreibungsmaßnahmen*).[35]

The inclusion of Aussiedler in this definition opened the expellee law to the future and to (potential) Germans from a circumscribed area abroad. In doing so, it corresponded to the stipulations of Article 116: if a "German according to the Basic Law" could be someone who found reception in the Federal Republic "as an expellee or refugee" even after the expulsion, then the definition of *expellee* had to be temporally open-ended as well.[36] But adding this category also had practical reasons. As the Federal Expellee Ministry and the Bundestag Committee for Expellees were drafting the BVFG beginning in 1950, the first Aussiedler from Poland were already arriving in the Federal Republic under family reunification schemes. The first major plan for family reunification, "Operation Link" in 1950–1951, brought 76,000 people from the former German Eastern Territories to both German states, 42,500 of whom were registered in West Germany.[37] By 1956, as many as 180,000 applications for resettlement were submitted from Poland alone, many of which would soon be granted by the Polish authorities in the large family reunification campaign that lasted from 1956 until 1958.[38] The legal category of Aussiedler as "expellees after the expulsion" thus came into being as the result of preexisting legal definitions and actual events on the ground.

THE LIMITED SCOPE OF AUSSIEDLUNG

The absence of an explicit law of return corresponded to the absence of an underlying comprehensive diaspora return ideology or overriding ethnic commitment in the making of Aussiedler policy. The scope of West German co-ethnic engagement had significant limits that made it fall short of the universal and time-transcending homeland stance expressed in the Israeli Law of Return. The first such limitation of the German co-ethnic migration regime's scope was temporal and resulted from the fact that ethnic German resettlement remained tied to the events of the Second World War and the mass expulsion of the Germans, even as the regime's time horizon gradually shifted toward the future with the legal codification of the Aussiedler category.

Aware that the legal fiction of people being expellees without having been expelled was problematic, the legislature introduced a separate explanation why Aussiedlung, despite its basically nonforced character, could still be considered to have a causal link to the events of the Second World War. As stated in the comments to the draft of November 26, 1951, "Flight, eviction and Aussiedlung are subsumed under the heading of 'expulsion' if they took place in the context of the events of the war. This context must not be defined too narrowly. Even though in many instances there is no more immediate force used to make people leave their homes, the reception of Germans from the expulsion area for example in the course of 'Operation Link' has to be considered as Aussiedlung in the context of the events of the war, as people cannot be expected to stay there, given the circumstances created by the war."[39] Seen from the perspective of 1951, stipulating this causal link was not too far-fetched, because the events of the war could still be felt. But it was also clear that this link would weaken over time. This construction of "expulsion after the expulsion" indicates that political actors did not anticipate long-term migratory movements. This is also suggested by the use of the term *Spätaussiedler* ("late resettlers") already in the 1950s.[40] Introduced as an official legal category in the reformed Federal Expellee Law of 1993, the term is used today to differentiate resettlers who were coming "late" (after 1992) from those who had immigrated before. The early usage of the term in the 1950s indicates that an end of the Aussiedler problem was anticipated sooner rather than later, as the ethnic Germans immigrating then were already considered to be "coming late" not even ten years after the end of the general expulsion campaign. A resettlement campaign of ethnic Germans from Eastern Europe stretching over decades was certainly not on the horizon in the 1950s, not least because the Germans in the Soviet Union, who would make up the vast majority of Aussiedler during the 1990s, were not yet on the German migration regime's radar.

The still limited time horizon of West German Aussiedler policy in the 1950s corresponded to the narrow confines of its conceptual and ideological scope. Contrary to the claims of some important literature on postwar German migration history, the Federal Republic did not embrace an ideology of returning to the homeland when dealing with ethnic Germans from Eastern Europe.[41] Nor did the country keep an unconditionally open door for this group of people and therefore did not treat them as "long distance citizens."[42] The contemporary deliberations about appropriate terminology to describe co-ethnic migration are instructive in this regard. In a January 1954 meeting at the Federal Expellee Ministry, several high-level federal institutions discussed the resettlement of Germans from the "Polish administrated German Eastern Territories and from Poland," the main regions of origin of the Aussiedler at the time and for subsequent decades.[43] Remarkably, both the Ministry for All-German Questions and the Foreign Office opposed the widespread use in legal texts of the term *repatriation* (*Rückführung*) for cases of Aussiedlung, because it was "factually wrong" and "politically problematic."[44] They also refused the term *resettlement* (*Umsiedlung*) because of its use by the German Democratic Republic government as a euphemism for the expulsion of the Germans. But not even the term *Aussiedlung*, which had already been introduced into official legal language through the BVFG, met with general agreement, as it was thought to imply renouncing the Eastern Territories, which, according to the West German standpoint, were merely under Polish administration. *Family reunification* could not be used as a substitute term, because it was identified as just one aspect of the wider problem—though the most important one. What remained in the consensual opinion of the discussants was the term *takeover* (*Übernahme*), as it was thought to be factually correct and politically neutral.[45] At the same time, it supposedly implied no obligation whatsoever on the side of the state and rather stressed the fact that the people in question were in need of help. Generally, *Übernahme* was to be preferred over *Aussiedlung* unless there was explicit reference to the BVFG and its Aussiedler clauses.

The intricate connection between Aussiedlung and the question of the Eastern Territories thus did not allow contemporary West German political actors to conceptualize this migration as return or repatriation—in contrast to the Israeli notion of "return to Zion" that found its expression in the 1950 Law of Return. The migration of Aussiedler to the Federal Republic of Germany could not be considered repatriation, since their rightful homeland was in the former—according to the West German view, still German—Eastern Territories of the Reich.[46] As expellee politician Hans-Christoph Seebohm phrased it in a letter to Expellee Minister Theodor Oberländer in December 1956, at the beginning of the great emigration wave from Poland shortly after Gomulka's ascent to power, the use of return terminology created the impression that it was "the repatriation of people who belonged in the Federal Republic anyhow."[47] According to Chancellor Adenauer, the exodus of the remaining Germans threatened any West German claim to the Reich's Eastern Territories. Oberländer even feared a "second expulsion of the Germans from beyond the Oder-Neisse line."[48] Their reception in West Germany—the "free part of the fatherland," as it was referred to in Cold War terms—was hence not the result of an ideologically motivated diaspora resettlement campaign but a consequence of the assumption that conditions in the old homeland under foreign and communist rule had become unbearable.[49]

It is also clear from the analyzed discussion that the open door the Federal Republic offered to Aussiedler from Eastern Europe was not unconditionally open from the outset. That the participants of this meeting insisted on a neutral term implying no obligation to take anyone in indicates that accepting Aussiedler was meant as a humanitarian gesture rather than a state obligation or an entitlement for migrants. Their arrival was not actively pursued by the state, on the contrary: When the German mining industry suggested recruiting Transylvanian Saxons from Austria as laborers in 1952, the Foreign Office and the Interior and Expellee Ministries all opposed this initiative for fear of setting a precedent for other ethnic Germans living abroad.[50] In later administrative documents, too, it was stressed that non-German citizens had no automatic right to settle in West Germany. The takeover guidelines of 1968, which are discussed in detail in chapter 4, clearly stated that "[Germans from Eastern Europe] who are not German citizens and cannot claim family reunification have no legal entitlement to admission to the Federal Republic of Germany. However, it has always been an important concern of the federal government and federal parliament to enable also those people to be admitted to the Federal Republic of Germany if they explicitly wish so."[51] In other words, at the time, the ethnic Germans in the East were seen not as long-distance citizens but as poor kinsfolk in need of help.[52]

This observation links to another conceptual limitation of Aussiedlung: the restrictive definition of the circle of eligible people. The first restriction in this regard resulted from considerations of political geography and was contained in section 1 of the BVFG. An Aussiedler could not be a German from anywhere in the world but had to hail from one of the communist countries of Eastern Europe, including Albania, which had never been home to a "German minority." From 1957, the definition was even extended to include China.[53] This exclusive focus on communist countries in the definition of the expulsion area has correctly been attributed to the Cold War context.[54] It shows that West Germany received Aussiedler not simply on account of being German but also, and crucially, for being victims of communism.

The 1954 meeting brought another point to the fore: people who were not legally entitled to immigration for lack of German citizenship would be taken in because they were in need of help. Aussiedler reception was thus intended as an ethno-humanitarian measure to reunify families torn apart by the war rather than an ethnically motivated resettlement campaign. For the first two decades of Aussiedler migration, this reserved stance concerning the scope of Aussiedlung prevailed. To some extent, this position was dictated by the fact that the very possibility of Aussiedler migration depended on bilateral cooperation with the socialist states in Eastern Europe. And these states would only accept emigration within the framework of internationally regulated humanitarian family reunification or, as in the Soviet case since 1958, as the resettlement of mutually recognized German citizens in West Germany.

Significantly, however, the West German governmental authorities employed such cautious humanitarian rhetoric not only within the international arena but also domestically when facing pressure from the vocal expellee lobby. From the early 1960s, the chancellor and the ministries encountered aggressive lobbying by various associations of Germans from Romania in West Germany that pushed the government to extend the scope of Aussiedlung from family reunification to a "proper" resettlement campaign on an ethnic basis in order to save their ethnic kinspeople from assimilation and doom.[55] They cited Romanian Jews, who had been literally ransomed from Romania with private financial initiatives, as an example to follow.[56] As the Association of Danube Swabians proposed, the money otherwise invested in the recruitment and accommodation of foreign workers could be used for this purpose. The German economy would also benefit from this additional labor force. Of course, they argued, the resettlement suggested here was not akin to the resettlement policies of the Nazis, but rather the realization of the human right to free movement, change of residence, and emigration as stipulated by the Universal Declaration of Human Rights.[57]

The government was unimpressed by this call for a more extensive resettlement campaign and insisted on the humanitarian logic of the refugee state. As an official from the Ministry for All-German Questions argued in an internal memorandum for the Federal Chancellery, the idea of Romanian Germans being an additional labor force for the German market was prone to disturb the humanitarian endeavors of the federal government and the Red Cross.[58] While the Foreign Office displayed some willingness to address the issue of Romanian Germans under the heading of "extended family reunification" in trade negotiations with the Romanian government, its representatives generally insisted that the issue should not be framed as a "resettlement campaign" (*Aussiedlungsaktion*) but as "genuine family reunification" (*echte Familienzusammenführung*). This should also be the government's position toward the expellee associations (*Landsmannschaften*).[59] In a meeting of the Parliamentary Committee for Expellee Questions in 1965, a Foreign Office official made the same point, arguing that, otherwise, the "wrong impression of a resuscitation of German minority policies" might be created.[60] In yet another meeting in 1966, Secretary of State Karl Carstens (the future president of the Federal Republic) used the term "VDA-reminiscences" to describe the possible negative reactions to an overt German attempt to resettle entire ethnic groups rather than just reunifying divided families. In general, he claimed, the problem was of a humanitarian rather than political-territorial nature.[61]

Carstens's reference to the VDA, the old *Verein für das Deutschtum im Ausland* (Association for Germans Abroad) and present-day *Verein für Deutsche Kulturbeziehungen im Ausland* (Association for German Cultural Relations Abroad), was not coincidental. In the mid-1950s, this infamous organization had been resurrected against stiff opposition from the Foreign Office.[62] After several years of negotiations, the government gave up its total opposition but kept its distance from the association.[63] In 1966, it still used the reference to the VDA to quell calls for a more extensive resettlement policy. In fact, the state's joining of forces with this association in the field of Aussiedler migration did not take place until the Kohl era in the 1980s.[64] And despite the continuous and persistent pressure by some of the expellee associations, transcending the concept of Aussiedler migration as family reunification towards a "proper" ethnic resettlement campaign was not on the agenda. As will be examined in chapter 4, this only began to change under the impression of developments on the ground in the 1970s.

WHO IS A GERMAN? DEFINING ETHNICITY BY LAW

The ethno-humanitarian laws of the West German refugee state provided political integration and welfare benefits based on belonging. As mentioned before, recognition as German according to the Basic Law and hence eligibility for benefits under the Federal Expellee Law was doubly coded: an applicant had to be both an expellee and either a German citizen or an ethnic German (*deutscher Volkszugehöriger*). Expellees could also be Aussiedler, defined as people who left their homeland in Eastern Europe after the expulsions but still in the context of the events of the war. If they were not German citizens already, both "real" expellees and Aussiedler had to fulfill the criteria of German *Volkszugehörigkeit*, which section 6 of the law defined as follows: "A German *Volkszugehöriger* according to this law is someone who has identified in his country of origin as belonging to the German *Volkstum*, provided that this self-identification (*Bekenntnis*) is backed up by certain characteristics like descent, language, upbringing, culture."[65] This definition was taken almost verbatim from a March 1939 Reich Interior Ministry circular concerning the ethnic classification of the newly created Protectorate of Bohemia and Moravia, though it excluded the obviously racist second part of the 1939 version, which had stated in accordance with Nazi ideology: "Persons of foreign blood (*artfremden Blutes*), especially Jews, are never such *Volkszugehörige*, even if they have so far referred to themselves as such."[66]

The adoption of this apparently Nazi-inspired definition met with frequent criticism in future decades, especially during the mass immigration wave from Poland and the Soviet Union that began in the late 1980s, when Aussiedler immigration became the object of public contestation.[67] Among the contemporaries, the *Allgemeine Wochenzeitung der Juden in Deutschland* articulated such criticism. In a January 1955 article titled "Old Norms in New Laws," the official organ of the Central Council of Jews in Germany condemned the supposedly National Socialist character of section 6 BVFG. In his reply to the editor in chief, Karl Marx, Expellee Minister Theodor Oberländer—himself a former member of the Nazi Party, prominent *Ostforscher* ("researcher of the East"), and suspected war criminal—admitted to this legacy of the section but turned the argument around.[68] He reasoned that it had been introduced into the law precisely to avoid reference to the 1939 definition, the only hitherto existing legal definition of German *Volkszugehörigkeit*. He further contended that this definition in fact preceded the Nazi era, just like the problem of German minorities.[69] In a parliamentary debate about the Federal Expellee Law,

Oberländer's predecessor Hans Lukaschek simply stated that "this version of section 6 adopted here is the formulation used in the literature"—a statement that brings into focus the complete lack of awareness among government officials that the legal literature on citizenship produced during the Nazi era might be problematic in any way.[70]

Although it comes as no surprise that a former *Ostforscher* and *völkisch* ideologue such as Oberländer should have had no problem with a definition of ethnicity used in a Nazi circular, he was in fact correct to point to its pre-Nazi origins, which also lay outside the borders of the German Reich. In this context, it is significant that the 1939 circular referred to the specific circumstances of the newly occupied Bohemian lands with their long tradition of ethnic and linguistic ambiguity. Tara Zahra has noted that, to classify the local population, the German occupiers used local definitions. Because of the blurred boundaries between Germans, Czechs, and other nationalities in the region, "officials were frequently forced to rely on long-standing civic definitions of Germanness that had been promoted by German nationalists since the late nineteenth century in order to implement the new policies of racial classification."[71]

As will be further developed in chapter 3, the definition of German *Volkszugehörigkeit* that later found its way into expellee law was precisely such a civic definition, as it placed emphasis on personal subjective identification that had to be "confirmed" by certain "objective" criteria. With its peculiar blend of subjective and objective components of ethnic belonging, the 1939 definition in fact connected to the late nineteenth-century legal tradition of Austrian jurisdiction on individual ethnic belonging. Its only genuinely National Socialist component was the explicit exclusion of Jews from identification with Germanness—who, as the circular implicitly acknowledged, did in fact identify as Germans in many instances.[72]

The genealogy of the definition's "civic" core part, by contrast, harks back to the Habsburg Empire. As the supreme Austrian administrative court stated in a January 1881 ruling: "Surely an individual member of a nationality will speak the language of that nation and likely share its customs, while it is certain that this might also be the case for a third party, a foreigner, which is why these criteria are not sufficient to determine nationality. Therefore, if an individual person's nationality is doubtful and he is lacking outward manifestations of national consciousness, there will be no other choice but to ask him for his nationality and treat him as a member of the nationality with which he chooses to identify."[73] This early ruling privileged individual self-identification over seemingly objective characteristics and thus firmly established the so-called *Bekenntnisprinzip* for the determination of individual ethnic belonging. Subsequent jurisdiction by Austrian courts, by contrast, often tried to use more objective criteria, which in the Austrian context revolved around the issues of "language of everyday use" (*Umgangssprache*) and "native language" (*Muttersprache*).[74] While Habsburg law never actually codified individual ethnic belonging, this characteristic (and ever dynamic) mixture of the two components—known in the Austrian legal world as *Willensmerkmale* and *Wesensmerkmale*—provided the foundation for the official definition of *Volkszugehörigkeit* in post–Second World War West Germany.

Although the *Volkszugehörigkeit* section generally aroused little contestation in the course of drafting the expellee law, the suggested blend of subjective and objective definitions did not go unchallenged in parliament. Both challengers were liberal party members of parliament with Eastern German backgrounds. One was Dr. Josef Trischler, a former minority politician and member of parliament in Yugoslavia and Hungary during the interwar period. He was joined by Axel de Vries, a German minority politician and member of parliament from Estonia, who, during the Second World War, had been in charge of agrarian affairs in the military administration of occupied Belarus.[75] These two men opposed the confirmation of the *Bekenntnis* by the proposed objective characteristics and instead suggested adding the following sentence: "Expulsion is to be considered as proof for identification with German *Volkstum* in the homeland."[76] In his explanation of the proposal, de Vries argued that neither descent nor language were suitable criteria to determine ethnic belonging, pointing to his own trilingualism. The criterion of culture he dismissed as simply too complex to make it useable for the purpose of this law. The objective criteria would thus only complicate the implementation of section 6. *Volkszugehörigkeit*, de Vries concluded on an almost postmodern note, should be recognized as the "inalienable human right of a free personality"; hence, "belonging to *Volkstum* should be the free decision of each individual."[77]

Expellee Minister Lukaschek's reaction to the proposal and his subsequent exchange with de Vries captures the complexity of the double definition of a German as an expellee and as a German *Volkszugehöriger*. Though generally agreeing with the proposal, Lukaschek asked for the motion to be withdrawn.[78] To substantiate his rejection of the idea to take expulsion for proof of *Bekenntnis*, he pointed to the case of Franz (František) Kroupa, the former mayor (or "commissar," according to a contemporary press report) of Czechoslovak Joachimsthal/Jáchymov who sought refuge from communism in West Germany but was accused of having tortured Sudeten Germans in the course of the expulsion.[79] Lukaschek argued that someone like Kroupa should not be recognized as an expellee just because he was expelled from his homeland. De

Vries interjected at this point: "As a German, Herr Minister!" To which Lukaschek replied: "Well, you know, my name is Lukaschek and I have a Polish name. These are difficult moments. I believe if I give you this assurance, you might be willing to withdraw your motion."[80] De Vries agreed and withdrew the motion.

Though somewhat cryptic, on closer examination, this exchange between de Vries and Lukaschek reveals two possible ways of interpreting the notion of German expellee. Lukaschek obviously understood de Vries's interjection "as a German" as referring to the issue of *Volkszugehörigkeit,* which he presumably identified with descent when pointing to his Polish surname. Yet what de Vries meant was that a German, in order to be expelled *as* a German, had to be expelled *because of* being German. And this could not be the case for a person like Kroupa, who had fled Czechoslovakia for political reasons.

The question of whether "as" was equivalent to "because of" would soon be an important issue discussed at court.[81] It became especially pertinent to the legal category of Aussiedler, who were considered expellees by the law but were not actually expelled by force. While de Vries and Trischler were able to give part of the defining power to the expelling state for actual expellees, this would no longer work for Aussiedler. Lawmakers at the time were aware of this problem and tried to resolve it with the notion of Aussiedlung as emigration in the context of the events of the war. This construction was realistic enough for the early 1950s, but it became more difficult to sustain with the passing of time, as will be shown in the discussions of generational extension in chapter 4 and of the creation and contestation of the notion of "expulsion pressure" (*Vertreibungsdruck*) in chapter 5.

The other key problem of the expellee law definition of ethnicity that Trischler and de Vries's proposal and the subsequent discussion brought to the fore concerned the question of how to assess whether someone had self-identified as German—that is, if they had made a *Bekenntnis.* This issue had already been discussed in a session of the responsible parliamentary committee but without any tangible outcome. Everyone merely agreed that the proof was indeed difficult to establish.[82] However, it was decided not to follow the Bundesrat suggestion to also require a *Bekenntnis* after the beginning of the expulsion in order to avoid even further complications. By not asking for a post-expulsion *Bekenntnis,* the legislature clearly established that a German *Volkszugehöriger* could only be someone who had identified as German before 1945, thus firmly rooting these notions in a specific temporal context. A person's subsequent behavior would make no difference, for better or for worse.

As is clear from the Braun case cited at the beginning of this chapter, the *Bekenntnis* question was anything but theoretical. Stephan Braun was objectively German in the eyes of the law, having perfect command of the language and being clearly of German descent.[83] The problem was with his self-identification. Could a Hungarian police officer have been a publicly self-avowed German? Given the dominant restrictive interpretation that a *Bekenntnis* could only be to one *Volkstum* at a time, this seemed highly doubtful.[84] At the same time, there was awareness among the commentators on the expellee law that identification with the Hungarian state did not necessarily imply identification with Magyar *Volkstum*.[85] Moreover, and contrary to the legislature's intuition, having to prove the *Bekenntnis* only for the time before 1945 did not facilitate the process: all of the 19 witnesses heard during the investigation of Braun's case possessed information only about the time after 1945, which was all but irrelevant. Braun's personal paperwork was also not helpful, because the Hungarian state, unlike some of the multinational states in Central and Eastern Europe, did not differentiate its individual citizens according to ethnicity.[86]

At the same time, it was not clear what a classification as German by the state of origin would have meant. Since it was up to the German state to identify German *Volkszugehörige* according to its own legal definitions, such a classification should have been irrelevant.[87] Nevertheless, identification as German—or at least as a speaker of German—in an official context such as a state census was identified from early on as one of the key ways to prove a *Bekenntnis*.[88] In the absence of such documentation and lacking relevant witnesses, retrospectively establishing *Volkszugehörigkeit* was already a difficult, if not impossible, task for the administration with less than ten years' distance from the events. With Aussiedler immigration extending into the future, proving the past *Bekenntnis* was sure to become even more complicated.

WHO DECIDES WHO IS A GERMAN? INSTITUTIONS AND GATEKEEPERS

Expellees and Aussiedler had to be German to qualify for political and social inclusion in the West German refugee state. This Germanness—whether expressed in political citizenship or ethnic *Volkszugehörigkeit*—was ascertained by the refugee administration. These special offices outside the regular state administration were the key institutional component of the regime administering the presence of the forced migrants in the country. Created at the Land level during the immediate postwar period, these agencies were tasked with integrating the millions of German refugees in the country, whom international care bodies such as the United Nations Relief and Rehabilitation Administration and, subsequently, the International Refugee Organization refused to deal with.[89]

The refugee administration's screening practices mirrored those of the international organizations, which also scrutinized applicants' life stories for hints that they were German, but with the opposite intention of excluding them from help.[90] Officially recognized expellees received an "expellee card" (*Vertriebenenausweis*) that identified them as eligible for integration benefits and, if they were foreign citizens, for German citizenship. As expellee migration evolved into Aussiedler migration during the 1950s, the regime of presence was supplemented by a regime of admission, as the refugee administration became integrated into the multitier bureaucratic process regulating the transfer of people from countries of the Eastern Bloc across the Iron Curtain to West Germany. It thus became one of the gatekeepers of co-ethnic migration within the evolving Aussiedler migration regime, which persisted in its basic form until 1990.

Since West Germany did not establish diplomatic ties with most socialist states harboring German minorities until later in the 1960s (Romania in 1967) or even the 1970s (Poland 1972, Czechoslovakia 1973), diplomatic missions, which in other contexts would be a first point of reference—and possibly a first obstacle—for prospective migrants, played a limited role in the resettlement process at the time. Instead, the German Red Cross tracing service came to play an important part as an intermediary and enabler in the migration process. It was the main organ of the migration regime institutions to reach out to Germans in Eastern Europe, as it provided a link between relatives divided by the Iron Curtain as well as with the German state institutions.[91] The German Red Cross also negotiated with the Red Cross societies of the socialist countries, reached agreements about emigration, and submitted lists of candidates.[92] Furthermore, the organization kept the state institutions up to date about the development of Aussiedler migration with frequent reports.

Consular institutions were far less important. Although the Foreign Office (*Auswärtiges Amt*) had two departments dedicated to questions of Germans abroad, the lack of consulates in most countries of origin meant that immigration requests could not be processed through regular consular channels. The two exceptions to this rule were Yugoslavia and the Soviet Union, where West Germany established embassies in 1952 and 1955, respectively. Consular institutions gained greater importance once people managed to leave their homeland on a different pretext and then reported to a West German consulate in a third country (in many instances, Austria).

Would-be Aussiedler had to pass several bureaucratic obstacles on their way west. The first—and, given the anti-emigration stance of state socialism, most difficult—step was to leave the country of origin in Eastern Europe, which often involved arbitrary and time-consuming emigration procedures.[93] After that, the entry procedure into Germany—which, despite the notion that migration controls on the German side of the migration channel were "lax" and that the country kept an "open door" for German co-ethnics—involved considerable bureaucracy.[94]

Contrary to what the adjective *open* implies, the door to the Federal Republic of Germany was guarded by intricate control mechanisms. In fact, it consisted of two consecutive gateways—one external and one internal—with no less than three rounds of examination, all of which, ideally, a candidate had to pass. The first two of these examinations were carried out by the institutions of the regular internal administration. The "takeover procedure" (*Übernahmeverfahren*), also known by its bureaucratic abbreviation D1, fulfilled the purpose of providing prospective Aussiedler with an entry permit for West Germany. Predicated on the idea that Aussiedler migration was family reunification, the application was supposed to be filed at local authorities by relatives already living in Germany.[95] Its processing was a collaborative effort of the Federal Interior Ministry (BMI) and local, regional, and Land-level institutions. As of 1960, the Federal Administration Office (*Bundesverwaltungsamt*, BVA) as an executive organ of the BMI was put in charge of the overall process, deciding individual cases based on input from these other institutions.

The BVA was also in charge of the second step of ethnic immigration control, the so-called distribution procedure (*Verteilungsverfahren*). As a link between the external and internal procedures, this step took place in the transit camps in Friedland and Nuremberg (and, until its dismantling in 1962, also in the Piding camp in Bavaria), where Aussiedler first reported to West German authorities on arrival. Whereas D1 used the available documentation on paper to check candidates' general eligibility for immigration, the distribution procedure fulfilled a complementary function by interviewing those who had managed to migrate. In the event of a positive evaluation, the immigrant was registered and received a registration certificate (*Registrierschein*). He or she was then assigned to a federal state, where the eventual recognition as an expellee, marked by the issuing of an expellee card, took place in the internal procedure carried out by the local refugee administration.

Though organizationally separate, the external and internal procedures assessed the same crucial criterion for the eligibility of candidates: their German *Volkszugehörigkeit* according to section 6 BVFG or their German citizenship. Expulsion, the second component of the doubly coded definition of a German expellee, was not explicitly controlled for, since the authorities took it for granted that a German who emigrated from Eastern Europe did so in the context of the events of the war, and hence as an expellee. As an official commentary to the Federal Expellee Law stated, "the legislature does not expect the

Figure 1.1. The administrative archive of Friedland transit camp, with hundreds of thousands of Aussiedler registration files on record. Reprinted with permission from Gesine Wallem and Bundesinstitut für Kultur und Geschichte der Deutschen im Östlichen Europa (BKGE).

Germans who stayed or who are held back in those states to remain there under the current circumstances, and given that the biggest part of the ethnic group (*Volksgruppe*) has been expelled."[96] But as the Braun case already indicated, assessing individual ethnicity in a bureaucratic procedure was a complicated business. Given the multiple individual and collective naturalizations of *Volksdeutsche* by Nazi authorities before and during the war, the same was true for identifying a German citizen.

The amount of information gathered in the questionnaires used in the various procedures testifies to the complexity of the task. The D1 form introduced for the external procedure in 1956 mainly asked for clues indicating that an applicant may have been a German citizen by birth or become a German citizen by association with the expanding and contracting German Reich at war. Apart from citizenship at birth and current citizenship (to be proved by documents), the form asked for places of residence at different points in time as well as for membership in German military formations (Wehrmacht or Waffen-SS), police, *Reichsarbeitsdienst, Organisation Todt,* or others as well as possible internment as a prisoner of war.[97] *Volkszugehörigkeit* was also among the items asked for on the form, but no additional information was requested to back up the claim to German ethnicity.

The form used in the internal procedure, which was in use from 1953, asked for more detail to assess whether an applicant fulfilled the subjective and objective criteria of section 6 BVFG. It requested information about the applicant's native language, possible attendance at German schools, and membership in German associations as well as the *Volkszugehörigkeit* of the person's parents and spouse.[98] This questionnaire, which was produced with a view to the expellees of the immediate postwar period, was later amended for the purposes of Aussiedler recognition through an additional form requesting a great deal of supplementary detail on places of residence, languages spoken, schools attended, military service, possible internment, expropriation, membership in an association, names of children, and possible witnesses to confirm this information—all with the aim of being able to judge the "overall behavior (*Gesamtverhalten*) of the applicant."[99] As Aussiedlung continued and the newcomers appeared less clearly German than before, more information was required to fit them into the categories of expellee law.

From the beginning, the institutions involved in the various steps of the screening process also relied on certain nonstate or semistate expert institutions for information on which they could base their judgment: the *Heimatortskarteien* (HOK) and *Heimatauskunftstellen* (HASt). The HOK were card indexes of the German refugee population operated by church charity organizations Caritas and Diakonie. In addition to helping with the tracing of missing individuals, the organizations used their extensive name record of ethnic Germans to assist the refugee administration in determining who among the Aussiedler was an ethnic German or descended from ethnic Germans.[100] The 34 HASt, each of which was responsible for a particular region of the German East, originally served to assess applications for indemnity by expellees in the context of the Equalization of Burdens Act (*Lastenausgleichsgesetz*). With the continuous influx of Aussiedler, it became an increasingly important part of their work to provide expertise on the question of the *Volkszugehörigkeit* of immigrants applying for an expellee card with the refugee administration. For this purpose, the HASt made use of networks of people with "intimate knowledge" of the expellees' regions of origin, especially former officials. Expellee associations cooperated with the HASt by providing them with names and addresses of such experts, and with staff for the offices.[101] Through the HASt, the expellee associations became indirect gatekeepers of the German refugee state. As described in subsequent chapters, their relationship with the state apparatus oscillated between cooperation and competition as they repeatedly attempted to assert their defining power over the question of who was to be considered German over the next decades.

LOST BETWEEN THE GATES: THE GULF BETWEEN THE INTERNAL AND EXTERNAL PROCEDURES

In addition to being organizationally separate, the external and internal procedures worked according to different logics, which resulted in varying degrees of strictness of control and a growing gulf between them. The case of Irma L. and her husband illustrates how the different gateways of the Aussiedler migration regime, though using the same code of admission, did not necessarily produce coherent results, as recognition in the external procedure did not necessarily entail recognition in the internal procedure.[102] Irma was born in 1911 in Slovak Banská Bystrica (German: Neusohl; Hungarian: Besztercebánya), then part of Habsburg Hungary, into a German-speaking family originally from Transylvania. In 1940, she married Stefan L., whose parents were of German and Hungarian origin. In 1969, the couple applied for a D1 immigration permit through Irma's cousin Hans, who lived in Berlin. The application was granted, and the couple moved from Czechoslovakia to West Germany in March 1971. When interviewed by BVA officials for the distribution procedure in the Nuremberg transit camp, Irma stated that she had identified as an ethnic German before the Czechoslovak authorities but then changed her identification to Slovak so as not to endanger her husband's job as a financial inspector. Stefan claimed to have always identified as Slovak. Because of the resulting doubts regarding the couple's German identity, the authorities suspended the distribution procedure.

Irma and Stefan then unsuccessfully applied for an expellee card with the refugee administration in Mannheim, which took their statements in Nuremberg as the indication of a lacking *Bekenntnis*. An administrative complaint was also unsuccessful. After Stefan passed away in March 1972, Irma took the case to court on her own and was initially vindicated. The Karlsruhe Administrative Court decided that she was entitled to an expellee card—not because she was an ethnic German expellee (the court thought she was not) but because the screening authorities at the external gate had treated her as such when accepting her. In the court's opinion, this created a justified expectation on her part that the same would happen at the internal gate, where she would be granted citizenship and pension rights. After all, it was with this expectation that she had left her homeland and had forfeited her previous citizenship and pension. However, both the Administrative Court of Baden-Württemberg and the Federal Administrative Court disagreed with this view and ruled that acceptance in the D1 procedure did not create any legal entitlement to subsequent recognition as an expellee in the internal procedure.[103] The courts argued that the external procedure only assessed whether there was any indication that the applicant was *not* an ethnic German expellee. The definitive decision was reserved for the internal procedure. For this reason, Irma L. was not recognized as German, even though she had been accepted into the country as such.

Irma L.'s case underscores the fundamentally different logic of the external and internal procedures. Despite the Federal Interior Ministry's concern to avoid the impression that D1 visas were issued arbitrarily to help people leave communist Eastern Europe, this is essentially what the external procedure did.[104] In the words of the Baden-Württemberg Administrative Court: "The preliminary examination of the applicant's case should enable him to immigrate for humanitarian reasons."[105] Under the impact of these Cold War–induced conditions, the external procedure was hence relatively lax. The internal procedure, by contrast, ruled on immigrants' eligibility for substantial financial benefits. The representatives of the *Länder* refugee administrations therefore agreed with the ruling on Irma L.'s case, because they saw it as an opportunity to correct the decisions of the external procedure which they viewed as potentially too generous.[106]

In fact, it had been the expellee department of the Interior Ministry of Baden-Württemberg that had appealed against the decision of the first court, according to which an expellee card should have been issued on the basis of the legal precedent created by the D1 takeover visa. If this rule applied, the ministry argued, the D1 procedure would have to become a great deal more restrictive.[107] Instead, closer examination of the cases was left to the internal procedure—though, due to its decentralized nature, the degree of strictness could vary substantially between offices. A remark by the Expellee Ministry of Baden-Württemberg in December 1958 that "the examination of the *Volkszugehörigkeit* of applicants with foreign citizenship is often not conducted with the necessary care" certainly indicates that some internal offices were lax in their practices, too.[108] At the same time, the admonition shows that the official intention was more restrictive, as the refugee state was unwilling to pay for "undeserving" benefit seekers.

ISRAEL: BETWEEN INGATHERING THE EXILES AND BUILDING THE STATE

In contrast to West Germany, Israel established itself clearly as the homeland of the Jewish people by means of a universal, time-transcending, and ideologically grounded Law of Return. Based on the 1948 Declaration of Independence, which affirmed that the Jewish state "will be open for Jewish immigration and for the Ingathering of the Exiles," the Law of Return asserted the right of every Jew to immigrate to Israel.[109] Unlike German Aussiedlung, which admitted "latecomers" to a discrete historical period and was thought of as a temporary relief measure, the Israeli invitation to world Jewry had no expiration date, other than perhaps some imaginary moment in the future when the "ingathering of exiles" (*kibbutz galuyot*) would be accomplished. The intention of complete Jewish resettlement certainly existed.[110] For some communities that were transferred to Israel almost in their entirety—such as those from Bulgaria, Libya, and Iraq—total resettlement was turned into practice. The vocabulary chosen in this regard is quite telling. Communities that could not be upheld were subject to "liquidation" (*chisul*)—a term that in this situation denotes not physical annihilation through killing but definitive dissolution and resettlement.

Zionism was the ideological foundation of this universal invitation to the Jews of the world to come to their resurrected historical homeland and build the Jewish state. A heterogeneous movement straddling various left-right and religious-secular cleavages among different Jewries, the basic objective of Zionism since the 1917 Balfour Declaration had been the establishment of a Jewish homeland in Palestine, also known as *Eretz Israel* (Land of Israel). While statehood was not necessarily implied as the ultimate aim, Zionism did entail the "negation of the diaspora" (*shlilat ha-golah*) as the Jewish condition of being.[111]

The resulting terminology to describe Jewish immigration, which was adopted in Israeli legal vocabulary, was itself ideological: Aliyah ("ascent") and the related term for immigrant, Oleh (plural: Olim), originated in the context of religious pilgrimage. This vocabulary was subsequently appropriated by Zionism to attribute a sense of individual elevation to the act of moving to the Land of Israel—a process that Zionists in the early twentieth century still matter-of-factly called *immigratziah*.[112] In this, it contrasted sharply with the German terminology of *Aussiedlung* and *Übernahme*, which, though transferred to a new context, had its roots in the technical vocabulary of Nazi population engineering intent on deindividualizing the people being resettled.

The notion of return was introduced into the legal discussion only shortly before the Law of Return was enacted, but it was uncontested in its substance.[113] The previously considered name, "Ingathering of the Exiles Law" (*chok kibbutz ha-galuyot*), conveyed a similar idea: the ingathering of and hence the return from the diaspora. Unlike the situation in Germany, where people left what was perceived to be their rightful place, their *Heimat*, Zionist ideology posited that Jews were finally returning to their rightful place that had been taken from them by force after the destruction of the Second Temple almost two thousand years before. For this reason, positive value was attached to the notion of the liquidation of the diaspora. Once the Jewish state was established in 1948, there was no doubt where the legitimate Jewish *Heimat* was.

Yet despite the temporal and geographical universality of Aliyah and its ideological significance, there were limits to it as far as the circle of eligible people was concerned. These limits resulted from the dual character of Israel as a state-building project dedicated to the ingathering of the diaspora—which Zionists after the Shoah perceived as an act of rescue even more acutely than before. These two dimensions of statehood, termed *binyan* (building) and *hatzalah* (rescue) by Israeli historian Avi Picard, were not necessarily congruent in their aims.[114] The tension between them accounts for many of the immigration dynamics in the late 1940s and throughout the 1950s. While Israel forcefully claimed the role of homeland from day one and actively pursued the immigration of Jews, its character as a nation-building enterprise made the issue of selectivity loom large during the first 10 to 15 years of the state's existence. Though every Jew had the right to come to Israel, eligibility for immigration depended on whether he or she was deemed fit for the task of settlement. Relevant restrictions found their way into the Law of Return. Section 2b excluded people who were "likely to endanger public health or the security of the State" or were "engaged in activity directed against the Jewish people." Further restrictions against people with a "criminal past, likely to endanger public welfare" were introduced after lengthy discussions among the government ministries and in the Knesset in 1954.[115]

While the health and security restrictions appeared to dwindle in importance in the debates about the Law of Return compared with the powerful assertion of Israel's will to ingather the exiles and the right of every Jew to immigrate to the country, they actually pointed to significant preexisting differences of opinion among the new leadership of the state and the Jewish Agency about the scope of Aliyah, which had been anything but resolved by the time the Law of Return was enacted. Supporters of unrestricted mass Aliyah were pitted against those who preferred gradual, controlled, and selected migration. This cleavage cut across other political divides, both left-right and secular-religious. Instead, this rift coincided, by and large, with the division between ministers and Jewish Agency officials active in Aliyah and hence in bringing migrants into Israel, and those active in absorption (*klitah*)—the latter responsible for managing the difficulties immigrant masses faced after the opening of the borders in 1948.[116]

The opposition between proponents of unrestricted immigration and supporters of selective immigration went back to the beginning of the settlement project in Palestine. The options of mass Aliyah versus selective Aliyah had already been discussed by early Zionists during the first and second Aliyot in the early twentieth century.[117] In 1919, Zionism's chief settlement planner, the sociologist Arthur Ruppin, vehemently argued for a careful "choice of the human material" to be allowed into the country, "a conscious and programmatic immigration policy" intent on securing "among the immigrants a maximum percentage of those persons who, by occupation, health, and character are best fitted to serve the Jewish community in Palestine, and a minimum percentage of those who are unfitted."[118] This, of course, was a reaction to the general absence of such a selective policy up to that point.

The Zionist approach to mass immigration remained ambivalent under the British Mandate.[119] The pioneering enterprise of building the Yishuv necessitated the immigration of young, able-bodied people, *chalutzim* (pioneers).[120] Moreover, due to restrictions on Jewish immigration in the wake of the 1922 British White Paper, the Yishuv was forced to selectively award immigration permits during the Mandate period.[121] It was only under the impression of further British restrictions on Jewish immigration in the 1939 White Paper that the Zionists started demanding the Mandate authorities to unconditionally open Palestine's gates for Jewish immigration.[122] Ben-Gurion had already advocated nonselective mass immigration of Jews to Palestine before the war, because he considered changing the demographic balance of the country a way to achieve statehood.[123] During the war, he radicalized this approach, claiming that the only rescue for European Jewry would be mass emigration to Palestine. He even had a planning committee develop elaborate strategies for the transfer and absorption of one million immigrants within 18 months.[124]

Out of demographic concerns, the future prime minister carried this expansive approach into the postwar period, planning for the complete resettlement of Jews from Muslim countries, most West European Jews, and as many East European Jews as possible.[125] In a speech in late 1947, four days after the United Nations partition plan for Palestine had been announced, Ben-Gurion uttered the concern that, since the Jews had been a people without a state for such a long time, the new Jewish state might end up without people—Jewish people, that is.[126] Getting as many Jews as possible into the country as quickly as possible was hence imperative—and it became more so after March 1949, when the first elected government, headed by Ben-Gurion, announced its aim of doubling the Jewish population within the next four years.[127]

Yet others—in fact the majority—within the government and the Jewish Agency Executive preferred a more gradual and cautious approach. Prominent among these were Health and Aliyah Minister Chaim-Moshe Shapira, Minister of Finance Eliezer Kaplan, the head of the Jewish Agency Settlement Department Levi Eshkol, and the head of the Klitah Department Giora Josephthal.[128] They were intent on controlling immigration by introducing quantitative and qualitative restrictions—that is, quotas—as well as tight medical screening of immigrants.[129] As Kaplan put it during a Jewish Agency Executive meeting in June 1949, only a few months after the end of the War of Independence, Israel needed "workers and fighters."[130] Discussions about health restrictions had already started in late 1948, and Aliyah officers were instructed to prevent the immigration of sick people from Displaced Person camps in Europe.[131] As this apparently did not yield satisfactory results, the government decided in May 1949 that "the entry of people suffering from tuberculosis, of mentally ill and of people suffering from contagious diseases is forbidden."[132]

Despite the barring of a tuberculosis patient like Misa Giulia B. from immigration, the skyrocketing immigration numbers around the years 1948–1949 suggest that these restrictive instructions were generally all but ignored by the emissaries on the ground.[133] In this the emissaries were supported by Ben-Gurion.[134] Continuous mass Aliyah was also supported by Yitzhak Rafael, the head of the Aliyah Department of the Jewish Agency.[135] Attempts to introduce numerical quotas as of 1949 failed because of external pressures derived from the precarious nature of many of the migrations at the time. Jews from Romania, Poland, Yemen, Libya, Iran, and Iraq were arbitrarily allowed by their governments to leave after having been held back for a long time. Once they were leaving, the Israeli authorities did not dare to impose quotas on their immigration or screen them for fear of endangering the whole Aliyah. In this way, the immigrant population kept growing without the absorption network being up to the challenge. The results included a dramatic housing crisis and abysmal living conditions in the transit camps, the so-called *maabarot*.[136]

Against this backdrop, official selection guidelines were eventually endorsed in November of 1951 by the Jewish Agency Executive and then also by the Coordination Committee (*mosad la-teum*), a joint organ of the Jewish Agency and the government created in May 1950.[137] They established an important principle: selection should take place "*in the countries where a choosing of candidates is possible,* such as Morocco, Tunisia, Algeria, Turkey, Persia, India, [and] the countries of Central and Western Europe."[138] Cases of urgent "rescue Aliyah" (*aliyat hatzalah*) and "liquidation Aliyah" (*aliyat chisul*) were to be exempt, as were candidates "with means" (*baalei emtzaim*). Transcending the previously established focus on the medical supervision of potential immigrants, these guidelines combined medical, social, professional, age, and class criteria that are discussed in more detail in chapter 2. A comprehensive selection was thus introduced that was fully centered on the needs of the emerging state.

Different authors provide diverging explanations as to the reasons for and the timing of the issuing of these guidelines. Dvora Hacohen attributes their creation to the experiences with "adverse selection"—that is, the disproportionally high immigration of sick, old, or disabled people to Israel who strained the absorption and welfare capacities of the young state while their able-bodied relatives stayed abroad.[139] Haim Malka, by contrast, sees these material difficulties as secondary in importance, stressing instead the fear among the state leadership that the mass immigration of so-called Oriental (*mizrachi*) Jews would precipitate demographic change and endanger the Ashkenazi majority in the country.[140]

Avi Picard occupies a middle ground between these approaches. He acknowledges the importance of material difficulties and the impact of "negative selection" on the opinion of the decision makers.[141] Yet Picard concurs with Malka on the reasons for the timing: after the dissolution of the Displaced Person camps in Europe and the sealing of the borders of the socialist countries, North Africa and Morocco in particular had become the main reservoir for Jewish immigrants by 1951. Moroccan Jews were the object of intense stereotypes by the Ashkenazi establishment in Israel. Hence, Picard argues, it was not coincidental that they had to bear the brunt of the new selective policy, which was supposed to counterbalance the "unproductive" immigration from Romania that had been going on uncontrolled.[142] The "orientalist" as well as other dimensions of selective Aliyah policy will be further developed in the next chapter, where the discourses and practices of selection are examined. For the time being, it can be stated that the experiences with mass immigration had strengthened the position of the proponents of a more restrictive approach to an extent that selectivity became consensual.

How does selectivity square with the powerful ethos of *Kibbutz Galuyot*? It is in this confrontation that the tension between the building and the rescue dimensions of Israeli statehood becomes apparent. Put simply, according to the logic of nation building, the consolidation of the State of Israel had priority over the well-being—even the rescue—of the diaspora. Hence, "good human material" had to be selected, at least for now, to contribute to the building effort. As discussed in the next chapter, this logic was taken to its extreme in the early 1950s by representatives of the Health Ministry, who denied the legitimacy of *Kibbutz Galuyot* in general and placed the interest of the settlement project above everything.[143] According to the ingathering logic, on the other hand, the rescue of the diaspora was more important, even if it complicated the state-building effort. This latter position was emphatically expressed by Golda Meir in a government meeting in May 1949: "The state has been founded for the sole purpose of absorbing Aliyah. If it was not created for this purpose, it is not necessary. Discussions about restricting Aliyah are not acceptable."[144]

According to Avi Picard, the selection guidelines represented what could be called a distinctly Zionist version of selectivity as expressed in the Law of Return, which saw the overriding importance of *Kibbutz Galuyot* but still insisted on some qualitative restrictions to ensure that immigrants would be productive and would contribute to the building of the state. Picard distills this idea to a formula of "selective but unrestricted Aliyah," with "unrestricted" referring to the absence of numerical restrictions. Originally coined by Jewish Agency Executive member Eliyahu Dobkin, this formula supposedly provided the best of both worlds: immigration that was large in quantity and of good quality. It thus combined the two fundamental tenets of Zionist ideology: Aliyah (which was related to the diaspora dimension of statehood) and *Chalutziyut* or "pioneership" (related to the nation-building dimension).[145] This formula, Picard argues, was generally accepted among the Zionist and state leaders by the end of 1951, including advocates of mass immigration such as Ben-Gurion.[146] The quota set for 1952—120,000 new immigrants—was not seen as a restriction but as a realistic number of people that would pass selection.[147] As will be seen in chapter 2, this formula would not last as selection policy radicalized both qualitatively and quantitatively.

In addition to selective but unrestricted Aliyah, the contemporary decision makers found another elegant formula that helped solve the apparent contradiction between the ethos of Aliyah as expressed in the Law of Return and the simultaneous restrictions of the selection guidelines. As future president Zalman Shazar argued in the discussions concerning the guidelines, the Law of Return was about the right to come (*laalot,* literally "to ascend") to Israel, not to be brought (*lehaalot,* literally "to be brought up") to Israel.[148] Since the guidelines were for agencies whose task it was to bring people into the country, it was perfectly legitimate for them to select according to established criteria. This was reiterated on other occasions by different state officials, such as then

Prime Minister Moshe Sharett in the Knesset in 1955. In his words, "It never happened . . . that a Jew arrived to the country's gates and found them locked before him. . . . But here we are [discussing Olim] that the Jewish Agency brings following their request."[149] Here, too, the next chapter reveals that this formula was all but ignored when later selection guidelines called for stricter border controls to prevent the infiltration of undesired people without Oleh visas.

WHO IS A JEW? ETHNICITY IN THE LAW OF RETURN AND THE POPULATION REGISTRY

The Law of Return stipulated the right of every Jew to immigrate to Israel. But due to the secular-religious stalemate within the government, the law did not provide a definition of the term *Jew* despite its obvious centrality.[150] In the parliamentary discussion about the Law of Return, it was not discussed at all whether the term *Jew* should be defined in the law. It had been debated before in the Constitution and Legislation Committee of the Knesset and within the government. The issue was raised by the minister of religion, Rabbi Yehuda Leib Maimon of the United Religious Front. Rabbi Levin of the ultra-Orthodox Agudat Yisrael suggested introducing the definition given by religious law—the halacha—which defines a Jew as someone born of a Jewish mother or converted to Judaism according to the Orthodox ritual.[151] Yet this motion did not even gain the support of another religious minister in the government.[152] It was explicitly opposed by the prime minister, David Ben-Gurion, and the attorney general, Haim Cohn.[153] The Knesset Committee voted 10–2 against introducing any definition into the law. Instead, for the purposes of both immigration and registration, a Jew should be someone who gave a bona fide declaration that he or she was Jewish.[154]

Beyond the political constellation of secular and religious forces, the striking absence of a definition of the key term *Jew* in the Law of Return points to an important difference between the Israeli and German situations at that point in time. German Expellee Law provided access to ethnically coded material benefits. The Law of Return provided ethnically coded access to a state in the making that had little to offer and demanded much. The likelihood that anyone would claim access to Israel on false pretenses was quite slim. For this reason, the Law of Return could do without a stringent definition of its key concept. Instead, as noted earlier and as chapter 2 will describe in more detail, other, non-ethnic criteria for immigration control were much more important at the time.

The Law of Return was closely intertwined with another important Israeli state institution that utilized the term *Jew*: the Population Registry (*mirsham ha-ochlusin*). This conceptual link was institutionalized when the Aliyah and Registration Departments of the internal administration were merged in 1957.[155] The registry was created in the context of the first national census, carried out under conditions of war in November 1948, and was officially instituted by Registration of Inhabitants Ordinance 5709-1949.[156] Under the same heading, the registry asked for the citizenship, religion, and *Leom* of the country's inhabitants.

Leom is an ethno-national category not equivalent to political citizenship (*ezrachut* in Hebrew) and therefore not adequately captured by the English term *nationality*, which is usually identified with (national) citizenship.[157] It is closer to the German notion of *Nationalität* as it was used, for instance, in the Habsburg context of the *Nationalitätenproblem*, or, indeed, the Russian term *natsional'nost'*—both of which are understood as distinct from political citizenship. The derived adjective, *leumi*, is the equivalent of "national" in Modern Hebrew. The registration of the population according to (ethno-) national categories other than citizenship, which was a consequence of the intense ethno-demographic politics vis-à-vis the Palestinian Arabs, had no equivalent in Germany.[158] German citizenry was and is not structured according to ethnic groups, unlike Israel's variety of ethnic categories to classify its citizens (Jewish, Arab, Druze, etc.) and unlike, for instance, the citizenry of the Habsburg Empire after the recognition of its "tribes" (*Volksstämme*) in the 1867 state law.[159] In this sense, the German state institutions were ethnicity-conscious toward the outside but ethnicity blind toward the inside. For Israeli institutions, formal ethnic categories mattered in both dimensions.[160]

It was in the context of the Population Registry that the first major "Who is a Jew?" debate in the State of Israel took place, which resulted in the first official codification of a definition of the term. The debate was triggered by guidelines that Interior Minister Israel Bar-Yehuda of the left-wing secular Achdut Ha-Avodah issued in 1958. These guidelines, which codified the bona fide principle for the Population Registry, prompted the two religious ministers, Yosef Burg and Chaim-Moshe Shapira, to resign from the government on May 24, 1958. To resolve the crisis, Prime Minister Ben-Gurion summoned 45 Jewish scholars from Israel and the world, the *Chachamei* Yisrael or "Sages of Israel," to give their opinion on "the course which we should pursue in the registration of the children of mixed marriages both of whose parents—both the Jewish father and the non-Jewish mother—wish to register their children as Jews."[161] The result was that 37 of the 45 "sages" favored applying the halachic principle that only a child born of a Jewish mother could be considered Jewish. This was not surprising given the selection bias in the group toward religious or traditionalist scholars that historian Yigal Elam has noted.[162] The religious definition was then introduced into the January 1960 administrative guidelines for the Population Registry.[163] It would take another decade before it became part of the Law of Return.

WHO DECIDES WHO IS A JEW? INSTITUTIONS AND GATEKEEPERS

In the absence of a clear and binding definition of who exactly was a Jew in the eyes of the state during the first decade of statehood, the question of who was going to oversee the immigration gate and conduct the screening of immigrants became even more important and remained contentious. There appears to have been no formalized external gateway akin to the German D1 procedure. Especially during the years of mass Aliyah, between 1948 and 1951, the immigration process in Israel was characterized by bureaucratic chaos.[164] Over time, however, certain procedures crystalized that can be reconstructed from the archives.

A distinction between external and internal gateways can be made, yet with a somewhat more complex structure than was the case in Germany. For one thing, especially in the 1950s, the Israeli focus on nation building with its active seeking of immigrants and non-ethnic screening for health and ability had significant institutional consequences at the external gate that have no equivalent in the case of West Germany. But in terms of ethnic recognition, the process was simpler in theory, since passing the external gate was sufficient to become an Israeli citizen. The Oleh visa (*eshrat oleh*) needed to enter the country and the Oleh certificate (*teudat oleh*) that could be obtained inside the country were treated as equivalent by the Law of Return. Yet the bureaucratic processing of Aliyah at both gates was intricately linked with the symbolic internal gate of the Population Registry, which acquired importance because of the layered nature of Israeli citizenship: all Jews could be citizens, but not every citizen was a Jew, and certain obligations (army service) and rights (land leasing) were exclusive to Jewish citizens.[165] It was at the internal gate that the religious subsystem first tried to assert its gatekeeping competence. Because of the linkage between registration and Aliyah, this had repercussions for the immigration process as well.

Especially during the first years of statehood, the different configuration of the external procedure in Israel and Germany underscores the differing logics of Israeli state building as opposed to German ethno-humanitarian asylum. In the German case, the tracing service of the Red Cross—a humanitarian institution—provided a link between relatives divided by the Iron Curtain as well as with the state institutions. In the Israeli case, the intermediary was the Jewish Agency, which had been founded to settle the "Land of Israel" with Jews. The immigration procedure started in the Jewish Agency's Eretz Israel offices, which examined the cases and approved or rejected the Aliyah bid in cooperation with the consular authorities. This included medical examinations and social screening that are examined in greater detail in chapter 2.[166] In 1952, the responsibility for these examinations—at least in North Africa, which was the main theater of selective Aliyah—was transferred to the Health Ministry, which thus became an additional gatekeeper of the Zionist settlement enterprise.[167]

The bureaucratic processing of the ethnic part of the screening, in turn, was a joint enterprise of the Jewish Agency, the Interior Ministry (or, until its abolition in 1951, the Aliyah Ministry), and the Foreign Ministry, which since 1952 was officially in charge of implementing the Law of Return abroad.[168] The Interior Ministry processing was done by the Aliyah and Registration (*aliyah u-mirsham*) Branch (in this combined form since 1957). The Foreign Ministry had a consular department that corresponded with the embassies. All of these institutions also communicated with one another. If there was an embassy or consulate present in the country, it issued the Oleh visa that qualified the candidate for entry under the Law of Return.[169]

In a nonindependent country like Morocco, where there was no Israeli embassy, the Jewish Agency arranged for the migrants to be brought to their transit stations in France or Italy, where they received their visas. In Romania and Poland, two important emigration countries during the 1950s, the situation was reversed: there was an embassy but no Jewish Agency representation. The embassy directly issued visas to Aliyah candidates; the Jewish Agency then became a kind of travel agency and brought Jews to Israel, usually via Vienna.[170] As a rule, Oleh visas were not supposed to be issued at the border.[171] An exception was made, for example, in the case of Olim from Morocco, if there was a lack of time during the transit stopover in Italy.[172] In such cases, an arrangement with the Interior Ministry was made in which the Jewish Agency could certify the list of immigrants and the visas would then be issued at the border—either at the Port of Haifa or at Lod Airport.

Gilbert A.'s case illustrates how the ethnic and medical screening could work in practice. A native of Alexandria, Egypt, Gilbert came to Italy in 1959 as a stateless refugee with the help of the Red Cross, which had paid for his trip and procured for him a transit visa for the country.[173] From Italy, he planned to immigrate to Israel. After filling out a Demande de Visa d'Immigrant for Israel on August 25, Gilbert underwent a medical examination a few days later, which certified that he was currently well ("*sta bene*") and did not suffer from any permanent medical conditions.[174] The consulate general in Milan meanwhile made inquiries regarding Gilbert's Jewishness. For this purpose, the consulate sought advice from the Council of Egyptian Olim in Israel—a practice that somewhat resembled the involvement of the *Heimatauskunftstellen* and the expellee associations in the recognition process of ethnic Germans, without, however, being institutionalized to the same degree. As the consulate reported to the Jewish Agency Office in Rome (Ufficio Palestinese) on September 8, the Egyptian Olim Council had confirmed that Gilbert was known to them "as a good Jew" and recommended issuing him the visa.[175] Based on this information and Gilbert A.'s positive health evaluation, the Ufficio Palestinese asked the consulate to issue the Oleh visa.[176] Because Gilbert was penniless, the Jewish Agency's Naples office paid for his fare from Naples to Israel, while the Jewish community in Genoa helped move his luggage from Genoa, his port of arrival, to Naples, his port of departure.[177] On October 8, Gilbert boarded a ship to Israel.

The different questionnaires used at different times, in different places, and by different institutions to determine eligibility for immigration generally made do with relatively little information on the ethnic belonging of candidates. The standard form for the Demande de Visa d'Immigrant, which Gilbert A. had to complete, asked for religion and current and past citizenships but not for *Leom* or "ethnicity," however defined.[178] The Aliyah Ministry Olim registration form that Misa Giulia B. filled out in 1951 was exceptional in that it explicitly asked for *Leom*—tellingly, though, with "*Leom* and religion" under the same item, with an explanatory footnote: "If not Jewish, separate." For Jews, ethnicity and religion were supposed to coincide so that they could respond to the item in one word, like Misa Giulia B.: "Jewish."[179] Surprisingly, the form that the Israeli embassy in Bucharest gave to Aliyah candidates from Romania until 1958 asked for neither religion nor *Leom*.[180] This might be explained by the fact that the form was titled "request for entry visa (*eshrat knisah*)," which, unlike the Oleh visa, was not conditional on the applicant's Jewishness. However, the accompanying letter clearly stated that "the questionnaires were used by the embassy for the awarding of Oleh visas."[181]

In contrast to German immigration and recognition forms, the Israeli questionnaires made little effort to assess an individual's ethnic belonging by recreating his or her trajectory in time and space before and during the war or by asking for membership in institutions such as cultural associations or the army.

The only somewhat comparable questions referred to a physical relationship to the Land of Israel. All forms contained a similar question concerning relatives already in the country, while the immigrant visa form also asked under number 17: "Has the applicant already been to Palestine/Israel as an immigrant or as a tourist? During which time period?" No further information was requested to ascertain a "typical" Jewish life trajectory, be it membership in a Jewish community or a Zionist organization or internment in a ghetto or concentration camp. The most relevant piece of information regarding Jewishness was religion. In the embassy in Bucharest, the very fact that a person would request immigration to Israel at all was apparently sufficient to vouch for his or her Jewishness.

The Aliyah and Registration offices of the Interior Ministry were in charge of the internal recognition procedure. Apart from awarding Oleh certificates, these offices also registered newcomers in the Population Registry, which entailed the registration of their religion (*dat*) and their ethnicity (*leom*). Although these offices were part of the regular secular state structure, their registration practice was subject to the influence of the religious subsystem—the religious parties and the chief rabbinate—which coexisted with the majoritarian secular state institutions within the institutional framework that historian Yigal Elam has termed the *maatefet* ("cloak" or "mantle").[182] This framework, which was the outcome of the 1947 status quo agreement between the Labor Zionists and the Orthodox parties, assigned the religious subsystem certain essential functions, such as control over personal status law.[183]

Beyond these functions, this subsystem also repeatedly tried to assert its influence over the definition of the concept of Jewishness, most explicitly so in the 1958 "Who is a Jew?" controversy. There was no institutional foundation for religious influence, as the religious institutions were not assigned an official role in the screening process—unlike the expellee-controlled *Heimatauskunftstellen* in the German case. The affiliation of the interior minister might be assumed to have played a role in determining the recognition practice.[184] During the 1950s, the office was held by both secularist (Yitzhak Gruenbaum 1948–1949, Israel Rokach 1952–1955, Israel Bar-Yehuda 1955–1959) and religious politicians (Chaim-Moshe Shapira 1949–1952, again in 1955, and from late 1959).

However, the available sources give no clear picture of the administrative practice that prevailed during that decade. In theory, applicants were supposed to state their belonging in good faith, and the registrars were supposed to register them accordingly. Yet the practical evidence of this is contradictory. It appears that registration practices varied among registration offices, since nothing seems to have been officially codified.[185] When Interior Minister Bar-Yehuda introduced his contentious bona fide Population Registry guidelines in 1958, he maintained that chaos had reigned in the registration offices in the absence of clear instructions—a charge naturally denied by the heads of the local offices.[186] At the same time, Bar-Yehuda claimed that there were preexisting guidelines stating the bona fide principle that had been in force even when the religious politician Chaim-Moshe Shapira (*Hapoel Ha-Mizrachi*) was in charge of the Interior Ministry. Shapira had claimed the opposite: halachic guidelines had been issued even under Bar-Yehuda.[187] Yigal Elam argues that, because so much depended on the lower officials, a de facto halachic practice is conceivable since the officials, like most other Israelis, thought about Judaism and Jewishness in halachic terms—that is, in terms of maternal descent.[188] This impression is reinforced by a discussion about the 1958 guidelines among the responsible officials, in which an official raised doubt whether such an important declaration could be made in good faith at all.[189] This particular clerk certainly did not apply the bona fide principle.

By triggering the creation of the halachic Population Registry guidelines of 1960, the 1958 controversy over who is a Jew brought about the unequivocally religious codification of the internal gate. According to Elam, the walkout of the religious ministers had less to do with the actual practices of registration—after all, the religious parties had participated in the government for a decade without insisting on a halachic definition of Jewishness in the law—and more with their determination to assert their place in the secular-religious status quo arrangement. According to this argument, there was no substantial disagreement between secular and religious circles over the definition of Judaism. An authoritative definition of Jewishness was the one thing the religious subsystem could offer to the state, which otherwise was fully in the hands of the laborite secularists—a fact the religious ministers drove home with their dramatic exit in 1958.[190] With the introduction of the halachic principle into the administrative guidelines in 1960, the religious camp had clearly asserted its definitional power in the field of Jewishness, and thus its role as gatekeeper of the nation. It additionally held exclusive sway over marriage and divorce, which made interreligious marriage impossible.

BETWEEN BONA FIDE AND HALACHA: THE GULF BETWEEN THE INTERNAL AND EXTERNAL PROCEDURES

In a striking parallel to Irma and Stefan L.'s troubled resettlement in Germany, in Israel, too, a gulf existed between the practices and hence—potentially—the decisions of the external and internal gates that resulted from their different logics and purposes. This gulf became apparent, for example, in the case of George H., a Jewish-born convert from Romania, and his Christian wife, Alma Cornelia.

George and Alma had received Oleh visas from the Bucharest embassy in December 1958. When they went to the Population Registry, it turned out that they were not covered by the Law of Return, because they were not Jewish. In their defense, they claimed that no one at the embassy had asked them if they were Jewish—a plausible scenario, given that the questionnaire used by the embassy for Romanian Olim until 1958 contained no question about religion or ethnicity. Now they were intent on leaving Israel again. To Y. Goldin, deputy general commander of the Aliyah and Registration Branch, this situation was unacceptable, as he elaborated in a letter to L. Alon of the Consular Department. He reminded his interlocutor of their repeated discussions regarding the processing of Oleh visa requests in Warsaw, Bucharest, Belgrade, and Vienna and on their agreement that "the control *needs to be done*, needs to be *effective*, and needs to be based on a written declaration by the person or other documents which confirm the person's linkage to the Law of Return."[191] This was necessary to prevent cases such as George and Alma's. Goldin suggested "that we ought to set clear procedural guidelines according to which the person asking for an Oleh visa within the framework of the Law of Return needs to prove that he is Jewish by means of a declaration signed by his own hand, or by means of documents from the Jewish community, the local rabbi etc. Perhaps it is possible to have a joint discussion to draw up procedural guidelines."[192]

In his response to Goldin, Alon agreed that this was a "troublesome problem" well known to the people in the embassies, but he added that "the conditions and the circumstances under which they work do not always allow for the full implementation of the instructions." In Bucharest and Moscow, the embassy staff did not actually see the applicants. Alon asked: "And what is the embassy staff supposed to do if, according to the request, it seems that the petitioner is Jewish bona fide and wishes to make Aliyah to Israel, and afterwards it turns out that they were deceived and the person is not Jewish? The people in the embassy do what they can to facilitate and speed up Aliyah and always act with the fear that if they start with questions and controls they might jeopardize the Aliyah of many Jews to Israel."[193]

The same day, Alon forwarded Goldin's letter to the embassy in Bucharest, adding that he had also received complaints from the Ministry of Religions.[194] Ambassador Shmuel Bendor responded a month later. He confirmed what Alon had told Goldin:

> We receive the travel documents from the [Romanian] Foreign Ministry and return them after the visa has been granted. We do not get to see the people and hence we cannot ask them for kosher certificates (*teudot kashrut*). The Romanian Foreign Ministry assumes that those documents

> belong to Jews and that is also our assumption. If it turns out that a non-Jew sneaks into the country here and there—this does not make it worthwhile to ask the Romanian Foreign Ministry to request from each Oleh to Israel another document for us in addition to all the documents and payments which the local authorities request from them anyhow. . . . The main thing is that the Jews get out of here as soon as possible.[195]

As it did in Germany, pressure on the external gate resulted in superficial controls that were intent mainly on helping people leave their home countries. The external gatekeepers were therefore ready to yield some of their defining power for that purpose. The fact that the Romanian authorities treated someone as Jewish was enough evidence for Ambassador Bendor. The internal gatekeepers—in this case, the Interior Ministry and the Ministry of Religions, both strongholds of the religious establishment after Chaim-Moshe Shapira had returned to the office of interior minister in 1959—were neither satisfied by such a foreign imposed definition nor by a bona fide declaration by the candidate. They insisted on evidence for Jewishness. Yet tellingly, this "objective" proof could be a written declaration or, preferably, a "kosher certificate" by a local rabbi, which points to the notorious difficulty of objectivizing Jewishness.

The persistently vexing problem of mixed families was structured along the same lines: they could pass the external gate but encountered problems at the internal gate.[196] Non-Jewish family members were not covered by the Law of Return and were relegated to the Law of Entry to Israel. This meant that they passed a different external gate but eventually had to pass the same symbolic internal gate of the Population Registry. As is evident in the 1958 debate, the issue of how the offspring of a Jewish father and a non-Jewish mother should be registered was especially irksome. The issue resurfaced on various occasions after that controversy and in extreme cases led to calls for revoking Israeli citizenship granted by virtue of the Law of Return. A particularly acrimonious case in 1964–1965 involved Rina Eitani, a city council member in Nazareth Illit for the ruling Mapai.[197] She was the daughter of a Polish Jewish father and a Protestant German mother. The mother had survived the war in a concentration camp after her Jewish husband had been murdered, and then immigrated to Palestine with her daughters. In Israel, Eitani was registered bona fide as a Jew and was issued a passport under the Law of Return. In the wake of a political controversy in the city council, the National Religious Party discovered her non-Jewish origin. For that reason the Interior Ministry demanded that she surrender her passport and apply for Israeli citizenship as a regular alien. Eitani threatened to take the matter to the Supreme Court.

The affair generated debates in the government (consisting of Mapai and the NRP at the time) and the Knesset and arrived at a compromise. Eitani was allowed to keep her passport, but she agreed to undergo a facilitated conversion to Judaism to prevent her children from being considered non-Jewish by the rabbinate.

As will be seen in chapter 4, the issue of mixed families was finally addressed in the 1970 amendment of the Law of Return, which had been triggered by another contentious case of the registration of mixed offspring, the Shalit case. This amendment included non-Jewish family members (both spouse and offspring) in the Law of Return, thus finally making them enter through the same external gate. This very image was used by Golda Meir in her discussion of the amendment in the Knesset.[198] Yet by also introducing the halachic definition of Jewishness by maternal descent both in the Law of Return and the Population Registry Law, the gulf between the external and internal procedures became official and was perpetuated.

This chapter emphasizes the dissimilar origins, purposes, and practices of the German and Israeli co-ethnic immigration regimes during the early postwar decades. Their main similarity was structural: In both countries, immigrants passed through external and internal gateways that operated by divergent logics. The external gate provided entry to the respective country and was relatively easy to pass as long as migrants hailed from countries on the other side of the Iron Curtain or, in the Israeli case, came from hostile countries in the Arab world. As the next chapter will show, in the absence of such conflict-related pressures, passage through this gate could turn into a real process of selection. The internal gate, in turn, provided access to the "nation" in its different meanings. In Germany, the claim to citizenship and ethnically coded integration benefits was decided in the internal recognition procedure. In Israel, the issue at stake in the internal registration process was recognition that the would-be citizen belonged to the state-bearing Jewish nation. To a much greater extent than the external gate, the internal gate was subject to influence from various gatekeepers claiming definitional power over national belonging. In Germany, those were the expellee associations, which had a quasi-institutionalized role in the internal recognition procedure. In Israel, it was the religious subsystem within the state, which did not play an institutionalized role in co-ethnic recognition but repeatedly tried to assert its halachic definition of Jewishness over the secular bona fide principle. As will be seen in subsequent chapters, gatekeeper struggles over definitions remained a constant feature in both countries at different points in time and with different degrees of publicity.

NOTES

1. All information about Stephan Braun's life is taken from Regierungspräsidium (RP) Nordbaden an Innenministerium Baden-Württemberg (IM BW), June 22, 1953, BArch, B 106/47357.

2. Grundgesetz, Art. 131, http://dejure.org/gesetze/GG/131.html, and "Gesetz zur Regelung der Rechtsverhältnisse der unter Artikel 131 des Grundgesetzes fallenden Personen," Bundesgesetzblatt, Teil I, No. 22, May 13, 1951, http://www.bgbl.de/xaver/bgbl/start.xav?startbk=Bundesanzeiger_BGBl&jumpTo=bgbl151s0307.pdf.

3. Ungarndeutsche Landsmannschaft, Dr. Heinrich Mühl, an Bundesinnenministerium (BMI), Dr. Lehr, July 22, 1952, BArch, B 106/47357.

4. RP Nordbaden an IM BW, June 22, 1953, BArch, B 106/47357.

5. Misa Giulia B.'s story is reconstructed from various documents contained in her personal file, which is preserved in CZA, L16/588-1.

6. Marzano, "Relief and Rehabiliation." See also Joint Distribution Committee, Photo Galleries, Italy: Grottaferrata, https://archives.jdc.org/project/italy-grottaferrata/.

7. For the notion of "originating similarities," see Levy, "Introduction," 3.

8. For coping with the logistics of accommodating such large numbers of people in a short time, the experience with large-scale resettlement and mass camps (including concentration camps) during the Nazi period did, of course, prove to be crucial. For a related argument regarding the health dimension of refugee accommodation, see Riecken, *Migration und Gesundheitspolitik*.

9. About the politically charged meanings of these (and other) contemporary terms to describe the Germans from Eastern Europe in postwar Germany, see Beer, "Flüchtlinge."

10. Rogge, "Eingliederung," 186–187.

11. Rogge, "Eingliederung," 230, uses the term "konnationales Asyl."

12. Steinert, *Migration und Politik*, 29, 136–143, 175–195; Sternberg, *Auswanderungsland Bundesrepublik*, 151–163.

13. Hacohen, "Immigration Policy," 288.

14. Gerard Cohen, *In War's Wake*, 110, 115.

15. Veidlinger, "One Doesn't Make Out Much," 244, 248.

16. The use of the term *human material* to refer to the immigrants had been common among—though by no means exclusive to—the Zionist movement since the early twentieth century. See, for example, Ruppin, "Selection of the Fittest." For the treatment of Displaced Persons as human material by international institutions after the war, see Gerard Cohen, *In War's Wake*, 108.

17. On the extension of the Geneva Convention in the context of the 1956 Hungarian refugee crisis, see Gatrell, *Making of the Modern Refugee*, 111–113.

18. Levy, "Introduction," 5.

19. Hacohen, *Immigrants in Turmoil*, 267.

20. For the creation of these institutions in West Germany, see Vogel, *Westdeutschland*, 459–485. About expellee integration in East Germany, see Ther, *Deutsche und polnische Vertriebene*.

21. The number is calculated from Der Bundesminister für Vertriebene [BMVt] (III 2a), Schätzung der Zahlen der im Bundesgebiet in Betracht kommenden Personenkreise, January 14, 1954, Materialien zum Gesetz zur Regelung von Fragen der Staatsangehörigkeit, Bundestagsarchiv (II/108), No. 60.

22. Heinrich von Brentano, "Schriftlicher Bericht zum Entwurf des Grundgesetzes für die Bundesrepublik Deutschland, XI. Übergangs- und Schlussbestimmungen," in *Parlamentarischer Rat*, 94–95.

23. Grundgesetz, Art. 116, https://dejure.org/gesetze/GG/116.html.

24. von Brentano, "Schriftlicher Bericht," in *Parlamentarischer Rat*, 95.

25. See the intervention by the expellee deputy Hans-Christoph Seebohm in Parlamentarischer Rat, Hauptausschuss, 20th session, December 7, 1948, in *Parlamentarischer Rat*, 226.

26. Hoffmann, *Gesetz zur Regelung von Fragen der Staatsangehörigkeit*, 21–30.

27. This reasoning was already established by the Federal Constitutional Court in 1952 in its verdict on the case of an ethnic German from Czechoslovakia (the so-called Czastka verdict). See BVerfG–1 BvR 213/51, May 28, 1952, *Entscheidungen des Bundesverfassungsgerichts* (BVerfGE), 1, 322.

28. For contemporary doubts on this topic, see Seeler, *Staatsangehörigkeit der Volksdeutschen*, 10–11.

29. Hoffmann, *Gesetz zur Regelung von Fragen der Staatsangehörigkeit*, 14.

30. For the notion of "claimed co-ethnics," see Stjepanovic, "Claimed Co-ethnics."

31. BMVt (III 2a), Schätzung, January 14, 1954, Materialien zum Gesetz zur Regelung von Fragen der Staatsangehörigkeit, Bundestagsarchiv (II/108), No. 60.

32. BMVt an Bund der Vertriebenen (BdV), December 23, 1955, HStAS EA 12/201, Az. 2552, No. 4 (2605/11).

33. Urban, *Deutsche in Polen*, 57; Hoffmann, *Kurzer Grundriss*, 21–22.

34. The exact percentage of the 2.8 million interwar Polish citizens on the *Volksliste* who were "rehabilitated" is not known but can be assumed to be significant; of the one million inhabitants of Eastern Upper Silesia, for instance, an estimated 85 percent could stay. See Service, "'Upper Silesia."

35. Werber, Bode, and Ehrenforth, *Bundesvertriebenengesetz* (1953), 61–62. About the creation of the peculiar legal category of *Fiktivvertriebene* in the context of the struggle for Jewish compensation, see Nachum, "Reconstructing Life."

36. Bundestag Heimatvertriebenenausschuss, 1st period, 48th session, January 9, 1952, Bundestagsarchiv (3113).

37. Stola, *Kraj bez wyjścia*, 73, 480. See also Schießl, "Im Niemandsland."

38. Dr. Curt Porella, Referat über die polnische Minderheitenpolitik und den innerpolitischen Umbruch in Polen, gehalten vor den Abgeordneten des Bundestages am 12.10.1956 im Osteuropa-Institut der Freien Universität Berlin, Bundestag Heimatvertriebenenausschuss, 2nd period, 31st session, October 12, 1956, Bundestagsarchiv (3113); Stola, *Kraj bez wyjścia*, chap. 5.

39. Bundestag Heimatvertriebenenausschuss, Unterausschuss I, Bundesvertriebenengesetz, DS No. 2872 (November 26, 1951), Bundestagsarchiv (3113).

40. The earliest documented use that I have found is in a report by the representative of Baden-Württemberg at the transit camp in Uelzen to the Expellee Ministry of that *Land* on January 31, 1956, referring to Germans from Poland. See HStAS EA 12/201, Az. 2267, No. 34. See also the semi-official publication by the Arbeits- und Sozialminister des Landes Nordrhein-Westfalen, *Das Dritte Problem*.

41. Joppke, *Selecting by Origin*, 171; Klusmeyer and Papademetriou, *Immigration Policy*, 53.

42. Münz and Ohliger, "Long Distance Citizens."

43. Besprechung im BMVt am 8. Januar 1954 betreffend Übernahme von Deutschen aus den von Polen verwalteten deutschen Ostgebieten und aus Polen, February 5, 1954, BArch, B 136/9437. The participants included representatives of the Federal President's Office (*Bundespräsidialamt*), the Federal Chancellery (*Bundeskanzleramt*, BKA), the Foreign Office (*Auswärtiges Amt*, AA), the Ministry of the Interior (*Bundesministerium des Innern*, BMI), the Ministry for All-German Questions (*Bundesministerium für gesamtdeutsche Fragen*, BMGF), the Family Ministry, the Federal Office for Citizenship Issues at the Interior Ministry (*Bundesstelle für Staatsangehörigkeitsangelegenheiten*), the Federal Office for Residence Permits at the Interior Ministry (*Büro für Aufenthaltsgenehmigungen*), and the Tracing Service (*Suchdienst*) of the Red Cross.

44. Bericht über die Besprechung am 8. Januar 1954, February 5, 1954, BArch, B 136/9437.

45. In fact, the term had previously been used by the Nazi resettlement authorities for *Volksdeutsche* and was thus of doubtful neutrality. See Aly, *"Endlösung,"* 85.

46. Demshuk, *Lost German East*.

47. See the exchange of letters between Oberländer and Seebohm on December 11 and 22, 1956, BArch, B 136/9437. Oberländer agreed with Seebohm's criticism and blamed the occasional confusion on the fact that repatriating prisoners of war and ethnic Germans arrived on the same trains.

48. Protokoll der 170. Kabinettssitzung, February 6, 1957, BArch online, http://www.bundesarchiv.de/cocoon/barch/0000/k/k1957k/kap1_2/kap2_7/para3_1.html. I thank Sascha Schießl for directing me to this document.

49. For the formulation of "free part of the fatherland," see, for example, the Expellee Minister of Lower Saxony, Herbert Hellmann, at an Advent celebration with Aussiedler in the Friedland transit camp, December 11, 1967, HStAS EA 12/201, Az. 2266, No. 159.

50. Steinert, *Migration und Politik*, 214.

51. BMI an Bundesverwaltungsamt (BVA), July 19, 1968, BArch, B 106/28627.

52. For the notion of long-distance citizens, see Münz and Ohliger, "Long Distance Citizens."

53. Fascinating individual cases of Germans from China who fled to Germany after the communist takeover in 1949 are documented in Politisches Archiv des Auswärtigen Amts (PAAA) B85 937.

54. Brubaker and Kim, "Transborder Membership Politics," 39.

55. Verband der Donauschwaben (Vereinigung der Deutschen aus Jugoslawien, Rumänien und Ungarn) an Herrn Bundeskanzler Konrad Adenauer, March 20, 1961, with the "Weißbuch über die Aussiedlungswünsche der Donauschwaben aus Rumänien, Ungarn und anderen Ländern" attached; Aufzeichnung über die Vorsprache der Vertreter der rumäniendeutschen Landsmannschaften beim Kanzler, May 22, 1962; Memorandum der Landsmannschaften der Banater Schwaben und Siebenbürger Sachsen in Deutschland an die Regierung der Bundesrepublik Deutschland, December 17, 1962, all in BArch, B 136/6470.

56. About this case, see Ioanid, *Ransom of the Jews.*

57. Verband der Donauschwaben an Bundeskanzler Adenauer, March 20, 1961, BArch, B 136/6470.

58. Dr. Chyla, BMGF an Dr. Schnekenburger, BKA, November 26, 1962, BArch, B 136/6470.

59. AA an BKA, November 27, 1963; Vermerk von Referat 4 zur Ressortbesprechung im AA mit Vertretern des BMGF, BMVt und BKA, March 4, 1965, both in BArch, B 136/6470.

60. Bundestag Heimatvertriebenenausschuss, 4th period, 53rd session, March 11, 1965, Bundestagsarchiv (3113).

61. BMI, Unterabteilungsleiter I B an Staatssekretär Dr. Schäfer, March 11, 1966, BArch, B 106/39937.

62. See the documentation in BArch B 136/6475, Az. 31211 (Verein für das Deutschtum im Ausland).

63. BMI, Bericht über das Gespräch vom 12.7.61, July 12, 1961, BArch, B 136/6475.

64. von Goldendach and Minow, *"Deutschtum erwache!,"* chap. 6.

65. Bundesgesetzblatt, Teil I, No. 22, May 22, 1953, http://www.bgbl.de/xaver/bgbl/start.xav?startbk=Bundesanzeiger_BGBl&jumpTo=bgbl153022.pdf.

66. Silagi, *Vertreibung und Staatsangehörigkeit*, 117.

67. Otto, "Aussiedler," 21.

68. About "Ostforschung," see the classic study by Burleigh, *Germany Turns Eastwards*.

69. Dr. Theodor Oberländer an Karl Marx, January 13, 1955, HStAS EA 12/201, Az. 2552, No. 4 (2605/4).

70. Bundestag, 1st period, 250th session, February 25, 1953, 11985.

71. Zahra, *Kidnapped Souls*, 186.

72. See also Čapková, *Czechs, Germans, Jews*, chap. 3.

73. Quoted after Kann, *Nationalitätenproblem*, 396.

74. Brix, *Umgangssprachen*, 27–30, 36–66.

75. There, de Vries was prominently involved in the persecution and killing of "partisans" and Jews, whom in late 1941 he characterized as "mortal enemies" who had to be "annihilated." See Gerlach, *Kalkulierte Morde*, 686–687.

76. "Die Vertreibung ist als Beweis für das erfolgte Bekenntnis zum deutschen Volkstum in der Heimat anzusehen." Bundestag, 1st period, 250th session, February 25, 1953, 11984.

77. Ibid., 11985.

78. Ibid.

79. See the debate in Bundestag, 1st period, 164th session, September 26, 1951, 6687–6694. His characterization as "commissar" is from: "Straflose Unmenschlichkeit," *Die Zeit*, December 15, 1949.

80. Bundestag, 1st period, 250th session, February 25, 1953, 11985.

81. See, for instance, BVerwG Urteil vom 12.6.69 – VIII C 125.67, HStAS EA 12/201, 2555, No. 160.

82. Bundestag Heimatvertriebenenausschuss, 1st period, 49th session, January 16, 1952, Bundestagsarchiv (3113).

83. RP Nordbaden an IM BW, June 22, 1953, BArch, B 106/47357.

84. Straßmann, Rösler, and Krüzner, *Bundesvertriebenengesetz*, 37.

85. Werber, Bode, and Ehrenforth, *Bundesvertriebenengesetz* (1954), 35.

86. Hungarian censuses in 1920 and 1930 asked only for mother tongue, not ethnic belonging. Only in the 1941 census did Hungarian citizens also have to state their ethnicity. See Swanson, *Tangible Belonging*.

87. Straßmann, Rösler, and Krüzner, *Bundesvertriebenengesetz*, 35.

88. Werber, Bode, and Ehrenforth, *Bundesvertriebenengesetz* (1954), 36.

89. For the *Land* of Hesse, see Messerschmidt, " Flüchtlingsfrage." About the international institutions' refusal to deal with German refugees, see Shephard, *Long Road Home*, chap. 7.

90. Gerard Cohen, *In War's Wake*, 44–46.

91. Deutsches Rotes Kreuz, Generalsekretariat, *60 Jahre Suchdienst*.

92. Stola, *Kraj bez wyjścia*, 110–115.

93. About the bureaucratic hurdles erected by the Polish passport authorities for prospective Aussiedler, see Stola, *Kraj bez wyjścia*, esp. chap. 6. According to the statistics in Pfundtner, *Spätaussiedler*, 96, the average number of applications that

Aussiedler who left Poland in 1976 and 1977 had to submit until they were granted emigration was between 6 and 8.2. Around the same time, Joseph Schnurr reported that more than 60 percent of Soviet German Aussiedler succeeded in obtaining an exit permit after submitting "only" one to three applications, though in more than one-third of the cases, ten years elapsed between the first and the successful applications. See Schnurr, "Aussiedler aus dem sowjetischen Bereich." About the troubles of prospective emigrants from the Soviet Union, see also Armborst, *Ablösung von der Sowjetunion*, 112–131.

94. For the notion of lax controls, see Joppke, *Selecting by Origin*, 174.

95. Baden-Württemberg, IM und Vertriebenenministerium an RPs, July 14, 1956, HStAS EA 12/201, Az. 2250, No. 90.

96. Werber, Bode, and Ehrenforth, *Bundesvertriebenengesetz* (1954), 22.

97. Attachment to BMI an die Herren Innenminister (-senatoren) der Länder, May 22, 1956, BArch B 106/39937.

98. Antrag auf Ausstellung eines Ausweises für Vertriebene und Flüchtlinge, BArch, B 150/889.

99. IM BW an RPs, August 1, 1967, HStAS EA 12/201 Az. 2555, No. 157.

100. *HOK—50 Jahre Kirchlicher Suchdienst*, 24, 26. See also "Kirchlicher Suchdienst, Heimatortskarteien der Kirchlichen Wohlfahrtsverbände, Exposé zu den Aufgaben der Heimatortskarteien in Vergangenheit und Zukunft (1958)," BArch, B 136/9437.

101. *25 Jahre Heimatauskunftstellen in Schleswig-Holstein*, Kiel 1978; *20 Jahre Heimatauskunftstellen in Baden-Württemberg*, Stuttgart [1973].

102. Information about this case is taken from HStAS EA 12/201, Az. 2552, No. 35.

103. BVerwG VIII C 64.75, August 25, 1976, *BVerwGE* 51, 101. The ruling by the Baden-Württemberg court of November 6, 1974, is documented in HStAS EA 12/201, Az. 2552, No. 35.

104. Argeflü-Rechtsausschuss, Öhringen, April 1–2, 1976, HStAS EA 2/811, Az. 2558, No. 1.

105. Urteil des Verwaltungsgerichtshofs Stuttgart, November 6, 1974, HStAS EA 12/201, Az. 2552, No. 35.

106. Argeflü-Rechtsausschuss, Eltville, March 24–25, 1977, HStAS EA 2/811, Az. 2558, No. 8.

107. IM BW, Hauptabteilung Vertriebene, Flüchtlinge und Kriegsgeschädigte, an den Vorsitzenden des Rechtsausschusses der Argeflü, Dr. Dengler, München, February 21, 1974, HStAS EA 2/811, Az. 2572, No. 35.

108. Ministerium für Vertriebene, Flüchtlinge und Kriegsgeschädigte Baden-Württemberg (MVFK BW) an RP Südbaden, December 11, 1958, HStAS EA 12/201, Az. 2261, No. 90.

109. For the Declaration of Independence and the Law of Return, see Rabinovich and Reinharz, *Israel in the Middle East*, 72–74, 102–103.

110. Hacohen, "Ben-Gurion," 266.

111. Schweid, "Rejection of the Diaspora."

112. Alroey, *Immigrants*, 21.

113. The only objection documented in the archives was in the letter of a certain Israel Erlich to Ben-Gurion on July 13, 1950. Yet the objection was on philological grounds; in his view, the use of the term *shvut* for "return" was based on a misreading of the Bible, where *shvut* in fact meant "captivity." Erlich suggested calling the law Aliyah Law instead. Ben-Gurion responded on August 27, conceding that *chok shivat ha-shvut* (Law for the Return from Captivity) would be more accurate but also too long. He argued that, in any event, the law was not an Aliyah law that dealt with the technicalities of immigration but a law that codified the right of the Jewish people to return from exile. The exchange of letters is documented in ISA 43.0.6.2833 (=5421/24-ג).

114. See Picard, *Cut to Measure*.

115. The internal discussions are documented in ISA 43.0.6.2833 (=5421/24-ג); for the discussions within the Knesset legislation committee, see ISA 60.0.15.262 (=72/11-כ).

116. Hacohen, "Immigration Policy," 291.

117. Shilo, "Immigration Policy." The Hebrew version of this article states the dilemma more clearly: "Mass Immigration or Selective Immigration?"

118. Ruppin, "Selection of the Fittest," 95, 97–98.

119. Halamish, *Dual Race against Time*; Gelber, "Difficulties and Changes."

120. Hacohen, "Mass Aliyah," 357.

121. Sachar, *History of Israel*, 146.

122. Hacohen, "Mass Aliyah," 358.

123. Hacohen, "Ben-Gurion," 250, 252.

124. Ibid., 262.

125. Ibid., 263.

126. Hacohen, *Immigrants in Turmoil*, 46.

127. Hacohen, "Immigration Policy," 293.

128. Ibid., 285, 290–291; Hacohen, *Immigrants in Turmoil*, 46.

129. Hacohen, *Immigrants in Turmoil*, 48–57.

130. Segev, *1949*, 117.

131. For selection practices of the Jewish Agency in Displaced Person camps, see Weindling, "Belsenitis," 414; see also Davidovitch and Shvarts, "Health and Zionist Ideology."

132. Hacohen, "Immigration Policy," 289–291.

133. Ibid., 292; Hacohen, *Immigrants in Turmoil*, 107–108, 126.

134. Hacohen, "Immigration Policy," 292.

135. About Rafael's stance and his leadership of the Aliyah Department, see Ben Ariye, "Immigration Policy."

136. Hacohen, *Immigrants in Turmoil*, chap. 4; Segev, *1949*, chap. 5.

137. Picard, "Beginning of Selective Immigration."

138. Ibid., 377 (emphasis added).

139. Hacohen, *Immigrants in Turmoil*, 234.

140. Malka, *Selection*.

141. Picard, "Beginning of Selective Immigration," 350–351.

142. Picard, "Immigration, Health, and Social Control," 40; Picard, "Beginning of Selective Immigration," 352–363.

143. Picard, "Immigration, Health, and Social Control," 44–45.

144. Hacohen, "Immigration Policy," 292.

145. Picard, "Beginning of Selective Immigration," 374; Picard, "Immigration, Health, and Social Control," 51.

146. Picard, "Beginning of Selective Immigration," 381.

147. Ibid., 371.

148. Malka, *Selection*, 75.

149. Quoted after Mor, "'Ableism and Orientalism," section C.

150. Hacohen, "Law of Return," 85–86.

151. Ibid., 85.

152. Elam, *Judaism as Status Quo*, 9.

153. Hacohen, "Law of Return," 86.

154. Legal Advisor to the Government to Vice Minister of Religions, June 18, 1952, ISA 98.0.4.1241 (=4770/8-ג).

155. See the meeting minutes of the head of the Aliyah and Registration Department with the heads of offices on March 4, July 10, and October 21, 1957, ISA 56.0.62.121 (=12045/4-גל).

156. Leibler and Breslau, "The Uncounted," 888.

157. Kraines, *Impossible Dilemma*, 20. And yet that is precisely how it is translated in Litvin and Hoenig, *Jewish Identity*.

158. Leibler and Breslau, "The Uncounted," 885–888.

159. Article 19 of the Staatsgrundgesetz zur Gleichberechtigung der Nationalitäten, http://alex.onb.ac.at/cgi-content/alex?aid=rgb&datum=1867&size=45&page=424.

160. See also Joppke, *Selecting by Origin*, 171–172, who argues that "the ethnic dimension of the (West) German state became internally invisible, as it was transferred into the future . . . and extraterritorialized (as the commitment to admit coethnics)."

161. Litvin and Hoenig, *Jewish Identity*, 15.

162. Elam, *Judaism as Status Quo*, 8.

163. Kraines, *Impossible Dilemma*, 20.

164. Segev, *1949*, 105.

165. Fisher, "Who Is a Jew in Israel?," 131.

166. CZA L16/588–1, and Picard, "Immigration, Health, and Social Control," 41.

167. Picard, "Immigration, Health, and Social Control," 42, 45ff. Its role is discussed in more detail in chapter 2.

168. This was based on a government decision of October 16, 1952. See Legal Counselor of the Foreign Ministry to the Government Secretary, October 21, 1954, ISA 43.0.6.2833 (=5421/24-ג).

169. See the documentation from Rome (1962), ISA 93.20.1.279 (=286/12-חצ).

170. See the related documentation regarding Aliyah from Romania in CZA S6/6054.

171. Aliyah and Registration Meeting Minutes, November 19, 1958, ISA 56.0.62.121 (=12045/4-גל).

172. Consular Division of the Foreign Ministry to Embassy Rome, June 13, 1962, ISA 93.20.1.279 (=286/12-חצ).

173. Gilbert A. to Ufficio Palestine, Roma, September 17, 1959 (Italian), CZA L16/588–1.

174. Modulo per le visite mediche, September 3, 1959 (Italian), CZA L16/588–1.

175. Israeli Consulate, Milan to Jewish Agency, Rome, September 8, 1959, CZA L16/588-1.

176. Ufficio Palestinese, Roma to Consolato d'Israele, Milano, 13 September 1959 (Italian), in CZA L16/588-1.

177. Ufficio Palestinese, Roma to Gilbert A., September 25, 1959, and Gilbert A. to Ufficio Palestinese, Roma, September 28, 1959 (Italian), both in CZA L16/588-1.

178. See also the forms in ISA 93.20.1.279 (=286/12-חצ) (Rome), CZA L16/670–1 (Rome), ISA 93.17.1.26 (=1897/4-חצ) (Amsterdam).

179. CZA L16/588–1.

180. Attachment to letter from Embassy Bucharest to Consular Department, January 15, 1960, ISA 93.34.1.40 (= 313/6-חצ).

181. Letter Embassy Bucharest to Consular Department, January 15, 1960, ISA 93.34.1.40 (= 313/6-חצ).

182. Elam, *Judaism as Status Quo.*

183. Abramov, *Perpetual Dilemma*, 127. For the original text, see The Status Quo Agreements (1947), in Kaplan and Penslar, *Origins of Israel*, 368–371.

184. Hacohen, "Law of Return," 86–87.

185. This at least was claimed by the Legal Advisor to the Government when challenged by Zerach Wahrhaftig on this point. See Legal Advisor to the Government to Vice Minister of Religions, June 18, 1952, ISA 98.0.4.1241. Archival research for this book has revealed no written guidelines.

186. Elam, *Judaism*, 19, and Aliyah and Registration Meeting Minutes, March 20, 1958, ISA 56.0.62.121 (=12045/4-גל).

187. Elam, *Judaism as Status Quo*, 17.

188. Ibid., 18. Thirty years later, Zerach Wahrhaftig claimed that the common practice had been to register people according to halacha and that there had been broad legal and public consensus on this. See Wahrhaftig, *Constitution for Israel*, 154–155. See also Fisher, "Who Is a Jew in Israel," 132.

189. Aliyah and Registration Meeting Minutes, March 20, 1958, ISA 56.0.62.121 (=12045/4-גל).

190. Elam, *Judaism as Status Quo*, 10.

191. Goldin to Alon, October 3, 1960, ISA 93.34.1.38 (=313/4-חצ), emphasis in the original.

192. Ibid.

193. Alon to Goldin, October 9, 1960, ISA 93.34.1.38 (=313/4-חצ).

194. Alon to Ambassador Bendor, Bucharest, October 9, 1960, ISA 93.34.1.38 (=313/4-חצ).

195. Ambassador Bendor, Bucharest to Alon, November 10, 1960, ISA 93.34.1.38 (=313/4-חצ).

196. In the discussions preceding the creation of the Law of Return, it had been contested whether to allow the immigration of mixed families at all. When Aliyah from Poland started in summer 1949, mixed families were taken in, although the diplomats in Poland were supposed to supervise them and report them to the Aliyah ministry. See the discussion in Hacohen, "Law of Return," 69–73.

197. The case is described in Kraines, *Impossible Dilemma*, 34–37, and Abramov, *Perpetual Dilemma*, 295–298. It even made it into the pages of *Time* magazine (February 12, 1965).

198. 7th Knesset, Session 38, February 10, 1970, 116, ISA 60.0.23.139 (=183/7-כ).

TWO

FREE TO CHOOSE

DR. WERNER KANEIN, A MINISTERIAL official and specialist in immigration law in the Bavarian Interior Ministry, certainly did not mince his words when he criticized the external immigration procedure for ethnic Germans—the D1 procedure discussed in chapter 1—in a letter to the Federal Administration Office in March 1965. D1 was "in urgent need of revision," he argued, since "the humanitarian endeavors of the Federal Republic have been abused in the most outrageous manner" by deceitful Aussiedler candidates. Kanein believed that "there is no need to uphold the facilitations once introduced out of humanitarian considerations. Applications have to be checked much more critically, since there has been a conspicuous increase in applications where the wish to resettle in the Federal Republic is the result of economic considerations. This may be acceptable if people are undoubtedly ethnic Germans and there is reason to assume that they feel a special connection to the German people and the Federal Republic of Germany. Yet in many instances this is not the case."[1]

Kanein elaborated his criticism in September of the same year: "The observation that applicants for immigration feel increasingly attracted by the effects of German welfare laws should give us reason to closely check their eligibility for takeover. . . . Considering that takeover entails economic advantages which are exclusively reserved for ethnic Germans, meticulous controls cannot be avoided to prevent abuse. Given the current conditions and the increasing normalization of [the applicants'] living circumstances there is no reason to continue the formerly justified practice to do without any documentation or evidence."[2]

The latter statement brings into focus a mechanism that I refer to in this book as the "normalization-contestation nexus": once conditions in the countries of origin appeared to normalize, the open door for purported co-ethnics was questioned and stricter immigration controls were added to the agenda. This was the fundamental mechanism restricting co-ethnic immigration in both Germany and Israel. As discussed in the previous chapter, both countries envisioned potential restrictions on their proclaimed openness toward co-ethnics abroad. Although ethnic German Aussiedler had immediate access to German citizenship once inside the country, they had no a priori legal entitlement to immigration. Their reception into the hands of the German state depended on the discretion of multiple state authorities. Israel, in turn, had codified the legal entitlement of every Jew in the world to come to Israel in the 1950 Law of Return, but it relativized this commitment by establishing health and security provisions. With the introduction of the 1951 selection guidelines, selective Aliyah became the rule and remained in place until the 1960s. As these guidelines clearly stated, medical and social selection among immigrants had to be carried out wherever possible. After the country had received a largely uncontrolled influx of some 700,000 immigrants between 1948 and 1951, Aliyah would henceforth be unrestricted only if it could be defined as exceptional, as "rescue Aliyah" (*aliyat hatzalah*), or "liquidation Aliyah" (*aliyat chisul*).

In both West Germany and Israel, exceptionality was thus the key to a generous co-ethnic immigration regime. In most instances during the postwar decades, the potentially restrictive thrust of each regime was neutralized by conflict-induced pressure against its external gates, which in turn helped keep these gates open. Most co-ethnic migration movements in the postwar era went "across enemy lines" as migrants crossed the fault lines of the Cold War, which affected both West Germany and Israel, and of the Israeli-Arab conflict. These movements were thus exceptional and hence not subject to strict immigration controls. Because emigration was rare and precarious, immigration policies that could have jeopardized the flow of people were not an option. German Aussiedlung as a special form of priority immigration was in fact built on the fundamental premise that it was an exceptional relocation of a particular group of people—separated family members of expelled Germans—from supposedly hostile communist countries. Israel differed from this approach in the sense that Aliyah was not exceptional per se; rather, it was the very foundation of the state. However, in practice, most Jews immigrating to the Jewish state since its foundation in 1948 came from "the other side" of these two major international conflicts.

In the absence of external pressure related to international conflict, the external gate turned into a site of thorough immigration control. When migrations were not exceptional, rare, and taking place "across enemy lines," but normal, steady, and not from an obviously inimical state, both the possibility and the need for immigration controls arose. The first two postwar decades saw two main types of nonexceptional co-ethnic migration to each country: the Aussiedlung of ethnic Germans from Yugoslavia to the Federal Republic of Germany and the Aliyah of Jews from colonial North Africa—mainly Morocco and Tunisia—to Israel. Although geographically disparate, these migrations share two important elements: migration flows were not hampered by emigration restrictions, and the conditions in the sending states/regions allowed the receiving states to choose freely among applicants for immigration.

Due to its policy of nonalignment, Yugoslavia was not clearly on the other side of the East–West divide, unlike all the other socialist states defined as the "expulsion area" by the Federal Expellee Law. The country maintained diplomatic relations with West Germany from 1951 and placed virtually no restrictions on the emigration of its remaining German minority. Moreover, in contrast, for instance, to the quarter-million Aussiedler coming from Poland between 1956 and 1959, ethnic Germans in Yugoslavia had not been German citizens before the war and—with the exception of those living in parts of Slovenia annexed to the Reich in 1941—had not been naturalized during German occupation.[3] Hence, the FRG saw no legal obligation to take them in.

Morocco and Tunisia remained under French (and, in the case of Morocco, also Spanish) colonial rule until their independence in 1956. Because the two nations were not immediately involved in the conflict between Israel and its Arab neighbors, Israel was less eager to hasten the emigration of Jews from these countries. This stance was quite different from Israel's approach to Jews from Arab League states such as Iraq or Yemen, who had been moved to Israel almost in their entirety in large-scale resettlement actions in 1950–1951. In addition, after 1948, the French rulers allowed Israeli and Zionist institutions to act freely and openly in these territories to recruit, select, and reject potential migrants.

The juxtaposition of these two case studies allows for an analysis of the different ways the migration regime institutions of the German ethnic refugee state and the Israeli diasporic nation-building project implemented selectivity in co-ethnic immigration, the different border regimes they instituted, and the different ways they envisaged their ideal co-ethnic immigrant.

Triggered in part by discussions surrounding Yugoslav Aussiedlung, Werner Kanein deplored what he felt was the abuse of the West German refugee state's ethno-humanitarian endeavors by economic migrants who were not genuine ethnic Germans. Immigration facilitations were justified only in case of a humanitarian emergency, while the "normalization of circumstances" rendered obsolete the benefit of the doubt that ethnic Germans received in immigration matters. Since Aussiedler were by definition refugees, the economic migration motives that Kanein presumed were also unacceptable. Yet unlike political refugees, whose claim to individual persecution would have been the object of state investigation, with ethnic refugees there needed to be stricter controls of the one decisive criterion of eligibility for asylum provided by the law: ethnicity (*Volkszugehörigkeit*).

This is precisely what happened in the case of purported Germans from Yugoslavia, whose ethnic belonging came under increasingly close scrutiny in the second half of the 1950s. Studying this case thus offers insights into how the ethnic immigration code was interpreted in the bureaucratic practice of the German co-ethnic migration regime. As will be seen, the assessment of ethnicity in individual cases was primarily focused on ethnic (endogamy), cultural (language), and political criteria. In contrast, social criteria and aspects of utility such as age, health, and the ability to work did not enter the equation at all, or they did so only marginally. Utility in West Germany was in a different compartment of the migration regime overall—namely, the guest worker regime, which began to take off around the same time and which explicitly targeted labor migrants for their economic value.[4]

Israel, by contrast, conceptualized Aliyah as "real" immigration that bolstered its settlement and state-building project and therefore cared very much about aspects of utility. As Yehuda Braginsky of the Jewish Agency put it during the discussions surrounding the selection guidelines, "only the healthiest material of today's Jewry" was to be brought in for that purpose.[5] Codified in the 1951 selection guidelines, the screening of previously identified Jewish Aliyah candidates in colonial North Africa therefore focused precisely on the utilitarian immigration criteria absent from the German selection practices. Like other immigrant nations that had come into being during the nineteenth century, Israel thus erected a "medical border," which, to an increasing degree, also fulfilled the function of social selection and screened according to criteria of health, fitness, class, and ethnic origin.[6] The selective Aliyah regime strove to keep out those deemed a burden on society, the sick and poor—who often were identified with "Oriental" (*mizrachi*) and, in particular, Moroccan Jewry—and allow entry to those considered useful. These would include young people, agricultural workers, "people with (economic) means," and those of Ashkenazi middle-class background from the United States or from Eastern Europe.

These categories of people point to the twofold dimension of Israeli nation building: the traditional Zionist ideological project of pioneering settlement combined with the creation of an urban middle class, which was deemed indispensable for a modern nation-state. Israel thus turned into what Aristide

Zolberg has called a "nation by design"—"a nation of immigrants, to be sure, but not just any immigrants."[7] Selectivity was the main tool for this designing process. The candidates' Jewishness was not contested at that point, because in the confessionally stratified societies of colonial North Africa, they were easily identified as Jews qua religion. While the intra-Jewish hierarchizations of Ashkenazim over Mizrachim mattered for this selective migration regime—which combined "ableism" with "orientalism" and class bias—the candidates' Jewishness remained unquestioned. This situation was quite unlike that of Ethiopian Jews discussed in chapter 5, who gained prominence from the 1970s onward and whose Jewish identity was the object of many discussions.[8]

Beyond these significant differences in terms of content were certain structural features in the functioning of the normalization-contestation nexus that these cases shared with each other and with other historical migration regimes. The two countries not only turned their external gates into mechanisms of proper control but also shifted this first "line of defense" as far away from the countries' borders as possible and into the countries of origin. Arguably, the model for this externalization of immigration control was the 1924 US Immigration Restriction Act, which made the departure of prospective immigrants for the United States conditional on a visa to be granted by an American consular office abroad and the granting of the visa conditional on passing a medical inspection—previously conducted at Ellis Island—in the country of origin.[9] West Germany took steps in this direction, starting in 1957, by gradually introducing candidate interviews at diplomatic missions in Belgrade and Zagreb to assess eligibility for acceptance, an option that did not exist in other European countries where the FRG had no embassies or consulates. Israel had already fully emulated the US model in 1952, when Aliyah from Morocco was made conditional on a successful examination in the country of origin, thus ensuring that no unwanted candidate could make his or her way to Israel. It will become clear that this externalization went so far that the possibility even arose—in theory unthinkable under the Law of Return—that a Jew deemed unsuitable for Aliyah could be turned away at the border.

Another common pattern that will emerge in this analysis is the mediated nature of the normalization-contestation nexus. The key mediating factor was institutional in that the question of precisely which institution would mount a more general challenge to co-ethnic immigration depended on the intrinsic logic of that very institution. Thus, Werner Kanein of the Bavarian Interior Ministry merely took the logic of his institution—securing the country's borders against foreigners—to an extreme by also applying it to (purported) Germans. The same was true for Dr. Eliezer Matan, an emissary doctor of the Israeli

Health Ministry in charge of screening migrants on the ground in Morocco, who mounted a radical challenge to Israel's open Aliyah gates in 1952 (which will be discussed later in more detail). Matan's categorical statement that "the doors are basically closed if we are to implement selective immigration as we understand it" was a consequent interpretation of the ministry's self-ascribed role of "gatekeeper of the land."[10] Their respective opponents—Hans Schütz of the Bavarian Labor Ministry, who was in charge of expellee affairs, and Yitzhak Rafael of the Jewish Agency Aliyah Department, who was in charge of promoting immigration—did the same in the reverse, defending generous immigration rules as part of their institutional mission. Institutional differences were thus important in determining how the normalization-contestation nexus would play out. As will be seen in the Israeli case, prioritizing certain immigrant groups (Polish Jews) over others (Moroccan Jews) could be an additional factor impacting the way that normalization—or, in the case of decolonizing Morocco, denormalization—of migration conditions would influence the generosity of the immigration regime.

GERMANY: SIFTING GERMANS FROM YUGOSLAVS

In December 1959, readers of *Der Donauschwabe*, a weekly newspaper of German expellees from Yugoslavia, were presented with the following statement on the newspaper's front page:

> On every working day, there is a motley crew of people queuing in front of a noble three-story building in the busy Kneza Miloša Street of Belgrade. Peasants with fur caps wait next to elegant ladies and men in dirty working gear. Even though there is a big sign announcing that the door of the building will not open until ten o'clock, the first contenders take their spots already before dawn, sometimes even at three o'clock at night. . . . There is something that distinguishes the people in the queue from the Yugoslav passersby: they speak only German among each other. They are ethnic Germans (*Volksdeutsche*) who have been released from Yugoslav citizenship, and the building belongs to the embassy of the Federal Republic of Germany. There they receive their immigration permit, which allows them to say good-bye to the dull everyday life of the Yugoslav people's democracy. Since the break of diplomatic ties between Belgrade and Bonn there is no ambassador of the Federal Republic in Belgrade anymore. France represents the Federal Republic's interests in Belgrade and also takes care of the ethnic Germans in Yugoslavia, but there are still German officials in the

> building of the former embassy and they try to support the ethnic Germans in their sometimes quite complicated struggle with bureaucracy to emigrate from Yugoslavia.[11]

This scene evokes images that are commonly associated with Moscow in the late 1980s: members of an ethnic minority queuing outside the embassy of their kin state to leave their socialist home country and start a new life in the West. Yet this scene took place in Belgrade, not Moscow, and the year was 1959, not 1989. Ethnic Germans from Yugoslavia were the first *Volksdeutsche* (or *folksdojčeri*, as they were called in Serbo-Croatian) who were able to freely emigrate from a socialist country to the West, and they did so in comparatively large numbers. In late 1959, at the time that the *Donauschwabe* article appeared, over 57,000 former Yugoslav citizens had been received as Aussiedler in the Federal Republic of Germany, making them the decade's second largest group of co-ethnic immigrants (after those from Poland). By the time of Yugoslavia's breakup in 1991, this number had reached almost 90,000, most of whom had already emigrated by the end of the 1960s.[12]

Challenging the notion that immigration controls for ethnic Germans were lax and that their resettlement was generally uncontroversial before the 1980s, this chapter explains that, already in the 1950s and 1960s, this relatively large and unrestricted flow of migrants led to fairly strict immigration controls and a contestation of Aussiedler migration from Yugoslavia and in general within the West German state apparatus.[13] The German authorities found that many of the applicants did not fulfill the criteria set by German law defining an ethnic German, especially if they lived in mixed marriages or had otherwise doubtful German credentials. In 1960, the Federal Administration Office (*Bundesverwaltungsamt*) rejected 23.3 percent of all applications for resettlement. In both 1963 and 1964, this ratio reached 29 percent—unthinkably high rejection rates in other contexts of Aussiedlung.[14] It was here that the external gate that was the takeover procedure—which, in the case of German emigrants from more restrictive socialist countries, was indeed a mere formality—turned into an actual site of selection.

Because the German refugee state framed Aussiedler reception as co-ethnic asylum, the method of controlling Aussiedler influx was to check candidates' eligibility under the main criterion provided for by expellee law: German ethnicity (*Volkszugehörigkeit*). For the historian, this provides a rare window into the process of administrative ethnic screening and thus an opportunity to closely examine the practice of ethnic selection. The selecting institutions—diplomatic missions, the Federal Administrative Office, and local authorities—did not accept Aussiedler from Yugoslavia as German merely on the basis of their German descent. Both cultural (especially linguistic) and political arguments were used to include or exclude applicants, while social criteria played only a marginal auxiliary role. At the same time, the structure of the takeover procedure allowed for a flexible handling of doubtful cases when it was deemed necessary. The expellee associations (*Landsmannschaften*) provided an additional voice that attempted to influence the state institutions' application of the ethnic immigration code. As they did so, these associations tried to assert their own role as gatekeepers in the immigration process—a phenomenon that will also be encountered in later chapters of this book.

On a more general level, the constant flow of Yugoslav Aussiedler led to calls for stricter immigration control. Parts of the state apparatus involved in the immigration process even went so far as to challenge the very notion of preferential immigration for ethnic Germans. Some state agencies—most notably the German mission in Belgrade and the Foreign Office—argued for a generally restrictive approach to Aussiedler immigration from Yugoslavia. Contrary to what the author of the *Donauschwabe* article claimed, the German officials in the former embassy did not support the ethnic Germans in their struggle against the obstructive Yugoslav authorities but, rather, tried on several occasions to restrict their access to the Federal Republic of Germany. The Bavarian State Ministry of the Interior even went so far as to demand the restriction of Aussiedler immigration from Eastern Europe altogether. Amid signs indicating normalization in the socialist East, the restrictive approach of the West German state to immigration in general was also extended to co-ethnic immigration.

AUSSIEDLUNG FROM YUGOSLAVIA

According to the logic of the normalization-contestation nexus, the exceptionally restrictive handling of Aussiedlung from Yugoslavia was a result of both the perceived necessity to control a migration stream that was not subject to the severe exit controls of other socialist states and the actual opportunity to do so in the absence of any Cold War–related pressures. In addition, the handling of Aussiedlung resulted from a mismatch between some of the structural characteristics of the formerly large German minority in Yugoslavia and the requirements of German expellee law. The majority of Yugoslav Germans were so-called Danube Swabians, or *Donauschwaben* (hence the expellee paper's title) from the Serbian part of the Banat known as the Vojvodina. There, and in neighboring Slavonia, some 440,000 people had declared their native language to be German in the 1931 census.[15] In these ethnically mixed regions, they were hardly an insular population, and many (former) German speakers assimilated to the surrounding dominant Hungarian and Croatian cultures—especially in Slavonia, where German settlement was less compact than in the Vojvodina. The lack of confessional barriers facilitated what were considered "mixed" marriages with members of these other linguistic groups. During the interwar period, "nationally conscious" Germans organized themselves in the so called Swabian German Kulturbund, which in the late 1930s became increasingly Nazified. Yet, especially in Croatia, the ensuing "awakening" on the level of ethnic self-declaration translated into neither a better knowledge of the (especially written) German language among the population nor a separation from the surrounding non-German population.[16] These blurry ethnic borders, which already troubled the *völkisch* activists of the time, were also problematic for German expellee law with its emphasis on unequivocal belonging and identification.

Both the expulsion and the Aussiedlung of Germans from Yugoslavia differed in significant ways from the developments in other affected countries. Yugoslavia was not included in the Potsdam agreement and hence could not rid itself of its German minority with Allied blessing. Direct expulsions took place only in Slovenia and parts of Slavonia.[17] In Croatia, the few Germans who had not been evacuated by the retreating Wehrmacht toward the end of the war were interned with the aim of expelling them afterward, which proved impossible. In 1946, all those were liberated who had not been Kulturbund members, had not exposed themselves as collaborators, lived in mixed marriages, or had assimilated linguistically—some 90 percent of those interned.[18] In the Vojvodina, the new communist government also dispossessed and interned the remaining Germans.[19] Until 1947, as many as 40,000 internees fled the camps with the implicit approval of the authorities in a process that Hans-Ulrich Wehler has called "indirect deportation."[20] In 1948, the remaining camp inmates were released but were forced to work on state farms for another three years. From 1950 on, family reunification became possible under a special agreement between the Yugoslav and German Red Cross societies.[21] After 1951, Yugoslav Germans could emigrate within a standardized and fairly reliable procedure.[22]

The consistency and relatively liberal nature of the emigration regime distinguished Aussiedlung from Yugoslavia from that of other socialist states. Tito's socialist but nonaligned Yugoslavia was the only one among the countries defined as the expulsion area, which not only allowed humanitarian family reunification of ethnic minorities but also increasingly permitted regular labor migration, often to West Germany.[23] Consequently, Aussiedler emigration was not limited to cases of family reunification, though in practice most Aussiedler did have relatives in West Germany. Any ethnic German living in Yugoslavia could apply for resettlement in the FRG, with which the country had maintained diplomatic relations since 1951. To migrate, the applicant needed permission to leave Yugoslavia, combined with a release from Yugoslav citizenship, and approval to immigrate to the FRG with the guarantee of receiving German citizenship on arrival (the so-called certificate of equalization, or *Gleichstellungsbescheinigung*).[24] The approval to immigrate and the guarantee of German citizenship were granted after the applicant's eligibility had been positively assessed by the German authorities in the takeover procedure. Unlike in other countries, where prospective Aussiedler had to rely on relatives in West Germany to launch the procedure, applicants in Yugoslavia could file their applications in the embassy in Belgrade or at the consulate general in Zagreb. The resulting migration channel was kept open even after the severing of diplomatic ties between the FRG and Yugoslavia in 1957, when the French embassy in Belgrade took over the representation of West German interests.

Although—or indeed, because—emigration from Yugoslavia was easier than from any other socialist state, the immigration procedure to West Germany turned into a major bureaucratic obstacle for potential resettlers. In 1954, a standard application that did not face major complications took about half a year to be processed by the local, regional, state, and federal institutions involved in the screening process.[25] By 1964, the average duration had reached one year, and complicated cases could take considerably longer.[26] The ultimate decision about admittance lay with the Federal Interior Ministry and, from 1960 onward, with the Federal Administration Office (BVA) as its executive branch. In their decision making, these federal institutions had to rely on (possibly contradictory) information about the applicant that had been gathered by other authorities. If the applicant's relatives in Germany filed the takeover application at their local expellee office, they were the main source of information for this office to assess whether someone matched the criteria of expellee law. The authorities were able to obtain further evidence from the *Heimatortskarteien* and *Heimatauskunftstellen* (already familiar from chap. 1), which were the main sources of institutionalized knowledge on ethnic Germans. In case of doubt, the embassy in Belgrade or the consulate general in Zagreb could be asked to summon the potential immigrants to the embassy to examine their credentials in a personal interview. This happened increasingly often from 1957 onward. If a prospective Aussiedler directly filed an application at a West German mission in Yugoslavia, a personal interview was compulsory. Indeed, in 1964, the BVA suggested accepting applications from relatives in Germany in exceptional cases only; the standard procedure should always start with the diplomatic mission in Yugoslavia.[27] This shift of the external gate to the country of origin, which we will encounter again in the discussion of Israel below, served to keep out unwanted candidates who may have immigrated through another channel—usually illegally via Austria—and then claimed recognition as ethnic Germans by the expellee authorities once they reached Germany.[28]

The personal interview of a prospective Aussiedler by diplomatic staff represented the most intimate encounter between state and migrant in the entire external immigration procedure. Whereas the takeover procedure launched from inside the country involved the assessment of information on paper provided by a third party, here officials and migrants faced each other. From the personal encounter, the diplomats were expected to decide whether they were in favor of accepting or rejecting the applicant. The items listed on the two-page form that summarized the personal interview detail how the examiners were to recognize an "ethnic German." The form included information about descent (*Abstammung*), ethnicity (*Volkszugehörigkeit*) according to Yugoslav identification, upbringing (*Erziehung*), level of German language skills, language spoken at home, membership in the Kulturbund, membership in the Wehrmacht, captivity as a prisoner of war, internment, and expropriation. Based on these facts, the examining officials were to state whether they believed that German *Volkstum* prevailed in the family, whether the applicant had self-identified as German (that is, made a *Bekenntnis* to German *Volkstum*), whether the criteria of section 6 of the BVFG were fulfilled, and hence whether the applicant should be accepted.[29] These were the pieces of a puzzle that, on completion, were supposed to produce an image of German *Volkszugehörigkeit*.

The cases analyzed below reveal how this ethnic puzzle was assembled in bureaucratic practice, both on paper and in personal interviews. The ideal Aussiedler will thus obtain some sharper contours. It will become clear that, for a long time, the institutions involved did not make their decisions strictly by the letter of the law. The complex definition given in section 6 of the BVFG, with its strong emphasis on subjective *Bekenntnis* in the past—*before* the expulsion—was in practice often reduced to the comparatively easy-to-handle and "objective" criterion of present language skills. In mixed families, where the issue of *Volkszugehörigkeit* was generally most contentious, the use of the German language was taken as evidence for the prevalence of German *Volkstum* and therefore as a precondition for immigration—but only after the practice of generally rejecting mixed families had ceased. In addition, a significant political aspect to *Volkszugehörigkeit* gained importance for ethnic Germans who had sided with the Yugoslav partisans against the Nazi occupiers. Social criteria, on the other hand, played only a complementary role, and at no point were medical examinations or other considerations of the prospective immigrants' physique used to decide on their applications.[30]

SCREENING MIXED FAMILIES

In April 1960, the *Donauschwabe* reported from the transit camp of Piding in Bavaria: "More than before the repatriation of members of so-called mixed marriages became noticeable. Among them there are people who do not speak a word of German."[31] During the preceding years, the authorities had already been grappling with the question of whether to allow the immigration of ethnically mixed families and, if so, based on which criteria. The approach changed over time, shifting from outright rejection to a flexible handling of cases that focused on the "prevailing of German *Volkstum*"—which usually meant speaking the German language—in the family.

Before 1959 there were several documented cases of mixed families that were denied entry into West Germany. In all these cases, it was the women who claimed to be German. The fact that they had "intermarried" was seen as the renunciation of their German *Volkstum*. For example, a mother and her son were rejected by the authorities in 1956 because the woman had been married to a non-German, despite her having relatives in the Federal Republic. The husband's non-German ethnicity was deduced from the facts that he had not served in the Wehrmacht, that his wife had not been interned despite her German ethnicity, and that their son did not bear a German first name.[32] In 1957, three other women were granted an immigration visa only after they had been divorced from their non-German husbands.[33] In March 1959, Elisabeth B., another German woman who had married a non-German, was granted an immigration visa "on purely humanitarian grounds" after someone had intervened at the Committee of Petitions of the German Bundestag. As it turned out, she and her mother, who already lived in West Germany, had made "exceptionally heavy sacrifices" (*außergewöhnlich schwere Opfer*) because of their German *Volkstum*, which eventually made them worthy of being admitted to the FRG as citizens.[34]

The available documentation that only German women married to non-German men were denied recognition as ethnic Germans indicates a likely gender bias in the authorities' assessment of German *Volkszugehörigkeit*. The officials may have assumed that the husband's *Volkstum* automatically dictated that of his wife, analogous to the long-standing rules of German citizenship law. This law stated that a woman lost her German citizenship if she married a foreigner and that a foreign woman acquired the German citizenship of her husband—a rule that had only recently been abolished between 1953 and 1957.[35] This parallel reasoning is not explicitly mentioned in the sources, but against the legal background it seems probable.

The practice of rejecting mixed families' applications out of hand ceased with an instruction given by the Federal Interior Ministry in July 1959. The instruction stated:

> Just because an ethnic German (*deutscher Volkszugehöriger*), no matter if man or woman, has married a foreigner of non-German ethnicity, does not mean he or she can be denied recognition of German *Volkszugehörigkeit*.... In mixed marriages, one partner usually has an ethnically dominating influence (*einen volkstumsmäßig bestimmenden Einfluss*) on the other partner.... Evidence for the prevalence of the *Bekenntnis* to German *Volkstum* can be found in the use of the German language within the family, in the choice of typically German names for the children, in the German upbringing of the children and in the acquaintance of family members with German citizens or ethnic Germans. In mixed marriages it should be thoroughly checked whether German *Volkstum* prevails in the family.[36]

From July 1959 onward, the screening of mixed families involved proving the German partner—regardless of gender—had been the primary source of cultural influence in the family. In several documented cases, mixed families were not accepted into West Germany because the German *Volkstum* of the one partner had not been found to be dominant. In practice, this was assessed by checking whether the family spoke German at home or used another language, usually Serbo-Croatian or Hungarian. For example, in 1965, the family of Josef K.—who, according to the BVA, was an ethnic German born in 1927 to two German parents—was not granted an entry visa because his non-German wife, Djurdja, did not speak any German and the children had "typically Slavic first names."[37] The fact that past applicants from their hometown Sokolovac in Croatia had had a good knowledge of the German language was held against this candidate. In a similar case in 1964, Emil S. and his wife, Jelka, from Slavonian Vukovar were denied entry despite the "typically German" first names of their three children—Josef, Emmerich, and Karl—because Jelka's Croatian *Volkstum* was judged to be dominant in the family.[38] In contrast, Stefan V., a Hungarian German man from Czerwenka (Crvenka) in Serbia was accepted, even though he had his father's typically Hungarian surname and was registered as

Hungarian in his Yugoslav identification. His son Tibor bore an equally Hungarian first name. Yet Stefan and his children spoke excellent German and, according to the embassy in Belgrade, "made a very good impression." Therefore, their application was granted without hesitation.[39]

Contrary to the idea that anyone with even remotely German descent would be recognized as ethnically German, German ancestry at times counted for very little compared with language skills in the family. This can be seen in the case of Barbara and Marko K. from Komletinci in Croatian Syrmia. Their first application, filed in 1963, to relocate to West Germany with their four sons was rejected even though both partners had German mothers and Barbara even spoke German quite well. Over a year after the family had filed their application for the second time in 1968, they received a letter from the BVA explaining that they were in fact not German *Volkszugehörige*, because this required a *Bekenntnis*. And the "most reliable evidence" for this *Bekenntnis*—according to the BVA—was the use of the German language in the family. Since the consulate in Zagreb had revealed that the family spoke Croatian at home, they had to be considered ethnically Croatian and were therefore denied permission to immigrate.[40] This outright identification of language and *Bekenntnis*, which was not covered by section 6 of the BVFG, had become common administrative practice for Germans from Yugoslavia. In the overall system of co-ethnic immigration to the FRG, it was not until the large-scale Russian German immigration of the 1990s that language skills obtained such an important status.

However, other cases indicate that no clear policy existed for keeping out mixed families, even if the personal interview revealed that German *Volkstum* did not prevail in the family. Sometimes applicants were given a second chance. This worked, for example, for a Hungarian German family whose application had been rejected in April 1959. When they were reexamined by the embassy in Belgrade in June 1961, it was determined that "the German *Volkstum* of [the mother] by now prevails in the family. The husband, who is of Hungarian descent and spoke little German in early 1959, has apparently made an effort to assimilate to German *Volkstum* (*im deutschen Volkstum aufzugehen*) and now speaks German. The daughter also speaks German—apparently she is raised the German way (*offenbar wird sie deutsch erzogen*)."[41] This dynamic approach to *Volkstum* was taken even further in a case in 1962, when Anton P. and his family were granted an immigration permit based on the embassy's judgment that "German *Volkstum* will soon prevail in the family."[42] One local office took this approach to its logical consequence when it supported the application of Johann and Katharina M., arguing that the husband's German *Volkstum* could prevail over that of his Hungarian wife only if they came to live with his relatives in Germany.[43] In yet other instances, families that had received an unequivocally negative ruling by the embassy were taken in with a special permit according to the Aliens Police Act (*Ausländerpolizeiverordnung*) issued by the local authorities at the place of residence of the applicants' relatives.[44]

Even so, applicants with questionable credentials did not automatically receive the benefit of the doubt. Much depended on the goodwill of the authorities at the applicants' prospective destinations.[45] Social considerations, while not the core of the screening process, could tip the scale for or against a candidate. The availability of sufficient housing was one of the relevant criteria in the takeover procedure. In 1964, for example, Roman and Maria T. were taken in despite their lacking German *Bekenntnis* and their "mixed Romanian-German-Hungarian-Serbian" *Volkstum*. Apart from the fact that they both spoke German, it was held in their favor that Maria's mother was already in West Germany and that their accommodation was secured.[46] In contrast, in 1961, two other families that did not fulfill the criteria for *Volkszugehörigkeit* were also denied a special permit because, among other reasons, they had not secured accommodation.[47] In 1956, the Federal Expellee Ministry made the takeover of Maria W. and her daughter Adelheide explicitly conditional on secured housing, "since without such an assurance there are no reasons why we should accept the person concerned."[48] In the case of Ferdinand and Maria T. and their children Slavia and Dezider, the authorities in Baden-Württemberg agreed to take them in only on the condition that the Land would receive adequate funding for housing construction.[49]

In general, it seems that the local institutions were more generous in their immigration decisions if they incurred no additional costs or if these costs were covered by additional funding. Although not engaging in positive social selection akin to what took place in Israel, a federal state like Baden-Württemberg was interested in not incurring additional welfare costs caused by the immigration of people whose relatives did not have sufficient means to accommodate them. Concerns about "negative selection" and the disproportionate allocation of welfare cases are also documented for the central distribution procedure at the transit camp in Friedland. In 1963, for example, the Baden-Württemberg Expellee Ministry suggested the full-time presence of a Land representative in the camp, since the current part-time solution entailed the danger of Baden-Württemberg "being disadvantaged compared to other federal states with regard to the professional and age-structure of the allocated Aussiedler, as well as with regard to the allocation of welfare cases."[50] This suggestion illustrates that, while co-ethnic immigrants were not generally selected by social criteria, such considerations were of interest when it came to distributing Aussiedler among the federal states.

In fact, the external selection practice, with its emphasis on language skills and critical approach toward mixed marriages, caused a certain amount of negative selection in the age structure of migrants. Younger candidates who had spent a significant part of their lives in postwar Yugoslavia had more trouble passing the interview in the embassy for lack of German language skills and a higher likelihood of living in a mixed marriage. In one striking case in the late 1950s, Franz K., who was in his early 50s at the time, and his wife, Anna, were taken in, but their daughter Veronika was rejected because she had not made German *Volkstum* dominant in her marriage with her Hungarian husband (himself in his late 20s).[51] The practice of letting people reapply after they had made German *Volkstum* prevail in their family similarly implied that age did not matter, as the applicants would inevitably grow older in the meantime. In an extreme case, Simon S. and his family were rejected in 1959, when he was 30, because of his lack of German language skills. In 1968, the family's takeover was finally granted.[52] Unlike the Israeli nation-building institutions, the German refugee state clearly did not seek out young and fit people from among the pool of potential co-ethnics, remarkably at a time when foreign *Gastarbeiter* were already being recruited for the German economy.[53]

THE POLITICAL DIMENSION OF *VOLKSZUGEHÖRIGKEIT*

Whereas social screening among Aussiedler remained marginal and largely implicit, the assessment of *Volkszugehörigkeit* could obtain an explicitly political character. This type of political screening is demonstrated in the case of Blagorodovac, a small Croatian village located between Zagreb and Osijek. In late 1959, the Federal Office for Administrative Matters (the precursor to the Federal Administration Office) reported that the consulate general in Zagreb had been anonymously tipped off about certain applicants from the village having fought for the communist partisans during the Second World War.[54] Unlike other Germans, they had not suffered internment or persecution after the war. In a personal interview in the consulate, one applicant claimed that the inhabitants of the village had had to serve with the partisans under the threat of execution. The association (*Landsmannschaft*) of Germans from Yugoslavia doubted this allegation and stated that it had been possible for the Germans of Blagorodovac to flee from the partisans. The office contacted the Federal Interior Ministry to clarify whether this engagement with the partisans allowed for a positive judgment of their *Bekenntnis*—their "objective" Germanness according to the law was not in question.

After having inquired into the matter more deeply and having heard witnesses, in March 1961 the consulate general in Zagreb reported that the inhabitants of Blagorodovac, 99 percent of whom were Germans, had indeed served with the partisans. Whether this had happened under coercion was deemed irrelevant, since "given the support for the partisans, for whatever reason and of whatever kind, we certainly cannot assume a *Bekenntnis* to German *Volkstum* anymore. For this reason, we suggest to reject all applicants from Blagorodovac unless it is proved that the individual applicant has *not* collaborated with the partisans."[55] Although it is unknown whether this ban was ever enforced, it is remarkable that such a measure was even suggested.[56] In principle, pro-Nazi engagement was not supposed to constitute a *Bekenntnis* to German *Volkstum*; yet this is precisely how applications from Blagorodovac were to be judged. While the villager Johann A., who had served in the Waffen-SS, was accepted as an Aussiedler in 1959, those who had fought the German occupying army in Yugoslavia had allegedly renounced their Germanness—despite the fact that the people in question had at no point denied being German and were still registered as Germans in their passports.[57] In fact, Blagorodovac was the symbol of a specifically German resistance to Nazi occupation and supposedly the place where the partisan army's German-manned Thälmann battalion had first raised its banner.[58] At this point, the meaning of *Bekenntnis* transforms into a strong political statement. This testifies to a politicized view of what and who was supposed to be German that neatly combined an apologetic view of the Nazi past with the anticommunist *raison d'état* of the West German state. An ethnic German after 1945 was supposed to have been a victim of communism, not a communist.

MIGRANT AGENCY: THE CASE OF FAMILY T.

Contrary to what the contemporary term *Übernahmeverfahren* and the analytical term *ethnic screening* might suggest, the migrants were not merely passive objects in the migration process. Their agency in positioning themselves vis-à-vis the requirements of the ethnically coded migration regime can be gauged from some of the administrative documentation. Given that Yugoslavia offered emigration options other than ethnic family reunification, the very attempt to come to Germany as an Aussiedler constituted a conscious choice. This channel of migration offered obvious advantages—the promise of German citizenship and integration benefits—but posed the challenge of having to prove German *Volkszugehörigkeit*. Some tried to bypass this hurdle by moving to the FRG as "guest workers" and then applying for Aussiedler status in the internal procedure after acquiring some language skills that could bolster their claim to being ethnic Germans.[59] Others struggled through the takeover procedure, attempting along the way to make their profile match its requirements.

The case of family T. from Croatia is instructive in this regard. In 1958, Elisabeth T., born in 1902, and her three sons applied for resettlement in West Germany. While the Baden-Württemberg interior ministry supported their application, the Federal Administrative Office rejected it in early 1960, based on information the Belgrade mission had obtained from the family members in the personal interview. It appeared that they did not fulfill the criteria for *Volkszugehörigkeit*:

> Elisabeth T. and her son Nikola speak German, but in their IDs they are registered as Croatian. Contrary to what her sister—now resident in the FRG—states in her application, they have not been interned in a camp, probably because they posed as Croats. Her son Hans, whose signature was "Ivan T.," does not speak German. His wife is an ethnic Hungarian and speaks no German. The family vernacular is Croatian. The couple's children are thus arguably being raised within a foreign *Volkstum* (*im fremden Volkstum erzogen*). The interests section further found out that their expropriation in 1947 was not due to their ethnicity but happened as part of the overall agrarian reform in Yugoslavia.[60]

Based on this negative assessment, the interior ministry withdrew its support. The application was finally rejected in October 1962.

Having awaited a final decision for four years, Elisabeth T. wasted no time and filed a new application in December 1962. Her son Johann—as he was called now—had been dropped from the application, arguably so his Hungarian Croatian family would not endanger the family's overall migration project. The consulate general in Zagreb conducted an interview with the family in January 1963 and reached a positive conclusion regarding their German *Volkszugehörigkeit*, given that Elisabeth and her sons Nikolas [*sic*], born in 1931, and Andreas, born in 1944, were supposedly ethnic Germans and spoke German. The BVA thus confirmed their approval for resettlement in July 1963—only to revoke it again in 1965 for the elder son, because his wife, Stojanka, was not German. Nikolaus [*sic*]—as he was called in his mother's renewed application—was eventually allowed to come in 1968.[61] By that time, the new takeover guidelines—which are discussed in more detail in chapter 4—decreed that for descendants of ethnic Germans who had not been of age at the end of the war and hence had had no chance to make a *Bekenntnis* of their own, the application for resettlement in Germany should count as such.[62]

Over ten years, the T. family managed to successfully complete their family migration project. To achieve this outcome, they had to convince the German authorities that, despite their obvious integration into local society and their lacking internment as Germans in the past, they were actually to be considered ethnically German. This argument involved several strategic moves. The most fundamental of these was the persistent filing of applications—a strategy that Aussiedler from other socialist countries with more restrictive emigration regimes used to obtain an exit permit. By trying this for long enough, they would eventually reach the desired result.[63] The applications were, however, not simply repetitive but adjusted to the situation: Hans/Johann/Ivan was dropped, because his non-German wife and poor language skills made him a hopeless candidate. The successive Germanization of his name and even more of Nikolas/Nikolaus's name can furthermore be interpreted as part of the strategy to outwardly appear more German, thus working toward the requirement that "the choice of typically German names for their children" could indicate the dominance of German *Volkstum* in the family. This performative aspect of *Volkszugehörigkeit* is developed further in the next chapter with regard to recognition practices at the internal gate.

WHO DEFINES WHOM? ENTER THE LANDSMANNSCHAFTEN

In addition to these grassroots practices that shaped the outcomes of the migration regime's proceedings, the Landsmannschaft of Germans from Yugoslavia as the organized representation of a previous wave of immigrants also tried to assert their own position in the regime and the ethnic screening procedure. Landsmannschaft interventions in the gatekeeping process were a recurrent phenomenon in the history of Aussiedler migration. These expellee associations were assigned an official gatekeeping function by the state authorities. For instance, when the Federal Interior Ministry ordered thorough controls of the prevalence of German *Volkstum* in mixed families in 1959, it suggested "involving the refugee administrations of the Länder and consulting the Landsmannschaften."[64] In addition, these associations publicly intervened on occasion, complaining about the admission of Aussiedler with Slavic names who had supported the partisans during the war or deploring the deportation of Yugoslav Germans who had entered the Federal Republic illegally.[65]

The crucial point was that the Landsmannschaft wanted only people they thought to be "real" ethnic Germans admitted to Germany. To be sure, there was significant tension between the two poles of the culturally German but politically undesirable communist partisans on the one side and desirable *Volksdeutsche* with little knowledge of the German language on the other. Regardless of these contradictions, what truly mattered was to establish the power to define who was ethnically German—or at least to gain some influence on the state offices that possessed this power. For instance, in early 1969, Florian Krämer of the Landsmannschaft's Bavarian chapter complained to the Federal Interior Ministry that in years past, many candidates for immigration had been rejected because of excessive emphasis on language over *Volkszugehörigkeit.* Yet his main concern lay not so much with the rejections as with the fact that the Landsmannschaft had no say in the decision: "When an applicant has sold all his belongings and has cut all ties with the homeland, we [i.e., the Landsmannschaft] cannot give an opinion anymore. *What is supposed to happen with an applicant who we would have rejected?* It would be irresponsible to cause the applicants any trouble after their entry into the Federal Republic. We have to find a way that avoids faits accomplis.[66] The plan Krämer had in mind was to strengthen the role of "our *Heimatauskunftstellen*" in the screening process. This would, no doubt, result in higher expenses for these institutions, "but this procedure would still be cheaper than having unworthy people (*Unwürdige*), non-Germans, and spies coming to the Federal Republic and paying for them with the taxpayer's money."[67]

At this point, it becomes clear that Krämer's aim was to impose his association's definition of an ethnic German onto the administrative procedure. The Federal Interior Ministry was not thrilled by this attempt of the Landsmannschaft to enhance its gatekeeper role. While a ministerial official commented on Krämer's reference to "higher expenses" for the *Heimatauskunftstellen* with a dry "So they want money!" on the margin of the original letter, in the response to Krämer, Dr. Heuer from the ministry fended off Krämer's definitional challenge.[68] Heuer justified the practice of recognition from a legal point of view and specified that neither German descent nor knowledge of the German language alone was sufficient to be recognized as German. Nevertheless, the use of the German language indicated which *Volkstum* applicants identified with. "Whoever has assimilated into another *Volkstum* is not a German *Volkszugehöriger,* in spite of German descent."[69] This episode reveals that, for the time being, the state bureaucracy was not willing to yield any more of its power concerning the definition of *Volkszugehörigkeit* to the expellee associations than what was already common through the involvement of the *Heimatauskunftstellen.* But as chapter 5 will illustrate, the definitional power and gatekeeping function of these institutions and associations remained contentious until the 1980s.

CONTESTING AUSSIEDLUNG

Ethnic German immigration from Yugoslavia had caused internal and public irritation on several occasions since the late 1950s. Recurring instances of corruption in the emigration procedure had led to suspended sentences for some of the immigrants charged for using fraudulent documentation to prove their Germanness.[70] The politically motivated initiative of the Zagreb consulate to halt immigration from Blagorodovac was also embedded in a wider contestation of ethnic German resettlement from Yugoslavia. The consulate closed its report with the supposition that German emigration from Yugoslavia was, by then, primarily economically motivated, which should lead to stricter standards in the assessment of the applicants' *Volkszugehörigkeit*—or even to the end of the resettlement campaign.[71] In March 1963, the *Donauschwabe* claimed that 75 percent of the newcomers at the time had doubtful German credentials.[72] As it transpired, this was only the prelude to a more general internal contestation of resettlement from Yugoslavia, which subsequently turned into a challenge of the very concept of ethnic German Aussiedlung.

The challenge against Yugoslav German Aussiedlung started with a letter from the West German interests section (*Schutzmachtvertretung*) in the French embassy in Belgrade to the Foreign Office in Bonn in July 1963. The head of the interests section, Hans Bock, admonished the Foreign Office to "reconsider the foundation and the motivation of the resettlement." He suspected that the increase in applications was due to the fact that more mixed families had been taken into consideration and the criterion of "prevailing German *Volkstum*" in the family was not being applied rigorously. Bock also criticized the common practice of letting people reapply after having acquired only a modest knowledge of German. He concluded that "the inevitable result of this generous practice is that even such categories of former ethnic Germans (*ehemalige Volksdeutsche*) who had long ago adapted to Yugoslav society and had no intention to emigrate before, are now virtually encouraged to emigrate."[73] With this latter statement, Bock anticipated Rogers Brubaker's observation about the "non-Euclidean demography" of co-ethnic migration—the phenomenon that with increased co-ethnic emigration to an attractive country, the pool of potential migrants does not decrease but increases as more people "rediscover" their origins.[74] The concern was clear: while the initial purpose of the resettlement campaign had been to enable the emigration of the "rearguard" of former German minorities in Eastern and Southeastern Europe, the embassy surmised that the current practice tended to attract more people with increasingly tenuous links to German *Volkstum*.

In another report in January 1965, the West German delegation in Belgrade was even more explicit in its criticism of the application of immigration policies regarding Yugoslav *Volksdeutsche*.[75] Countering the BVA's defense that it had rejected more than a third of the applications from Yugoslavia, the interests section complained that the percentage of "real" Germans among the Aussiedler was down to only 10 percent, while most of the families were of mixed ethnic background with the foreign element being predominant.[76] The criteria set by law were hardly applicable under the given conditions. A former *Bekenntnis* was hard to prove for lack of documentation, as was German descent in cases of mixed families, especially if they no longer carried German names. Crucially, given the predominant recognition practice, the author of the report argued that language could not be considered a valid criterion to identify a German, because many *Volksdeutsche* no longer spoke German while many non-Germans did. With this last manageable criterion for identification gone, the embassy representative proposed to set a deadline after which a resettlement from Yugoslavia to the FRG should no longer be possible.

As a reaction to this outright challenge of Yugoslav Aussiedlung, representatives of the Foreign Office, the Federal Administrative Office, and the Federal Expellee Ministry met in March 1965.[77] The Foreign Office officials supported the embassy's recent report. They regretted that the resettlement campaign could not be terminated anytime soon and criticized the BVA's broad definition of *volksdeutsch*. The BVA representatives in turn rejected the accusations made in particular cases. Instead, they blamed the Länder authorities and local expellee offices for not being strict enough in rejecting applications.[78] The general discussion reached the following conclusions: a deadline for new applications could not be set, because this was against the Federal Expellee Law. There was no majority in parliament to change the law, as the general political line was to keep the door open for ethnic Germans from socialist countries. However, it was suggested to advise the Interior Ministry to limit the certificates of equalization to two years—a measure that was eventually implemented in August 1966.[79] Furthermore, the federal states should be encouraged to use stricter standards in the context of family reunification. But other than that, the forceful contestation started by the Interests Section in Belgrade and supported by the Foreign Office yielded no tangible results.

Despite its inconclusiveness, this discussion is important for two reasons. It provides clear evidence that the politically imposed open door for ethnic Germans was not as uncontested during the 1960s as it would seem on the surface. Both the West German interests section at the French embassy in Belgrade and the Foreign Office were, in fact, in favor of closing this door to Germans from Yugoslavia. However, since this was a political rather than a bureaucratic decision, they could not act against the majority in parliament that wanted to keep the gates open. This discussion also resulted in a game of passing the buck between different institutions on different levels. The embassy blamed the BVA for being too generous. The BVA rejected this charge. But rather than defending its purported generosity—which, after all, could have been justified with the plight of ethnic Germans in Yugoslavia and the danger of their assimilation—its representatives pointed to their own restrictive record and indicated that the origin of the problem was to be found in the generosity of the Länder and expellee authorities.

This episode thus shows that, by the mid-1960s, restrictiveness had become a virtue among the higher authorities involved in co-ethnic immigration procedures from Yugoslavia. The liberal Yugoslav emigration regime and the apparent normalization of living conditions in the country made the exceptionally generous co-ethnic immigration regime appear unnecessary to some West German institutions. This impression was presumably reinforced by the hundreds of visa applications submitted by Yugoslav citizens wanting to become guest workers in West Germany that had been flooding the German delegations in Yugoslavia since the early 1960s.[80] Hence, a restrictive immigration regime more in line with the general stance toward the influx of foreigners was suggested. But for political reasons, this restrictive standpoint was not fully implemented. In 1969, the embassy in Belgrade complained once again that the BVA was too generous in granting immigration permits.[81] Unlike 1965, no controversial discussion followed. This time, not even a departmental meeting was scheduled to consider the issues.

THE BAVARIAN INTERVENTION

As discussed earlier in this chapter, the controversy surrounding Yugoslav migration triggered parallel discussions starting in March 1965 about the overall legitimacy of the special co-ethnic immigration regime. Here, too, the perceived normalization of conditions in socialist Eastern Europe led to questioning the alleged humanitarian emergency that had provided the basis for generous Aussiedler reception. For the main challenger, Werner Kanein of the Bavarian State Ministry of the Interior, anything that reduced the exceptionality of ethnic German migration from the East—first and foremost the suspected economic migration motives of many Aussiedler—prompted the restrictive stance that he, one of West Germany's leading experts on aliens' law, and his institution generally held toward "normal" immigration.[82] He urged the Federal Administration Office to revise its supposedly overly generous takeover procedure and even took unilateral measures to undermine the office's position.[83] Denying the BVA's competence to decide on immigration applications of ethnic Germans from Eastern Europe traveling via "free countries" such as Austria—a phenomenon that also troubled the federal authorities—Kanein's office assigned the processing of such applications to local aliens authorities.[84] That he was serious about eliminating this form of illegal immigration became clear in the case of Julius Kiener, a purported ethnic German from the Serbian town of Vršac, who was deported to Austria after entering West Germany illegally with a friend and trying to settle in Munich.[85]

Following up on Kanein's second letter to the BVA in September, in which he further explicated his "normalization" argument, the Bavarian Interior Ministry issued guidelines to the regional authorities in November, asking them for stricter admission practice.[86] The interior ministers of the other Länder were asked to follow suit. The guidelines made an exception only for Germans from the Soviet Union, whose difficult situation made it impossible to demand documentation proving *Volkszugehörigkeit*. Nor was such evidence needed, since the restrictive Soviet emigration practice supported the assumption "that the USSR will grant resettlement permits for the Federal Republic of Germany only to Germans."[87] In apparently more "liberal" states such as Poland, there was no such preselection of candidates, which necessitated stricter controls. Germans immigrating via Western countries were to be treated according to regular aliens' law.

Kanein's restrictive stance found some support among the Federal Interior Ministry and certain Länder interior ministries.[88] It was opposed by the Foreign Office, which had been in favor of restricting Aussiedler immigration from Yugoslavia but now took the Cold War context into consideration and expressed concern about humanitarian issues as well as the damaging effect it would have for the West German image abroad if ethnic Germans were deported to the Eastern Bloc.[89] Yet the harshest critique came from the Bavarian State Ministry for Labor and Social Welfare under conservative politician and expellee activist Hans Schütz.[90] Schütz rejected the notion that conditions in socialist states other than Yugoslavia had normalized to the extent that

Kanein suggested. The extensive evidence that the new guidelines demanded would lead to a drastic reduction of Aussiedler migration. This was politically problematic, Schütz argued, because it interfered with the policy of the federal government, "which undertakes many efforts to enable the Germans still living behind the Iron Curtain to migrate to Germany. . . . The Länder expellee ministers agree with the Federal Ministers that all existing possibilities for resettlement should be used and even extended."[91]

Reacting to this criticism, the Bavarian Interior Ministry mobilized a series of Cold War and *Deutschlandpolitik*-related arguments for its case against the privileged reception of Aussiedler, which normally served to justify its continuation. An April 1966 letter to the Federal Interior Ministry and the interior ministers of the federal states painted a grim picture of "subversion of the Federal Republic by people who, even if they are not pronounced supporters of communism, still represent a significant danger for the internal security of the Federal Republic."[92] After repeating the allegation that Aussiedler mainly came for economic reasons and criticizing the supposedly lax immigration controls, the ministry picked up the fundamental policy point Schütz had made in his letter: "It is a significant political question whether the attempts to make use of all possibilities for resettlement and even extend them are compatible with German foreign policy which tries to reduce the differences with the states of the Eastern Bloc, and whether it is desirable to strip the Eastern Territories of the last German elements. This problem cannot be discussed in detail here, but it has to be seen."[93] The ministry thus turned Schütz's argument for generous Aussiedler reception on its head. Extensive Aussiedlung would not serve West German interests, it claimed. Rather than saving their brethren in the East from communist oppression, it would bring in subversive elements; rather than furthering détente, it would obstruct it; and rather than serving the obligation of the West German state toward the Germans who had remained in the lost territories in the East, it would strip these very territories of their remaining German population.

Beyond the generally valid mechanism of normalization in the East causing stricter controls and contestation of co-ethnic immigration, the Bavarian Interior Ministry's intervention demonstrates that this normalization-contestation nexus was institutionally mediated. An institution's position toward Aussiedler migration in the face of changing circumstances was shaped by certain intrinsic motivations. In the interior ministry, the motivation was a general preference for immigration control and restriction, which was extended to the "special case" of ethnic German immigration due to the perceived signs of normalization in the Eastern Bloc. In the labor ministry, the motivation was the commitment to a particular clientele—expellees and their relatives—that made an increased resettlement effort imperative.

Working from these different assumptions, the same arguments could be mobilized to argue for the extension or restriction of Aussiedler reception. The link between the Cold War, *Deutschlandpolitik*, and co-ethnic immigration was thus more complex than Rogers Brubaker claims when he cites "Cold War and nationalist commitments" as being at the foundation of "the expansive embrace of transborder Germans."[94] Every institution in West Germany had to argue within this framework, and still the outcomes could be very different. The importance of institutional logics for the assumption of a particular stance toward co-ethnic immigration also mattered in the discussions surrounding selective Aliyah from North Africa to Israel, to which we will turn next.

ISRAEL: NOT JUST ANY IMMIGRANTS—SELECTIVE ALIYAH FROM NORTH AFRICA

In 1951, journalist Maurice Carr witnessed this scene taking place in the Jewish Agency immigration office in Casablanca:

> The screening process is a nerve-racking business.... The men, women and children arrive well-washed and in their Sabbath finery for this occasion.... Since birth certificates were a thing unknown until a couple of years ago, no family head admits to being above forty-five and no youth to being under eighteen.... Some of the rowdiest and most pathetic scenes occur when an aged and widowed mother, or elderly parents whose sons and daughters have preceded them to Israel, are turned away because the thoughtlessly drafted regulations require that a family breadwinner be on hand in the Diaspora at the time of application. The old folk weep and shout, demanding why they, who may have sons in Israel, in the Army, be penalized as against other people whose children are still in Morocco....
>
> When asked to state his trade, the breadwinner almost invariably replies, "I can do anything," and when further pressed, adds that he is a cobbler or a tailor or a peddler, or confesses that he has no trade. To ingratiate himself, he will give the Israelis behind the table a military salute or throw himself forward to kiss their hands....
>
> And then comes the most awesome day of judgment; the final decision is taken by a panel headed by a doctor sent over from the Israel Ministry of Health.... The families are not told immediately what the outcome of the selection is, but they always guess, infallibly. The rejected ones often

> dissolve in tears, fly into fits of rage. As I watched these scenes, and I attended a dozen such selections, I was moved as never before. It needs supreme callousness to remain dry-eyed.[95]

This account testifies to a phenomenon that characterized migration to Israel from North Africa during the 1950s: selective Aliyah. After the relatively uncontrolled influx of about 700,000 new immigrants between 1948 and 1951, it was the clearest expression of the young state's willingness to implement a proactive immigration policy and keep the gates of the country well guarded, despite the solemn declaration that Israel was open for Jewish immigration and despite the Law of Return. As outlined in chapter 1, proponents and opponents of selectivity faced each other within the Jewish Agency and state leaderships, with the proponents gradually gaining the upper hand. In an explicit manifestation of the normalization-contestation nexus, the November 1951 guidelines asserted that selection should take place wherever circumstances would allow it—a principle that was upheld until the 1960s. Exceptions were only to be made under urgent conditions, in cases defined as "rescue Aliyah" (*aliyat hatzalah*) or "liquidation Aliyah" (*aliyat chisul*). If the State of Israel could select, it did.

North Africa, and more specifically Morocco and Tunisia, was the only region where selective Aliyah was implemented fully over several years, and thus it provides an ideal context for understanding how selection played out in theory and practice.[96] The region, home to some 600,000 Jews by the late 1940s, was the center of much migration activity during the 1950s, supplying almost half (roughly 142,000 of 297,000) of all immigrants to Israel between 1952 and 1960, most of whom (almost 96,000) were from Morocco.[97] When selectivity was at its strictest during 1952–1953, rejection rates were as high as 70 percent; during 1954–1956, still one-third of Aliyah candidates were not approved.[98] At the "medical border" that Israel erected to control immigration, the scope of selection criteria widened over time from predominantly medical criteria to encompass a mix of medical and social elements that involved the fundamental issues of health, fitness to work, and hence the ability to contribute to the national construction effort. An integral part of these considerations was age. Facilitations for immigrants "with means" (*baalei emtzaim*) or with a certain amount of capital (*baalei hon*) were among the explicitly class-related social components that came to be introduced.

All of these criteria were in line with an instrumentalist state-building logic that involved both the settling of the land and the creation of a functioning national economy. These utilitarian criteria stand in contrast to the selection criteria employed by the ethnic refugee state in Germany, which cared about ethnically based entitlement to welfare state benefits rather than an immigration candidate's contribution to the economy. It will become clear below that they also came into conflict with the imperatives of the diaspora state, which postulated the unrestricted and unconditional reception of diaspora Jews based on the sole ethnic criterion of their Jewishness—to the point that some of the gatekeepers would contest the very legitimacy of the open gate created by the Law of Return.

WHY NORTH AFRICA? OPPORTUNITY, ABLEISM, AND ORIENTALISM

The focus of the Israeli selection effort on North Africa was a result of opportunity—unlike in other places, selection was actually possible—but also of a distinctly negative image of North African, and especially Moroccan, immigrants among Israeli and Zionist elites. This latter point contributed to an important variation on the generally valid principle that, while a normalization of conditions in the country of origin would result in stricter immigration controls, a worsening of these conditions should trigger a softening or abolition of these restrictions. As discussed below, the imminent independence of Morocco and Tunisia in 1955–1956—which, given experiences with other Arab states, carried with it the risk of restrictions or even a total ban on Jewish emigration—did not result in the abrogation of selection and the implementation of unrestricted rescue Aliyah. Although the strain on the Israeli absorption apparatus doubtlessly played a role in this, too, the simultaneous unrestricted reception of immigrants from Poland after the opening of emigration gates in 1956 suggests that the cultural imagery representing "Oriental" immigrants as backward, lazy, and prone to sickness was a key factor in the persistence of selectivity in North Africa, even beyond the closing of the emigration gates.

Unlike in other countries, whether communist or Arab, in the colonial Maghreb the Israeli and Jewish institutions could roam freely and select immigrants according to their own prerogatives after the French authorities had lifted their emigration restrictions in March 1949. Before the Second World War, North Africa had hardly been a center of Zionism, which had largely remained an elite phenomenon.[99] Its mass influence grew afterward due to a combination of reasons that made more Jews receptive to Zionist ideas and the option of Aliyah. Important factors included growing Muslim hostility toward Jews as a result of nationalist mobilization, the creation of Israel, rampant poverty, and the ongoing refusal of citizenship by the French as well as negative experiences with the anti-Semitic Vichy regime during the war.[100] Tension with the Muslim majority population started to grow in Morocco in 1947 against the backdrop of the war in Palestine. Following the June 1948 pogroms in Oudjda and Djérada in eastern Morocco on the border with Algeria, emigration of Jews from Morocco to Israel became a more widespread phenomenon.[101] When the French colonial rulers realized that the constant illegal flow of migrants could not be stopped, they allowed for the organized emigration of Jews, giving the Jewish Agency free rein in processing and selecting the migrants. For this purpose, the Jewish Agency–operated *Kadima* (forward) office was created in April of that year.[102] A similar office had operated in Tunis since the second half of 1948, when the French authorities had started tolerating, if initially not fully legalizing, Aliyah.[103]

As a significant body of recent scholarship has demonstrated, the selective Aliyah policy that these offices and additional Israeli emissaries implemented in North Africa was embedded in a cultural imagery among Israeli and Zionist elites that construed immigrants from the countries of the Muslim and Arab "Orient" (*mizrach*) as distinct from and inferior to the European Jews who, during the pre-state period, had made up the vast majority of the Zionist Yishuv.[104] This literature suggests that the elite fear of "Levantinization" caused by an uncontrolled influx of "backward," "primitive," "violent," "lazy," and "sick" Olim from Oriental countries was one of the key factors in selective Aliyah's focus on Oriental Jewry in general and within this heterogeneous group on North African—mainly Moroccan—Jewry in particular. Oriental Jewries were distinguished from the hitherto dominant European population of the Yishuv by labeling them as *edot ha-mizrach*, which roughly translates as "ethnic groups of the Orient." Although this designation as ethnic groups did not imply a questioning of their Jewishness—as would be the case with the Ethiopian "Falashas" in later years—it certainly gave expression to a sense of separateness and differentiation among the Jewish people. As Sami Shalom Chetrit points out, only Oriental Jewries were called ethnic groups (*edot*), and the adjective ethnic (*adati*) would only be used in reference to them, especially in a political context.[105] Hence, the term "ethnic problem" (*beayah adatit*) described the problems related to their immigration and absorption.[106]

The state leadership and the Jewish Agency feared for Israel's character as a European pioneering society if Oriental immigration was to continue unchecked. The expected demographic change that would result from mass immigration from Oriental countries was at the heart of this fear. Such preoccupations were enhanced by the fact that, following the destruction of most of European Jewry, North Africa had become the main reservoir for new immigrants.[107] As Yaron Tsur argues, this fear was partially material for the political decision makers. The Labor establishment was afraid that the new immigrants would strengthen the ranks of the Revisionist opposition.[108] Yet fear of Levantinization was not simply a matter of quantitative aspects of Mizrachi immigration; it was also associated with qualitative aspects of what Ashkenazi officials imagined to be a "Levantine" way of life. In closed forums, they quite openly discussed the anticipated negative consequences for Israeli state building. During the discussions regarding selection guidelines for 1953, Giora Josephthal, the head of the Klitah (Absorption) Department of the Jewish Agency, stated, for instance: "I say that this land is in danger, its ethical and social existence are in danger because of this Aliyah [from Oriental countries]. . . . They say that life in Israel will obtain a Levantine character, I am convinced that some of us are already afraid of the immigrants."[109]

A central concern with the Levantine way of life revolved around traditional family structures, which supposedly obstructed the Oriental immigrants' transformation into Israelis. Thus, Moshe Kol, the head of the Jewish Agency's Youth Aliyah Department, argued in favor of bringing in North African youngsters without their families within the framework of Youth Aliyah: "By the time the families come to Israel after two or three years the absorption work will be a lot easier. If we don't do this, all the families will come by themselves and the state will turn into an exile (*galut*). . . . If we first bring the young, we can take care of them. . . . If not, we are likely to drown in a sea of Levantinism (*levantiniyut*) and Israel will turn into a country of the Levant."[110] In Kol's view, the uncontrolled immigration of entire Oriental Jewish families thus threatened to destroy the dividing line between the old way of life in the *Galut* and the new Jewish way of being that was supposed to be Israel. But in contrast to more radical members of the Zionist leadership, Kol was in favor of eventually bringing in entire families. When he argued for family unity in a meeting of the Coordination Committee between the Jewish Agency and the government (*mosad la-teum*) in May 1954, he received a blunt response from Finance Minister Levi Eshkol: "I want to say very clearly and frankly: we are not interested in the parents if we can get the children here, and if it is possible to prevent the coming of the parents we should do that."[111]

To Yehuda Braginsky of the Klitah Department, Oriental family structures affected the immigrants' productivity:

> If we talk about people with whom you can do something—this can only be about those who come from the countries of the East (*mizrach*). Them I can throw into settlement and to all the other places. . . . As to the small communities [of southern Morocco and Tunisia], if there is good material

> in them, we'll take it, but to bring all the Jews together—there is no logic to that. . . . Those who come in a patriarchic way to Israel, the way they come in clans (*chamulot*), there is no hope for them. . . . Of today's Jewish people you need to bring the healthiest material.[112]

This last point provides the link between the negative image of the *Edot Ha-Mizrach* and the actual focus of selective Aliyah on North African countries. Oriental immigration was welcome in principle, but only on the condition that the immigrants would cease to be Oriental—captured by the notion of the clan (*chamulot*) as the symbol of a supposed Oriental lifestyle. And because of this negative image of the collective, the useful individual—"the good material"—needed to be selected carefully.

In the framework of Israeli nation building, cultural and material concerns thus reinforced each other, merging into a discourse that—in the words of legal scholar Sagit Mor—combined "ableism" with "orientalism."[113] It placed migrants in a hierarchy according to their ability, health, and class, but also according to origin. Ableism came first. In principle, the young state cherished productivity and abhorred those who could not contribute to the building effort: people who were sick, handicapped, or old and "social cases" (*mikrim sotzialiim*). Orientalism became apparent in the sense that this type of "inferior human material" was considered to be widespread among Jews from North Africa.[114] The result was a conception of the stereotypically sick, poor, and lazy Oriental immigrant who was of little value to the state-building enterprise and was to be kept out. This did not preclude the immigration of Oriental capitalists (*baalei hon*), which was to be facilitated.

The flip side of the coin was the positive imagination of Ashkenazi immigrants as diligent and productive members of the middle class holding great value to the state-building enterprise. The fusion of ability, class, and ethnicity thus worked either way. American immigrants in particular were exempted from selection policies. Immigrants from Poland received privileged treatment when they were competing with Moroccans for scarce absorption resources in 1956. The state and the Jewish Agency leadership also deliberated on various occasions about how to actively promote Western immigration and/or "middle-class immigration," especially after the liberal bourgeois General Zionists had participated in the government for the first time in December 1952, and in subsequent years.[115] This happened at a time when great effort was made to restrict the bulk of Moroccan immigration. A press conference that Dr. Nachum Goldman of the World Jewish Congress gave in May 1956 is emblematic in this regard: after announcing that selection would continue to be implemented in Morocco despite its independence and the possibility that emigration gates would close, he also declared the need to invest more money in and create special institutions for Aliyah work in the West in order to increase pioneer or middle-class immigration.[116]

SCREENING MIGRANTS, CONTESTING IMMIGRATION

While not becoming fully institutionalized until the adoption of selection guidelines in November 1951, post-1948 selective Aliyah began with the attempt to gain medical oversight over the new immigrants during the period of mass immigration from 1948 to 1951. Conceptually, it is possible to discern a shift of emphasis over this period from purely medical screening to explicitly social selection. This shift went hand in hand with a toughening of the selection practice, which was in turn linked to the increased influence of the "selectionists" in the government and the Jewish Agency Executive, and with institutional shifts in the immigration control apparatus. Ironically, the movement toward more pronouncedly social screening was initially related to the greater influence of the Health Ministry, which understood itself as the supreme gatekeeper of Israel.

The basic rationale behind medical selection was established through the "Medical Guidelines for the Approval of Aliyah," which the medical department of the Aliyah Ministry issued at the height of mass immigration in January 1949.[117] Though never consistently implemented, the guidelines' fundamental postulates were of considerable importance for the shaping of subsequent selection policies. The document's primary demand was that "every Oleh needs to be healthy in body and soul and fit for work."[118] For that reason, no immigrants with—extensively enumerated—contagious, acute, or chronic diseases or other impairments that would reduce their ability to work would be accepted. This rule was justified as follows: "This land cannot allow itself the entry of masses of chronically ill people or invalids, who are not able to take part in the task of building the land and will fill the hospitals and public institutions."[119] Although not denying the right of these people to immigrate in principle, the document stressed the necessity that their entry be in accordance with the "absorption capacity" of the country—a term taken straight out the British Mandate authorities' 1922 White Paper, which had stipulated that Jewish immigration must not "exceed whatever may be the economic capacity of the country at the time to absorb new arrivals."[120] Among the contagious diseases, tuberculosis was identified as "the central problem in the medical supervision of Aliyah."[121] It was this condition that kept Misa Giulia B., whose story is described in chapter 1, from entering Israel for three years. Yet eventually she was allowed to immigrate in 1951; significantly, the 1949 medical guidelines did not call for rejecting candidates on the grounds of health, but rather "postponing" or "delaying" their entry.[122] This system thus allowed for a cure to be found or health to be regained.

The Jewish Agency Executive and the Coordination Committee officially established selection as a comprehensive process of medical and explicitly social screening by passing selection guidelines in November 1951. As discussed in chapter 1, this process was supposed to ensure what historian Avi Picard has called "selective but unrestricted Aliyah"—that is, the immigration of large numbers of useful migrants. The following five selection principles illustrate the advanced stage of fusion between medical screening and social selection according to age, profession, and ability:

1. 80 percent of the immigrants from these countries [where selection is to apply] need to be selected from among Youth Aliyah candidates, pioneers, settlement nuclei, professionals (*baalei miktzoa*) up to the age of 35, or families where the breadwinner (*mefarnes*) is not older than 35.
2. The above mentioned candidates—with the exception of professionals or people with sufficient means for housing—must sign a written obligation to agricultural labor for two years.
3. The above mentioned candidates will only be approved after a fundamental medical examination under the supervision of a doctor from Israel.
4. Not more than 20 percent of the Olim from these countries can be above the age of 35 and from outside categories included in [section 1], if they are in the company of families whose breadwinner is young and able to work, or if they are requested by relatives in Israel who will receive them.
5. Immigrants who are requested by their relatives in Israel will only be approved by the Aliyah Department after an examination by the Klitah Department and on the basis of a notification about the willingness and ability of the relative to receive them.[123]

In principle, the document stated that selection should be carried out in any country where it was actually possible to select candidates. The countries explicitly listed were Morocco, Tunisia, Algeria, Turkey, Persia, India, and the countries of Central and Western Europe. The cases of rescue Aliyah that would be determined by the Coordination Committee were explicitly excluded.[124] The class component of selection was clearly present in the decision to also exempt "people with means" (*baalei emtzaim*), and implicit in the choice not to include the Americas in the list of regions where selection would be implemented in order not to deter the "handful of Jews who would be interested in making Aliyah from there," as Levi Eshkol put it.[125]

The dominance of Oriental countries on this list is not accidental. As Avi Picard points out, the new guidelines, which were approved by the Coordination Committee on November 27, 1951, only codified what had been ongoing practice in North Africa since 1949.[126] In addition to the negative stereotypes about North African immigration discussed above, there was a utilitarian rationale behind this decision. In the words of Yehuda Braginsky of the Klitah Department, "if today there are many old people coming from Romania, we need to search for their neutralization in a different place, by enhancing the Aliyah of young people."[127] And these young people were to be found in North Africa. "Old" Oriental Jews (i.e., people over age 35) thus had to pay the price for the fact that large numbers of old and infirm Jews from Romania—a country beyond the Iron Curtain where no active selection was feasible—were coming to Israel at the time.

The practical implementation of selection in North Africa experienced significant organizational changes after the introduction of the selection guidelines, which resulted in the Health Ministry being placed in charge of the process. Until then, doctors of the Aliyah Department's medical service had carried out examinations on the ground in the country of origin before departure. In accordance with the 1949 medical guidelines, their priority was the treatment rather than the blocking of potential immigrants. The Health Ministry doctors only saw the immigrants once they reached the transit camp in Marseilles.[128] Dr. Chaim Sheba, director general of the Health Ministry since April 1951 and today the namesake of Israel's largest hospital in Tel Hashomer, was dissatisfied with this arrangement. He suspected the Jewish Agency's Aliyah Department—and in particular its representatives in North Africa—of being too lax and allowing too many sick people in, which put an increasing strain on the health system.[129] Despite the fact that, as both Haim Malka and Avi Picard have pointed out, most hospitalized immigrants did not come from North Africa at that time, Sheba was successful in his lobbying with Ben-Gurion and others for the reassignment of responsibilities in the selection of North African immigrants.[130] The Health Ministry assumed responsibility for Aliyah preparations in North Africa in a June 1952 agreement with the Jewish Agency Aliyah Department.[131] Both the Aliyah Department and the "doctors of trust" (*rofei imun*) on the ground, some of whom had worked for the Aliyah Department before, were to follow its instructions. Families interested in emigrating had to first undergo an examination by the representatives of the Aliyah Department about their age structure and family composition. Subsequently, they were examined by a doctor of trust of the Health Ministry, who was authorized to approve or reject their Aliyah bid.[132] No Oleh was able to come to

Israel without obtaining official medical approval.[133] Like the West German insistence on embassy interviews with prospective Aussiedler from Yugoslavia since 1964, the external gate of North African immigration to Israel was literally externalized as far as possible, to the migrants' countries of origin. However, in the Israeli case, the main gatekeeper was no diplomatic mission but rather the Health Ministry.

With the Health Ministry in charge of the external gate, selection practice became significantly stricter. Health and social control took absolute precedence over any other concern. According to the approach taken by Sheba and his successor, Dr. Shimeon Batish, medical and social selection basically merged into one—a phenomenon known from other historical contexts of immigration control.[134] As Batish pointed out, the goal of medical selectivity was to prevent "the immigration of people who, from a *social* standpoint, are a burden on the community."[135] Eliezer Matan, who was sent to Morocco as *Rofe Imun* in October 1952, also "regarded medical oversight as a vehicle for social control."[136] In his own words, the Health Ministry performed "a global selection that did not ignore the immigrants' social background."[137]

Under Matan's aegis, the global selection approach in Morocco was taken to an extreme. His thinking, which was influenced by his previous experience as a medical official in charge of the notoriously overcrowded immigrant camps (*maabarot*) in Israel, epitomized an approach that favored the building of the state over the rescue of the diaspora. He rejected mass immigration from Morocco without adequate means of absorption, stating in December 1952 that "we must not bring Moroccan Jewry to Israel en masse, no matter what happens here [in Morocco]."[138] A few months later, he wrote to Sheba: "[Israel should] stop all Zionism and concern itself only with affairs of state. . . . The Jewish Agency should be finished with; immigration is the government's business. . . . Anyone who wants to engage in the luxury (and today it is a luxury) of ingathering the exiles for its own sake should be aware that there are extremely clear terms of selectivity. Not relative but absolute."[139] As quoted earlier, on another occasion Matan had summed up his position even more succinctly: "*The doors are basically closed* if we are to implement selective immigration as we understand it."[140] This signals a qualitative shift in the thinking of the "bouncer": instead of keeping the door open and closing it if someone did not match the expectations of the "club," now the door was closed and would only be opened if a candidate matched the—rather high—expectations of the club, which this bouncer thought was already full. This was the radical version of selective Aliyah, which went beyond its "moderate" Zionist version expressed in the restrictions included in the Law of Return.

Matan, like Kanein in West Germany 13 years later, thus took the logic of his institution to an extreme and questioned the very concept of preferential co-ethnic immigration to his country. As in the German case, this initiative triggered strong reactions from differently minded state agencies. Matan's radical stance caused conflicts between the Health Ministry and the Aliyah Department of the Jewish Agency, which was still interested in bringing in large numbers of immigrants.[141] The most vocal opposition came from the Aliyah Department's head, Yitzhak Rafael, who criticized the Health Ministry's hijacking of social selection tasks.[142] Sheba, by contrast, defended the merging of medical and social selection before the Coordination Committee. He praised the Health Ministry as "the strictest border guard" and stated categorically: "If there is a social case, we need to treat it like a health case."[143]

While this altercation represented a clash of state-building and diaspora ingathering logics, the most contentious issue between the institutions concerned the Health Ministry's obstruction of settlement objectives through its disqualification of young people for Youth Aliyah because of cases of sickness or disability in their families. This practice was based on the fear that "sick" families would send one young and healthy member to Israel via Youth Aliyah and later apply for family reunification, thus circumventing the selection guidelines.[144] This, of course, ran counter to the Jewish Agency's intention of bringing young Moroccans to Israel without their families to mold them into pioneers—a key concern of the settlement effort. The practice was harshly criticized and eventually abolished by the Coordination Committee in June 1953.[145]

The June 1953 guidelines for selective Aliyah, issued jointly by the Health Ministry and the Aliyah Department of the Jewish Agency to the *rofei imun* of the Health Ministry and to the local offices of the Aliyah Department, were an attempt to reduce the tension between the two institutions and take the edge off some of the Health Ministry's more extreme practices.[146] To accommodate the Health Ministry's radicalized stance on medical selection, the guidelines became considerably harsher than what had been decided in 1949. People suffering from contagious diseases, mental illnesses, or conditions that required continued treatment in an institution were strictly disqualified from immigration. The uncompromising statement read: "If the family is not willing to leave this person behind, it will not be able to make Aliyah."[147]

In contrast, on the issue of social selection these new guidelines were more lenient than past instructions and included some easements that Yitzhak Rafael had been struggling to obtain since the selection guidelines had come into being. They introduced the principle of "family selection" (*selektziah mishpachtit*), which essentially reversed the previous selection practice of the Health

Ministry. Henceforth, a family would no longer be disqualified because of a family member in need of support. Rafael had blamed low immigration numbers on this practice since North African families did not want to be separated and therefore chose not to migrate if one member was disqualified.[148] The permissible age of the family breadwinner was raised from 35 to 40, or even to 45 for people who could perform "hard physical labor" or had a profession that would allow them to support themselves in Israel. In February 1954, the respective age limits were raised to 45 and 50. Anyone older than 50 needed to be received by relatives in Israel or was required to possess US$7,000 worth of capital.[149]

IMMIGRANTS INTO PIONEERS: "FROM THE SHIP TO THE VILLAGE"

When the selection guidelines were introduced in late 1951, policy makers believed that they would be able to select among an unabated stream of immigrants. But in fact, the mass Aliyah of 1948–1951 was followed by a dramatic slump in immigration numbers during the following two years. In 1952, 23,375 immigrants came from all countries, and a mere 10,347 in 1953.[150] In Eastern Europe, this was evidently due to the closing of the emigration gates, but the reasons for the countries of North Africa, where emigration was free, had to be sought elsewhere. Selection was one factor; in both years, more than two-thirds of the candidates from Morocco were rejected. Yet, as Avi Picard has pointed out, even without selection, the number of applicants would not have been sufficient to fulfill the quotas of 17,500 and 25,000 migrants set for the respective years.[151] Contemporaries suspected that the policy of selectivity had deterred many potential candidates from applying in the first place, as did the spreading of knowledge that absorption conditions in Israel were anything but good.[152] Moreover, the economic and security situation in North Africa had improved to the point that fewer Jews were interested in making Aliyah. According to French Protectorate sources, 2,466 Jews who had gone to Israel even returned to Morocco between 1949 and 1953.[153] By 1954, the fear that immigration might stop altogether had reached the Aliyah Department of the Jewish Agency.[154]

Because the aim of the selection policy was to achieve the right kind of immigration rather than have no immigration at all, the state institutions and the Jewish Agency started developing schemes for a proactive policy that would enhance Aliyah again. But they did so strictly in accordance with the absorption capacities of the country and with its settlement needs. In addition to taking facilitating measures such as raising the breadwinner's age, these plans included tapping the remaining pool of potential immigrants from Tunisia and Morocco, especially from the remote and isolated villages of the south.[155] The initiative came from Shlomo Zalman Shragai, who had taken over as head of the Aliyah Department from Yitzhak Rafael in late 1953.[156] Under the label "from the ship to the village" (*me-ha-aniyah el ha-kfar*), the Coordination Committee designed a program that combined medical and social selection with monthly and yearly immigrant quotas and a program of direct resettlement in agriculture or development towns to process this anticipated new immigration.[157] The overriding imperative was that Aliyah should be in accordance with absorption capacities to avoid repetition of the traumatic scenario of immigrants crowding in the *Maabarot*, which by 1954 still held a population of 108,000—hence the direct resettlement.[158] Sending the new immigrants straight to remote towns and agricultural settlements (*moshavim*) also contributed to the policy of population dispersion, which strove to fortify Israel's claim to its new peripheries in the Negev desert and the Galilee region.[159] To match the absorption capacities of the country, yearly and monthly quotas were introduced: from August 1954 to September 1955, a total of 47,000 Olim were expected to come, including 40,000 from North Africa.[160] For 1955–1956, the quota was set at 45,000.[161] To resettle them directly, the immigrants needed to be capable of agricultural work, which partially accounts for the fascination with the southern villages.[162] This idea was not new, but this time it was pursued with greater vigor, and it added a new control mechanism at the external gate: "selection teams" (*chuliot miun*).

The selection teams, tasked with choosing suitable candidates for agricultural settlement, were created in July 1954, following a suggestion by Giora Josephthal.[163] The teams were to consist of representatives of the Aliyah, Klitah, and Settlement Departments of the Jewish Agency. The division of labor within the teams was as follows: the representative of the Aliyah Department made sure that candidates conformed with the general selection criteria to avoid the immigration of "social cases," and the Klitah and Settlement representatives were in charge of finding suitable candidates for settlement in agriculture and "development areas." Only those candidates fulfilling the selection team's criteria would reach the next level: medical examination.[164] As Shragai pointed out in a letter to Josephthal, the main task of the teams was to provide the prospective immigrants with basic knowledge about their possibilities of absorption in Israel. The ultimate decision about their immigration remained with the Aliyah Department and the government's doctor of trust.[165] In practice, contrary to Shragai's wishes and in agreement with Josephthal's ideas, the teams established themselves as independent final arbiters in selection questions.[166]

In addition to the selection teams in the countries of origin, there was an escort on each immigrant ship consisting of officials from the Aliyah, Klitah, and

Settlement Departments as well as the Health Ministry. The officials on the ships did the sorting of candidates and preparation for settlement, which until then had been done at the Shaar Ha-Aliyah transit camp or at the port of Haifa.[167] In line with the overall class-orientated selection policy, middle-class Olim did not have to pass the selection teams but went straight to the medical examination. Their journeys were organized by Rassco, the Rural and Suburban Settlement Company that specialized in middle-class immigration.[168] The Jewish Agency trained the prospective selection team members in Israel and sent the first contingent to Morocco and Tunisia toward the end of 1954.[169] They stayed until 1956.

Parallel to the efforts of the selection teams, the "liquidation" (*chisul*) of Jewish villages in the Atlas Mountains between 1954 and early 1956 was carried out on behalf of the Jewish Agency and the agricultural movements by the brothers Yitzhak and Yehuda Grinker.[170] In addition to concerns about the security of these remote and isolated villages, their inhabitants were seen as the "best and most suitable human elements for settlement" in agriculture, in mountainous regions and in the Negev region.[171] This made them most desirable for the "from the ship to the village" absorption approach. "Social cases" living in their midst, who did not pass selection, were to be resettled in larger urban communities in Morocco and taken care of by the American Joint Distribution Committee.[172] According to statistics from March 1956, by the end of January that year, 31 villages with 806 families (or 3,261 inhabitants) had been "liquidated" in Morocco. Another 36 villages with 1,066 families (or 5,928 inhabitants) had been registered and examined by the selection team.[173] The Grinker brothers reported about 28 villages (646 families/3,577 inhabitants) that had been liquidated and 36 villages (1,346 families/7,584 inhabitants) that had passed the selection team. On average, 20 percent of all candidates were rejected; in some villages, this percentage was as high as 50 percent. Some 30 villages with 300 to 350 families were still left in different regions at that point.[174] After the Grinker brothers' departure in early 1956, the regular selection team continued the *Chisul* and was strict about it; in Marrakesh, for example, up to 45 percent of all applicants were rejected in January and February 1956.[175]

The selection teams' general rejection rates were not quite as high. According to statistics compiled in June 1956 for Morocco, until May 1, 1956, the selection teams endorsed 45,100 people for immigration altogether, 20,000 of whom were from Casablanca.[176] Although these aggregate statistics do not mention the number of people who were rejected, other records provide further insight. Between January 1 and September 30, 1955, 6,628 of 7,447 examined families, or 89 percent, were endorsed, which amounted to 37,136 individuals.[177] In December of that year, 567 of 658 families, or 86.1 percent, were endorsed, which amounted to 3,220 individuals.[178] In January, the rate was 88.5 percent of all families, or 1,786 individuals.[179] Based on contemporary newspaper reports, Avi Picard estimates an average rejection rate of 20 percent of the candidates, while another 10 percent failed the subsequent medical exam.[180] With about one-third of candidates not passing selection, rejection rates during the reign of the selection teams were thus considerably below the numbers of the preceding years 1952 to 1953. Picard attributes this to the "better quality" of the candidates, since the selection guidelines had not changed in principle.[181] What these statistics do not reveal, however, is the—according to Picard, considerable—number of potential migrants who were deterred by the selection process itself and therefore did not even apply.

In addition, these statistics cannot capture how the people affected by the selection process, especially those who were rejected, perceived the selection team's activities. It was reported that Moroccan Jews greeted the "Poles who came to obstruct Aliyah" with suspicion—a reflection of the fact that all selectors were of European extraction.[182] According to a contemporary newspaper report, encounters were brief and superficial; the selectors would check 100 to 200 families in one day, choosing suitable ones according to their apparent physical strength.[183] In some instances, those rejected responded with despair and aggression. An article titled "Rescue or Selection?" published in early 1955 in the Jewish newspaper *Ha-Mevasser* (The Messenger) from Djerba in Tunisia vividly recounts one family's rejection:

> It happened to be on a rainy day that we learned about the arrival of four Israelis who came in a giant airplane from Marseilles to Tunis.... Four of them sitting around a table.... The instruction has been given not to give a final permit to any Oleh who has not come through here.... A family has completed all the formalities, has passed all the circles of hell and waits for the final moment in which they will receive the instruction to board a ship and leave the place. At that point the family is asked to pass the "selection team," [first] the head of the family, an accountant by profession, who does not know what is expected from him, and after him his wife and his 16-year-old son who finished middle school, and also their eight children.... After all the questions to the head of the family they ask his wife if she knows how to milk a cow and if she ever learnt how to plow etc. etc., and after all the registrations comes the verdict: According to the law in our hands, [each family needs] one breadwinner for five persons, not for eight. You cannot make Aliyah. The responses by the head of the family and his wife do not convince the team. Scandal in the office. Immediately the young servant is called who ejects the troublemakers by force.[184]

Shmuel Marcuse of the Jewish Agency Office in Tunis even reported violent attacks by rejected candidates who would visit his office and break furniture and windows.[185] Other aspiring migrants used more creative strategies, forging marriage certificates and inventing breadwinners to circumvent the selection guidelines.[186] In the spring of 1955, 90 villagers from southern Morocco who had been disqualified for Aliyah and were to be resettled under miserable conditions in Marrakesh, turned to the local pasha to mediate between them and the Zionists. The pasha likened the right of Jews to make Aliyah with the right of Muslims to go on a pilgrimage to Mecca and hence determined that these people should be taken to Israel.[187] Whether the Jewish Agency abided by the pasha's ruling is not known, but it seems doubtful.

The selection practice of the teams remained a bone of contention between proponents and opponents of selectivity. Marcuse in Tunis and Baruch Duvdevany of the Aliyah Department in Paris complained about what they perceived to be excessively strict selection, which complicated the bureaucratic process, slowed down the migration process, and caused despair among the potential Olim.[188] The representatives of the selection teams, in turn, believed that the Jewish Agency emissaries (*shlichim*) and Aliyah Department members were too lax in their approach to selective Aliyah and actively bypassed the guidelines. Chaim Tolczynski, the head of the Moroccan team, complained to his boss, Avraham Ziegel of the Klitah Department in March 1955: "The 'infiltration' (*histanenut*) will continue since the Aliyah Department people cannot do otherwise, and sometimes it is a matter of prestige of the State of Israel to them. . . . Mr. Duvdevany excels in particular, since he does this [bypasses the selection guidelines] with great intelligence and, I need to note, also with full faith that every Jew needs to be brought to Israel on account of being Jewish."[189] This quote is striking for its wording and content. The use of the term *histanenut* usually described the "infiltration" of Palestinian refugees into Israel. Here, the term moves unselected immigration from Morocco into the rhetorical vicinity of what was perceived as one of the major security threats of the day; in fact, a special anti-infiltration law had been introduced just a few months before, in August 1954. While this may be seen as rhetorical hyperbole, Tolczynski's latter statement underscores how little the Declaration of Independence and the Law of Return meant to some practitioners of selective Aliyah, who worked according to a very different logic than that of "ingathering the exiles." Duvdevany's faith in these declarations, which captured the essence of Israel's diasporic ingathering, seemed bewildering to the guardians of its pioneering settlement project.

Despite their competing agendas, the rival institutions eventually found a modus vivendi and cooperated successfully in the selection of suitable immigrants and their direct resettlement in agriculture.[190] The joint effort of the gatekeepers allowed them to successfully follow their quotas and resettle two-thirds of the new immigrants in agricultural settlements in the central and northern Negev, around Kiryat Gat (located between Ashkelon on the coast and the Judean Mountains in the east), and in the southern Jezreel Valley in the Galilee region. The remainder ended up in so-called development towns (*ayarot pituach*).[191] And yet, as the historian Yishai Arnon points out, this success came at a price: when Morocco and Tunisia became independent in 1956, tens of thousands of Jews who had registered for Aliyah were still in these countries.[192]

A MATTER OF PRIORITY: SELECTION AND THE CLOSING OF THE MOROCCAN EMIGRATION GATES

By the second half of 1955, Israeli officials on the ground in Morocco realized that political change was imminent. Baruch Duvdevany warned Shragai in September 1955 that, in view of the formation of a Moroccan government, Aliyah quotas needed to be increased. "The feeling is that we missed the boat in evacuating Jews from Morocco and the continuation of Aliyah from here is a question of limited time."[193] Independence talks between the Moroccan Istiklal party and the French colonial rulers had been going on since the summer, resulting in calls for an enlarged quota and the implementation of rescue Aliyah during the Zionist leadership discussions of the 1955–1956 quota.[194] In the end, these bodies decided that the danger to free emigration was not immediate and that no policy change was necessary.[195] Even so, the calls for more and faster Aliyah in view of the exacerbated situation did not die down.[196]

Inverting the logic that normalization of migration conditions led to a more restrictive immigration practice, the manifest deterioration of conditions should have had the opposite effect—that is, a more lenient, less selective immigration practice. But this was not the case for Moroccan Aliyah, at least not immediately. The Jewish Agency and diplomatic officials in Paris (Duvdevany, Ambassador Yaakov Tsur) were in close contact with the officials in Morocco and were in favor of increased and accelerated Aliyah. But Shragai in Jerusalem had other plans. As he told Duvdevany in January 1956, less than two months from Moroccan independence, the number of Moroccan Jews (25,000) that had come to Israel by December 1955 had, in fact, necessitated the reduction of monthly quotas as of April to stay within the yearly quota of 45,000 that had been set for the period October 1955 to September 1956.[197] Duvdevany saw this as harmful for Moroccan Aliyah.[198] Tsur, too, felt that immigration restrictions from the Israeli side would lend support to those among the Moroccan Jewish elite who were ready to sacrifice Aliyah to strengthen their own position.[199] But Shragai was not impressed. As he told Moroccan Zionist leader Paul Calamaro in early February 1956, the scheduled 45,000 immigrants were hard enough for Israel to handle; an increase of the quota was out of the question, despite the seriousness of the situation in Morocco.[200] When writing these lines, he was probably under the influence of reports such as those of Alexander Easterman of the World Jewish Congress, who—in line with his organization's general assessment of the situation—told Shragai that Moroccan interference with the organization of Aliyah was unlikely.[201]

The selection practice on the ground also remained unaffected by political developments.[202] A report from Chaim Tolczynski of the selection team for the months of January and February 1956 reveals that the team's work continued as usual, with rejection rates reaching the already mentioned 45 percent around Marrakesh.[203] Few immigrants were to be expected from Spanish Morocco, he wrote, since most of them were sick and hence not eligible under the current selection criteria. During March and April, selection was meant to continue—mainly in small towns and villages but also in larger cities. Tolczynski drew up his report on March 5, three days after Morocco had achieved independence from France. He cautioned that the new situation required increased attention and that a revision of current practices might be necessary. But as the reactions over the next few months indicated, this did not imply an immediate abrogation of selection. Responding to public pressure, in May 1956, the Aliyah quota for the following three to four months was increased from 15,000 to 30,000. Yet selection was to be continued even though it had become all but impossible by then, because doctors were increasingly refusing to participate in the medical examinations for fear of possible repercussions.[204] On May 21, 1956, Shragai still informed the Aliyah Council in Tangiers that the community of Alcazarquivir in Spanish Morocco would only be brought to Israel after undergoing selection; "social cases" would have to be taken care of in cooperation with the American Joint Distribution Committee.[205]

By that point, the principle of selectivity had become entrenched to such an extent that not even the closing of the Jewish Agency Kadima Office and the prohibition of all organized Aliyah activity on June 11, 1956, put an immediate end to selection.[206] Considerations to implement selection continued even during the liquidation of the remaining Aliyah camp in Casablanca, which supposedly contained up to 1,200 "social cases."[207] Chaim Tolczynski was one of the proponents of this idea; his selection team colleague Ovadiah Bijou even stated categorically that "the camp and the material in it are not worth the effort being made for them."[208] It was not until the end of August that the easement of selection was officially endorsed at all levels, including the Klitah Department.[209] By then, the Jewish Agency and the Israeli authorities gave full priority to the liquidation of the Jewish Agency camp in Casablanca, the transportation of Jews from Morocco to the transit camp in Marseilles, and the desperate attempts at keeping the camp from overcrowding.

The slow response of the Israeli state and its institutions to the worsening conditions in independent Morocco and the closing emigration gates contrasts with the same institutions' reaction toward the opening of Poland's emigration gates a few months later, in October 1956.[210] The handling of "Gomulka's Aliyah" reinforces the impression that immigration from Morocco did not enjoy a high priority for the Israeli state. Although there can be little doubt that previous concerns about the lack of absorption capacities for Moroccan immigrants in Israel were genuine, this concern was more easily overcome for Polish Olim. The consensus in an extensive meeting of the Coordination Committee in December was that this Aliyah had to be brought in at all costs, given that it was unclear how long this window of opportunity would be open. Shragai underscored the necessity of prioritizing Polish Aliyah by referring to the example of the 120,000 Moroccan Jews who had not been brought to Israel and were now "lost."[211] For the Moroccan Jews who had made it out of the country and were at that time waiting in the Marseilles transit camp, the Polish priority meant that they had to continue waiting.[212]

The immigrants coming from Poland also received preferential housing treatment: new accommodation was to be built which had to be acceptable to people who had lived in "European" flats with at least two rooms, bathroom and shower. In the words of Yehuda Braginsky: "We cannot put the Poles just anywhere with a thousand Moroccans. . . . We cannot put the Poles into huts. We fear that they will start writing letters to the country of origin and complain about the conditions. We need to give them more or less acceptable accommodation. . . . I cannot put a Pole into a tent. . . . I cannot send a Pole to *Shaar Ha-Aliyah*."[213]

Israel Barzilai, the former ambassador in Warsaw, urged for stricter medical controls, but this time not with the aim to keep sick people out but to make sure that they would receive adequate treatment. Toward the end of the meeting, Zalman Shazar summed up the overall approach that prioritized Polish Aliyah and pushed Moroccan Aliyah to the margins: "We need this Aliyah . . . to introduce elements other than the ones we have thus far. The matter is desirable for the country also from a demographic viewpoint."[214] Given that Shragai had reported in the beginning of the meeting that 85,000 of the 112,000 new immigrants in the past 27 months had been from North Africa, the reference was clear. The supposedly excellent age and professional structure of the Polish immigration was seen as an additional asset. Once again, ethnic and class considerations were combined and prioritized one group of immigrants over another.

CONDITIONALLY OPEN GATES

Most accounts of selective Aliyah end in 1956. Yet this policy did not cease with the Moroccan emigration gates closing. On the contrary, the principle became even more deeply entrenched as its scope widened and developed into the 1960s. As the revised guidelines stipulated in 1958, and again in 1963, selection was still supposed to be the rule, both in countries with free and restricted exit.[215] When selection was not implemented—for instance, in cases of rescue Aliyah from countries such as Libya, Lebanon, Syria, Iraq, Yemen, Afghanistan, Egypt, and Romania—this was justified not with humanitarian considerations but "in light of the impossibility to carry out organized activities there."[216] The revisions were carried out on behalf of the Coordination Committee in 1958 and starting from late 1962 by the Health, Labor (in 1958) and Aid (1962) Ministries as well as the Aliyah and Klitah Departments of the Jewish Agency. Based on considerations of the needs of the state, absorption capacities, experience with the social and health makeup of ongoing immigration, and the specific circumstances in each country of origin, both revisions reaffirmed the aims of selective Aliyah policy: to obtain more able-bodied immigrants; to prevent the immigration of individuals or families that might endanger public peace from a social or health point of view; and to limit the number of people who might become welfare dependent once in Israel. The guiding principles to achieve these aims involved adjusting the guidelines according to the conditions in each country, implementing "family selection" (*miun mishpachti*), and selecting individuals according to their economic and social adaptability in Israel. The guidelines provided detailed instructions about where and how medical and social selection was to be implemented.

A deeper analysis of the revisions reveals three important points. First, in what appears to be the logical extension of the differential treatment of Polish and Moroccan immigrations in 1956, Eastern Europe received ever greater priority in the hierarchy of migrant countries of origin that were not considered rescue Aliyah—again notably when compared to Morocco. In the 1963 guidelines, section 3c regarding Eastern Europe stated explicitly that "these guidelines were established from the desire that the social situation of the candidate does not worsen due to his Aliyah."[217] Sick, old, and handicapped people could all be brought to Israel, provided that they had been assured a hospital or care place. For Hungary and Czechoslovakia, it was added: "Family reunification needs to be enabled without restrictions."[218]

For Morocco, on the other hand, section 3d stated that in principle the guidelines did not apply there; yet several caveats were added in which the authors of the guidelines displayed much less sympathy for the weaker members of Moroccan Jewish society. No divided families were to be brought to Israel that did not comprise the healthy members of the family; no sick, handicapped, or old people were to be allowed to migrate together with anyone other than their own families; and the immigration of a working-age individual would be dependent on the candidate having a "reasonable work-capacity." Other restrictions applied to the sick, the blind, the handicapped, and the old.

These restrictions were anything but theoretical: thanks to "Operation Yakhin"—a half-clandestine Aliyah enterprise organized jointly by the Mossad, the Jewish Agency, the Hebrew Immigrant Aid Society, and King Hasan II—Morocco had once again become the main supplier of Olim starting in 1961, with immigration numbers reaching 11,517 in 1961, 36,821 in 1962, and as many as 37,078 in 1963. In each year, this amounted to more than half of the total number of new arrivals to Israel.[219] Historian Michael Laskier reports that selective Aliyah was implemented during this operation, which lasted from 1961 to 1966, although his sources did not allow him to assess whether this was true consistently over the whole period.[220] What is certain is that on August 8, 1963, the same subcommittee responsible for drafting the new guidelines decided on an immigration freeze from southern Morocco for September, October, and November. In addition, it was decided to not facilitate Aliyah from Marrakesh, Rabat, and Casablanca and to halt the immigration of blind people, mentally handicapped children (*yeladim mefagrim*), widows, and paupers with children up to the age of ten.[221]

Second, the principle of social selection was universalized, elaborated, and deepened in conjunction with a continued and growing emphasis on promoting middle-class Aliyah from the West. Appendix D to the 1958 guidelines elaborated on the definition of social selection. In "Western countries," the Jewish Agency's controls were to focus on "Aliyah candidates whose personality and past raise doubts if their mental strength will allow them to adapt to life in Israel." A definition of murky terms such as "personality" and "mental strength" was lacking, however. Yehuda Braginsky, by then the lone opponent of selective Aliyah, had suggested removing some of the more arbitrary social selection provisions, but he was outvoted in the drafting committee.[222] In countries experiencing "economic distress" (*metzukah kalkalit*), the concern was about "other motivations for Aliyah," which suggests an aim to keep out refugees from poverty. This was the logical extension of the persistent and growing concern with promoting middle-class immigration from the West, which was also on the agenda of the same Coordination Committee meeting in October 1958 that endorsed the revised guidelines and which the Jewish Agency tried to attract with the help of a new program.[223]

Third, when immigrants tried to circumvent selection by trying to immigrate on their own account, they ran the risk of being turned back, which put the very notion of open Aliyah gates into question. Section 4 of the 1963 guidelines was most explicit in this regard:

> The committee sees the need to stop the trend towards bypassing the selection guidelines by coming to Israel without an Oleh visa and thus confronting the authorities with a fait accompli. Logic dictates that the guidelines applying to Aliyah candidates in their countries of origin shall apply also to those who come to Israel without an Oleh visa (but just with a visitor's visa, a permanent residence visa or no visa at all). . . . *The Interior Ministry will order a stricter supervision at the borders of the country to prevent the entry of mentally ill, those suffering from retardedness and those suffering from contagious diseases if they come to Israel's borders without an Oleh visa.*[224]

According to this suggestion, it could very well happen that a Jew who was found to suffer from any of the mentioned conditions would arrive at the gates of Israel and find them closed. To avoid such a situation, the committee stressed the importance of medical examinations of the migrants before they came to Israel, either in their countries of origin or in the transit stations (section 6). But it was clear that loopholes were not to be tolerated and that even someone who made it to Israel's gate by his or her own devices might be turned away.

At this point, the guidelines rendered obsolete the alleged difference mentioned in chapter 1 between unrestricted "making Aliyah" (*laalot*) and legitimately restricted "being brought to Israel" (*lehaalot*). It was the ultimate denial of the principle of open Aliyah gates that the Law of Return so forcefully put forward. Given that the committee's report containing these provisions was endorsed by the Coordination Committee in August 1963, the Israeli state's intention to keep Jews from entering the country is certain.[225] However, there is no clear evidence whether any Jew was actually ever rejected at the border. It might have already been the case in 1961, when the Jewish Agency rejected the Aliyah bid of Giacobbe Romano from Rome and his sister Sara because of their "advanced age" (58 and 45, respectively) and Sara's purported mental illness. Due to a lack of communication between the Jewish Agency and the Israeli embassy in Rome, the embassy nonetheless issued the siblings tourist visas for Israel. Once the embassy found out that they had previously been disqualified for immigration, it alerted the Consular Department of the Foreign Office and asked to warn the authorities in Israel about the Romanos possibly trying to change their tourist visas into an Oleh visa.[226] It is therefore possible that Giacobbe and Sara were rejected as Olim after their arrival in Israel, but there is no documentary proof.

What did the ideal co-ethnic immigrant look like when West Germany and Israel were free to choose? As portrayed in this chapter's case studies, the ideal profiles differed radically as they reflected the preferences of the respective migration regime institutions and, to some degree, the self-image of the two nations at large. In line with the West German postwar narrative of victimhood, a German Aussiedler from Yugoslavia was an endogamous German-speaking victim of communism—a profile that would reappear with striking similarity to define a Soviet German Aussiedler in the early 1990s. He or she was not just someone of German descent but someone who, in addition and most crucially, spoke German. In the (undesirable but frequent) case that a spouse was not German, families were expected to use German as the dominant language. The overriding importance of language was only canceled out by political criteria—namely pro-partisan engagement during the Second World War, which could jeopardize the immigration of otherwise undoubtedly ethnic Germans. In contrast, having been a member of the Nazi-controlled Kulturbund or having been interned and suffered at the hands of Yugoslav communists undoubtedly worked in an applicant's favor. Here the narrative of victimhood and an apologetic view of National Socialism complemented each other perfectly. At the same time, for the migration regime, an ethnic German was virtually a noncorporeal being, with no specific age, no particular health requirements, and no predetermined social features. Advanced age could actually be an advantage, because it often implied better language skills. Social criteria only mattered when the refugee state institutions, operating according to a welfare state logic, tried to prevent excessive spending on benefit seekers and hence took into consideration whether immigrants had sufficient accommodation on arrival in Germany—preferably provided by their relatives or at least paid for by the federal government.

The image of the ideal Oleh to Israel was shaped by the classic Zionist vision of settling and building the country through hard physical labor and by the aspiration to be a Western or European country in oriental surroundings. In contrast to the bodiless Aussiedler, the Oleh was very much a physical being—a "muscle Jew" and "pioneer" (*halutz*), as it were.[227] The selection guidelines insisted that he or she should be healthy, young, and able to work. While the age criterion was softened over time by raising the age limit for a family's breadwinner from 35 to 40 and then 45, these easements always remained conditional on the capacity for physical labor. Yet the ideal immigrant could be more than a toiler: in the interest of the maturing state-building project, class could be as important as health and fitness. An ideal Oleh could thus alternatively also be economically well-to-do, a person "with means" (*baal emtzaim*) or "with capital" (*baal hon*), or an educated member of the middle class. These qualities were supposedly found predominantly among Ashkenazi Jews in the West and the East, as demonstrated in the repeated deliberations about how to attract immigrants from the West and from the preference given to Polish over Moroccan immigrants in 1956. The Moroccans, by contrast, were imagined, by and large, as being poor, sick, and uncultured. Their uncontrolled influx raised the specter of Israel turning into a country of the "Levant." Yet they were welcome as immigrants if they shed their "oriental" and "Levantine" characteristics once settled in Israel. This intra-Jewish "ethnic criterion" was not part of the official guidelines but figured prominently in the internal discussions of the decision makers. In designing their nation, the Israeli and Zionist leaderships thus combined criteria of fitness, ethnicity, and class with the goal of building the state both at the periphery—its northern and southern frontiers in the Galilee and the Negev regions—and in the cities.

NOTES

1. Dr. Kanein, Bayerisches Staatsministerium des Innern (BSMI) an Dr. Reuscher, BVA, March 29, 1965, BArch, B 106/39948.

2. BSMI an BVA, nachrichtl. an das BMI und die Innenminister der Länder, September 13, 1965, HStAS EA 12/201, Az. 2250, No. 309.

3. Little research has been done on this first massive wave of Aussiedlung from Poland. For the Polish side of the story, see Stola, *Kraj bez wyjścia*, chap. 5. See also Arbeits- und Sozialminister des Landes Nordrhein-Westfalen (ed.), *Das Dritte Problem*.

4. About the guest worker regime, see Oltmer, Kreienbrink, and Sanz Díaz, *Das "Gastarbeiter"-System*.

5. Jewish Agency Executive (JAE) Minutes, November 4, 1951, quoted in Picard, "Beginning of Selective Immigration," 376.

6. About the concept of "medical border," see Davidovitch and Zalashik, "Medical Borders."

7. Zolberg, *Nation by Design*, 1.

8. For the notions of ableism and orientalism as features of Israeli immigration policy, see Mor, "Ableism and Orientalism."

9. Fairchild, "Rise and Fall of the Medical Gaze," 346.

10. Quoted in Picard, "Immigration, Health, and Social Control," 45.

11. Franz Xaver Engelbert, "Pankow 'entdeckt' die Volksdeutschen: 'Abwerbung' volksdeutscher Ärzte, Ingenieure und Künstler—Rosen für eine Primaballerina—Jugoslawien dementiert Menschenhandelsabkommen mit Pankow," *Der Donauschwabe*, no. 47, November 22, 1959, 1.

12. See "(Spät-)Aussiedler und ihre Angehörigen. Zeitreihe 1950–2017," https://www.bva.bund.de/SharedDocs/Downloads/DE/Buerger/Migration-Integration/Spaetaussiedler/Statistik/Zeitreihe_1950_2017.pdf?_blob=publicationFile&v=5. Gerhard Reichling argues that the number for the 1950s did not exceed 40,000. He explains the difference with the fact that the official statistics incorrectly also counted former German prisoners of war who had stayed in Yugoslavia after the war and returned to Germany during the 1950s. See Reichling, *Deutsche Vertriebene*, 41–43.

13. The argument for the noncontroversial nature of Aussiedler migration during the Cold War was most recently made by Brubaker and Kim, "Transborder Membership Politics," 51.

14. For 1960, see BVA an BMI, June 6, 1961; for 1963 and 1964, see BVA an BMI, January 8, 1965, both in BArch, B 106/39940.

15. All numbers are from Wehler, *Nationalitätenpolitik in Jugoslawien*, 107.

16. Bethke, "'Erweckung' und Distanz." That engagement in the Kulturbund did not necessarily imply a good knowledge of written German can be seen from the rather "Croatian" orthography used in the reports of local activists in Croatia quoted in Bethke, "'Erweckung' und Distanz," 194, 196.

17. Wehler, *Nationalitätenpolitik in Jugoslawien*, 85. The expellees included ethnic Germans from the Gottschee region and Bosnia, who had already been displaced by the Nazi occupiers during the war.

18. Bethke, "Von der 'Umsiedlung' zur 'Aussiedlung'," 35–37.

19. In addition to Wehler's classic study, see the more recent works on the topic by Portmann, *Kommunistische Revolution*, and Janjetovic, *Between Hitler and Tito*.

20. Wehler, *Nationalitätenpolitik in Jugoslawien*, 92.

21. Ibid., 93.

22. Ibid., 93–94, and Portmann, *Kommunistische Revolution*, 266–267.

23. Goeke, "Yugoslav Labor Migrants."

24. Wehler, *Nationalitätenpolitik in Jugoslawien*, 93, and RP Südbaden an die Kreisverwaltungen, Kreisämter für Umsiedlung, January 9, 1954, HStAS EA

12/201, Az. 2250, No. 32. Yugoslavia's demanding proof of prospective Aussiedler being admitted by their country of destination harks back to older paternalistic traditions of emigration countries seeking to limit departures while protecting their citizens. See Torpey, *Invention of the Passport*, 66.

25. See, for example, the procedure documented in HStAS EA 12/201, Az. 2257, No. 36.

26. Schutzmachtvertretung (SMV) Belgrad an AA, November 3, 1964, PAAA B 85 938.

27. BVA an IM Baden-Württemberg, August 15, 1964, HStAS EA 12/201, Az. 2250, No. 286(307).

28. This suspicion had been uttered by the Federal Interior Ministry already in 1960. See BMI an AA, April 29, 1960, BArch, B 106/39948.

29. See SMV Belgrad an AA, February 25, 1963, PAAA B 85 938. The items investigated during the interview were the same that the form filled out by the relatives in the Germany-based procedure was supposed to reveal. See BMVt an MVFK BW, July 23, 1954, HStAS EA 12/201, Az. 2257, No. 22.

30. About health examinations in the Friedland transit camp once in Germany, see Schießl, *Tor zur Freiheit*.

31. "Pforte zu einem neuen, besseren Leben: Interessante Zahlen aus dem Grenzdurchgangslager Piding Obb." *Der Donauschwabe*, no. 16, April 17, 1960, 13.

32. HStAS EA12/201, Az. 2257, No. 81.

33. HStAS EA12/201, Az. 2257, Nos. 108, 111, and 114.

34. Bundesstelle für Verwaltungsangelegenheiten des Bundesministers des Innern (BSVA) an AA, February 23, 1959, quoted in BMVt an MVFK BW, March 23, 1959, HStAS EA12/201, Az. 2257, No. 116.

35. Nathans, *Politics of Citizenship*, 209–212, 238–239.

36. BMI an BSVA, July 11, 1959, PAAA B 85 938.

37. BVA an AA, February 13, 1964, and BVA an IM BW, September 20, 1965, both in HStAS EA12/201, Az. 2257, No. 299.

38. HStAS EA12/201, Az. 2257, No. 294.

39. HStAS EA12/201, Az. 2257, No. 306.

40. HStAS EA12/201, Az. 2257, No. 286.

41. BVA an AA, May 3, 1962, HStAS EA12/201, Az. 2257, No. 228.

42. HStAS EA12/201, Az. 2257, No. 256.

43. HStAS EA12/201, Az. 2257, No. 316.

44. Such cases from the 1960s are documented in HStAS EA12/201, Az. 2257, Nos. 175, 214, 296, 306, and 310.

45. Cases from 1963–1964 in which a local office (the district council of Tettnang) denied the special permits are documented in HStAS EA12/201, Az. 2257, Nos. 266 and 283.

46. BVA an AA, March 5, 1964, HStAS EA12/201, Az. 2257, No. 285 (includes the protocol sheet of their interview at the interests section in Belgrade on January 23, 1964).

47. BVA an IM BW, September 28, 1961, HStAS EA12/201, Az. 2257, No. 220.

48. HStAS EA12/201, Az. 2257, No. 85.

49. HStAS EA12/201, Az. 2257, No. 201.

50. IM BW, Abteilung Vertriebene, Flüchtlinge und Kriegsgeschädigte, an Abteilung I, September 12, 1963, HStAS EA 12/201, Az. 2266, No. 145.

51. HStAS EA 12/201, Az. 2257, No. 135.

52. HStAS EA 12/201, Az. 2257, No. 307.

53. About the recruitment of foreign workers starting from the German-Italian 1955 recruitment agreement, see Herbert, *History of Foreign Labor.*

54. BSVA an BMI, November 30, 1959, PAAA B 85 938.

55. Generalkonsulat (GK) der Bundesrepublik Deutschland in Zagreb an AA, March 16, 1961, PAAA B 85 938 (emphasis added).

56. The lists of German immigrants from Yugoslavia published in *Der Donauschwabe* show that in October 1963, on several occasions in 1966, and as late as 1968, people from Blagorodovac entered the FRG through the Piding transit camp. Therefore, it is possible that this ban was not actually enforced.

57. For the case of Johann A., see BMI an AA, March 25, 1960, PAAA B 85 938.

58. Kühnrich and Hitze, *Deutsche bei Titos Partisanen 1941–1945.*

59. See Ministerialrat Dr. Wottge an BVA, May 23, 1973, HStAS EA 12/201, Az. 2250, No. 373, as well as the case reported by RP Südenwürttemberg-Hohenzollern an IM BW, February 1, 1973, HStAS EA 12/201, Az. 2552, No. 28.

60. BVA an IM BW, December 21, 1961, HStAS EA 12/201, Az. 2257, No. 223.

61. IM BW an RP Nordwürttemberg, September 3, 1968, HStAS EA 12/201, Az. 2257, No. 223.

62. BMI an BVA, July 19, 1968, BArch B 106/28627.

63. For Poland, see Stola, *Kraj bez wyjścia,* 204, 250.

64. BMI an BSVA, July 11, 1959, PAAA B 85 938.

65. "So was gibt es auch! Vorsicht bei Ausstellung von Volkszugehörigkeitsbestätigungen," *Der Donauschwabe,* no. 23, June 7, 1959, 2. "Missbrauchte Sozialgesetzgebung: Aussiedler ohne Ende aus Jugoslawien," *Der Donauschwabe,* no. 9, March 3, 1963, 1–2; "Volksdeutscher aus Bayern ausgewiesen: Rat der Südostdeutschen protestiert gegen diese Ungeheuerlichkeit," *Der Donauschwabe,* no. 15/16, Ostern 1963, 5; "Kein Aufenthaltsrecht für einreisende Volksdeutsche: Unbefriedigende Stellungnahme des bayerischen Innenministeriums," *Der Donauschwabe,* no. 35, September 1, 1963, 1, 4.

66. Landsmannschaft der Deutschen aus Jugoslawien (Florian Krämer) an BMI, February 18, 1969, BArch, B 106/39940 (emphasis added).

67. Ibid.

68. BMI an Krämer (May 7, 1969), BArch, B 106/39940.

69. Ibid.

70. Those are documented in BArch, B 106/39940.

71. GK Zagreb an AA, March 16, 1961, PAAA B 85 938.

72. "Missbrauchte Sozialgesetzgebung."

73. All quotes are from SMV Belgrad an AA, July 10, 1963, BArch, B 106/39940.

74. Brubaker, "Migrations of Ethnic Unmixing," 1053.

75. See SMV Belgrad an AA, January 21, 1965, BArch, B 106/39940.

76. For the BVA's defense, see BVA an BMI, January 8, 1965, BArch, B 106/39940.

77. Vermerk Ressortbesprechung, March 19, 1965, PAAA B 85 938.

78. The BVA had already rejected the charge of "frivolous generosity" in January, arguing that it rejected more than one-third of the applications from Yugoslavia. BVA an BMI, January 8, 1965, BArch B 106/39940.

79. AA an SMV Belgrad und GK Zagreb, August 3, 1966, PAAA B 85 938.

80. Kaja Shonick mentions 150–200 visa applications per day in the consulate general in Zagreb in 1962. In 1963, 2,000 Yugoslav citizens arrived in Germany each month. From 1961 to 1968, the overall number of Yugoslav guest workers reached 100,000. See Shonick, "Politics, Culture, and Economics," 727.

81. Botschaft der Bundesrepublik Deutschland, Belgrad an AA, May 17, 1969, PAAA B 85 812.

82. Kanein was the founder of West Germany's most important textbook on aliens' law, *Ausländerrecht*, published by Beck in Munich. For his stance in *Gastarbeiter* affairs in the early 1960s, see, for instance, Mattes, *"Gastarbeiterinnen"*, 150.

83. Dr. Kanein, BSMI an Dr. Reuscher, BVA, March 29, 1965, BArch, B 106/39948.

84. See BVA an BMI, October 6, 1964, and June 3, 1965, both in BArch, B 106/39948.

85. BVA an BMI, June 3, 1965, BArch, B 106/39948; see also the articles in *Der Donauschwabe*, no. 15/16, Ostern 1963, 5, and no. 35, September 1, 1963, 1, 4.

86. BSMI an die Regierungen, sowie in Abschrift an das BMI, das BVA und die Innenminister der Länder, November 10, 1965, HStAS EA 12/201, Az. 2250, No. 311.

87. Ibid.

88. The BMI backed the restrictions against ethnic Germans traveling via third countries but was more reserved regarding the overall guidelines. See BMI an AA, May 26, 1966, BArch, B 106/39938. See also BMI an BSMI, December 28, 1965, HStAS EA 12/201, Az. 2250, No. 311. The Interior Ministry of Schleswig-Holstein gave a positive response and suggested that the Länder interior ministries discuss the Bavarian proposal. See IM Schleswig Holstein an BMI und die Innenminister der Länder, April 4, 1966, HStAS EA 12/201, Az. 2250, No. 311.

89. BMI an AA, May 26, 1966, BArch, B 106/39938.

90. About Schütz and his expelle activism, see Ackermann-Gemeinde, *Hans Schütz.*

91. Bayerisches Staatsministerium für Arbeit und Soziale Fürsorge (BSASF) an BSMI, December 22, 1965, HStAS EA 12/201, Az. 2250, No. 311.

92. BSMI an BMI und die Innenminister der Länder, April 14, 1966, HStAS EA 12/201, Az. 2250, No. 310.

93. Ibid.

94. Brubaker and Kim, "Transborder Membership Politics," 40.

95. Quoted in Schechtman, *On Wings of Eagles*, 289–290.

96. Recent Hebrew-language monographs dealing with Aliyah from this region in general and selectivity in particular include Picard, *Cut to Measure*; Laskier, *Israel and Jewish Immigration*; and Malka, *Selection*.

97. For the total number of Jews in the region, see DellaPergola, "Global Context," 17. For Aliyah numbers, see Central Bureau of Statistics, State of Israel, "Immigrants, by Period of Immigration, Country of Birth and Last Country of Residence," http://www.cbs.gov.il/reader/shnaton/templ_shnaton_e.html?num_tab=st04_04&CYear=2011 (link no longer active, document in the possession of the author).

98. Picard, *Cut to Measure*, 170, 190. For 1952, Picard mentions 5,000 immigrants out of 16,500 candidates; for 1953, 3,600 of 11,000.

99. Laskier, *North African Jewry*, 34, 37.

100. Ibid., 85.

101. Ibid., 102.

102. Ibid., 106–113.

103. Ibid., 265–266.

104. Picard, *Cut to Measure*; Malka, *Selection*; Mor, "Ableism and Orientalism"; Tsur, "Ethnic Problem"; Tsur, "Carnival Fears"; Lissak, "Demographic-Social Revolution;" Chetrit, *Mizrahi Struggle*; Segev, *1949*. For an interpretation of this Ashkenazi orientalism as the result of the internalization of European prejudices against Jews in general, see Khazzoom, "Great Chain of Orientalism."

105. Chetrit, *Mizrahi Struggle*, 45.

106. Tsur, "Ethnic Problem."

107. Emphasized by Picard, "Beginning of Selective Immigration," 386; Malka, *Selection*, 58–62; Tsur, "Ethnic Problem," 97.

108. Tsur, "Carnival Fears," 99.

109. Josephthal at the JAE Meeting, November 13, 1952, quoted in Picard, "Beginning of Selective Immigration," 388.

110. JAE Minutes, November 4, 1951, quoted in Tsur, "Ethnic Problem," 92–93.

111. Minutes of the Coordination Committee (CC) between the Jewish Agency and the Government, May 24, 1954, ISA 43.0.6.2089 (=5383/16-ג).

112. JAE Minutes, November 4, 1951, quoted in Picard, "Beginning of Selective Immigration," 376.

113. Mor, "Ableism and Orientalism."

114. Levi Eshkol in Jewish Agency Executive Plenum, March 13, 1952, quoted in Malka, *Selection,* 97. See also Hacohen, *Immigrants in Turmoil,* 113.

115. Hacohen, "Immigration Policy," 304.

116. Goldman press conference, May 17, 1956, CZA S6/10025.

117. Partially reprinted in Malka, *Selection,* appendix 1, 230–232. The full guidelines are reprinted in Malka's MA thesis. See Malka, "Selection in Immigration," 254–272.

118. Malka, *Selection,* 231.

119. Ibid.

120. Ibid. The 1922 White Paper is reprinted at Avalon Project, http://avalon.law.yale.edu/20th_century/brwh1922.asp.

121. Malka, "Selection in Immigration," 262.

122. Ibid., 260ff.

123. Picard, "Beginning of Selective Immigration," 377–378.

124. Ibid.

125. JAE Minutes, November 18, 1951, quoted in Malka, *Selection,* 73.

126. Picard, "Beginning of Selective Immigration," 381. In fact, social and health selection had already been part of the Juin-Gershuni agreement about Moroccan Aliyah in March 1949. See Laskier, *North African Jewry,* 110.

127. JAE Minutes, November 4, 1951, quoted in Picard, "Beginning of Selective Immigration," 376.

128. Picard, "Immigration, Health, and Social Control," 42.

129. Sheba in the JAE, June 10, 1952, quoted in Malka, *Selection,* 132–133.

130. Malka, *Selection,* 133, and Picard, "Immigration, Health, and Social Control," 39.

131. Picard, "Immigration, Health, and Social Control," 42.

132. Ibid.

133. Malka, *Selection,* 134.

134. For Argentina, see, for instance, Rodriguez, "Inoculating against Barbarism."

135. Batish to Shragai, April 5, 1954, quoted in Picard, "Immigration, Health and Social Control," 46 (emphasis in the original).

136. Picard, "Immigration, Health, and Social Control," 46.

137. Dr. Matan to Dr. Brakha, March 6, 1954, quoted in Picard, "Immigration, Health, and Social Control," 47.

138. Dr. Matan to Sternberg, December 12, 1952, quoted in Picard, "Immigration, Health, and Social Control," 44.

139. Dr. Matan to Dr. Sheba, May 6, 1953, quoted in Picard, "Immigration, Health, and Social Control," 44.

140. Picard, "Immigration, Health, and Social Control," 45 (emphasis added).

141. Ibid., 42–43.

142. Rafael in JAE Plenum, March 9, 1953, quoted in Malka, *Selection*, 100.

143. CC, March 15, 1953, quoted in Malka, *Selection*, 102.

144. Picard, "Immigration, Health, and Social Control," 47–49.

145. CC Minutes, June 14, 1953, ISA 43.0.6.263 (=5384/ 2-ג).

146. Picard, "Immigration, Health, and Social Control," 51; the guidelines are documented in full in ISA 43.0.6.263 (=5384/ 2-ג), and Malka, *Selection*, appendix 4, 238–239.

147. Malka, *Selection*, 238.

148. CC, March 15, 1953, quoted in Malka, *Selection*, 101.

149. Malka, *Selection*, 95–96, and Decisions of the JAE, February 15, 1954, posted to the CC for decision on February 16, 1954, ISA 43.0.6.263 (=5384/ 2-ג).

150. Hacohen, "Immigration Policy," 304.

151. Picard, *Cut to Measure*, 170.

152. Hacohen, "Immigration Policy," 305.

153. Laskier, *North African Jewry*, 123–124.

154. "The Fear of an Aliyah Stop," January 25, 1954, ISA 43.0.6.263 (=5384/ 2-ג), and ensuing decisions by the JAE.

155. Arnon, "Immigration and Absorption Policy," 317.

156. CC Minutes, May 24, 1954, ISA 43.0.6.2089 (=5383/16-ג). Giving priority to these villages had been promoted by Zeev Chaklai, head of the Jewish Agency offices in Casablanca 1952–1955; see Laskier, *North African Jewry*, 122.

157. Picard, *Cut to Measure*, 164–165. See also Picard, "Reluctant Soldiers."

158. Arnon, "Immigration and Absorption Policy," 322.

159. Picard, "Reluctant Soldiers," 30.

160. Arnon, "Immigration and Absorption Policy," 322.

161. Ibid., 334.

162. Laskier, *North African Jewry*, 129–130.

163. Picard, *Cut to Measure*, 196.

164. Malka, *Selection*, 111–112. Malka bases his account on the protocol of a JAE meeting in December 1954. Picard, *Cut to Measure*, 196–197, gives a slightly different division of tasks based on a February 1954 letter from Yehuda Braginsky's personal archive. According to that source, the Aliyah Department was expected to insist on the right of Jews to make Aliyah; the Klitah Department prevented the immigration of those whose absorption would strain the state; and the Settlement Department chose candidates for the new agricultural settlements.

165. Shragai to Josephthal, October 20, 1954, CZA S6/6002.

166. Picard, *Cut to Measure*, 197.

167. Shragai to Duvdevany, September 6, 1954, CZA S6/6002.

168. Dr. Rapp (Casablanca) to Dr. Pechthold (Jerusalem), April 8, 1956, CZA S6/10025. In this letter, Rapp criticized this practice.

169. Picard, *Cut to Measure*, 197. Their activities are extensively documented in CZA S6/6002. According to this file, such teams also existed in Persia and Italy, but they left a considerably smaller paper trail. The main focus was on Morocco and Tunisia.

170. Their activities are described by Laskier, *North African Jewry*, 128–130.

171. Ibid., 130.

172. Picard, *Cut to Measure*, 164, 210–216.

173. Duvdevany to Shragai, March 15, 1956, CZA S6/7260.

174. Grinker report, January 30, 1956, CZA S6/7260.

175. Selection team monthly report for January and February, March, 1956, CZA S6/7260.

176. Shragai to Jerusalem, June 14, 1956, CZA S6/10024.

177. Statistics attached to "Selection Team News from Morocco," No. 8 (November 9, 1955), CZA S6/6002.

178. Selection team report for December 1955, sent by the Kadima Office in Casablanca to Duvdevany in Paris, January 23, 1956, CZA S6/6002.

179. Numerical report on the selection of Olim, January 1956, CZA S6/7260.

180. Picard, *Cut to Measure*, 199–200.

181. Ibid., 190.

182. Ibid., 198. The European origins of the selection team members are pointed out by Malka, *Selection*, 112. The Moroccan team consisted of Chaim Tolczynski, Yehuda Kastelen, Zelig Nahumi, and the Aliyah Department representative in Morocco. For the Tunisian team, Malka lists the names of Hannah Hefetz, Menachem Vilner, Arieh Feuerstein, and Moshe Reber.

183. Article by Uri Oren in *Davar*, December 23, 1955, quoted in Picard, *Cut to Measure*, 200.

184. Quoted in Malka, *Selection*, 113. See also Kaufman to Shragai, February 2, 1955, CZA S6/6002. It appears that such complaints did not remain without consequences: in the new guidelines of June 12, 1955, the number of persons with each *mefarnes* was raised from five to seven.

185. Arnon, "Immigration and Absorption Policy," 331.

186. Picard, *Cut to Measure*, 201–202.

187. Recounted in Picard, *Cut to Measure*, 213.

188. Arnon, "Immigration and Absorption Policy," 326–327.

189. Quoted in Arnon, "Immigration and Absorption Policy," 328.

190. Arnon, "Immigration and Absorption Policy," 328.

191. Ibid., 339. See also Khazzoom, "Did the Israeli State."

192. Arnon, "Immigration and Absorption Policy," 340.

193. Duvedvany to Shragai, September 13, 1955, quoted in Laskier, *North African Jewry*, 131.

194. Picard, *Cut to Measure*, 301.

195. Arnon, "Immigration and Absorption Policy," 334.

196. Picard, *Cut to Measure*, 313–320.

197. Shragai to Duvdevany, January 19, 1956, CZA S6/7261.

198. Duvdevany to Shragai, January 24, 1956, CZA S6/7261.

199. Ambassador Tsur, Paris to Aliyah Department, Jerusalem, February 1, 1956, CZA S6/7261. In other sources, these integrationists, who called themselves Al-Wifaq ("the Agreement") in Arabic, are pejoratively referred to as the "*yevsektzia*," alluding to prominent Jews in the Soviet Union who made common cause with the regime and obstructed Aliyah. About Al-Wifaq and Aliyah, see also Picard, *Cut to Measure*, 306–309.

200. Shragai to Calamaro, February 9, 1956, CZA S6/7261.

201. Easterman to Shragai, January 30, 1956, CZA S6/7261; see also Picard, *Cut to Measure*, 303.

202. Picard, *Cut to Measure*, 328–330.

203. Monthly report for January and February, March, 1956, CZA S6/7260.

204. Picard, *Cut to Measure*, 321; Goldman press conference, May 17, 1956, CZA S6/10025; about the practical difficulties with selection, see Picard, *Cut to Measure*, 309–311, and Duvdevany confidential memorandum, undated (must be early May 1956), CZA S6/10025.

205. Shragai to Aliyah Council, Tangier, May 21, 1956, CZA S6/10025.

206. Shragai, Paris to Jerusalem, June 11, 1956, CZA S6/10025.

207. Shragai to Shazar, July 5, 1956, CZA S6/10024.

208. Picard, *Cut to Measure*, 345.

209. Dominitz to Shragai, August 30, 1956, CZA S6/10030.

210. About the background and development of "Gomulka's Aliyah," see Stola, *Kraj bez wyjścia*, chap. 6.

211. CC Minutes, December 10, 1956, CZA S100/513.

212. Naftali, CC Minutes, December 10, 1956, CZA S100/513. See also Picard, *Cut to Measure*, 349–351.

213. Braginsky, CC Minutes, December 10, 1956, CZA S100/513.

214. Shazar, CC Minutes, December 10, 1956, CZA S100/513.

215. For the 1958 guidelines, see ISA 43.0.6.262 (=5384/1-ג). For the 1963 revision, see Report by the Sub-committee on Immigrant Health, June 13, 1963, ISA 130.3.2.254 (=4326/25-חצ).

216. Report by the Sub-committee on Immigrant Health, June 13, 1963, section 3b, ISA 130.3.2.254 (=4326/25-חצ).

217. Ibid.

218. Ibid.

219. Aliyah from Morocco, CZA S6/10382 Laskier, *North African Jewry*, 238.

220. Laskier, *North African Jewry*, 240.

221. Protocol of the Meeting of the Sub-Committee on Aliyah Matters of the CC, instituted on August 6, 1963, with the participation of Burg, Sapir, Zisling, and Shragai, August 8, 1963, ISA 130.3.2.254 (=4326/25-חצ).

222. Braginsky to Shragai, August 1, 1958, and Shragai to Ben-Gurion, August 20, 1958, both in ISA 43.0.6.262 (=5384/1-ג).

223. CC Minutes, October 15, 1958, ISA 43.0.6.262 (=5384/1-ג).The attempts of the Jewish Agency to design a program to attract middle-class Aliyah in 1958–1959 are documented in CZA S6/6429.

224. Report by the Sub-committee on Immigrant Health, June 13, 1963, ISA 130.3.2.254 (=4326/25-חצ), emphasis added.

225. CC Minutes, August 27, 1963, ISA 130.3.2.254 (=4326/25-חצ).

226. Embassy Rome to Consular Department, April 26, 1961, ISA 93.20.1.280 (=286/13-חצ).

227. On "muscle Jews" and *chalutzim*, see Presner, *Muscular Judaism*, and Meira Weiss, *Chosen Body*. Some authors interpret this focus on physical fitness in the process of settlement as part of a eugenic enterprise. See Falk, "Settlement of Israel." Such an interpretation is consistent with the more general propensity of twentieth-century "communitarian-organic" socialists to embrace eugenics that Leo Lucassen has identified. See Lucassen, "Brave New World."

THREE

PROBLEMATIC OTHERS

ISIDOR B. CAME TO WEST Germany in February 1962. He had previously left his native country, Romania, for Israel, where he acquired citizenship. After settling in Mannheim, he applied for an expellee card and thus for recognition as an ethnic German Aussiedler. When Isidor's initial bid was rejected by the expellee authorities, he mounted a successful appeal, which involved a personal conversation with the city's mayor, Karl-Otto Watzinger. The mayor was impressed by Isidor's flawless, Austrian-inflected German and instructed the local administration to grant him an expellee card after all.[1] Yet the administratively superior North Baden Regional Council (*Regierungspräsidium*) contested the mayor's decision. Although the council did not question Isidor's knowledge of the German language, it doubted that he had identified as ethnically German back in his homeland, as required by the law. The reason for the council's doubt was Isidor's Jewish creed: Working on the assumption that "belonging to the Mosaic faith almost invariably justifies the assumption of belonging to the Jewish people as well," the regional council bureaucrats considered it unlikely that Isidor had been one of the 980 self-declared Germans living in his native Iaşi according to the 1930 census, when 34,662 of his coreligionists had identified as Jews. For the regional council, this meant that it would have to be assumed that "he lived within his Jewish *Volksgemeinschaft*" to which he was "affiliated by birth." Hence, Isidor B. could not be considered an ethnic German.[2]

Beyond the regional council's irritatingly unabashed use of *völkisch* vocabulary, the case of Isidor B. points to a general difficulty with the ethnic recognition process at the internal gate when different classifications and identifications of belonging came into conflict. Ideally, ethnic recognition could be quite straightforward when all sides—the receiving state, the sending state, and the migrants themselves—agreed on how to categorize a person in ethnic terms, the meaning of the categories used, and when the person adhered to the prescribed pathways and procedures of the co-ethnic migration regime. A 1958 commentary on the German Federal Expellee Law provided an example of a hypothetical person from one of the traditional German areas of settlement in Romania (Transylvania and the Banat), who would arguably have few problems satisfying the legal criteria of German *Volkszugehörigkeit.*[3] Such a person would have been part of a well-established national minority with its own German-language schools, would therefore speak German well, and would most likely have migrated to Germany under an official family reunification scheme to join relatives in Germany who had already been recognized as Germans. This migrant would easily meet both the subjective (*Bekenntnis*) and the objective requirements of German law.

The recognition process became much more complex when someone like Isidor B. strayed from the prestructured pathways of the ethnically coded East–West migration regime and did not fit neatly into these seemingly simple and consensual classifications. In such cases, divergent interpretations of ethnic categories became evident. As Isidor B.'s case demonstrates, the meaning of "Jewishness" was particularly contentious in this context. Harking back to the pre-Nazi notion of a "German citizen of the Jewish faith" as well as to Habsburg conceptions of nationality by self-declaration, the Federal Expellee Law did not generally exclude the possibility that a Jew by religion could be an ethnic German. The same 1958 commentary stated: "Contrary to the national socialist view, membership of the Mosaic confession or descent from a person who professed the Jewish faith does not preclude German ethnicity (*Volkszugehörigkeit*)."[4] Yet there were context-specific limitations to this open definition concerning the ambiguous nature of modern Jewishness as religion or ethnonationality: "Those Jews cannot be considered German *Volkszugehörige* who belonged to a separate minority which existed alongside the German minority (as, for example, in Galicia and Romania)."[5] A Jew in an ethno-national sense could thus not be an ethnic German according to German law, because "it is impossible to identify with two ethnic groups at once."[6]

Against the backdrop of this exclusive definition of German *Volkszugehörigkeit,* cases such as Isidor B.'s—which involved ambiguous categories, multiple migrant self-identifications, and classifications by different actors—represented a particular challenge for the authorities at the internal gate. Isidor B. was Jewish by religion, which the regional council took to indicate his identification as Jewish also in an ethno-national sense. The Romanian state certainly considered him as such when it let him emigrate to Israel. The State of

Israel agreed with this classification and provided him with Israeli citizenship. But after his subsequent migration to West Germany, Isidor claimed to be German and to have professed an exclusive *Bekenntnis* to German *Volkstum* back in Romania, just as expellee law required. Isidor's "objective" cultural credentials—fluent knowledge of the German language—were not in doubt; the question was whether his Jewish religion and the existence of a strong Jewish national minority in his hometown a priori precluded the possibility that he had identified as German—a Romanian citizen of German ethnicity and Jewish faith, as it were. As several thousand Eastern European Jews, especially from Romania but also from other Central and Eastern European states, immigrated to West Germany during the 1960s, this question was deliberated within the administration and at court on multiple occasions, some of which will be analyzed in this chapter.

In Israel, too, the relationship between Jewish national belonging and the Jewish religion could become a contentious issue, yet in a reverse constellation. The question here was how to determine which category should be used for people who defined themselves as Jewish or were defined by their country of origin as Jewish but lacked one essential characteristic: belonging to the Jewish faith. The most challenging constellation was provided by Jewish converts to Christianity: once converted, did they qualify for citizenship under the Law of Return? The famous case of Brother Daniel, alias Oswald Rufeisen, a Jewish-born convert to Catholicism who claimed recognition as a Jew under the Law of Return, brought this issue to the fore in the early 1960s. Here, too, it became the task of a court to determine the national belonging of an individual. In contrast to the German examples, which attracted minimal media attention and cannot be said to have had considerable social repercussions, the Brother Daniel case was a significant cause célèbre, because it touched on Israel's very self-understanding as a Jewish yet secular state. Indeed, many decades later, its protagonist inspired an award-winning novel by Russian author Ludmila Ulitskaya.[7]

Despite their different degrees of publicity, these cases are compared here because they have two key issues in common: the application of definitions of co-ethnic belonging in practice and the secular and religious meanings of modern Jewishness. In each instance, the discrepancies between conflicting classifications of belonging complicated the process of ethnic recognition, while the hybrid and ambiguous nature of the applicants' biographical profiles seriously tested the respective recognition mechanisms in both states. A comparative analysis thus makes it possible to reconstruct the techniques that judges and administrators used to assess ethno-national belonging in contentious borderline cases. It also sheds light on how the gatekeeping administrators and judges constructed ethno-national belonging in relation to both religion and each nation's "problematic other." At that point, the entangled nature of the comparative cases comes into sharp focus.

EAST–WEST MIGRATION PATHWAYS

Migration from Eastern to Western Europe under Cold War conditions was restricted, because socialist states generally did not allow emigration, and the—not only metaphorical—Iron Curtain provided a very real obstacle to mobility. The main legal way to permanently emigrate from one's homeland was through what this book refers to as ethnically coded family reunification, available mainly for citizens identified as Germans and Jews. In the highly regulated and strictly supervised East–West migration system that had been established by the early 1960s, legal emigration followed a prestructured path that led from the official exit gate of the country of origin to the official external immigration gate of the receiving country, passing through certain fixed routes and nodal points on the way. As long as people went through these official channels, control procedures were relatively simple. As a rule, an exit visa entitling its holder to enter Germany or Israel signaled to the receiving state that the sending state considered the migrant either German or Jewish. The receiving states relied on their external migration procedures to provide the additional safeguard that incoming migrants conformed to their definitions of co-ethnicity.

As soon as people strayed from this prestructured path and bypassed at least one of the official gates, the process became more complex from the state's point of view. On the one hand, there were people from Eastern European countries who managed to leave their home country legally (for instance, on a tourist visa) or illegally and then reported to German diplomatic representations in the West, seeking to immigrate as Germans. When this occurred, the German authorities had to assess the migrants' eligibility for preferential immigration outside of the official external procedure. On the other hand were people who left their home countries on a "Jewish ticket" but then "dropped out" on their way to Israel. This phenomenon was aided by the more complicated logistics of Jewish migration to Israel, the emigrants' extended family networks, and alternative migration channels. It was this early experience of *Neshirah* (as the dropout phenomenon became known in the 1970s) as well as the use of Israel as a transit country by Eastern European Jews planning to go elsewhere—notably, West Germany—that brought about the entanglement of German and Jewish migrations, and all the ensuing complications this implied.

The logistics of Aussiedler immigration to Germany were relatively straightforward: the Federal Republic was physically close to the countries of origin, and transport links existed across the Iron Curtain. The ease of transportation to Germany contrasts sharply with the difficulties of travel to Israel. Migrants coming from Poland and the Soviet Union entered West Germany through the Friedland transit camp in Lower Saxony, which was located right on the zonal border to East Germany and earned the epithet "gate to freedom."[8] Migrants from the southeast (Czechoslovakia, Romania, Yugoslavia) entered through transit camps in Nuremberg or Piding, a small town in Upper Bavaria on the Austrian border. Usually by the time migrants reached these camps, they would have passed the regular takeover procedure which ascertained that they were most likely ethnic Germans according to the law.

Bureaucratic problems occurred when citizens of Eastern European countries reported to a West German consulate in a Western country and claimed to be of German ethnicity or to hold German citizenship. Most of these people came from Yugoslavia, Romania, and occasionally from Poland, and they reported to German missions in Austria.[9] In other documented cases from the early to mid-1960s, passengers defected from Polish cruise ships that anchored in Copenhagen and Helsinki and contacted the German representation there.[10] Since none of the applicants were certified for takeover, the embassies and consulates faced the problem of having to validate German citizenship or *Volkszugehörigkeit* with a sufficient degree of certainty in a relatively short period. The time limit was set by the Federal Expellee Law, which stipulated that an ethnic German could be recognized as an expellee only if he or she entered West Germany less than six months after having left the expulsion area. A longer examination could thus have led to a mismatch between external and internal recognition, since the latter would have become impossible with the passing of the deadline. A shorter and less thorough examination, on the other hand, could have opened the gates of the country to aliens who, in the eyes of the state, were not entitled to enter.

The treatment of Hungarian citizen Jozsef E. offers an example of the process. In August 1964, Jozsef reported to the consulate general in Milan with his wife, Jozefine, and daughter Agnes.[11] According to the consulate, Jozsef spoke fluent German. He also presented evidence of his German descent (including his father's certificate of baptism, an old school report from Vienna, and pictures of his mother's restaurant, also in Vienna). Nevertheless, his application was rejected by the Federal Interior Ministry. The grounds for rejection related to the crucial issue of *Bekenntnis*: Agnes's knowledge of German was very limited, and Jozefine spoke no German at all. Therefore, it was to be assumed that

Hungarian *Volkstum* prevailed in the family. Similar to the practice in Yugoslavia analyzed in chapter 2, the authorities interpreted these factors as opposing a *Bekenntnis* to German *Volkstum*. Therefore, the Interior Ministry deemed it impossible to permit the family to enter Germany.[12]

The internal authorities were unwilling to take any chances on candidates who arrived outside of the official takeover procedure, even if the candidates obviously fulfilled some of the legal criteria for entitlement. When the consulate general in Salzburg suggested the examination of such unofficial Aussiedler in the Piding transit camp, both the Federal and Bavarian Interior Ministries disagreed.[13] The decisive argument was that, by law, German *Volkszugehörige* only became Germans according to the Basic Law on entry into the Federal Republic. To enter the country, they needed a valid passport or an entry visa, which these illegal transit migrants did not possess. The Federal Interior Ministry saw a clear danger here: "The procedure suggested by the consulate general in Salzburg would lead to the circumvention of the takeover regulations. Foreigners (*Ausländer*) whose takeover has been rejected or who are not able to prove their German ethnicity would obtain the possibility to enter the Federal Republic."[14] Similarly, the same ministry rejected an ad hoc procedure adopted by the West German trade mission in Helsinki, which had issued short-term entry passports for the Federal Republic to people—like Jozsef E.—whose origin (*Herkunft*) and language skills suggested that they were ethnic Germans.[15] The Federal Interior Ministry argued that, in general, the regular D1 takeover procedure could not be skipped. Origin and language were generally not sufficient to grant entry visas. The *Bekenntnis* would have to be established as well to make the takeover compatible with section 6 BVFG.[16]

The interior authorities' concern was to keep the external gate guarded and to prevent the entry of aliens who might claim recognition in the internal procedure—or who, in any event, could hardly be deported to their country of origin in the Eastern Bloc. Since they were already outside the Eastern Bloc at the time they made their application, the "state of exception" that facilitated their direct takeover from the "expulsion territories" no longer applied, thus following the pattern established in chapter 2. But controlling the external gate became more difficult if Eastern European citizens chose not to report to a German consulate, but rather entered West Germany legally on a western passport and then sought recognition as Aussiedler. Some of them obtained western passports in another important transit country on the way from Eastern Europe to West Germany: Israel.

Israel, of course, was not a transit country due to its geographical location, but due to its designation as the default destination for Eastern European

Jews—not all of whom planned on staying there. In fact, some of them never made it to the Jewish state at all. The logistics of transporting migrants to Israel were more complicated than to Germany; hence, it was more likely that people "got lost" on the way. Organized Jewish migrants used routes that were determined by Jewish Agency travel arrangements. An important relay in this migration arrangement was the port of Naples, where the streams of Eastern European and North African migrants to Israel converged. Naples had replaced Marseilles as the transit station for Jews from the Maghreb by the early 1960s due to the high concentration of North African Arabs in southern France and the resulting fear of friction this caused among the Israeli authorities.[17] Eastern European migrants were alternatively sent to Israel through Athens, or via a Black Sea route through Constanta, Varna, and Istanbul.[18] From Naples, the Olim were shipped directly to the port of Haifa.

A second, increasingly important relay for Eastern European migrants was Vienna. Strategically located between East and West, the Austrian capital became more prominent as Soviet Jewish migration grew in the 1970s. Much to Israel's concern, in Vienna migrants could quite easily redirect their journey, and there is evidence that some had already tried to do so in the late 1950s.[19] Some of those who sought to change their final destination in Vienna contacted the West German embassy with the goal of traveling on to the FRG. However, at that point, the embassy refused to assist them, because the Federal Republic wanted to avoid trouble with Israel, especially given that Israeli representatives tried to prevent such contact.[20] Although the available documentation does not reveal how the migrants to Germany who followed this path managed to enter the country, it is clear that some did. Some migrants even asked the expellee authorities to refund their travel expenses, though mostly without success.[21]

Beginning in the early 1960s, Jewish migration trajectories became more varied. Romania, one of the most significant sources of Jewish migrants at the time, began issuing exit visas to Jews for not just Israel but also other countries. During the second half of 1958, Aliyah from Romania had already increased dramatically when the authorities relaxed emigration restrictions, arguably to gain favor in the West.[22] When Romania started to issue exit visas for other Western countries, Israeli officials were initially very cautious about this move, as they were unsure about the underlying intentions. Some suspected that this was simply a tactical ploy by the communist authorities to have an alibi toward the Arab world, which opposed Jewish Aliyah. Others were concerned that this maneuver was intended to create confusion among Romanian Jews. Additionally, the Israeli authorities wondered whether they could force reluctant migrants to make Aliyah. After all, Western transit countries such as France requested the guarantee that migrants would not settle down—a guarantee that Israel could not give.[23] Despite these initial doubts, in February 1960, the Eastern European Department of the Israeli Foreign Ministry instructed the diplomatic representations in France, Italy, Belgium, the Netherlands, and Austria to find arrangements with the respective countries.[24] Henceforth, Jews in Romania were able to receive visas for any of those countries—even visas for permanent settlement—though the idea was that they would eventually move to Israel. By April 1960, the Eastern European Department still reported that the majority of Romanian Jews went directly to Israel via Vienna.[25]

Despite this reassuring report, cases multiplied in which migrants refused to make Aliyah. Alfred and Cesarina S., for example, had received a Belgian visa after the Israeli ambassador in Bucharest, Bendor, had intervened on the couple's behalf at the Belgian legation in March 1960.[26] By July it was clear that they had no intention of going to Israel, as they had registered as political refugees in Belgium.[27] The Belgian authorities, however, refused to grant them permanent residence and asked the Israelis to give them immigration visas instead. This, of course, was precisely what the Israelis wanted in the first place, and they promised to convince the couple to make Aliyah after all. Alfred S. accepted the invitation to the embassy but declared that he and his wife neither wanted to make Aliyah, nor did they plan to stay in Belgium. Instead they intended to settle in France or Germany. At that point, the Israeli officials could do nothing more, because they wielded no authority over the migrants, who were not Israeli citizens. In the opinion of the embassy, the Belgians "did not see a disaster in that one or two persons would exploit their kind-heartedness in order to travel to and settle in Belgium instead of continuing on their way to Israel."[28]

Similar situations were reported from the Netherlands: some Romanian Jews with Dutch visas went directly to Israel via Vienna; others came to the Netherlands with a visa for a third country, often in Latin America; and some tried to stay in Holland.[29] Although it is not clear which option Alfred and Cesarina S. or people in the reported cases from the Netherlands eventually chose—staying in the transit country, moving to another country, or making Aliyah after all—it is important to note that they possessed these different options once they had left Romania. As emigrants from the Eastern Bloc in the West, they were in a relatively comfortable position, since deportation back to socialist Eastern Europe was generally not an option for their host countries when bloc confrontation was at its peak.[30] The guaranteed possibility of being received in Israel as Jews constituted an additional safety net against the danger of ending up lost in transit.

The sidestepping of official migration paths thus affected West Germany and Israel in different ways. The FRG faced the additional immigration of purported co-ethnics, including Jews, who needed to be bureaucratically processed outside of the official takeover procedure. Israel, on the other hand, lost migrants this way. Those latter instances, in which migrants used Israel or Israeli visas as a stepping-stone to the West, resulted in the entanglement of the German and Jewish-Israeli migration systems and regimes. It is these physical connections and the resulting conceptual entanglement between the German and Jewish-Israeli definitions of ethnicity that we will turn to next.

JEWISH IMMIGRATION TO GERMANY IN THE 1950S AND 1960S

Contrary to the myth of Germany being a *terra prohibita* for Jews after the Holocaust and until the Russian-Jewish mass immigration of the 1990s, there was continuous Jewish immigration to the FRG in the postwar decades. In fact, the rate of Jewish immigration to the country was consistently above the respective emigration rate during these years.[31] The idea that Jews should not come to live in (or initially even travel to) Germany was an ideological stance that was shared by the State of Israel and Jewish representatives in Germany at the time. Early Israeli passports even contained a provision that they were valid for all countries except Germany.[32] Despite such obstacles, small West German Jewish communities—which, after the war, initially consisted of stranded Displaced Persons, people who had survived the Holocaust inside Germany, and returning émigrés—received several waves of immigration in the following years and decades. During the 1950s, most were German Jewish returnees from Israel or other countries, while others came directly from Eastern Europe. Prominent among the latter is the famous literary critic Marcel Reich-Ranicki, who left Poland in 1958 and came to Germany, where he had already lived in the 1930s.[33] Other Eastern European Jews had started using Israel as a transit country for other destinations by that time. Among these destinations, West Germany was perceived as so popular that, in 1958, the Israeli newspaper *Maariv* called it one of the "classic" destinations for Israeli migrants, many of whom were precisely such Eastern European newcomers.[34] Whereas few Jewish immigrants trickled into the country in the early 1960s, a second immigration wave from Eastern Europe and Israel brought another couple of thousand to West Germany between 1964 and 1967.[35]

In the absence of a regularized immigration regime, those immigrants who were not returnees and thus were not entitled to have their German citizenship reinstated had two options for obtaining permanent residence status: seeking asylum (which was likely to be unsuccessful for those who had already become Israeli citizens) or seeking recognition as a German expellee.[36] The second option was the most advantageous for those who, due to their language skills, could make a credible claim to ethnic Germanness, for it promised immediate German citizenship as well as substantial integration and retirement benefits. The granting of expellee status mainly hinged on one condition: the German *Volkszugehörigkeit* of the applicant, which was determined by German bureaucrats and, if the bureaucratic process yielded no satisfactory result, by German judges.

Who were these immigrants? In the process of assessing the validity of applicants' claims to German ethnicity, the expellee bureaucracy gathered data that can be used to reconstruct their origins and migration trajectories. For instance, a list of 236 Jews who lived in the city of Mannheim in 1970 and had received expellee cards or had pending applications has been preserved in the Baden-Württemberg state archives.[37] The purpose of the data collection—to ascertain eligibility for expellee status within the framework of the internal recognition procedure—determined the information contained in the list. In addition to the person's date of birth, it notes the place of residence in 1937 (relevant to establish whether someone had been living in the German Reich within the 1937 borders), the date of exit from the home country, the date of entry into the Federal Republic of Germany, and any countries where the person had lived in the meantime (all of which was relevant to assess whether the six-month deadline was met and whether the candidate had acquired another citizenship), and the person's current address in Germany. In almost half the cases, the immigrant's profession was also documented, even though it had no immediate relevance for the recognition process. By contrast, data regarding the fate of these people during the war and the Holocaust is lacking completely. In 92 of the 236 cases, this lacuna could be filled for the purposes of this study with data from the International Tracing Service (ITS) archives in Bad Arolsen, which hold extensive documentation on Nazi persecution and were an important reference for these migrants when they applied for compensation by the West German authorities. Together, the Mannheim list and the ITS data allow for the creation of a collective social and migratory profile of this particular sample of Jewish immigrants in 1960s West Germany and the reconstruction of many individual wartime persecution and postwar migration trajectories.

The 236 individuals on the Mannheim list originated from four geographically contiguous countries in Central, Eastern, and Southeastern Europe. Three-quarters of the people came from Romania (178); the countries of origin for the rest were Poland (31), Hungary (17), and Czechoslovakia (10). They were a fairly aged migrant population: More than two-thirds of the sample was older than 40 at the time of immigration to Germany, and more than one-third were over 50. By the time the list was compiled in 1970, the average age was 51 years, with the years of birth ranging from 1882 to 1954. Two-thirds had been born between 1908 and 1930. The professional profile was mixed: Of the 112 individuals whose profession is noted in the list, about 30 percent were technicians or craftspeople of some kind, including car mechanics, tailors, butchers, and goldsmiths. Another quarter consisted of merchants and traders. Some 20 percent worked in medical professions, mainly dentistry. The sample also comprised two rabbis and a lawyer specialized in compensation law.

In terms of the postwar migration trajectories, the vast majority of these immigrants (at least 205 of the 236 on the list, or almost 87 percent) immigrated to Germany during the 1960s. About two-thirds (155) came between 1964 and 1967 and thus belonged to the second immigration wave. At least 116 (49 percent) of the total number had previously spent time in Israel at some point. Among those whose stay in Israel can be reconstructed in some detail from the data, different migration patterns emerge. Some migrants used Israel for quick transit on their way to Western Europe—sometimes staying less than a month—while the majority tried to settle in the Jewish state at least initially before deciding to move on for reasons about which we can only speculate. The median time of residence of all migrants in Israel was between three and four years. Almost all of them acquired Israeli citizenship, which, even without the intention of permanent settlement, was a useful asset for further migration.

By contrast, at least 60 individuals (25 percent) immigrated to Germany via another Western country without going to Israel at all. Most transmigrated through the Western countries that provided Jews with entry visas to facilitate their exit from Romania or that were adjacent to the other countries of origin. The main transit countries were Belgium and Austria; others passed through France and Italy or a combination of these countries. Most of the transmigrants spent just a few months in their places of transit; others settled for more extended periods, up to eleven years. Migration trajectories moreover differed according to the country of origin. Among the Romanians, a majority (at least 57 percent) came via Israel, while the Hungarians and Czechs, except for one case, avoided the "detour" through the Jewish state entirely. Eight migrants from all four countries came directly to Germany during the 1950s and 1960s. Another ten, mostly from Poland, had been Displaced Persons in Germany at the end of the war and remained there.

While these postwar trajectories were shaped by the constraints of the ethnically coded East–West migration regime of the Cold War period as well as different national exit regimes, going back to the period before the Second

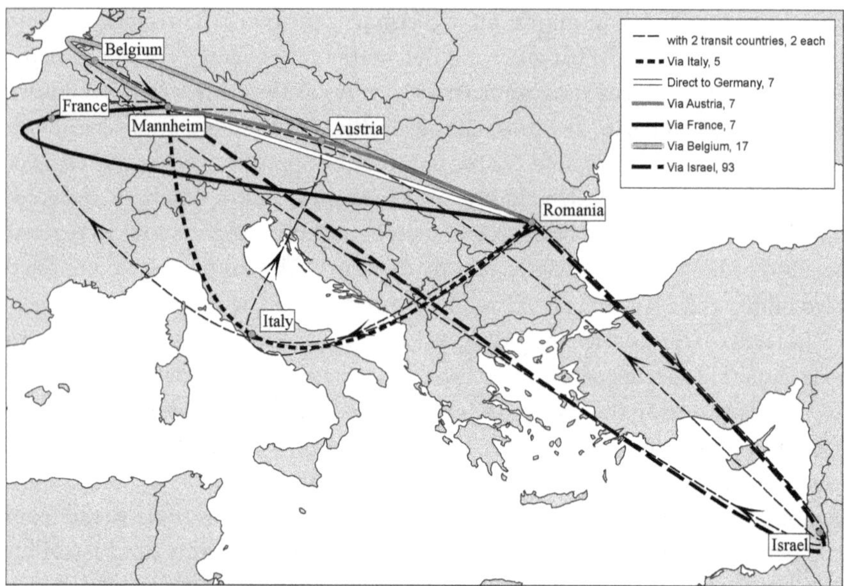

Map 3.1. Emigration trajectories of Romanian Jews on the Mannheim list. Map designed by Lukas Hennies, based on CShapes by Nils B. Weidmann, Doreen Kuse, and Kristian Skrede Gleditsch, "The Geography of the International System: The Cshapes Dataset," *International Interactions* 36, no 1 (2010): 86–106.

World War and considering the origins of the Mannheim Jews below the national level of their postwar countries of emigration allows us to capture some of the complexity that life trajectories assumed in Central and Eastern Europe as a result of the great upheavals of the twentieth century. These people mostly originated from contested multiethnic and multilingual regions of the former Austro-Hungarian Empire, which were subject to significant border shifts during the first decades of the twentieth century. More than half were born inside the historic borders of Habsburg Hungary. They mainly came from the Transylvania, Crişana/Körösvidék, Satu Mare/Szatmár, and Maramureş/Máramaros regions (all ceded to Romania in the 1920 Trianon treaty), but also from Slovakia, Transcarpathia (both part of Czechoslovakia after 1918) and from central Hungary. A few others were from formerly Austrian Bukovina, which was also awarded to Romania after the First World War. About one-third came from Romania within its pre-1918 borders (the Regat). The immigrants from Poland were mainly from formerly German Eastern Upper Silesia (Katowice/Kattowitz, Chorzów/Königshütte, and Będzin/Bendzin), the formerly Austrian southern part of Silesia (Bielsko/Bielitz), and from the western and eastern parts of the Habsburg province of Galicia—all of which became part of the resurrected Polish state in 1918. They thus originated from a geographical space—historical *Mitteleuropa* and its fringes—where, in the words of Dan Diner, "the German language had been the lingua franca, also and especially for the Jews."[38]

A comparison of birthplaces with the places of residence in 1937 and after the war shows different degrees of mobility among these inhabitants of the Central European borderlands. Most of them stayed within their regions of origin as those shifted national allegiance—borders moved over people in these cases. Others moved within the nation-states that their regions had been attached to. Frieda W., for example, was born in 1912 in Transylvanian Sibiu but lived in Bucharest in 1937; Joachim D., born in Kolomea (eastern Galicia) in 1911, moved to Upper Silesian Katowice; Heinrich G., born in 1920 in Užhorod/Ungvár in formerly Hungarian Transcarpathia, later lived in northern Bohemian Teplice, from where he emigrated in 1964. Yet others moved across new national boundaries within the old Habsburg space. Josef M., for instance, was born in 1909 in Transcarpathian Munkács/Mukačevo, then part of Habsburg Hungary and from 1919 onward part of Czechoslovakia. In 1937, he lived in formerly Austrian Czernowitz, capital of the Bukovina, which by then was part of Romania. After the war he lived in Transylvanian Sibiu. Another example, Paula W., was born in 1910 in Galician Sanok, which was then part of Austria and became part of Poland in 1919. In 1937, she lived in Transcarpathian Hust, a formerly Hungarian town which then belonged to Czechoslovakia and was occupied by fascist Hungary during the war. After the war and before moving to Belgium in 1961, she lived in Oradea, Romania. A third case, Dr. David L. was born in Transylvanian Gödemesterháza/Stânceni in 1905. By 1937, he resided in Prague, whereas after the war he lived in Hungary, from where he emigrated in 1967.

As borders shifted again during the Second World War and regions were occupied or annexed by states with different agendas regarding their Jewish populations, people's wartime trajectories greatly depended on the regions where they lived rather than the interwar nation-state. The differences in forced migration patterns between the Romanian Jews of different regional origins on the Mannheim list are particularly striking. Those from the formerly Hungarian territories in the north, which were re-awarded to Hungary in the 1940 Second Vienna Award, generally shared the fate of Hungarian Jewry, including the immigrants from Hungary to Mannheim. Some of the men were recruited for Hungarian labor battalions starting in 1942, while most of the women remained untouched until March 1944, when Hungary was occupied by Germany and Jews were forced into ghettos and deported. Of those on the list, only a few

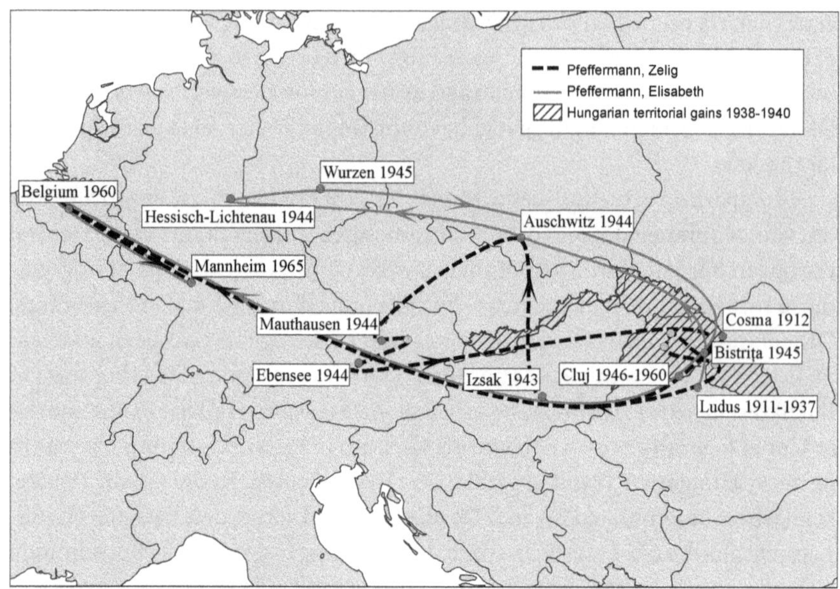

Map 3.2. Migration trajectory of Zelig and Elisabeth Pfeffermann.
Map designed by Lukas Hennies, based on CShapes by Nils B. Weidmann, Doreen Kuse, and Kristian Skrede Gleditsch, "The Geography of the International System: The Cshapes Dataset," *International Interactions* 36, no. 1 (2010): 86–106.

managed to escape deportation and go into hiding in Budapest, where the chances for survival were generally better.

More typical is the story of Zelig and Elisabeth Pfeffermann.[39] The couple, born in 1912 and 1911, respectively, had married in 1937 and lived in Transylvanian Bistrița. Zelig was arrested there in October 1942 and had to perform forced labor in different places in Maramureș and Transylvania. Elisabeth was arrested in the Bistrița ghetto in May 1944. Both were subsequently deported to Auschwitz, where most of Hungarian Jewry perished during the following months. At the ramp, Zelig and Elisabeth, who were both in their early 30s at that point, were obviously considered fit for work. Like most others from the list whose wartime fate can be reconstructed through the ITS archives, the Pfeffermanns embarked on a westward odyssey through the Nazi camp system that ended with liberation somewhere in Germany or Austria toward the end of the war. Both were liberated by the Americans in April 1945—Zelig in the Ebensee camp in Austria, Elisabeth in Wurzen near Leipzig. After liberation, Zelig and Elisabeth returned to Bistrița, which, after the war, once again belonged to Romania. They subsequently settled in Cluj, where they stayed until their emigration from Romania to Belgium in 1960. In 1965, they came to Germany.

The Jews from the Bukovina and the Regat—about 40 percent of the Romanian immigrants in Mannheim—fared quite differently. Most of the Regat Jews on the list have no wartime record in the ITS archives, arguably because they were among the majority of the Jews from Old Romania who were not deported by the Antonescu regime. The ones whose fate is documented followed a trajectory similar to their coreligionists from Bukovina. They were persecuted from 1941 but did not go through the German camps. Instead, they ended up in Transnistria, where fascist Romania deported Jews from Bukovina as well as from Bessarabia. Avram and Sofia Junger from Bucharest, for instance, were deported with their newborn son, Simon, to Mogilev in 1941 and subsequently to Iampol, where their other son, Reuven, was born in 1943.[40] After liberation, the family returned home to Bucharest, as did most other Romanian Jews from the list. Between 1961 and 1963, the family chain-migrated to West Germany via Israel. After leaving Romania together in April 1961, Avram was first to leave Israel for West Germany in December of the same year. In June 1962, Simon followed. In January 1963, they were joined by Sofia; and, finally, in July 1963, Reuven completed the move.

From among the small sample of Bukovina Jews, about half chose not to return to their homes after the war, which, if they were from the northern part of the region, were under Soviet rule. Artur Madfes, for instance, a native of Lemberg who had lived in Czernowitz in 1937, was living in Bucharest after the war. There, he married Sifra Iosupovici from Târgu Neamţ in September 1945. In 1948, they migrated to Uruguay, from where they moved to West Germany in 1964.[41] Other Bukovina Jews also left Romania during these immediate postwar years, while the bulk of the Regat Jews from the sample, just like the ones from the formerly Hungarian territories, generally did not emigrate until the early 1960s.[42]

In contrast to the Romanians, the small sample of Polish Jews registered on the Mannheim list shows no such regional differentiation. Their life stories reflect some of the common trajectories of Polish Jewish survivors during and after the Shoah. Irrespective of their regions of origin, they were arrested and ghettoized around 1939–1940 and subsequently went through various concentration camps in occupied Poland and Germany. After liberation, many of them did not return to Poland and chose to stay in occupied Germany as Displaced Persons. Others had survived the war in hiding or in the Soviet Union and fled Poland in 1945–1946 due to postwar anti-Jewish violence. They, too, became Displaced Persons, and their subsequent migration trajectories were subject to the contingencies of the postwar period.

David Chwat, who had survived different concentration camps and was liberated in Leonberg near Stuttgart in April 1945, stated Buenos Aires, Argentina, as his preferred destination in his September 1945 Displaced Person registration.[43] Yet it appears he never arrived; in April 1949, he was reported as having left for Israel.[44] In 1958, Chwat returned to Germany and settled in Mannheim. Mietek Finkelstein, a survivor of Auschwitz, Stutthof, and Natzweiler camps, still stated in his 1951 application for support by the International Refugee Organization that he, his Berlin-born wife, Genia, and their baby son planned to migrate to the United States.[45] Yet their emigration plans never came to pass and they stayed in Germany. Isak and Anna Krieger from Bielsko, who had survived the war pretending to be Christian Poles, stated in 1949 that they planned to go to Israel.[46] Instead, they stayed in Mannheim, a decision that was arguably aided by the fact that they had lived in Anna's nearby hometown of Worms until 1933, before moving to Isak's native Bielsko after the Nazis' rise to power.

Two additional Polish cases capture the interplay of contingent decisions, larger migratory trends, and constraints imposed by various migration regimes. Irene Resler, born in Bielsko in 1925, had survived the war in the Soviet Union. After her return to Poland, she moved on to occupied Germany in July 1946, likely under the impression of the Kielce pogrom, which triggered a major emigration wave of Polish survivors. Untypically, Resler returned to Bielsko in 1947 for reasons unknown. In 1957, she left Poland once more, this time headed for Israel as part of the post-1956 emigration wave, and settled in Ramat Chen near Tel Aviv. But again, this was not her final move. In 1961, she left the Jewish state and came to West Germany, where she settled first in Mannheim and then in Frankfurt.[47]

The second case, Michael Weiner, a native Galician who had survived in illegality and lived in Upper Silesian Zabrze (Hindenburg) from 1946, managed to dodge the Polish migration regime, which sent "Jews" to Israel and "Germans" to Germany. In 1958, he joined his Silesian neighbors—tens of thousands of whom were flocking from their homeland at the time—and entered West Germany through the Friedland transit camp like a "regular" Aussiedler.[48]

One last example concerns an individual with a relatively unspectacular emigration history. Filip Müller, born in Sered, Czechoslovakia, in 1922, came directly to Germany as an Aussiedler in 1969 and immediately received an expellee card. It was not his first visit to West Germany. In 1964, he had testified at the first Auschwitz trial in Frankfurt.[49] Müller had been imprisoned in Auschwitz in 1942 and worked in the *Sonderkommando* of Jewish prisoners charged with clearing the gas chambers of dead bodies and cremating them.[50] In 1979, he published his memoirs of his time in Auschwitz, and later appeared in Claude Lanzmann's monumental documentary *Shoah*.[51] His story is a powerful reminder that the cases on the Mannheim list are real people with dramatic fates during the war and the Holocaust.

JEWISH IMMIGRANTS IN GERMAN COURTS

Whatever their twisted individual trajectories and horrific wartime fates, once these people applied for German expellee status, none of these things mattered. To achieve recognition, they had to convince the German authorities (and possibly courts) that, despite moving across borders and borders moving over them, and despite their persecution by Germans, they had been nothing but German back in their homeland. This requirement had been imposed by the already known definition of a German *Volkszugehöriger* in section 6 of the Federal Expellee Law. This law defined someone as German if he or she was able to demonstrate a public self-identification (*Bekenntnis*) to German *Volkstum* in the past, which was supported by "objective" criteria such as descent, language, upbringing, and culture. Most of the Jewish applicants for a German expellee card easily overfulfilled these objective criteria, because they spoke German and were familiar with German culture. Given the multiple definitions of Jewishness as either religion or nationality, the problem lay in the unequivocal *Bekenntnis*. If an applicant had been Jewish in only a religious sense, he or she might still be considered German; but given the exclusive definition of *Bekenntnis*, under the law, any identification as Jewish in a national sense ruled out a simultaneous belonging to the German nation.

Precisely because of their ambiguous nature, Jewish cases disproportionately often forced the administration and subsequently the administrative courts to explicitly spell out their criteria against the background of an individual case—an exercise that brings the recognition techniques they applied into sharper focus. Based on the reading of individual cases, this section suggests the existence of two different models. The first case study will show that *Bekenntnis* could be "performed" by Jewish migrants by streamlining their biographical data with the requirements of German expellee law in order to conform to a certain narrative of national belonging. This meant presenting facts from their lives in a way that they could be endowed with "national" meaning. Given the complexity of the life trajectories of emigrants, this task entailed considerable difficulty. As the second case study analyzed in this chapter will show, in response to this ambivalent system, the administrative judges sought a clear-cut, unambiguous solution, which will be termed the "declarative model."

The third and fourth cases serve to investigate how the German legal system assessed the impact of Jewish religion on German *Volkszugehörigkeit.*

Performing Germanness: The Case of Valentina Colien

Valentina Colien was recognized by the Administrative Court of Hesse as an "ethnic German expellee" in January 1966.[52] She was born in Bucharest in 1906. At the beginning of the Second World War, she lived in Czernowitz, her mother's native city, where she had moved after divorcing her husband, Harry, in 1938. After the war, Colien returned to Bucharest. In 1960, she left Romania for France, which was also the preferred transit country of Regat Jews on the Mannheim list. From there she went on to Israel, where she acquired citizenship. In January 1962, Colien came to West Germany and took up residence in Frankfurt. She immediately applied for an expellee card, but her application was rejected by the city authorities, as was her first administrative appeal. When Colien took her case to the city's administrative court, she finally received the desired card. The city authorities appealed against this ruling at the Administrative Court of Hesse, but the verdict stood. Valentina Colien was recognized as an ethnic German expellee.

The final ruling of the state court reveals important insights into the workings of the bureaucratic and legal ethnic recognition process that regulated access to expellee status. Its reconstruction of the arguments brought forward on different levels of jurisdiction reveals an act of self-fashioning by Colien that served to prove to the courts that she had lived in Romania "as a German" and was thus entitled to an expellee card. This act of performing Germanness intensified as the case progressed through different levels of appeal and as Colien added detail to her life story to overcome the different courts' doubts. Already when submitting her application, she pointed to a range of biographical factors to substantiate the claim that she had lived in Romania as an ethnic German: Her mother descended from an Austrian family from Czernowitz; she and her sister had been educated "in the German manner" (*im deutschen Sinne erzogen worden*); at home, they spoke only German; outside home, she tried to speak as much German as possible; she attended German schools in Bucharest; and after the war, she tried to obtain permission to emigrate from Romania to Germany several times. These statements were confirmed by the affidavits of two other immigrants from Romania, Manuel Fuhrmann and Rivka Calmanovici.

Colien's original application was rejected because the city authorities believed that she was lacking a *Bekenntnis* to German *Volkstum*. The affidavits were considered too vague, and her German descent, the use of the German language, and attending German schools were deemed insufficient, especially since she had married a Romanian—a familiar theme from the external recognition practice among Germans from Yugoslavia. Colien appealed this decision. In her appeal, she provided two more affidavits. When this appeal was met with no success, she turned to the Administrative Court of the City of Frankfurt. There, she repeated the evidence she had already brought forward and added the following details: She participated regularly in German cultural events; she always read the German newspaper published in Bucharest; she was a member of a German gymnastic club (*Turnverein*); she owned a fashion parlor in Bucharest, and almost all her customers were German, because her German ethnicity was well known in town; she brought up her son Siegfried "in the German manner" and had obtained for him a private instructor, an ethnically German woman from the Banat; until he was seven, Siegfried spoke only German.

This evidence presented at court illustrates how Colien added to her self-biography to create a picture of her life as a German in Bucharest. Everything she did supposedly revolved around her German ethnicity—her fashion parlor, her cultural life, her membership in the most German of all associations, a *Turnverein,* and her son having the most German of names, Siegfried. Even so, the city authorities remained unconvinced and brought up another argument. Not only was she lacking a *Bekenntnis* and thus could not be considered German, they also claimed that she had left Romania because of the overall political situation rather than because of her alleged ethnicity. They based this on a statement she had made in front of a refugee authority in Frankfurt, where she declared that she was dissatisfied with the communist regime in Romania. According to this interpretation, familiar from chapter 1, leaving one's home country *as* a German was supposed to mean *because of* being German. And declaring an anticommunist stance was taken as evidence against the causal link between emigration and Germanness.[53]

Of course, Valentina Colien—or most likely her team of lawyers, which included Henry Ormond, a prominent legal representative of Jewish Holocaust survivors and participant in the first Auschwitz trial—were aware of this alleged contradiction between generic anticommunist politics and specific German suffering.[54] Therefore, she specified that what she had originally meant was that she had troubles with the communist system *because of* her public identification as German and because of her attempts to migrate to West Germany. To stay in Romania, she would have had to deny her German ethnicity, which she refused to do. Colien further stated that she had become increasingly isolated in Romania, because all her German friends had left—an allusion to the notion that the "solitarization" (*Vereinsamung*) that the Germans left behind suffered as a consequence of the general expulsion was part of their ongoing oppression and justified their treatment as expellees.[55]

The Frankfurt court's interpretation of the evidence presented by Valentina Colien contrasted with previous decisions of the local authorities. The judges agreed that she had been an ethnic German in Romania. In light of the evidence she gave about her close ties to German *Volkstum*, the court argued, it was not evident that she did not feel as a German, thus giving her the benefit of the doubt. In the court's opinion, an ethnic German could be someone who, back in the homeland, did not suppress or deny her ties to German *Volkstum* and set up her whole lifestyle accordingly. Moreover, the judges held the exact reasons why Colien left to be irrelevant. Thus, the administrative court of Frankfurt interpreted the same facts that had led the expellee administration to deny Colien's claim to German ethnicity in the exactly opposite way and decided she had been a declared German all along. Indeed, given their expectation to find somebody who had set up her whole lifestyle according to her ties to German *Volkstum*, they were satisfied with the evidence that Colien put forward.

Despite the Frankfurt court's decision in favor of the plaintiff, the city authorities did not relent. Although they now accepted the verdict that Colien had been a German back in Romania, they insisted that she should have left Romania *because of* her Germanness, and not because of her general dissatisfaction with the communist regime. Therefore, the case went to the superior Administrative Court of Hesse. There, Colien claimed that the exact reasons for her emigration from Romania were irrelevant, given that her German *Volkstum* had been established by the Frankfurt court. Nevertheless, she added that she had indeed left Romania because of her German ethnicity. Further evidence was gathered to reconstruct the circumstances of her departure. Another witness was heard in court, and Colien testified herself. She claimed that she had already applied for emigration from Romania to West Germany in 1948, then in 1953, 1955, and 1958.[56] In 1960, she was finally allowed to leave, but only to France, where she had relatives. From there she moved on to Israel, where she had to care for a sick aunt. When the aunt died, Colien immediately left the country for the FRG in January 1962.

The state court upheld the city court's decision in favor of Valentina Colien. In its ruling, the judges first concurred with the city court that Colien had lived in Romania "as an ethnic German." Once again, they positively evaluated all the evidence from her life story and found further corroborating evidence in the fact that she had credibly claimed to have brought up her son in a German way. In the judges' view, the boy's name, Siegfried, supported this claim. Her repeated attempts to leave Romania for Germany could also be seen as evidence for a *Bekenntnis* to German *Volkstum*. Even so, the judges did not agree with the view that this was enough to justify the status of ethnic German expellee. Like the city authorities, they also insisted on the necessity of a causal link between Colien's emigration and her Germanness. Yet contrary to the city authorities, they saw this link as given. Her repeated attempts to obtain permission to leave for Germany, despite all the difficulties this caused, were seen as evidence that she did not want to stay in Romania precisely because she identified herself as German. Neither her immigration to France, nor her stay in Israel spoke against this. Nor did the fact that she had acquired Israeli citizenship—according to her own testimony, this happened at the initiative of the Israeli authorities. Finally, Colien's generally anticommunist stance and her claim to have left Romania because of her German identity were seen as complementary rather than mutually exclusive. In this view, as she repeatedly applied for permission to leave Romania (because of her Germanness), the communist authorities made her life increasingly difficult—in this way the circle closed. In the words of the state court judges: "The very fact that she felt as a German and gave expression to this feeling by repeated applications for emigration had to have the effect that she rejected the political conditions in Romania."[57]

At the end of this multilevel dialogue between authorities, courts, and the plaintiff, Valentina Colien had successfully performed her German *Volkszugehörigkeit*. She was recognized as an ethnic German after convincing two courts that her entire life in Romania had revolved around her Germanness and that she had left Romania because of this ethnic identity. Even her opposition to the communist regime was supposedly derived from her being German, which for the German court had to be the prime motivation for all her actions. Remarkably, however, Colien's Jewish background was not discussed or even referred to at any point in this court matter. The only way that it can be understood from the ruling that Colien was Jewish is from the fact that she received Israeli citizenship while in Tel Aviv. As will be discussed below, as the number of Jewish applicants for expellee cards increased, the Jewish faith and its implications for German *Volkszugehörigkeit* became the object of more explicit controversy.

On a side note, it should be pointed out that it is neither possible nor important to know to what extent everything that Valentina Colien told the German bureaucrats and judges was true. There is no archival record of the documentation she provided to support her claims, nor does she have an entry in the ITS archives. Even assuming that everything she told the court about her life was true, it is remarkable how such details from a doubtlessly eventful life were streamlined to paint a picture of a true German identity. This becomes even more remarkable when reading between the lines and taking into consideration the parts of Colien's biography that she obviously left out. Especially the court's matter-of-fact statement that she lived in Czernowitz at the beginning of the Second World War raises considerable questions. When the city came back under Romanian control in June 1941 (after having been annexed by the Soviet Union in June 1940), more than 30,000 Jews were deported to Transnistria by the Romanian authorities in autumn 1941 and summer 1942.[58] Valentina Colien may have been one of them. If she stayed in Czernowitz, she lived in continuous fear of being deported or murdered. Perhaps she was among the 12,000 Jews who were saved by the intervention of mayor Traian Popovici.[59] Possibly she was interned and had to perform forced labor, like her witnesses Manuel Fuhrmann and Rivka Calmanovici.[60] The court verdict does not say anything about this, presumably because Colien did not mention anything in this regard. A story of suffering at the hands of Germans would have only disturbed her claim to German identity and *Volkszugehörigkeit.*

The Declarative Model: The Case of Chocolate Manufacturer Josef Floris

Valentina Colien's recognition as a German was not the last Jewish case to be examined by German courts—on the contrary. Soon after, in April 1967, the Federal Administrative Court (*Bundesverwaltungsgericht*), the highest court in administrative matters, ruled on three Jewish cases on the same day.[61] One of them was the case of chocolate manufacturer Josef Floris from Budapest, whom we encountered in the introduction to this book. It will be analyzed here in greater detail, because it constituted a landmark case for the reinforcement of the declarative model of proving German identification. Floris's ambiguous life story defied the streamlining that Valentina Colien had successfully employed in her battle with the courts. But it is this very ambiguity that makes Floris's case an exceptional illustration of how the legal system allocated identity through the practice of requiring proof of *Bekenntnis*. The first guiding principle that the Federal Administrative Court extracted from this case defined the *Bekenntnis* as a certain "behavior that gave expression to the conscience and the will to belong *to one particular and no other Volkstum* in a way that it could be perceived by a third party."[62] According to the second guiding principle, declarations of ethnic belonging in official contexts were the main indicator of a *Bekenntnis.*[63] It was precisely this reinforced claim of exclusiveness in conjunction with the reference to "official contexts" and hence the classifications and definitions of another state that made it particularly hard for Jewish applicants to prove their *Bekenntnis* to German *Volkstum*, especially if their vita was as ambiguous as this one.

The plaintiff, whose family name at birth was Steiner, was born to Jewish parents in Budapest in 1905. In court, he claimed German to be his native tongue, after having previously stated Hungarian. Steiner attended an evangelical grammar school in Budapest and converted to Catholicism in 1943. In 1944, he was deported to Mauthausen concentration camp. Following the camp's liberation, Steiner returned to Budapest in 1945. There, he changed his family name from Steiner to Floris, which was the name of the chocolate factory he had co-owned before the war. This factory was nationalized in 1949. In 1957, Floris and his wife, Elisabeth, left with official permission for Israel, from where they moved on to Wilhelmshaven in Germany in July 1958. In 1959, they moved to Munich, before settling in the Bavarian town of Forchheim in 1960, where Floris worked for the Piasten chocolate factory.[64]

In contrast to Valentina Colien's case, Floris's application for an expellee card was unsuccessful in both the administration and in two court hearings. In the second court hearing, the Bavarian Administrative Court argued that Floris had not made a *Bekenntnis* to German *Volkstum* back in Hungary. Although his parents might have been part of the "German linguistic and cultural sphere" (*deutscher Sprach- und Kulturkeis*)—as he claimed—and his ancestors might have come from German-speaking lands, this did not mean that they *were* Germans. Liberal Jews in interwar Hungary had cherished German language and culture, but, the court argued, this attitude resulted from a "cosmopolitan stance" (*weltbürgerliche Haltung*) and was not indicative of a person's "conscience and will to be German and to belong to no other people."[65] In this court's view, the plaintiff had not publicly identified himself as German. Rather, he had tried twice—once without success, then successfully—to change his German-sounding surname, Steiner, into the neutral-sounding Floris. The reasons for these actions were arguably economic (only by assuming this name could he continue using the brand name after the war, when the real Floris moved to England), yet the name change made clear that he did not value his German appearance in name. In the Bavarian court's view, Floris's emigration from Hungary had also been for economic reasons. Moreover, his wife, Elisabeth, was not clearly German either, even though she credibly stated that her maternal language was German and that she had been a member of the Mozart cultural association in Budapest, where she used to sing German songs and where she met her husband, with whom she always spoke German. She supposedly also lacked the *Bekenntnis*.[66]

Figure 3.1. Advertising poster for Floris chocolate manufacturers (Floris cukrászda), Budapest, 1929.
Magyar Kereskedelmi és Vendéglátóipari Múzeum (CC BY-NC-SA).

The Federal Administrative Court, as the highest court of revision, did not pass a clear verdict of its own on the case. It merely decided that the arguments used at the preceding level of jurisdiction to reject the plaintiff's claims were flawed and that new evidence had to be gathered. At the same time, it validated some of the general claims of the court of appeal. In the verdict, the judges first recalled the principle that, to be recognized as an ethnic German expellee, one needed to provide both a subjective *Bekenntnis* and fulfill certain objective criteria: descent, language, upbringing, culture. Crucially, they argued that the presence of the objective criteria did not and could not simultaneously constitute the subjective *Bekenntnis*; the two sets of criteria had to be conceptualized as legally distinct. Confusion might arise from the fact that the Federal Restitution Law (*Bundesentschädigungsgesetz*) contented itself with the applicant's belonging to the German linguistic and cultural sphere. However—and here they concurred with the lower court—this had no impact on the Federal Expellee Law, which always required a *Bekenntnis*. The federal judges went on to argue that this emphasis on subjective identification was in fact derived from the historical knowledge that in the multiethnic states of interwar Eastern Europe, people were identified as belonging to the one or the other ethnicity by personal declaration. This declaration had to result from "the conscience and the will to be German and to belong to no other people, and it had been made with the aim to be considered and treated as a German back in the homeland."[67] This statement implied that the applicant's German identity had to be observable by a third party. At which occasions this might have been the case—in national censuses, at the issuing of passports, when entering military service, and so on—was to be investigated by the examining court through the study of relevant historiography, by seeking expert advice, or from other suitable sources. Anyone who had stated any other nationality at these occasions could not be considered an ethnic German.[68]

In essence, the Federal Administrative Court thus argued that the mere fact that someone spoke German did not indicate that he or she identified as German. What was necessary was an explicit and observable self-identification as German, which had to be confirmed, for example, by knowledge of the German language. The judges admitted that providing suitable evidence for such an observable *Bekenntnis* caused great difficulties but that they could be overcome. If necessary, the examining court would have to make a decision based on an evaluation of the plaintiff's "overall behavior" (*Würdigung des Gesamtverhaltens*).[69]

Throughout this process, the "Mosaic faith" of the plaintiff should be irrelevant, because it was interpreted only as a religious confession, not as a

Volkstum. The Jewish confession should only be taken into consideration if it had caused the applicant to deny her or his German *Volkstum* in reaction to the propagation of National Socialist ideology among the German ethnic group (*Volksgruppe*) in the country of origin. If this was the case, the *Bekenntnis* to German *Volkstum* would have to be proven for a point in time before National Socialism could have factored in—that is, before 1933. Since none of these potentially decisive bodies of evidence had been looked for in the preceding hearings, the Federal Administrative Court sent the case back to the previous court, the Bavarian Administrative Court.[70] Based on new evidence, that court eventually recognized Floris as a German expellee in October 1968.[71]

The Federal Administrative Court verdict in the Floris case is instructive despite its inconclusiveness. There is enormous tension between the court's request for clarity and the ambiguity of the case. As quoted above, making a *Bekenntnis* to German *Volkstum* meant expressing "the conscience and the will to be German and *to belong to no other people*." This definition was based on a historical argument about the situation in Central and Eastern European states during the interwar period. Needless to say, it was completely at odds with the vita of an applicant like Floris, which was full of ambiguities and creative adaptation to different circumstances that defied the streamlining that Valentina Colien had managed for her own biography (though obviously also at the cost of a dramatic reduction of complexity). Precisely for that reason it does not seem to be so untypical for that time, that place, and, in this particular case, that class of society. Born a Hungarian Jew with a German name, Steiner/Floris attended a Christian school, changed his religious creed and his name, and apparently felt equally familiar in the Hungarian and German cultures and languages. Despite his conversion to Catholicism, he managed to immigrate to Israel—a phenomenon that in another instance described below caused headaches in Israeli courts—but then preferred to come to Germany.

It is no coincidence that it was such a messy Central European case that led to the strong affirmation of the *Bekenntnis* requirement as an explicit and official statement. As already explained in chapter 1, the very notion of *Volkszugehörigkeit* defined via self-avowal originated in this region, as Habsburg administrative courts and imperial officials and statisticians grappled with the question of how to determine individual belonging to one of the empire's officially recognized ethnic groups (*Volksstämme* or *Nationalitäten*). In Austrian jurisdiction and administrative practice, the relationship between subjective *Bekenntnis* and objective criteria like language and hence the question of whether nationality should be subjectively chosen or objectively ascribed always remained contested.[72]

The situation was hardly clearer in the multiethnic successor states, where national identification and linguistic usage still did not necessarily coincide. In her history of German-Jewish relations in interwar Romania, historian Hildrun Glass recounts significant examples to illustrate this point. One example is that the German *Autonomiepartei* in the Banat initially conducted its meetings in Hungarian, while the opening speech of the 1922 Zionist congress in Arad was held in German.[73] Neither the states nor interwar minority activists in different countries could definitively state which criterion should be decisive, because they were both potentially too exclusive and too inclusive at the same time. From the viewpoint of minority activists, a pure *Bekenntnis* nationality would potentially leave out nationally indifferent German speakers, while possibly inviting opportunistic identifications with the German nation. A single-minded focus on language would exclude self-identified Germans who did not speak German while including German-speaking Jews, who, in the increasingly anti-Semitic climate of the time, were not necessarily welcome additions to the ranks of the German minorities. The fact that many people—including Floris—could speak several languages equally well further complicated the use of language as a criterion. When objective circumstances were so chaotic, subjective declaration seemed like the only way out of the multicultural predicament.

The definition of *Volkszugehörigkeit* chosen for the Federal Expellee Law, which in this form was first coined by the Nazis to deal with the confusingly mixed and ambiguous population of the Czech protectorate, combined all these elements: subjective identification with a certain *Volkstum,* supported by objective criteria that were to be assessed by "experts."[74] In the Floris case, the experts were judges who gave both the subjective and the objective criteria a peculiar interpretation. By emphasizing the subjective *Bekenntnis* having to have been observable by a third party and uttered in an official context, the judges moved away from key postulates of the 1958 commentary to the Federal Expellee Law quoted earlier. Explaining the definitions of section 6, the commentators, all of whom were officials in the Bavarian Labor Ministry, stated that it was not decisive for the application of the law whether a person had been considered German by the state authorities in the country of origin.[75] The judges' emphasis on identification in official contexts seemed to suggest the opposite. Moreover, the commentators argued that "the *Bekenntnis* does not have to have been explicit. It is sufficient if the person in question has demonstrated through conclusive actions that he is a member of the German linguistic and cultural sphere and hence of German *Volkstum*."[76] In the Floris verdict, these cultural and ethnic spheres of belonging were explicitly defined as incongruent.

This separation of German culture and German *Volkstum* corresponded to certain underlying views on historical understandings of German nationality, which affected the assessment of Floris's belonging. By stating that the liberal and educated Jews of Hungary spoke German as a consequence of their cosmopolitan stance—here obviously constructed as antithetical to being German—the Bavarian administrative judges retrospectively delegitimized the imperial Habsburg notion of German as a supranational language of culture and civilization. Instead, they embraced the post-Habsburg "provincialized" (and indeed *völkisch*) view of German culture as being the authentic expression of the identity of a particular German *Volksgruppe*.[77] The Federal Administrative Court did not disagree with this conception, which already in the past had not corresponded to the social reality of multilingual hybrids like the chocolate manufacturer Steiner/Floris.

Neutrality of the "Mosaic Faith?"

While the previous two cases are enlightening in a discussion of the different performative and declarative methods of assessing German *Volkszugehörigkeit* in legal contexts, neither of them addresses the fundamental problem at the heart of many Jewish cases: the impact of the Jewish religion—or, as the official terminology in legal contexts referred to it, the "Mosaic faith"—on the assessment of an applicant's German *Volkszugehörigkeit*. The judges in the Floris case only broached this matter when they argued that the applicant's Mosaic faith should be deemed irrelevant when assessing his overall behavior "as German." This supposedly neutral role of the Jewish religion in matters of German *Volkstum* was at the center of another high court ruling in March 1968.[78] It also concerned an Eastern European Jewish immigrant, in this case from Łódź in Poland, who had already come to West Germany in 1954. The man was denied expellee status on several levels of jurisdiction, including the Federal Administrative Court. In the ruling, the relationship of Jewish religion and German *Volkszugehörigkeit* was discussed extensively.

In this case, too, the discussion revolved around the notion of *Bekenntnis*. The plaintiff argued that the judges on the lower levels of jurisdiction had misconceived the way in which a Jew could state a *Bekenntnis* to German *Volkstum* in Poland. The Federal Court rebutted this argument by affirming that, since religious confession was neutral for the assessment of ethnic belonging, the standards for a Jewish applicant could not be lower than in any other case. Hence, an explicit *Bekenntnis* was still necessary. This case involved the plaintiff's parents' *Bekenntnis*, because he had been only eleven years old in

1933—the decisive deadline for a Jew to prove a *Bekenntnis*. But, again, the court did not see any conclusive evidence. In the judges' opinion, the parents' attendance of German schools, the use of German as a family language, the German family name, the mother's German maiden name, and the fact that the plaintiff himself had allegedly been called "Jecke" (a mock term for a German Jew) by his peers did not count as a *Bekenntnis* because they did not present a definitive statement before a third party to be treated as Germans and Germans only.

Declaring the Jewish religion neutral on these premises amounted to discrimination under the guise of equality. The plaintiff captured the essence of the problem when he highlighted the difficulties that a Jew faced when trying to fulfill any of the criteria that would count as a *Bekenntnis* to German *Volkstum* under German law. Membership in a German organization or a German club, for example, would have counted, especially if the club in question checked the German ethnicity of its members. But even though the courts recognized that a Jew's *Bekenntnis* to German *Volkstum* could be expected only until 1933, rather than until 1945, it seems that it did not occur to the judges that Jewish membership in German *Volkstum* associations in Central or Eastern Europe may have been problematic even before that time.[79] Moreover, as was noted in a similar Polish-Jewish verdict six years later, it had to be an "association that pursued *Volkstum* political aims or engaged at least in cultural politics with a *Volkstum* tendency."[80] A chess club in Kraków that admitted Germans exclusively was therefore not relevant for the assessment of the German *Bekenntnis*, because "the game of chess is a hobby and has no relation to *Volkstum*."[81] In contrast to this logic, Chad Bryant notes, for instance, that Czech local officials in Prague who tried to identify Germans for expulsion after the Second World War resorted to lists of German theater subscribers, many of whom were in fact Jewish.[82] The *Volkstum* value of participation in cultural associations was thus by no means fixed, but always tended to be interpreted to the individual's disadvantage. Given the restrictive interpretation chosen by the West German administrative judges deciding on the mentioned cases, a Jew originating from interwar Eastern Europe had limited possibilities to prove his or her avowal to German *Volkstum* in a way that would have been acceptable to German bureaucracy and German courts 30 or 40 years later.

As already seen in the case of Isidor B. at the beginning of this chapter, belonging to the Mosaic faith was also not neutral when it was taken to indicate an individual's belonging to a Jewish minority in an ethno-national sense. The identification of Jewish religion with Jewish nationality could be another significant hurdle for Jewish applicants for German expellee status, especially if they originated from Romania. This issue, too, was deliberated in depth at court. Like many other Jewish cases, Joel Glinert's case made it to the highest level of administrative jurisdiction, the Federal Administrative Court. Glinert was born in Gura Humorului, Bukovina, in 1895. He was deported to Transnistria in October 1941 and performed forced labor in the Morafa, Trichati, and Nikolaev labor camps.[83] He returned to Bukovina in 1944 and emigrated from Romania to Israel in 1950. In 1962, he submitted a request for compensation under the Equalization of Burdens Act (*Lastenausgleichsgesetz*), which was conditional on his German citizenship or *Volkszugehörigkeit* according to the Federal Expellee Law.[84] This request was denied by the administration, and Glinert went to court.

Even though Glinert's case was not related to immigration, it is relevant for this discussion, because the assessment of *Volkszugehörigkeit* for compensation under the *Lastenausgleichsgesetz* followed the definitions of the BVFG and had repercussions for immigrants' applications for expellee status. On the first level of jurisdiction, the Bremen administrative court upheld the administrative rejection of Glinert's request in May 1967 with a remarkable justification that rendered the alleged neutrality of faith explicitly obsolete.[85] The judges argued that, since the beginning of the twentieth century, Jewish national ideas aimed at the separation of the Jewish and German *Volksgruppen* had spread widely throughout Bukovina. They based their assessment on a historical opinion by Martin Broszat (the future head of the Munich Institute for Contemporary History) as well as a two-volume German-language history of the Jews of the Bukovina published by historian and publisher Hugo Gold in Tel Aviv in 1962.[86] In light of this historical assessment, the court disregarded the applicant's German education and use of the German language and demanded that Glinert, whom they identified as a "Jew" in the ruling, provide evidence that he did not identify as a Jew in the national sense. With such an approach, religion was clearly not neutral, as it implied ethno-national belonging.

The Federal Administrative Court did not uphold this complete identification of Jewish religion and nationality. In its revision of the case in October 1968, it overturned the Bremen court's decision, arguing that "the creation or the existence of a Jewish minority does *not* justify the assumption that a persecuted Jew did *not* belong to German *Volkstum*."[87] With this double negation, the judges postulated that, just because Jews were generally recognized as a national group in a certain region, such as Bukovina, this did not mean that every person with a Jewish religious affiliation should automatically be considered a Jew in a national sense as well. While the court later specified in a different ruling that this did not mean, in turn, that German-speaking Jewish applicants should generally be considered German if they had not identified with another *Volkstum*, the 1968 ruling was nevertheless a significant move away from the Bremen court's approach according to which Jewish religious affiliation prejudiced Jewish national affiliation.[88] Nevertheless, as some of the arguments quoted in Isidor B.'s case indicate, the relationship between Jewish religion and nationality could be interpreted differently on the administrative level even afterward. When an administrator took a stance like the North Baden Regional Council did regarding Isidor B. and argued for the almost complete identity of Jewish religion and nationality as well as for the "natural attachment" of individuals to their ethnic groups, "German Jews" could appear only as an anomaly. In the decentralized recognition procedures of the internal gate, these views could prevail despite high-level jurisdiction intending the contrary. Consequently, the issue of Jewish applicants for German expellee status remained contentious throughout the following two decades.

JEWS, GERMANS, AND THE PLEBISCITE OF *BEKENNTNIS*

Two models for assessing an applicant's claim to German *Volkszugehörigkeit* have emerged from the above analyses of the Colien and Floris cases: a performative model and a declarative model. Both the performance and the declaration refer to the way in which the court attributed the required *Bekenntnis* to German *Volkstum* to each candidate—that is, the public and unequivocal self-identification as German. For Valentina Colien, performing Germanness implied arranging details from her life story in a certain way and thereby attributing national meaning to them in an attempt to convince the judges that she was the bearer of a genuine and publicly known German identity and that she had lived in and departed from Romania as a German.

This performative dimension of German refugee law has been addressed by anthropologist Stefan Senders in the context of Russian German Aussiedler migration in the 1990s. Based on a close reading of an administrative court ruling in another co-ethnic case, Senders noted a narrative of "likeness" or "similarity" produced by the court, and he used the category of "mimesis" to describe it. In Senders's words, "mimesis can be analysed in terms of the organisation and evaluation of identifications and perceived resemblance among people and between people and identity categories."[89] What mattered in this framework was not so much one's "ethnic descent" (erroneously identified in the article title as *jus sanguinis*) but one's performed resemblance with preconceived identity categories.

In contrast, the judges' insistence in the Floris case on an explicit declaration as his *Bekenntnis* put significant constraints on the performative dimension of

Germanness. While they allowed for inferences from the applicant's overall behavior, someone with a twisting and turning life story like that of the chocolate manufacturer from Budapest had little chance for a successful performance, given that mere knowledge of the German language and partaking in German culture were not deemed sufficient. Asking for an explicit declaration of Germanness—for example, in an official census or a document—seemed to be one way to avoid the difficult task of extracting an unambiguous *Bekenntnis* from ambiguous life stories.

While this demand for explicit self-identification supposedly facilitated the work of the administration and the courts, in the other cases discussed here—the anonymous "Jecke" from Łódź and Joel Glinert from the Bukovina—it did not solve two problems that applicants of the Jewish faith had to confront. First, their life stories were likely to be different from predefined "normal" ethnic German trajectories, which were expected to include membership in German *Volkstum* associations during the interwar period, among other things. According to the Federal Administrative Court, an applicant's Jewish religion could not lead to lower requirements in this regard despite the fact that, in the past, it had effectively lowered the person's chances of participating in any such organization. Second, their Jewish religion might have led to their classification as Jews in the national sense in their Eastern European state of origin, in which case German bureaucrats and judges might rule out their simultaneous belonging to the German minority. As noted earlier, in some instances, this was even taken for granted by the German authorities. Either way, then, belonging to the Jewish religion lowered one's chances of being recognized as a German in the present, precisely because this had already been practiced in the past.

The issue of whether an explicit declaration of *Bekenntnis* was indispensable in Jewish cases, and to what extent Jewish religion affected German *Volkszugehörigkeit*, remained contentious throughout the 1970s. In line with past definitions, such as the one given by the BVFG commentary in 1958, the 1980 ethnicity guidelines for the refugee administration stipulated that the *Bekenntnis* could result from either an explicit declaration or "conclusive behavior" (section 2.2), thus allowing for the declarative and the performative models.[90] In a similar vein, in December 1981, the Federal Constitutional Court affirmed the principle that cumulated objective criteria could indicate a *Bekenntnis*.[91] In addition, section 2.2 of the ethnicity guidelines stipulated that it should not be held against the applicant if his or her environment did not assess this *Bekenntnis* by "conclusive behavior" correctly. Similarly, section 2.5, which explicitly regulated the recognition of Jewish applicants, stated that the exclusion of Jews in the past should not be repeated in the present by disadvantaging individual applicants. In effect, this meant that just because a Jewish person was not perceived as German in the anti-Semitic climate of the interwar period, this should not mean that she or he could not be a German *Volkszugehöriger* now. The guidelines thus tried to facilitate the performance of Germanness for Jewish applicants.

On a more general note, the overriding importance of public self-identification in the legal definition of a German, which has become evident in this chapter through the analysis of Jewish borderline cases, confounds the stereotypical idea that the postwar German conception of nationhood was ethno-cultural—that is, based on descent and culture. In fact, the decisive criterion for admission into German nationhood via German expellee law was neither descent nor the mere partaking in German language and culture. Rather, it was public identification: *Bekenntnis*. Both descent and culture were merely auxiliary criteria. Ironically, then, the definition of German *Volkszugehörigkeit* according to the Federal Expellee Law, which emerged from the specific context of Habsburg and post-Habsburg Central Europe, was closer to an ideal-type "Renanian" definition of nationhood as a "daily plebiscite" than to the notion of a "community of descent." *Bekenntnis*-based *Volkszugehörigkeit* was thus a distinctly "civic" notion of belonging.[92] What the authorities and courts wanted was nothing less than a continued public plebiscite for the German nation to be seen and understood by all.

At the same time, it was precisely the overriding importance of the plebiscitary dimension of national belonging that made it more difficult for Jewish applicants to be recognized as Germans. Based on a purely cultural definition, most of them would, in fact, have been able to gain recognition without much trouble, because they could easily prove their belonging to the German linguistic and cultural sphere.[93] But this type of belonging was not identical with German *Volkszugehörigkeit* in the legal sense, which, as commentators on the law pointed out time and again, was also not to be confused with the ethnological notion of Germanness.[94] Belonging to the German linguistic and cultural sphere was sufficient for recognition according to the Federal Restitution Law but not for the purposes of the Federal Expellee Law with its requirement of a *Bekenntnis*.[95]

The Jewish Aussiedler cases thus underscore that even a civic, plebiscitary notion of national belonging does not necessarily imply a free vote. One reason for this is the intersubjective way that *Bekenntnis* was conceptualized. The identification as German had to have been properly understood by others in the past. It also needed to be deemed acceptable by "experts"—authorities and judges—several decades later, adding a strong ascriptive component.

Acceptance of the vote was thus conditional. A second reason involved the very structure of a compulsory plebiscite. Like most plebiscites, the question of national self-identification prestructures the voters' answer by offering a fixed set of mutually exclusive choices—in the present case, German or not German. It does not allow for hybridity and multiple loyalties, which characterized the social reality of the geographic space that German expellee law referred to and, in particular, the life stories of the individuals discussed here.

Nor did the national plebiscite allow for any indifference once it became compulsory in a nationalizing context. As Tara Zahra has pointed out for the late Habsburg Empire and after, "national agnosticism [became] less viable, particularly in regions affected by the so-called national compromises of the early twentieth century (Moravia, Galicia, Bukovina). Once citizens were forced to register their nationality in order to exercise basic civil rights such as the right to vote or to a primary school education, remaining on the national sidelines was no longer simple. The collapse of the Habsburg empire into self-declared nation states in 1918 rendered the outright refusal of nationality nearly impossible."[96] People from these regions, like the Jews discussed in this chapter, were thus forced to choose their national identification on several occasions during their lifetime—or had it chosen for them, especially in the context of anti-Semitic persecution. Becoming migrants after the Second World War, they had to choose again, as the East–West migration regime was largely predicated on ethnic terms. At that point, their ambiguous position yielded options and room for maneuver, as they could go to Israel as Jews and then claim recognition in the FRG as Germans. Yet the way in which these claims were assessed in practice—namely, by examining these people's lives during the interwar period through a specific historical prism of a provincialized or even outright *völkisch* notion of Germanness—tied the ultimate decision about their national belonging back to a historical context where choices of identification were neither free nor unrestricted, especially for Jews.

A "CHRISTIAN JEW" IN ISRAEL

As the above discussion reveals, the German legal system and state administrations held two positions on the *Volkszugehörigkeit* of Jewish applicants. According to the first position, belonging to the Mosaic faith was defined as precisely that: membership in a religious community that was compatible with membership in the German national community. The second, opposed, view, understood belonging to the Mosaic faith as equivalent to, or at least strongly indicative of, membership in the Jewish nation and therefore incompatible with membership in another national community (in this case, the German nation).

In Israel, a similar, if reversed question arose: To what extent could Jewish religion and Jewish ethno-national belonging be separated in the Jewish state? Whereas the German lawyers and administrators asked whether a Jew by religion could also be of a nationality other than Jewish, in Israel, the question was whether a Jew by nationality could be of a religion other than Jewish. Following the gradual emancipation of the Jews in Europe in the second half of the nineteenth century, members of the Jewish religion were also defined as belonging to other nations. In the German case, their nationality was identified as *deutsche Staatsbürger jüdischen Glaubens*, or German citizens of the Jewish faith. By contrast, with the rise of Zionism during the first half of the twentieth century, Jewishness also came to be conceived of in ethno-national terms. As a consequence, the Zionist Yishuv in Palestine defined itself as a national community, which also corresponded to the spirit of the Balfour Declaration with its call for a "national home for the Jewish people" in Palestine.[97] In this context, the question was debated: Could there be a secular Jewish nationality independent of the Jewish religion? If so, what would its defining features be?

In 1911, the writer Yosef Chaim Brenner had already asserted the possibility that a "national Jew" could believe in other religions, including Christianity. For him, the key component of modern Jewish national identity was language.[98] In a similar and even more radical vein, the "Canaanites"—a 1940s fringe movement within the Jewish Yishuv in Palestine—believed in a "Hebrew" nation in the land of Israel distinct from the religiously defined Jewish diaspora.[99] Mainstream Zionism, by contrast, although based on modern Hebrew language and culture and secular in nature, still sought a connection with historical (religious) Judaism. This was one of the motivations for the 1947 status quo agreement between Ben-Gurion and the religious parties, which assigned a fixed role to Orthodox Judaism in the Israeli government and everyday life.[100] When the population registry was introduced in 1948, the term introduced to describe the ethno-nationality (*leom*) of the Jewish inhabitants of the new state was *yehudi* (Jewish) rather than *ivri* (Hebrew) or *yisraeli*. Jewish nationality and religion were thus supposed to coincide. The separate registration of the categories *Leom* and religion was relevant with regard to the Arab inhabitants of the country, who could be Muslim, Christian, or, before their recognition as a separate *Leom* in 1955, Druze.[101]

In 1962, the Brother Daniel case raised a controversial issue: Could a person who had been born a Jew and had a Zionist past and who converted to Christianity but continued to regard himself as a Jew in the national sense become a citizen of the Jewish nation-state by virtue of the Law of Return's stipulation that "every Jew has the right to immigrate to this country?" Two previously mentioned cases of Jewish-born converts to Christianity who immigrated to Israel did not trigger similar discussions, because they did not intend to stay. Convert George H. and his gentile wife, Alma Cornelia, whose Aliyah from Romania in 1958 was mentioned in chapter 1, soon after declared their intention to leave Israel again.[102] Similarly, chocolate manufacturer Floris from Budapest, who was born Jewish but later converted to Catholicism, left Hungary for Israel together with other Olim in 1957 but moved on to Germany in 1958.

Brother Daniel's case was different, because he intended to stay in Israel and press his case of recognition as a national Jew of the Catholic faith. Born Oswald Rufeisen in the village of Zadziele in formerly Austrian Silesia in 1922, his origin was, in fact, quite similar to that of some of the Jewish Aussiedler in Germany. Growing up in a Polish Jewish multilingual family that spoke German at home and cherished German culture, young Oswald was an active Zionist in the Akiva movement.[103] Like Isak and Anna Krieger from the nearby town of Bielsko, he succeeded in concealing his Jewish origins after the German invasion of Poland, successfully passing for a Christian Pole and actually working as an interpreter for the German police. To explain his German-sounding name and excellent knowledge of German, Rufeisen invented a cover story of having a German father and a Polish mother.[104] While this story would have also given him the chance to identify as ethnically German (*volksdeutsch*)—which some authors claimed he did—his biographer, Holocaust scholar Nechama Tec, points out that Rufeisen preferred to claim a Polish identity, since a claim to German status could have implied a more thorough background check by the German authorities.[105] In his function as a collaborator with the German police, he managed to save many of the inhabitants of the ghetto of Mir, Belarus, tipping them off about their impending mass execution and organizing their escape into the woods. Rufeisen was then arrested, but he managed to escape. He hid in a Catholic monastery and decided to convert to Catholicism. After the war, he became a monk. As a member of the Carmelite order, he moved to the Carmelite Stella Maris monastery in Haifa, where he applied for Israeli citizenship under the Law of Return, arguing that, despite his conversion to Christianity, he was still a Jew in the national sense. When his request was rejected, he turned to the Israeli Supreme Court.

The Brother Daniel case was decided by five judges of the Israeli Supreme Court: Moshe Silberg, Hermann Haim Cohn, Moshe Landau, Eliyahu Many, and Zvi Berenson.[106] Technically speaking, in their ruling they did not assess Rufeisen's individual Jewishness but rather made a more fundamental decision

Figure 3.2. Brother Daniel aka Oswald Rufeisen in 1980.
By Eli Dotan / Creative Commons Attribution-Share Alike 3.0 Unported License.

on what a Jew was according to the Law of Return—and in particular, whether this definition included someone who converted to another religion but still considered himself Jewish. Hence, both the relationship between Jewish ethnicity and religion and the right to a subjective identification as Jewish—known in previous discussions as the bona fide principle—were at stake here. With the exception of Cohn, all the judges concurred that Brother Daniel was not to be considered Jewish under their respective interpretations of the concept in the Law of Return. Silberg, Landau, Berenson, and Cohn developed their arguments in detail, while Many restricted his opinion to concurring with Silberg and Landau. The four formulated opinions provide insight into the different techniques that were used to assess the case, which substantially differed from the performative and declarative models applied by German administrative judges. Following up on the deliberations of the "Sages of Israel" a few years earlier, in which Silberg and Cohn had participated, the judges consciously strove to produce a secular meaning for the term *Jew* in the context of the secular Law of Return. Their opinions thus included fundamental considerations of Jewish history, the place of Zionism and the State of Israel in this history, and the significance of religion in this matter. Yet it will become clear that, in the end, the majority opinion hinged on one rather simple concept: intuition.

Moshe Silberg, an Orthodox Jew from Lithuania who had studied law in Frankfurt and Marburg, began his opinion by expressing his sympathy with and admiration for the applicant's courage during the war years.[107] Still, he considered his personal sympathy irrelevant, because, in his opinion, the petitioner requested nothing less than the negation of Jewish history:

> I have reached the conclusion that what Brother Daniel is asking us to do is to erase the historical and sanctified significance of the term "Jew" and to deny all the spiritual values for which our people were killed during various periods of our long dispersion. For us to comply with his request would mean to dim the lustre and to darken the glory of the martyrs who sanctified the Holy Name in the Middle Ages to the extent of making them quite unrecognizable; it would make our history lose its unbroken continuity and our people begin counting its days from the emancipation which followed the French Revolution. A sacrifice such as this no one is entitled to ask of us, even one so meritorious as the petitioner before this Court.[108]

After this dramatic historic introduction, Silberg went on to more prosaic matters and formulated the underlying legal question at stake: "What is the meaning of the expression 'Jew' as used in the Law of Return, 1950, and [does] it also include a Jew who has changed his religion even though he has been baptized as a Christian, and still feels and regards himself as a Jew in spite of his conversion?" Starting with the observation that, according to religious law, the applicant would still be considered Jewish despite his conversion, the judge delved into rabbinical discussions to make a simple point: "Were I of the opinion that the term 'Jew' as used in the Law of Return bears the identical meaning which it bears in the Rabbinical Courts Jurisdiction (Marriage and Divorce) Law, that is to say, a Jew as *interpreted according to Jewish religious law*, then I would agree to grant the application of the petitioner."[109]

But Silberg's take on the matter was different. In his search for a secular meaning of Jewishness, the judge introduced the notion of intuition: "In the Law of Return the term 'Jew' has a secular meaning, that is, as it is usually understood by the man in the street." Given the absence of a definition in the law itself, he argued, "We must interpret its terms according to their ordinary meaning, taking into consideration, if departing from the ordinary sense, the legislative purpose behind its provisions."

At this point, this "ordinary meaning" of the term *Jew* was determined in the most circular of ways: "Because the Law of Return is an Israeli statute, enacted in the Hebrew language, and not translated into Hebrew, it stands to reason that the term 'Jew' in that statute is to be interpreted as understood by Jews, for they are nearest to the subject matter of the Law, and who better than they can know the significance and meaning of the term 'Jew'?"[110] The tautological nature of this argument is obvious: Who knows better what a Jew is than a Jew, or, more precisely, "the ordinary Jew in the street?" Silberg had a clear answer what "the Jew in the street" thinks: "A Jew who has become a Christian is *not* called a 'Jew'."[111] While acknowledging the range of extremely diverse opinions in Israel, he claimed that "there is one thing that is shared by *all* Jews who live in Israel (save for a mere handful) and that is that we do not sever ourselves from our historic past and we do not deny our heritage."[112] He went on to elaborate his speculations about the feelings of "ordinary Jews" on the one hand and Brother Daniel on the other hand:

> Whatever national attributes may be possessed by a Jew living in Israel—whether he is religious, non-religious or anti-religious—he is bound, willingly or unwillingly, by an umbilical cord to historical Judaism from which he draws his language and its idiom, whose festivals are his own to celebrate, and whose great thinkers and spiritual heroes . . . nourish his national pride. *Would a Jew who has become a Christian be able to feel at home in all this?* Would he not see through different eyes, would he not regard in a different light, our draining to the dregs the bitter cup from which we drank so deeply in those dark Middle Ages? I have not the least doubt that Brother Daniel will love Israel. This he has proved. *But this brother's love will be from without*—the love of a brother far away. He will not be a true part of this Jewish world. His living in Israel in the midst of the Jewish community and his sincere affection for it cannot take the place of absolute identification that can only come from within and which is absent."[113]

Silberg hastened to underscore that this view did not imply turning Israel into a "theocratic state." The opposite was true, he claimed, since Brother Daniel would indeed be considered Jewish under religious law. The judge followed this reasoning with a longer outline of what he meant when he spoke of the opinion of "ordinary people." Quoting three scholarly books that postulated the indivisibility of Jewish religion and nationhood, he identified "the healthy instinct of the (Jewish) people and its thirst for survival" as being responsible for the "axiomatic belief" that a convert to Christianity can never be a Jew.

The final question Silberg addressed in his opinion was which nation Brother Daniel belonged to. His answer demonstrates a remarkable conflation of terminology: "He does not belong to the Jewish nation, nor to the Polish, for he gave up Polish nationality before leaving Poland. If so, to which nation is he to be registered as belonging in his identity card? The answer is to neither the one nor the other. Brother Daniel is a man without a nation."[114] At this point, Silberg revealed that he not only identified Jewish nationhood with Jewish religion but also conflated political nationality (Rufeisen's Polish citizenship) and ethnic nationality (the *Leom* to be registered in his ID card).[115] Rather than producing a secular conception of Israeli Jewishness, Silberg thus essentially reproduced a traditionalist notion of the Jews as an ethno-religious community.

Like Silberg, Moshe Landau, the Danzig-born and London-trained judge who had presided over the Eichmann trial the previous year, invoked Jewish history to justify his rejection of Brother Daniel's request.[116] Having uttered some doubt regarding Silberg's contention that Brother Daniel would be considered a Jew under religious law, he expressed his full agreement that the Law of Return was a secular law and hence that the legislature had to determine what was meant by the term *Jew*. Rather than hypothesizing what the man in the street was thinking, Landau reflected on the great thinkers and texts of Zionism: Theodor Herzl, Ahad Ha'am, and the Declaration of Independence. In all these sources, he identified religion as being of particular importance and, in fact, inseparable from the nation: "The meaning of this Law cannot be severed from the sources of the past from which its content is derived, and in these sources nationalism and religion are inseparably interwoven."[117] His conclusion was clear: "A Jew who, by changing his religion, severs himself from the national past of his people ceases therefore to be a Jew in the national sense to which the Law of Return was meant to give expression. [The petitioner] has denied his national past, and can no longer be fully integrated into the organized body of the Jewish community as such. By changing his religion he has erected a barrier between himself and his brother Jews, especially as this change has assumed so extreme a form as entering the gates of a monastery."[118]

Haim Cohn, the only dissenter on the panel and the most ardent secularist, agreed with Silberg's assessment of religious law, on the secular nature of the Law of Return, and the continuity of Jewish history and heritage.[119] Nevertheless, he rejected the conclusion that Brother Daniel should therefore not be considered Jewish. After developing a dynamic account of Jewish history in which continuity meant "to *build* on the foundations of the past" and in which "times have changed and the wheels have come full circle," he asked: "There comes now to the State of Israel a man who regards Israel as his fatherland and who craves to find fulfillment within its borders, but his religion is Christian. Shall we close the gates because of this?"[120]

Cohn's negative response to this question was based on sober legal deliberations. Since the Law of Return contained no religious qualification at all, "the Law must be construed and applied as it is and as it reads, without adding to or subtracting from the term 'Jew' any religious qualification."[121] A declaration of good faith, as it had been stipulated in the 1958 population registry guidelines (which Cohn had partly drawn up himself), should be sufficient. Hence, Cohn's conclusion: "Since the declaration of the petitioner that he is a Jew was accepted as a declaration in good faith—and in view of the material which was before the Minister of the Interior and which is before us it could not have been accepted otherwise—the petitioner is entitled to an immigration certificate under the Law of Return, and is entitled to be registered as a Jew by nationality in the Register of Inhabitants."[122]

The three opinions discussed thus far—whether negative (Silberg, Landau) or positive (Cohn)—had one thing in common: they expressed little, if any, interest in Brother Daniel himself. As stated from the outset, the discussion was on a matter of principle: Could a convert to Christianity be a Jew? Justice Cohn said yes, as long as the convert declared his Jewishness in good faith. Justices Silberg and Landau said no, surmising that Brother Daniel could not be a "true part" of the Jewish community and could not "feel at home" in it. Yet despite their arguments about the applicant's "feelings" and his "denial of his national past," none of the judges tried to reconstruct these feelings in a narrative akin to the one that the administrative judges in Hesse had developed for Valentina Colien.

Justice Zvi Berenson, a British-educated native of Palestine, was the only one on this panel of judges to engage with the petitioner's life story.[123] He, too, denied Brother Daniel's Jewishness, but the way he reached this conclusion is remarkably different than the way his colleagues did. Berenson started his opinion not with considerations of principle but by discussing Brother Daniel's biography—much the way a German administrative judge in search of a performative *Bekenntnis* would have done. The petitioner, Berenson wrote, had not converted to Christianity for the well-known opportunistic reasons that made other converts cut off their ties to the Jewish people. Quite the opposite: "An exceptional man, to whom material comforts and worldly pleasures have no attraction, he is a Jew by birth and as a Jew he grew up, suffered and conducted himself. And even after he embraced Christianity he did not reject his people. Of himself he says, and his history proves it, that in his consciousness he has remained a Jew in the national sense and he claims that in the Christian faith which he has embraced there is nothing that prejudices his belonging nationally to the Jewish people."[124]

After reporting some episodes from Oswald Rufeisen's/Brother Daniel's life and his heroic conduct during the war and the Shoah, the judge recounted that the petitioner had attempted to emigrate from Poland to Israel several times after the war, and in 1958 he finally obtained an entry visa for Israel. Berenson quoted Brother Daniel's application to the Polish authorities for a passport and an exit permit in full, "because it shows clearly that even after he became a Christian he never ceased, both by inner conviction and in external appearance, to regard himself as a national Jew who was bound heart and soul to the Jewish people."[125]

Indeed, Brother Daniel's petition to the Polish authorities would have satisfied all the criteria for a declarative *Bekenntnis* to the Jewish nationality, had there been such a thing:

> I base this application on the ground of my belonging to the Jewish people, to which I have continued to belong although I embraced the Catholic faith in 1942 and joined a monastic order in 1945. *I have made this fact clear whenever it has been raised with me officially, as, for instance, when I received my military papers and identity card.*
>
> I chose an Order which has a Chapter in Israel in consideration of the fact that I would receive the leave of my superiors to travel to the land for which I have yearned since my childhood when I was a member of a Zionist Youth Organization. *My national allegiance is known to the Church.*[126]

Doubtlessly, then, Brother Daniel had identified with the Jewish people as a national group in a way that could be perceived by a third party, both the Polish authorities and the Catholic church. As Justice Berenson further acknowledged, the Polish authorities gave him an exit permit that was usually given only to Jews making Aliyah to Israel. "This means that as far as the land of his birth is concerned *the petitioner has immigrated to Israel as a Jew* who has severed his links with Poland without leaving himself a way of return."[127]

On the basis of all these positive assessments, Berenson stated that was he to follow "his own inclination," he would recognize Brother Daniel as Jewish. But at this point, he introduced a "Silbergian" notion into his argument: "To my regret however I am not free to do so but have to construe the word 'Jew' as used in the Law of Return not as I would like to construe it myself but as I believe it to be understood by those who enacted the Law or, more correctly, *according to the meaning of that term in common parlance in our time.*"[128]

Despite this first element of doubt, Berenson continued arguing in the petitioner's favor also on the conceptual level. Coming close to Haim Cohn's position, Berenson rejected the use of "national and spiritual leaders, historians, and famous scholars" in support of either argument, because these opinions might have been valid in their time but were no longer applicable. Nevertheless, he put forward two Zionist authorities, Eliezer Ben Yehuda and Arthur Ruppin, to show that they defined nation without any reference to religion. He also asked a crucial question for Israel after the Holocaust: Could Israel refuse to recognize someone as a Jew who would have been killed as such by the Nazis?

By that point, Justice Berenson had established a well-crafted argument that, both with regard to the individual case and in principle, Brother Daniel should be recognized as a Jew. To remove all doubts, he even referred to Ahad Ha'am—whom Justice Landau had quoted to reject the petitioner's claim to Jewishness—to bolster his claim that a Jew who had changed his or her religion did not cease being part of the Jewish people. And yet Berenson dismissed his entire previous elaboration with one Silbergian move:

> The people themselves, however, because of a well developed sense of preservation, have believed differently and have behaved differently throughout the centuries. In their opinion a Jew who has embraced another religion has withdrawn himself not only from the Jewish faith but also from the Jewish nation, and has left no further room for himself amongst the Jewish people. . . . *Simple people could never conceive of anyone being a Jew and a Christian at one and the same time* and certainly not a Jew who was a Catholic priest—to them that would be a contradiction in terms.[129]

To reinforce this claim, Berenson quoted Moshe Sharett (then still Shertok) when he spoke before the United Nations Special Committee for Palestine on behalf of the Jewish Agency in 1947. Sharett had stated that it was essential in the definition of a Jew that she or he had "not gone over to another religion." Berenson gathered that this "embodied the opinion commonly held and there is nothing to show that any change has taken place on the question in Jewish opinion since then, which is but some fifteen years ago."[130] And so he came to a negative conclusion:

> My final conclusion therefore is that a Jew who has changed his religion cannot be considered a Jew in the sense intended by the Knesset when it used this term in the Law of Return and as this word is understood today by the people at large. I do not believe that we as judges are entitled to make innovations as pioneers and to determine today what looks certain to come about in due course of time. It is Law that follows Life and not Life that follows Law. . . . It will take a long time still, so it seems, before convictions change and that sense of grievance so deeply felt by the Jews for all the

> wrong that Christianity has done to their people, whose history is soaked with the blood of martyrs who died in order to sanctify the Holy Name, will disappear. Until that day dawns it is not possible to recognize the petitioner as a Jew for the purposes of the Law of Return.[131]

In Berenson's judgment, the difference in recognition techniques between Germany and Israel becomes evident. Constructing a cross-case counterfactual argument, it could be said that if the performative model or the declarative model of German *Volkszugehörigkeit* had been applied to Brother Daniel's case, as it was recounted by Justice Berenson, there would have been no doubt that the petitioner belonged to the Jewish people. He had demonstrated a credible *Bekenntnis*, and it was acknowledged that he had left Poland as a Jew. But unfortunately for Brother Daniel, neither of these models applied in his case. For Justices Silberg and Berenson, "Jewish opinion" and conceptions of "the people at large" were decisive.

The Rufeisen case thus suggests a third, intuition-based model of co-ethnic recognition typical for Israel. It postulated that the concept of Jew was best understood by Jews themselves, by the man in the street. This circular construction was the model's main drawback. In this way it was not unlike the halachic definition of a Jew: that only someone born of a Jewish mother could be a Jew. According to the intuition-based model, a Jew is a Jew because he or she is defined as such by other Jews. This definition had no answer to the question of what identified other Jews as Jewish. The halachic definition faced the same problem: a Jew is a Jew because she or he is born of a Jewish mother. However, that definition offers no explanation for what defines the mother as Jewish. In the case of Brother Daniel, neither of these problems was resolved. As discussed in chapter 1, the only solution the Israeli authorities had to these dilemmas were "kosher certificates," which in practice allocated the definition of a person's Jewishness to the Jewish religious authorities. Since such certificates were not readily available in Eastern Europe, the intuition-based model found its way into the instructions for Aliyah and registration offices, as will be seen in the next chapter. Recognizing a Jew could then amount to being simply a matter of (Jewish) intuition.

On a more general level, it must be noted that, despite their claims, the judges in the Brother Daniel case failed to produce a truly secular notion of Israeli Jewishness. Religion remained the make-or-break criterion that drew the ultimate line defining who was *not* a Jew.[132] Oswald Rufeisen's conversion to Christianity was deemed to have precluded his recognition as Jewish, making it the equivalent of a *Gegenbekenntnis*, as it were—that is, a renunciation of belonging. At that point, secular Jewishness was constructed *ex negativo*—but all the more emphatically—against Christianity as Judaism's great historical foe and oppressor. Against the backdrop of twenty-first-century notions of an allegedly shared Judeo-Christian civilization, this radically exclusive construction deserves to be highlighted.

As the cases analyzed in this chapter have shown, the gatekeepers of the immigration process—mainly courts—employed three techniques to assess the merit of applications made by people whose profiles did not accord with the ways a "normal" case was conceptualized: the performative model, the declarative model, and the intuition-based model. The first two techniques were used to assess claims to German *Volkszugehörigkeit* based on public self-identification (*Bekenntnis*) and were in fact not mutually exclusive. The tools used by the performative model included the narration of life story details in a way that would produce a narrative of credible German identity. The declarative model asked for explicit statements of German identification in official contexts, which, given the complex nature of the German definition of *Volkszugehörigkeit*, still needed to be supported by objective criteria. The latter were also a constitutive element of the performative model. The intuition-based model, by contrast, moved co-ethnic recognition into the realm of intuition—in this case, Jewish intuition about who is a Jew. In Brother Daniel's case, this intuition invalidated the results of the performative and declarative techniques that Justice Berenson had attempted. Brother Daniel publicly declared his Jewishness even after his conversion, he left Poland as a Jew, and he was born of two Jewish parents, but, as a convert to Christianity, Brother Daniel simply was not a Jew.

This last point calls attention to a more general phenomenon: the construction of belonging by co-ethnic immigration regimes against "problematic others." Because they were thinking in historical categories of the (European) Jewish diaspora, for the Supreme Court judges, this problematic other was Christianity. Even in the Jewish state, a Jew was therefore someone who was not Christian. As will be discussed in chapter 5, in subsequent decades, and particularly in the context of the Russian Aliyah after 1987, the "non-Arab" dimension of Jewishness in Israel became more important.[133] For the German administrative judges, in turn, the Jews were the problematic historical other. Although the law did not a priori exclude the recognition of Jews by religion as ethnically German, German-speaking Jews who self-identified as Jews by nationality broke the supposedly homogeneous German linguistic and cultural sphere and created incongruity between this sphere and German *Volkstum*. Here, too, nationality was defined against a particular religion, as a non-Jewish speaker of German would not encounter the same doubts from the administration.

The reason for these doubts was the suspicion that Jewish religion would normally form the basis for national identification as Jewish. It was precisely at that point that the German and Israeli definitions of co-ethnicity intersected. When a German official stated that "belonging to the Mosaic faith almost invariably justifies the assumption of belonging to the Jewish people as well," he basically echoed the Israeli-Zionist standpoint on this matter. As the Brother Daniel ruling demonstrates, even in the markedly secular definition of Jewishness that Justice Silberg aspired to give in his ruling, Jewish nationality and Jewish religion remained inseparable. In the case of Brother Daniel, religion was, in effect, the sole decisive criterion, because it canceled out all his other impeccable Jewish-Zionist credentials as well as his descent from two Jewish parents.

This chapter also provides evidence that serves to problematize the very notions of ethno-cultural and descent-based conceptions of nationhood prevalent in the literature about Germany and Israel.[134] In practice, neither culture nor descent nor a combination of the two was a decisive criterion in either case. Had the German authorities and courts recognized people as German on the grounds of German culture, the Jewish applicants discussed here would have had little problem being accepted, since their belonging to the German linguistic and cultural sphere was not in doubt. Had the Israeli authorities and courts recognized people according to their descent, Brother Daniel should have been recognized as a Jew, as his Jewish genealogy had been acknowledged by the court. However, the German institutions cared more about public self-identification, thus turning German *Volkszugehörigkeit* into a plebiscite for the German nation. This plebiscite had to be confirmed, to be sure, by cultural elements, but those were insufficient by and for themselves.

The Israeli institutions, on the other hand, cared less about whether people were of Jewish descent and more about whether they were Jewish. And Brother Daniel was not, because he had the wrong religion. In that sense, the Law of Return was a lot less ethnic than critics might claim, because a person could drop out of the Jewish community of descent despite his or her Jewish origins. This view came with a paradox, of course: From the perspective of racial anti-Semitism, conversion did not protect someone from classification and persecution as a Jew. The same persecuted convert, however, was not Jewish enough to qualify for Israeli citizenship. Israel would thus not leave the power to define Jews to their persecutors. As the next chapter will show, the issue of descent—understood in its genealogical sense as opposed to a more abstract notion of ethnic origin—would acquire greater importance in each case with the generational extensions that took place in the late 1960s and early 1970s.

NOTES

1. Vermerk Watzinger, June 19, 1969, Stadtarchiv Mannheim, B-HR, Dezernatsregistratur 17/1993, No. 84.

2. RP Nordbaden an Oberbürgermeister Dr. Reschke, Mannheim, August 25, 1970, HStAS EA 12/201, Az. 2552, No. 14.

3. Straßmann, Rösler, and Krüzner, *Bundesvertriebenengesetz*, 36.

4. Ibid., 40.

5. Ibid.

6. Ibid., 37.

7. Ulitskaya, *Daniel Stein*.

8. See Schießl, *Tor zur Freiheit*.

9. AA an BMI, August 31, 1961, quoting Bericht GK Salzburg, May 19, 1961, BArch, B 106/39948.

10. For Copenhagen, see the correspondence between AA, BMI and BVA documented in BArch B 106/39942 (late 1962/early 1963). For Helsinki, see AA an BMI, April 1, 1964, ibid.

11. GK Milan an AA, August 20, 1964, BArch B106/39948.

12. BMI an AA, June 4, 1964, BArch B 106/39948.

13. The Foreign Office and the Federal Expellee Ministry, on the other hand, supported the plan. Bericht GK Salzburg, May 19, 1961; BMVt an BMI, February 22, 1962; and BMI an AA, May 14, 1962, all in BArch, B 106/39948.

14. BMI an AA, May 14, 1962, BArch B 106/39948.

15. AA an BMI, April 1, 1964, BArch B 106/39948.

16. BMI an AA, June 26, 1964, BArch B 106/39948.

17. Diken (Embassy Rome) to Maruz (Foreign Minister's Office), March 6, 1961, ISA 93.20.1.282 (=286/15-חצ).

18. See ample documentation from 1960 in ISA 93.34.1.40 (= 313/6-חצ).

19. Report by the Department for External Relations (secret), "Activities of Emigrants (*yordim*) and Other Elements in Vienna against Aliyah," August 25, 1958, CZA S60/334.

20. BMVt an AA, April 29, 1965, BArch, B 106/39938.

21. Ibid.

22. Ioanid, *Ransom of the Jews*, 76.

23. Eastern Europe Department of the Foreign Ministry to the Israeli Ambassador in Sydney, copy to the Ambassador in Bucharest, "Migration (*hagirah*) from Romania," January 12, 1960; Y. Lotan, Consul General Paris, to the Heads

of the Consular and Eastern Europe Departments, copy to the embassy supervisor Meir Rosen, "Aliyah from Romania," January 15, 1960; and Eastern Europe Department to the Israeli Ambassador Budapest, copy to the ambassador in Bucharest, Sh. Avigor, "The Problem of Aliyah from Romania," January 17, 1960, all in ISA 93.34.1.40 (= 313/6-חצ).

24. Eastern Europe Department to Ambassadors in Paris, Rome, Brussels, the Hague, and Vienna, "Help for the Exit of Romanian Jews," February 8, 1960, ISA 93.34.1.40 (= 313/6-חצ).

25. Eastern Europe Department to Consulate General Amsterdam, April 26, 1960, in ISA 93.17.1.26 (=1897/4-חצ).

26. The case is documented in ISA 93.34.1.41 (=313/7-חצ).

27. Eastern Europe Department to Embassy Bucharest, July 12, 1960, ISA 93.34.1.41 (=313/7-חצ).

28. Embassy Brussels to Eastern Europe Department, October 28, 1960, ISA 93.34.1.38 (=313/4-חצ).

29. Consulate Amsterdam to Embassy Bucharest et al., October 14, 1960, ISA 93.34.1.38 (=313/4-חצ).

30. Ibid.

31. Dietz, Lebok, and Polian, "Jewish Emigration," 41. That West Germany has been one of the main European destinations for Jewish migrants during the postwar decades has been noted by Karin Weiss, "Between Integration and Exclusion," 183.

32. About the ban (*cherem*) on Jewish life in Germany as well as its continuous infringement by Jews, see Diner, "Im Zeichen des Banns." Concerning the *prat Germania* provision of Israeli passports in the overall context of the initially restrictive Israeli emigration regime, see Rozin, "Negotiating the Right to Exit."

33. Precise numbers are difficult to establish from the existing historiography. Marita Krauss estimates as many as 30,000 Jewish returnees from all countries, only about 12,000 to 15,000 of whom registered with Jewish communities; see Krauss, "Jewish Remigration," 107. On German-Jewish remigration, see Panagiotidis, "Policy for the Future." About Reich-Ranicki's emigration and his recognition as German, see Reich-Ranicki, *Author of Himself*, 181–186.

34. Menachem Talmi, "In the Year of Israel's Tenth Anniversary—10,000 Émigrés," *Maariv*, October 17, 1958 (Hebrew), from the press collection in CZA S71/3135.

35. A 1970 report wrote of 3,000 recent immigrants from countries of the Eastern Bloc (Hedwig Biermann, "Juden in Deutschland: Beobachtungen zu einem aktuellen Thema," *Publik*, February 27, 1970, 3). The period 1964–1967 was suggested by the head of the Central Council, Hendrik G. van Dam, quoted in Lothar Labusch, "Das deutsche Verhältnis zu den Juden ist ein Testfall," *Kölner Stadt-Anzeiger*, September 20, 1968. Both articles are from the press collection on Jewish topics in Archiv für Christlich-Demokratische Politik (ACDP), 23/2.

36. "Germany Refuses Asylum to Israel Émigrés," *Jerusalem Post*, January 19, 1961; "Israel—A Liberal State," *Maariv*, January 20, 1961 (Hebrew) (both in CZA S71/3135). However, in 1973 a German court apparently did grant asylum to a "quarter Jew" from Poland who convinced the judges that he had been unable to integrate in Israel because there he was considered a non-Jew. See "Verwaltungsgericht billigte 'Vierteljuden' Asylrecht zu," *DPA*, August 21, 1973 (ACDP 23/2).

37. HStAS EA 12/201, Az. 2552, No. 14. All the data cited in the following paragraphs is extracted from this list unless otherwise noted.

38. Diner, "Im Zeichen des Banns," 44.

39. 6.3.3.3/82714117/International Tracing Service Digital Archive, Bad Arolsen (ITSDA).

40. 6.3.3.3/82711812/ITSDA.

41. 6.3.3.2/103787566 (Artur Madfes) and 6.3.3.3/83054810 (Sifra Iosupovici)/ITSDA.

42. About these different tendencies among Jews in postwar Romania see Ancel, "'New Jewish Invasion,'" 248.

43. 3.1.1.1/66796767/ITSDA.

44. 2.2.2.1/71804441/ITSDA.

45. 3.2.1.1/79085066/ITSDA.

46. 3.2.1.1/79346897/ITSDA.

47. 6.3.3.2/107734009/ITSDA.

48. 0.1/53189464/ITSDA.

49. Witness no. 97, http://www.auschwitz-prozess.de.

50. 6.3.3.2/104622105/ITSDA.

51. Müller, *Sonderbehandlung.*

52. The case with the full court ruling is documented in HStAS EA 12/201, Az. 2551, No. 82.

53. Werber, Bode, and Ehrenforth, *Bundesvertriebenengesetz* (1954), 22.

54. On Ormond see Rauschenberger and Renz, *Henry Ormond.*

55. The BVFG commentary by Werber/Bode/Ehrenforth already noted in 1954 that "The legislature does not expect the Germans who stayed or who are held back in those states to remain there under the current circumstances and given that the biggest part of the ethnic group (*Volksgruppe*) has been expelled." Werber, Bode, and Ehrenforth, *Bundesvertriebenengesetz* (1954), 22. In a 1967 court ruling, this idea was expressed by saying that people could not be expected to stay "in an environment stripped of Germans" ("in der von Deutschen entblößten Umgebung"). See BVerwG VIII C 66.66, April 26, 1967, *BVerwGE* 26, 352. The term *solitarization* (*Vereinsamung*) is mentioned in BVerwG VIII C 58.76, March 16, 1977, *BVerwGE* 52, 167.

56. This is quite possible. As of May 1958, there were 8,426 Jewish emigration requests for Germany pending with the Romanian authorities. See Ioanid, *Ransom of the Jews*, 74.

57. Urteil des Hessischen Verwaltungsgerichtshofs, II. Senat, OS II 50/65, January 5, 1966, 17, HStAS EA 12/201, AZ 2551, No. 82.

58. Ancel, "Chernovtsy."

59. Sha'ari, "Die jüdische Gemeinde von Czernowitz," 126.

60. See their biographical data sketched in the ITS digital archives 6.3.3.2/108391549 (Manuel Fuhrmann) and 6.3.3.3/82771839 (Rivka Calmanovici).

61. BVerwG VIII C 30.64 (*BVerwGE* 26, 344), BverwG VIII C 66.66 (*BVerwGE* 26, 352), BVerwG VIII C 49.64 (unpublished), all on April 26, 1967. All three are documented in HStAS 12/201, Az. 2552, Nos. 8–10.

62. BVerwG VIII C 30.64, *BVerwGE* 26, 344 (emphasis added).

63. Ibid.

64. Details of his life story are given in Bayerischer Verwaltungsgerichtshof, Urteil Nr. 61 VI 61, October 30, 1963, BArch, B 139/2105.

65. Ibid., 24.

66. Ibid., 25–28.

67. BVerwG VIII C 30.64, 11, BArch B 139/2105.

68. Ibid., 12–13.

69. Ibid., 13–14.

70. Ibid., 14–15.

71. Bayerischer Verwaltungsgerichtshof, Urteil Nr. 265 VI 67, October 15, 1968, BArch, B 139/2105.

72. Brix, *Umgangssprachen*; Zahra, *Kidnapped Souls*, chap. 1, esp. 32–39.

73. Glass, *Zerbrochene Nachbarschaft*, 162, 166.

74. Zahra, *Kidnapped Souls*, 186.

75. Straßmann, Rösler, and Krüzner, *Bundesvertriebenengesetz*, 35.

76. Ibid., 36.

77. For the post-Habsburg Bohemian context of provincialized Germandom, see Zahra, *Kidnapped Souls*, chap. 5.

78. BVerwG VIII C 36/65, March 14, 1968, HStAS 12/201, Az. 2552, No. 16.

79. In the cosmopolitan setting of Łódź, Jews actually were members of German associations before 1933. See Chu, *German Minority*, 159. For racialized notions of Germanness among German nationalist activists in Romania, by contrast see Glass, *Zerbrochene Nachbarschaft*, 151–155.

80. BVerwG VIII C 173.72, November 14, 1973, HStAS EA 12/201, Az. 2555, No. 181.

81. Ibid.

82. Bryant, "Either German or Czech," 700.

83. 0.1/50560060/ITSDA.

84. About Jewish compensation under the *Lastenausgleichsgesetz*, see Nachum, "Reconstructing Life."

85. Verwaltungsgericht Bremen, May 5, 1967, HStAS EA 12/201, Az. 2552, No. 7, attachment 7.

86. Gold, *Geschichte der Juden in der Bukovina*. Broszat's piece was published as Broszat, "Von der Kulturnation zur Volksgruppe."

87. BVerwGE III C 121.67, October 24, 1968, *BVerwGE* 30, 305 (emphasis added).

88. BVerwG III B113/69, January 20, 1970, HStAS 12/201, AZ 2552, No. 19.

89. Senders, "*Jus Sanguinis* or *Jus Mimesis*," 89.

90. "Richtlinien zur Anwendung des §6 des Bundesvertriebenengesetzes (BVFG) vom 20. Februar 1980," in Liesner, *Aussiedler*, 78–91.

91. 1 BvR 898, 1132, 1150, 1333, 1181/79, 83, 416/80, 1117/79, 603/80, December 16, 1981, *BVerfGE* 59, 1982, 128, here 161.

92. Zahra, *Kidnapped Souls*, 186.

93. For the inclusive use of cultural definitions of Germanness in Jewish naturalization cases in the Weimar Republic, see Sammartino, *Impossible Border*, chap. 7.

94. Silagi, *Vertreibung und Staatsangehörigkeit*, 129.

95. About this fascinating parallel case of ethnic recognition according to German law, see Brunner and Nachum, "'Vor dem Gesetz steht ein Türhüter'."

96. Zahra, "Imagined Noncommunities," 101.

97. Balfour Declaration, November 2, 1917, in Rabinovich and Reinharz, *Israel in the Middle East*, 29.

98. Biale, *Not in the Heavens*, 162–163.

99. Segev, *1949*, 244–245.

100. Elam, *Judaism as Status Quo*.

101. About the creation of the population registry in the context of the first national census and its particular focus on counting the Arab population, see Robinson, *Citizen Strangers*, chaps. 2, 3. About Druze ID nationality, see ibid, 55.

102. Documented in ISA 93.34.1.38 (=313/4-חצ).

103. His biography is recounted in Tec, *In the Lion's Den*.

104. Ibid., 47.

105. Ibid., 88.

106. State of Israel, the Supreme Court, *Judgment*. For other discussions of the case see Abramov, *Perpetual Dilemma*, 285–290, and Kraines, *Impossible Dilemma*, 22–28.

107. About Silberg, see Oz-Salzberger and Salzberger, "Hidden German Sources," 84.

108. State of Israel, the Supreme Court, *Judgment*, 2.

109. Ibid., 18 (emphasis in the original).

110. Ibid., 19.

111. Ibid., 20 (emphasis in the original).

112. Ibid. (emphasis in the original).

113. Ibid., 21–22 (emphasis added).

114. Ibid., 25–26.

115. About the confusion of terminology between English nationality and Hebrew citizenship (*ezrachut*) and ethnic nationality (*leom*), see Robinson, *Citizen Strangers*, 111. Even today, Israeli forms ask for *Leom* and *Ezrachut* and translate both as "nationality."

116. About Landau, see Oz-Salzberger and Salzberger, "Hidden German Sources," 85.

117. State of Israel, the Supreme Court, *Judgment*, 45–46.

118. Ibid., 46.

119. About Cohn, a native of Lübeck, see Oz-Salzberger and Salzberger, "Hidden German Sources," 85.

120. State of Israel, the Supreme Court, *Judgment*, 29, 31 (emphasis in the original).

121. Ibid., 34.

122. Ibid., 38.

123. About Berenson, see Oz-Salzberger and Salzberger, "Hidden German Sources," 84n12.

124. State of Israel, the Supreme Court, *Judgment*, 51.

125. Ibid., 54.

126. Ibid., 54–55 (emphasis added).

127. Ibid., 55 (emphasis added).

128. Ibid., 57 (emphasis added).

129. Ibid., 67–68 (emphasis added).

130. Ibid., 69.

131. Ibid., 70–71.

132. Kraines, *Impossible Dilemma*, 28.

133. For an interpretation of Israel as a "non-Arab state" see Lustick, "Israel as a Non-Arab State."

134. Levy, "Introduction," 3. See also Yfaat Weiss, "Golem and Its Creator," 84, 100.

FOUR

THE WATERSHED PERIOD

IN JANUARY 1967, EMIL SCHWANDTNER was permanently delegated to the Friedland transit camp as the Baden-Württemberg special representative. Over the preceding four years, his employer, the expellee department of the Baden-Württemberg Interior Ministry, had kept his appointment provisional. Schwandtner had first been sent to the camp near the inner German border in Lower Saxony in September 1963. Previously, in 1962, the ministry had decided that one representative was enough for both the Friedland and Giessen camps. The latter, known as the emergency reception center (*Notaufnahmestelle*) for refugees from the German Democratic Republic, had significantly less traffic after the Berlin Wall had been built in August 1961. Aussiedler numbers, too, had been steadily declining since the dramatic peak during the Polish exodus between 1956 and 1958, so it seemed that one official was enough to handle both camps.[1]

But during the summer of 1963, the ministry was already having second thoughts. The Giessen camp kept the representative busier than expected, which meant that the Baden-Württemberg representative, Franz Müller, could spend only one or two days a week in Friedland, where Aussiedler numbers were on the rise again. As seen in chapter 2, this led to fear among officials that the Land might end up with a negative selection of immigrants. Schwandtner's full-time presence was meant to prevent that. He was initially delegated only until the end of September, but his appointment was extended consecutively until January, April, and September 1964, as the Aussiedler kept coming. In November 1965, Schwandtner was informed that his full-time presence was still required.[2] But it was not until January 1967 that the ministry finally decided to make his position permanent. The reasoning given was the following: "So far we have refrained from giving a delegation order, because the future development of the [Aussiedler] influx was unclear. The current development suggests that the Friedland transit camp will continue to exist for a longer period of time."[3]

This episode from the life of a medium-level official reflects the uncertainties that the West German Aussiedler regime was dealing with during the 1960s amid shifting migration patterns. Would the emigration of Germans from Eastern Europe continue? The low numbers in the early years of that decade—less than 20,000 per year from all countries combined—gave little reason for optimism. Nor was it certain that it should continue, as clearly shown by the discussions surrounding Aussiedlung both from Yugoslavia and in general. Given the idea that Aussiedler were latecomers to the expulsion of Germans from Eastern Europe and hence a circumscribed group of people, continuing to resettle them indefinitely until an undefined point in the future was not necessarily on the agenda. Nevertheless, the influx never ceased completely, and from 1964 onward, numbers were on the rise again. The 27,813 new arrivals in 1966 were mostly from Poland and Czechoslovakia but also included 1,245 resettlers from the Soviet Union—an almost negligible quantity in absolute terms but a significant increase in percentage compared with previous years.

This new immigration peak, though modest in its overall size, proved to be a turning point, because it created the expectation that Aussiedlung would continue for the foreseeable future. It not only convinced the Baden-Württemberg expellee ministry that the Friedland camp was there to stay but also triggered the increased engagement of various state agencies with the phenomenon and placed the Germans of Eastern Europe higher on the government agenda. While the abolition of the Federal Expellee Ministry, which became a department of the Federal Interior Ministry in 1969, appeared to signal the diminishing importance of the expellee question inside the country, the issue of those left behind acquired new relevance. On the initiative of Dr. Kurt Wagner, head of the Red Cross Tracing Service, the Federal Chancellery (*Bundeskanzleramt*, or BKA) created the Interministerial Committee for the Coordination of Problems Related to the Germans in Eastern and Southeastern Europe. Comprising representatives of the Interior, Finance, Labor, Inner-German Relations, and Youth Ministries and led by the Foreign Office, this committee was officially constituted in February 1971.[4] Given the still sensitive nature of anything that could have resembled German minority politics and the fear of "undesirable misinterpretations regarding the past (*unerwünschte, vergangenheitsbezogene Fehlinterpretationen*)," it was supposed to operate outside the public eye and should not involve the highest ministerial echelons.[5] Still, it indicated the ongoing commitment to assisting German citizens and ethnic Germans in Eastern Europe—not necessarily only by helping them emigrate but also by providing them with the financial means to live a decent life where they were, which in turn would reduce emigration pressure and thus help the new social-liberal government's *Ostpolitik*.[6] Even so, it was the *Ostpolitik*-related rapprochement with Germany's eastern neighbors that enabled some 200,000 Germans from Poland as well as about 60,000 Germans from the Soviet Union to leave their home countries and immigrate to West Germany until the end of the decade.

Israel similarly experienced a change in immigration patterns during the 1960s and 1970s. The great exodus movements from Arab countries came to an end with the last major wave of immigration from Morocco, which occurred between 1961 and 1964 when approximately 100,000 Jews left Morocco for Israel.[7] From this point on, the focus of Aliyah shifted decisively toward the predominantly Ashkenazi Jewry from the United States, Western Europe, and the socialist countries of Eastern Europe. The Jewish state began receiving increasing numbers of immigrants from Western countries after the spectacular victory in the Six-Day War in 1967. Between 1968 and 1972, about 24,000 Olim came from France and Britain, and some 29,000 from the United States and Canada (compared with merely 28,000 from all these countries during the preceding two decades).[8] Israel simultaneously directed its attention toward the Soviet Union and Soviet Jewry, which, after the end of Arab-Jewish mass Aliyot, had become the main reservoir of potential immigrants from non-Western countries. Already between 1965 and 1967, a relatively high number of 4,500 Jews received exit permits from the Soviet authorities. This temporary slight liberalization was interrupted by the Six-Day War and the severing of diplomatic ties between the Soviet Union and Israel. But emigration soon resumed, and more than 2,900 people received an exit permit in 1969.[9] In the meantime, Soviet Jews had begun to display a national conscience and growing identification with Israel after the victory in 1967; Jews in Israel reciprocated with demonstrations of support.[10] This mobilization on both sides, alongside perceived cracks in the Iron Curtain, was enough to create the expectation that in the future more Soviet Jews would be permitted to leave the Soviet Union—an expectation that was soon to be fulfilled.

In the context of these actual and anticipated changes in migration patterns, both states ventured to adjust their migration regimes starting from the mid-1960s to be able to deal with the resulting challenges for practices involving recognition of co-ethnics. This chapter will analyze these transformations. In addition to changes to the international situation, dissimilar domestic triggers brought about these adjustments, and the processes of adjustment differed considerably in each country. In Germany, following the restrictive challenges discussed in chapter 2, changes were first introduced to the administrative framework of the external gate. Yet instead of tightening control or even closing the gate, as the Bavarian challengers had suggested, the gate was in fact opened for the younger generation of Aussiedler. In due course, the internal gate followed by including the postwar generation in the internal recognition practice through a protracted administrative and judicial process. Parallel to these internal developments, the extension of Aussiedlung to new groups of potential migrants in Poland and the Soviet Union—Germans with no relatives in West Germany or without mutually recognized German citizenship respectively—necessitated an adjustment of the screening process there as well. All these changes took place in the arcane and quiet realm of the administration and involved no changes to existing laws, arguably for the same reason that the interministerial committee was supposed to stay out of the public eye.

In Israel, by contrast, the stimulus for change was the much publicized Shalit case, which was decided by the Supreme Court in January 1970. The case itself was not actually migration related; rather, the issue at stake was the registration of children from mixed marriages in the population registry. However, that issue was fundamentally linked to the Law of Return, the institutions that administered it, and the meanings of the identity concepts defining it. So, too, subsequent debates were intrinsically related to the anticipated Soviet Aliyah and the expected increase in mixed families arriving in Israel. Combined, these factors resulted in a substantial change to the Law of Return. That change fundamentally altered the definition of who is a Jew in immigration practice. At the same time, it opened the gates of the country for two generations of non-Jewish immigration.

As this chapter argues, the period between the mid-1960s and the mid-1970s thus represents a watershed in the history of co-ethnic immigration to West Germany and Israel. During this decade, in both countries, the meanings of the key concepts underlying the co-ethnic migration regimes changed considerably. As a result, the two regimes—which, beyond the common element of accepting immigrants by ethnic origin, had been defined by significant differences in scope and rationale—came to resemble each other as they became more inclusive, less selective, and focused on migrants with conceptually more remote links to each nation. Transcending their original practices of the 1950s and early 1960s, both Germany and Israel began to target people who, rather than being Germans and Jews in their own right, could be identified as being of

German and Jewish descent—or, as they will be called here, derived Germans and Jews.

Moreover, Germany's conception of Aussiedlung began to resemble Israel's holistic approach to co-ethnic immigration, because from this point onward it could be legitimized purely in terms of shared ethnicity instead of having to rely on ethno-humanitarian family reunification or the repatriation of citizens. In this way, German co-ethnic asylum came to resemble Israeli co-ethnic resettlement. In a process of mutual convergence, Israeli co-ethnic resettlement also came to resemble German co-ethnic asylum as the changes in the geography of Jewish migrations and the concomitant stronger focus on emigration from the Soviet Union made Aliyah, like Aussiedlung, a predominantly Eastern European affair. This shift went hand in hand with the abandonment of selective Aliyah, which became obsolete in view of the arrival of "desired" immigrants and the progressing consolidation of the state, making the nation-building dimension of the Israeli migration regime recede into the background. Taken together, all these transformations during the watershed period laid the conceptual foundation for the mass immigration of the late 1980s and early 1990s.

GERMANY: AUSSIEDLER—THE NEXT GENERATION

By the mid-1960s, different actors in the West German co-ethnic migration regime became aware that Aussiedlung, once meant to be restricted to the temporally limited ingathering of one generation of would-have-been expellees, extended further into the future than the legislature would have imagined 10 or 15 years earlier. For some, like Werner Kanein from the Bavarian Interior Ministry familiar from chapter 2, the perpetuation of resettlement created suspicions that the Aussiedler regime, which offered citizenship and material benefits, actually attracted people who were not among the original target group. He therefore interpreted the increasing Aussiedler numbers of the mid-1960s as the result of "abuse" of German "generosity" and called for stricter immigration controls on the German side, or even an end to preferential co-ethnic immigration altogether.

But even to those who did not share Kanein's apprehensions and choice of words, it was clear that if Aussiedlung was to continue, its original scope would be subject to significant extension. In practice, there were two key aspects to this: first, Aussiedlung came to include postwar generations; and second, it transcended its original narrow focus on the reunification of families. As will be seen in this chapter, this extension was not the outcome of an explicit political decision in favor of continued Aussiedler migration. It was, rather, driven by migratory developments on the ground and was negotiated on the administrative level and by the courts for the external and internal gates. When the interministerial committee was created in 1971, the key decisions enabling the reception of Aussiedler beyond the original target group had already been taken.

GENERATIONAL EXTENSION AT THE EXTERNAL GATE

The administrative extension of the scope of Aussiedlung was codified in the new guidelines for the D1 procedure passed in July 1968.[11] Paradoxically, it was triggered by the Bavarian Interior Ministry's (BSMI) restrictive intervention discussed in chapter 2, which initiated a process of soul searching among the administration regarding fundamental questions related to the if and the how of continuous Aussiedler reception. In response to Bavaria's unilateral restrictions, the Federal Interior Ministry (BMI) hinted in December 1965 that the D1 procedure could be revised.[12] In June 1966, it went so far as to explicitly welcome the Bavarian initiative and suggested a meeting with the interior ministers of the Länder.[13] Discussions began in April 1967, when the BMI circulated a draft for new guidelines among the Länder interior ministers, the Federal Administration Office, the Foreign Office, and the Federal Expellee Ministry.[14] At the end of these intensive written and oral deliberations stood the official opening of the external gate to the postwar generation—a result diametrically opposed to the challenger's intention.

In the course of the discussions between federal and Länder institutions, interior ministries, aliens' authorities, and expellee ministries, the very existence of the D1 procedure as a special immigration procedure for an exceptional group of immigrants was called into question by the Bavarian Interior Ministry and like-minded ministries from other federal states. Questions such as the requirement for candidates to submit documentation to prove their eligibility for takeover, the involvement of the Federal Administration Office (BVA) in the procedure, and the very necessity of a special immigration procedure itself were at stake. On the first point, a consensus emerged among most discussants that written documentation could not generally be required from candidates. Apart from Bavaria, the interior ministry of Schleswig-Holstein had preferred stricter requirements in this regard, given that they perceived the takeover of Aussiedler as "real immigration" (*echte Einwanderung*). Yet they eventually conceded that this was not feasible for "political and humanitarian reasons."[15]

Cutting out the BVA or abolishing the D1 procedure altogether was on the agenda of the Bavarian and North Rhine-Westphalian interior ministries. Both ministries argued that these measures would speed up bureaucratic proceedings.[16] The Federal Interior Ministry had previously attempted to quell such calls by pointing out that, for "domestic reasons"—arguably the anticipated outrage of expellee organizations—giving up the special procedure for ethnic Germans and treating them like other aliens was not an option.[17] Nevertheless, Kanein from the BSMI suggested a visa procedure based on the 1965 Aliens' Act (*Ausländergesetz*), which he asserted would not be a restriction but an improvement: Applicants should simply present themselves at a German embassy, which could then reach a joint decision with a local aliens' authority in Germany about whether they were indeed ethnic Germans and accordingly grant or refuse them a visa.[18] This suggestion was rejected by all the other institutions involved, not least for practical reasons. As the Foreign Office pointed out, German missions in most of the Eastern countries were not authorized to process requests for Aussiedlung. The only exceptions were the missions in the Soviet Union, Romania, and Bulgaria—countries that saw little emigration activity at the time. The French embassies in Prague and Budapest and the US embassy in Warsaw, which were responsible for issuing visas for West Germany, were deemed unsuitable for the task of sifting Germans from non-Germans because of their exclusively non-German staff.[19] As a consequence, the D1 procedure remained untouched.

Yet the issue that triggered most discussions was generational change: How could young ethnic Germans be accommodated who had not been old enough in 1945 to have made a legally valid *Bekenntnis* of their own or had not even been born yet? Independently of the D1 revision, the Federal Interior Ministry and the Federal Expellee Ministry (BMVt) had been discussing this issue since 1966. The BMI wanted to amend section 6 of the Federal Expellee Law (BVFG) in a way that would place the *Bekenntnis* of a parent in lieu of a young Aussiedler's own *Bekenntnis*, thus making the parental *Bekenntnis* hereditary.[20] The BMVt, by contrast, preferred taking the application for takeover by a member of the younger generation as a *Bekenntnis*.[21] In the takeover procedure revision, the Committee of Refugee Administrations of the federal states (*Argeflü*) suggested a third option. The idea was to make analogous use of the draft guideline's suggested regulations for members of the older generation who, for different reasons, had had no chance to make a *Bekenntnis* and were, as an exception, to be judged by the presence of objective criteria (such as language and culture) or the—normally irrelevant—behavior after the end of the expulsion measures.[22] This solution was already familiar from the practice concerning Germans from Yugoslavia. Of these three options—hereditary parental *Bekenntnis*, emigration as *Bekenntnis*, or language skills instead of *Bekenntnis*—the second one was pursued. The final version of the D1 guidelines, which the Federal Interior Ministry circulated in June 1968, stipulated that the takeover application should be considered as a valid *Bekenntnis*.[23]

With this extension to new generations of applicants, the West German state took a decisive step in the transformation of Aussiedler migration from the mere ingathering of the ethnic Germans left behind after the expulsion to a perpetual ethnic priority immigration regime. This outcome was crucial, because it offered the potential to prolong the resettlement campaign indefinitely. As it appears, the Bavarian Interior Ministry was not aware of the profound implications of these changes. Between the meeting in Unna-Massen in September 1967 and the eventual circulation of the guidelines, it launched one last attempt to promote its original call for the abolition of the special immigration procedure. The argument the ministry used was that "the group of people who are supposed to receive the benefits of simplified and accelerated entry and of permanent residence is not big enough anymore to justify a special procedure."[24] Assuming a fixed quantity of ethnic Germans left in Eastern Europe after the expulsions, this argument was certainly valid. But with the opening of the external gate to the younger generations, it became obsolete.

De facto, of course, the young generation had already been included in the Aussiedler regime, as described in the Yugoslav immigration cases discussed in chapter 2. Many of the ethnic Germans from there had in fact been too young for a *Bekenntnis* before the expulsion. Their *Volkszugehörigkeit* had been judged according to their own behavior after the war. The solution proposed by the Argeflü would have been in a similar spirit, merely removing the necessity of an explicit *Bekenntnis*. The solution that was eventually accepted, by contrast, dodged the question of who was supposed to have declared what and when by introducing the circular logic of taking the application for resettlement as a substitute for a *Bekenntnis*. This opened the gates for many people who were not among the original target group of the expellee legislation. Consequently, the generational question became a crucial issue also in the internal procedure in the years to come, as will be discussed in the next section. At this point, the hereditary *Bekenntnis* that the Federal Interior Ministry had promoted since late 1966 was placed back on the agenda as well.

THE NEXT GENERATION AT THE INTERNAL GATE: WHO IS A GERMAN AND WHEN?

On a bureaucratic level, the revision of the D1 guidelines in 1968 had opened the external immigration gate for the second generation of Aussiedler who had either been children at the time of the "general expulsion measures" or had been born after the expulsion. An increasingly large share of the purported ethnic Germans from Eastern Europe who immigrated in the following years belonged to this category. Within the internal procedure, the external gate's circular logic to treat the application for Aussiedlung as a *Bekenntnis* was deemed unsatisfactory. The question of how someone who was born after the war or was a minor at the time of the expulsion could have the legally required *Bekenntnis* to German *Volkstum* before the beginning of the expulsions in 1944–1945 reappeared with renewed urgency. With the passing of time, a related question became even more pressing: How many generations of descendants should still be recognized as ethnic German expellees? And how was *Volkszugehörigkeit* supposed to be assessed among the members of these generations? In the absence of legislative change that could accommodate the new situation, it was the responsibility of the refugee administration (through its deliberative body, the Argeflü) and the Federal Administrative Court to find solutions for these vexing issues.

Making Bekenntnis *Hereditary: The Case of Margit C. (1976)*

One of the young Eastern European migrants making her way to West Germany after the D1 reform was Margit C. Born in Hungary in 1952 to a Hungarian father and an ethnically German ("Swabian") mother, she left the country in June 1970 and traveled via Yugoslavia to Italy, where her fiancé had already immigrated to in 1969. After their marriage in August, they moved on to West Germany, where Margit applied for expellee status. Her application was rejected by the administration and two levels of jurisdiction. The court of appeal, the Mannheim Administrative Court, justified its rejection by noting that Margit had been born after the Second World War and hence had not made a *Bekenntnis* to German *Volkstum* before the war as requested by the law. The Federal Administrative Court, which had to rule about Margit's case as the last instance of appeal, upheld the rejection in November 1976. However, importantly, the court refuted the argument that because of her postwar birth, Margit was a priori excluded from recognition as an expellee. Instead, the judges endorsed the recurrent idea of judging young applicants by the *Bekenntnis* of their parents, thus giving the construct of hereditary *Bekenntnis* authoritative judicial blessing.

Like the Jewish cases described in chapter 3, this, too, was an atypical case that pushed a court to establish a more general principle. Margit was one of only about 3,800 Aussiedler from Hungary who were registered in West Germany during the entire 1970s. Compared with the more than 200,000 new arrivals from Poland and over 70,000 from neighboring Romania during the same period, this was an almost negligible number—the lowest in all Eastern European countries from where ethnic Germans emigrated.

Yet precisely because it was marginal, Margit's case provided the judges with the opportunity to develop their conception of the relationship between the Federal Expellee Law and the postwar generation. Despite the apparent gap in the legislation concerning the descendants of the war generation, the judges argued that the law was generally open to include subsequent generations. In the past, other judicial courts had used the parental *Bekenntnis* to recognize people as ethnic German expellees who had been born before the war but had not been old enough to make a *Bekenntnis* of their own. The Federal Administrative Court now applied this construction to the generation born after the war. The underlying assumption was that they, like their parents and the children born before or during the war, suffered from the same "expulsion pressure" (*Vertreibungsdruck*). Historical experiences were passed on within the family. The judges went on to elaborate:

> For the children born after the war, who are identified by the surrounding environment with the *Volkstum* of their parents, the continuous process of tradition from the older to the younger generation also justifies the use of the *Bekenntnis* made by the parents or the parent that exerts dominant influence on them (*des sie prägenden Elternteils*). The connection to the *Bekenntnis* is mediated by the family unit (*der Familienverband vermittelt den Bekenntniszusammenhang*). . . . *Bekenntniszusammenhang* means that the children descend from parents who . . . have experienced the beginning of the general expulsion measures and who are German *Volkszugehörige*. The German *Volkszugehörigkeit* of the parent(s) is assessed according to section 6 BVFG. If they were still under age at the decisive point in time and hence could not make a *Bekenntnis*, their parents or the dominant parent are decisive.[25]

In other words, much like the Federal Interior Ministry had already suggested in 1966, the *Bekenntnis* of a person born after the war was replaced with the *Bekenntnis* of his or her parents. If the parents had been minors before the end of the war, their *Bekenntnis* could in turn be derived from their parents. The court considered it unreasonable to request a *Bekenntnis* from the young applicant herself but argued that it might be possible to take the applicant's behavior after the war that resembled a *Bekenntnis* (*bekenntnisähnliches Verhalten*) as indicative of the parents' former identification. However, the latter would be decisive in any event. The judges explicitly limited this construct to the first generation born after the war, deeming any more extensive use as "doubtful."

Writing about this "landmark ruling" in 2005, Christian Joppke identified the creation of a "strange construct of inheritable confession."[26] Sociologist Karl Otto even considered this "a new variant of the theory of evolution," since the *Bekenntnis* was passed on like a "genetic code."[27] Two arguments need to be made in this regard: First, the reference to a genetic code, which rhetorically associates Aussiedler policy with biology and, by extension, race, is misleading and unjustified, because the judges explicitly argued in terms of a *social* transmission of Germanness in the family unit that could be plausibly assumed only for the first postwar generation. Although the merit of this construct is open to question, it is certainly not based on genetics. Second, the notion of "inheritable *Bekenntnis*" needs to be contextualized. Contrary to what the terminology "genetic code" might suggest, in this ruling, the Federal Administrative Court in fact chose a restrictive rather than an expansive approach to the question of the BVFG and subsequent generations. This will become clear in the next section, which examines the discussions that occurred in the refugee administration both before and after the Federal Administrative Court ruling. At any rate, the judges ruled that Margit could not be considered ethnically German, because she had to be judged by the *Bekenntnis* of the "formative parent" (*prägender Elternteil*), which, in the court's reading, was her Hungarian father.

The Roads Not Taken: Discussions in the Argeflü (1974–1976)

Since the late 1960s, when the Federal Interior and Expellee Ministries failed to amend section 6 BVFG and the new D1 guidelines still included the younger generation of Aussiedler as eligible for immigration, two questions lingered: Who is (still) a German? How do we (still) recognize a German? This last question amounted to asking: *When* is a German—that is, when was he or she supposed to have made the *Bekenntnis* required by law? All these questions together amounted to asking: What is the nature of the Federal Expellee Law? Is it just an expellee law or an Aussiedler law, and hence an immigration law?

The refugee administration—which was responsible for the implementation of this law and hence was the guardian of the internal gate—developed some fairly radical solutions to tackle this issue in the years between 1974 and 1976, when the practical need to include young Aussiedler like Margit C. became increasingly urgent. The plan was essentially to turn the Federal Expellee Law into an Aussiedler law by decoupling wartime expulsion and postwar

Aussiedlung and moving forward the cutoff point for the *Bekenntnis* to any given moment in the present or future when a person would actually emigrate. This would have affected the adult war generation as well as those who had been too young to make a pre-expulsion *Bekenntnis*, and those like Margit who were born after the war. Such a solution would have cast aside all generational limits, thus overcoming the focus on the postwar expulsions as the vantage point in time, and hence creating a co-ethnic immigration regime without temporal limits—a "proper" Law of Return, as it were.

Based on discussions within the Argeflü, the Bavarian State Ministry for Labor and Social Order drew up two documents expounding ideas on how a presentist *Bekenntnis* could be implemented and justified from a legal point of view.[28] The basic premise of these deliberations was that Aussiedlung was not just a subcategory of actual expulsion but a legal phenomenon sui generis. As a rule, recognition of Aussiedler candidates as German should be based on their own self-identification, while the use of an indirect *Bekenntnis* derived from the parents should be the exception. Although it was conceded that it was unreasonable to ask for public self-avowal after the war, the first paper suggested that what mattered was the "inner will" (*innerer Bekenntniswille*) to be considered a German. If this will no longer existed, even a prior *Bekenntnis* could become void. The second paper expanded this line of argument, asserting that the required *Bekenntnis* "in the homeland" (*in der Heimat*) and "before the expulsion" did not necessarily have to date back to the time before the general expulsion measures of 1944–1945. Instead, by framing Aussiedlung itself as individual "voluntary expulsion," the paper reasoned that these formulations could also refer to each individual moment of emigration. In addition to this *Bekenntnis*, German descent in an "objective" sense—that is, not necessarily descent from a *Volkszugehöriger* in the legal sense—was considered the crucial objective backup criterion.

This theory of objective descent combined with the presentist *Bekenntnis* would have allowed ethnic Germans in Eastern Europe to reproduce into the future, very much like the remaining German citizens—for instance, those naturalized through the *Volksliste*—already did. The second Bavarian paper made this reasoning explicit, claiming that German *Volkszugehörigkeit* should be inheritable just like German *Staatsangehörigkeit* (citizenship), given that ethnic Germans and German citizens were equal under the Basic Law. This was perhaps the first time that ethnic Germans outside the Federal Republic of Germany, and hence outside the purview of the Basic Law, were considered "long-distance citizens" with a claim to equal treatment. Accepting this postulate and implementing the Bavarian proposals would have significantly changed the nature of the Federal Expellee Law, moving it closer to the post-1970 Israeli Law of Return, which will be discussed later in this chapter.

Although the sources do not reveal the explicit intentions behind this solution, which was completely at odds with current jurisdiction at the time, it may be surmised that the reasons were primarily of a practical nature. As a refugee administration official from Hamburg remarked in one of the relevant discussions, "existing social welfare laws have to be applied in a way that the basic conception intended by the legislature is realized. Since Aussiedlung is still a current problem, the realization of the purpose of the BVFG must not be obstructed by a very formalistic approach."[29] From the administration's point of view, the main goal was thus to find a practical solution for a pressing problem. In fact, ever since the external door had been opened for the younger generation of Aussiedler in 1968, the refugee administration had to deal with their recognition and integration. The goal, then, was to find an easy way to their legal inclusion. The idea behind the insistence on a present-day *Bekenntnis* could have been that it was easier to assess a person's behavior in the present than his or her ancestors' purported behavior in the past. Singling out German descent as the decisive objective criterion would have replaced the search for increasingly absent German language skills, upbringing, and culture. Looking for objective rather than subjective Germanness among the ancestor generation also might have been considered the easier exercise, even though some officials explicitly disagreed with this view.[30]

Whatever the motivation for the alternative proposals, the ruling about Margit C.'s case in November 1976 basically precluded any such inclusive and present-oriented medium-level administrative solution. In a decision with a clearly restrictive thrust compared with the administration's proposals, the highest administrative judges in the country decided that the concepts of *Volkszugehörigkeit* and *Bekenntnis* should remain firmly rooted in the past, limiting the circle of eligible people to prewar Germans and their first generation of descendants. The *Bekenntnis* of the descendants should always be derived from the parents—or, in exceptional cases, from the grandparents. A maximally inclusive subsequent Argeflü proposal in November 1977 that would have allowed the recognition of young Aussiedler based on their own present-day *Bekenntnis* (the Bavarian solution) or by that of their parents in the past (the Federal Administrative Court solution) stood no chance against this background.[31] The administrative judges had made it clear that the BVFG was still an expellee law and not an Aussiedler law. To be considered an expellee in the present, a candidate had to have been eligible to be considered an expellee in the past, or to have descended from such a person. That is why a *Bekenntnis* had to exist for the time before the general expulsion measures in 1944–1945, and its bequest was only permissible down to one generation. Thus, a clear time frame was set. If a solution was to be found for those future generations, the judges argued, the legislature, not the court, would have to discover it.[32]

As it happened, the legislature did not raise a finger to resolve the issue of postwar generations until the 1992 reform of the BVFG, which is analyzed in detail in chapter 5. For the time being, it was up to the Argeflü to turn the existing provisional model, developed by the Federal Administrative Court, into binding administrative instructions for the refugee administrations in all the Länder. It did so with the February 1980 "guidelines for the implementation of section 6 BVFG" ("ethnicity guidelines").[33] These guidelines offered nothing substantially new; they merely summarized the developments of the watershed period, which effectively had come to an end with the 1976 ruling. With their voting, the application of section 6 to subsequent generations was generally regulated. There were occasional discussions in later years about how to deal with the offspring of mixed marriages in determining which parent had had the dominant cultural influence on the child. The guidelines asked the authorities to assume a child's German upbringing in case of doubt. As some officials criticized in a May 1983 meeting, the local authorities were, however, inclined to assume a child's German upbringing in general, even if it was obvious that the non-German parent had been dominant. It was suggested to take a child's knowledge of the German language as an indicator of the extent to which the German parent had exerted significant influence.[34] But there and in later Argeflü sessions, no agreement was reached on how to assess formative parental influence. An amendment of the BVFG was considered the only possible solution.[35]

OSTPOLITIK, DÉTENTE, AND THE CONCEPTUAL EXTENSION OF AUSSIEDLUNG FROM POLAND AND THE SOVIET UNION

In addition to the generational extension, the watershed period between the mid-1960s and mid-1970s brought an additional conceptual widening of the scope of Aussiedlung from Poland and the Soviet Union. Poland—with its substantial German-Polish autochthonous population in Upper Silesia, Masuria, and other former Reich territories—had been the main source country of Aussiedler from the very beginning. But, generally, the Polish authorities granted official exit only for the ostensibly humanitarian purpose of ethnically coded family reunification—that is, the reunification of separated families in Germany—and not because of German ethnicity alone.

The Soviet Union, by contrast, had not been a significant supplier of such migrants for the first two postwar decades. The emigration of almost 13,000 Aussiedler between 1958 and 1960 under the German-Soviet repatriation agreement had been based not on their German ethnicity but on the mutually recognized

German citizenship that they held—either as residents of former East Prussia or as resettlers from Volhynia, Bessarabia, Galicia, Bukovina, and the Baltic States under the German-Soviet resettlement agreements concluded in the wake of the Hitler-Stalin pact of 1939 (*Vertragsumsiedler*).[36]

In both cases, the détente climate of the early 1970s and concomitant larger emigration numbers created the possibility of transcending this narrower focus on family members and mutually recognized citizens and putting resettlement on a more purely ethnic basis. The groundwork for the mass immigration of Polish and Soviet Aussiedler in the late 1980s was laid here.

This conceptual extension raised the question of how eligibility for such resettlement could be assessed in administrative practice. This section reconstructs the search for administrative solutions for ethnic recognition for prospective Aussiedler from Poland and the Soviet Union. Continuing from the discussions in previous chapters, the analysis here deals with many of the same questions: What kind of information was required to establish *Volkszugehörigkeit* with a sufficient degree of certainty before immigration? How could this information be reliably gathered in the absence of family connections in Germany? And to what extent was the exit permit given by the home authorities an indication of *Volkszugehörigkeit* and thus a valid preselection? The discussions surrounding the creation of the new questionnaires, as well as the questionnaires themselves, reveal how the watershed period brought about the creation of new conceptions and images of Aussiedler and Aussiedlung.

Poland: Overcoming Family Reunification

As mentioned above, both the challenge to and reform of the D1 procedure between 1965 and 1968 had taken place against the backdrop of increasing numbers of Aussiedler from Poland and Czechoslovakia starting in 1964. But no sooner had the reform been decided on by the interior administration than developments on the ground slowed down again. By the time the new guidelines went into force in mid-1968, the number of Aussiedler from Poland had dropped below 10,000 a year. The Soviet crushing of the Prague Spring in 1968 prompted another dramatic surge in the number of Aussiedler from Czechoslovakia. But because of these special circumstances, this group of people was not discussed in the context of the D1 reform. Rather, there was a consensus that there should be no bureaucratic obstacles for ethnic Germans fleeing Czechoslovakia, usually via Austria. In 1970, when this exceptional immigration wave was over, the total annual number of Aussiedler from all countries combined had dropped to roughly 19,000, the lowest number since 1963.[37]

The developments triggered by the *Ostpolitik* of the new social-liberal government under Willy Brandt, however, set Polish-German migration back into motion. On December 7, 1970, the West German and Polish governments signed the Warsaw Treaty about the normalization of relations between the two countries. In the treaty, the West German government de facto recognized the Oder-Neisse line as the western border of Poland. At the end of the negotiations, the Polish government issued a unilateral declaration. The so-called Information by the Government of the People's Republic of Poland stipulated that people of "undoubtedly German ethnicity," mixed families, and separated families would be allowed to emigrate from Poland.[38] This declaration was significant for the process of migration, because it overcame the exclusive focus on family reunification. In other words, for the first time since the expulsion, the Polish side showed a willingness to let people emigrate not only for humanitarian reasons but also explicitly based on their ethnicity.

On a theoretical level, this meant an important extension of the scope of Polish-German Aussiedler migration. On a practical level, the German authorities had to find a way to process this kind of immigration. The conventional D1 procedure was premised on the idea that each applicant for immigration had a relative or acquaintance already living in the FRG who would file the application on behalf of the would-be immigrant. This corresponded with the usual Polish insistence on an "invitation" (*zaproszenie*) that a citizen needed to apply for an exit visa. Even so, the theoretical possibility to decouple Aussiedlung from family reunification had been included in the 1968 revised D1 guidelines. Resettlement requests from candidates without relatives in West Germany were to be processed by the Federal Administration Office, which would sift out hopeless candidates and forward the more promising ones to the Red Cross, which would file the D1 application. As the Federal Interior Ministry remarked in the draft guidelines, "This solution can only be realized if the number of such applications will not substantially grow because of public promotion of this possibility."[39] Family reunification was thus still supposed to be the rule, arguably because it also functioned as a kind of safety valve for the ethnic selection process, since it could be assumed that a German's relatives were also Germans. Furthermore, relatives in West Germany could furnish information to the examining authorities, which would help assess whether the person in question matched the legal criteria defining a German. After the "Information," the authorities started to look for a way to enable this kind of extended migration while still controlling who was to come.

The method of choice to ensure an efficient processing of the expected immigration wave—which, according to initial Red Cross estimates, could comprise as many as 90,000 cases of family reunification and 180,000 cases of people willing to resettle who could not claim family reunification—was the new and simplified D1A procedure.[40] This procedure was supposed to be operated only by the Red Cross and the Federal Administration Office, thus excluding the normally involved lower authorities of the Länder. It caused protracted administrative discussions up to the ministerial level and tested the limits of the West German state's generosity with regard to the open door for purported co-ethnics from Poland. The reason for the perceived need to simplify and speed up the bureaucratic handling of the new immigration was political: As a representative of the Federal Interior Ministry underscored in a January 1971 meeting with representatives of the Federal Administration Office, the Foreign Office, the Red Cross, and the Länder interior ministries, the German willingness to take people in should not fall short of the increased Polish willingness to let people go.[41] The credibility of the Federal Republic's commitment to its co-ethnics and alleged citizens abroad was at stake.

The new procedure involved a set of problems that caused controversy among the responsible authorities, because they affected the state's aspiration to control immigration and the necessity to gather information to that end. The first of these problems related to the fact that application forms would now be filled out not by relatives in West Germany but directly by Aussiedler candidates in Poland. For this reason, the D1A form, which the Federal Interior Ministry and the Federal Administration Office created after the publication of the "Information" in December based on the existing D1 form, did not contain certain questions that presumably could cause the applicants in Poland trouble with the local authorities or that were deemed unnecessary. Hence, the form did not ask for:

- German name of the place of birth (thus avoiding, for example, that an applicant would have to write "Breslau" instead of "Wrocław");
- current citizenship (because the postwar citizenship status of the formerly German "autochthones" was a contentious issue; only citizenship before May 8, 1945 was kept);
- reasons for a possible change of citizenship;
- language currently spoken in the family;
- participation in German political, cultural, or other associations (all that was kept was the general question about *Volkszugehörigkeit* and native tongue, without these additional details);
- membership in the Waffen-SS or other Nazi organizations (membership in the Wehrmacht was deemed neutral enough to be kept);

- imprisonment as a prisoner of war or internment, possible expropriation as well as still existing property;
- all questions concerning relatives in the FRG.[42]

At the January meeting, the Foreign Office further suggested not asking the applicants for written documents. This proposal was rejected by both the BMI and the BVA representatives, who stressed that documentation was still necessary to assess an application. The Red Cross would create a list of the documents to be requested.[43]

A second contentious question was whether the German authorities should examine the applications at all. Here, too, the Foreign Office (supported by the Argeflü) took a generous line, asking for little or no control, while the Interior Ministry believed control was still both necessary and possible. The background of this discussion, which took place on the ministerial level, was the quick realization that the D1A procedure as envisioned in the January meeting was unfeasible in practice. The German Red Cross could not directly contact the ethnic Germans willing to emigrate and hence could not send them the necessary form.[44] An alternative scenario was the distribution and collection of the forms by the Travel Permit Office (TPO) at the US embassy in Warsaw, which was still in charge of West German consular affairs. In a June 1971 letter to the interior minister Hans-Dietrich Genscher, foreign minister Walter Scheel, a liberal democrat who had taken office with the rise to power of the new social-liberal coalition in 1969, rejected this scenario. Among his objections was the observation that the TPO staff were Poles and would not be able to help the applicants fill out the German forms correctly.[45] He also feared bureaucratic delays that could put the whole resettlement enterprise into question.

Scheel's alternative proposal amounted to nothing less than devolving to the Polish authorities the decision of who was to be defined as an ethnic German. He suggested that the TPO issue an entry visa for the FRG to anyone who had an exit permit that the Poles reserved for ethnic Germans. Scheel argued that this was unproblematic, since the Polish government had a very narrow conception of what the "undoubtedly German ethnicity" of the "Information" meant. For this reason, the German authorities could assume that only "actual German *Volkszugehörige*" would receive an exit permit. As in other urgent cases, such as those of Germans from Czechoslovakia after 1968 or Germans from the Soviet Union, the necessary examination could then take place in the transit camp at Friedland (i.e., within the framework of the distribution procedure). The same procedure was in place for ethnic Germans who came to West Germany as visitors with regular Polish passports and then applied for recognition as Aussiedler. People adhering to the legal procedure were not to be disadvantaged in comparison.

As might be expected, Scheel's laissez-faire proposal did not meet with the approval of the Federal Administration Office, whose advice the Interior Ministry had sought.[46] After dispelling Scheel's worries about delays in the procedure and the possible endangering of the resettlement campaign, the responding official, Dr. Even, explained in detail why he rejected the foreign minister's idea to use Polish emigration permits as proof of Germanness:

> I hold it to be very problematic to leave the decision about German ethnicity and citizenship exclusively to the Polish authorities for the sake of "simplification." First of all, we must not forget that during the great resettlement campaign of 1958 and 1959, Poland infiltrated people who were undesirable also for the Federal Republic, such as travelers (*Landfahrer*) and antisocial elements (*Asoziale*). The authorization of the Permit Office to give all people an entry visa who claim that they have no intermediary would certainly be extended to all those people who have not filed a D1-application yet and would put them in a better position compared to those Germans who for many years have had no success in obtaining an emigration permit, despite their entry permit. The knowledge that immigration is beyond prior control of the German authorities could be an incentive to decide upon exit permits based on Polish interests only. An ex post examination in the German transit camp is of limited value only, since it will hardly be possible to send an Aussiedler back to Poland, for political as well as for humanitarian reasons.[47]

In subsequent discussions, the Foreign Office and the Interior Ministry, which fully adopted the BVA's position, searched for a compromise solution that would reconcile the contradictory imperatives of a politically expedient speedy processing of the resettlement campaign on the one hand, and sovereign control of who was going to enter the country on the other hand.[48] The compromise solution the ministries found attempted to make use of the fact that many of the prospective resettlers were so-called *Alteingesessene*—that is, inhabitants of the German Eastern Territories who had been verified as Polish autochthones after the war but, according to the West German viewpoint, had retained their German citizenship.[49] They, as well as their descendants, should be automatically considered German citizens and immediately receive entry visas from the TPO. German staff should assist the TPO in identifying such candidates. Moreover, it was agreed to create a further reduced D1A form for the inhabitants of the Eastern Territories, which together with the regular D1A form should be translated into Polish and forwarded to the TPO. This form omitted questions about applicants' places of residence and occupations since December 31, 1937, and questions about *Volkszugehörigkeit* and native tongue; all these were deemed irrelevant for German citizens.[50] The applications of people who were not considered to belong to this group were still to be decided by the BVA.

Conceptually, then, resettlement from Poland had been extended to people with no relatives in the Federal Republic of Germany, thus transcending the formerly narrow focus on family reunification. The D1A procedure was the administrative expression of this reconceptualization; or put differently, it was the channel through which this extended co-ethnic migration was supposed to flow. The information that was requested to assess someone's eligibility to enter this channel was drastically reduced. Given the removal of the requirement of a family connection, which so far had served as a reassurance that the people taken in were actually Germans, this seems counterintuitive. The idea, however, was that the candidates should simply prove their descent from the Eastern Territories, which would make them German citizens in all likelihood. This is why the questions about *Volkszugehörigkeit* and language were removed from the form.

In practice, this supposedly elegant solution was met with severe difficulties. One such difficulty resulted from developments on the ground. Potential emigrants in Poland did not apply for Aussiedlung through the D1A channel as they either did not know about the "Information" issued by the government and the extended emigration possibilities it promised, or they could not benefit from it because the Polish authorities continued to insist on an invitation from relatives.[51] Frightened by the prospect of another "emigration psychosis" among the "autochthones," the restrictive faction among the Polish authorities prevailed in internal struggles over the emigration question, and the gate that had opened with the "Information" was closed again.[52] After a record 26,237 exit permits having been issued for West Germany in 1971—the highest number since 1958—numbers dropped back to below 5,000 by 1973.[53]

A second difficulty was of an administrative nature and related to problems with the assessment of individual eligibility for co-ethnic resettlement. It was soon revealed that the new and shorter D1A forms sometimes did not yield enough information after all to allow the authorities to reconstruct an applicant's life, looking for typical clues of German *Volkszugehörigkeit*.[54] In one case, the representative of the federal government at the transit camp in Friedland and the aliens' authorities of the Göttingen district were unable to assess the eligibility of Ladislaus/Władysław M. and of his Polish wife, Franciszka.

Ladislaus/Władysław had been born in then Austrian Galicia in 1915 and currently lived in Wrocław. According to his D1A application, he had lived in the "Sudetengau" on May 8, 1945, and had been a German citizen before that date.[55] Yet the representative in Friedland felt unable to assess the applicant's citizenship or *Volkszugehörigkeit* based on this information only and without any knowledge about his subsequent trajectory. Unknown were Ladislaus/Władysław's places of residence after 1937, his occupations during the war, how he had acquired German citizenship (e.g., via the *Volksliste*), and when and why his name had been Polonized.[56] The BVA, the Federal Interior Ministry, and the Foreign Office therefore created a new, expanded version of the D1A form.[57] It reintroduced all the previously dropped questions about places of residence and occupations since 1937, when and how German citizenship was acquired, as well as detailed information about the parents, and thus very much resembled the original D1 form. The final version of the longer form was endorsed by the Federal Interior Ministry in March 1975—just in time for the major emigration wave from Poland that was about to start in the wake of the Conference for Security and Cooperation in Europe negotiations in Helsinki in August and the ensuing Polish-German emigration protocol of October 9, 1975, which by 1979 would bring more than 125,000 Germans from Poland to West Germany.[58]

New Aussiedlung from the Soviet Union and the Making of "Russian Germans"

Simultaneously to, and even preceding the attempted reinvention of Polish-German Aussiedlung as an ethnic resettlement campaign that transcended humanitarian family reunification, the West German institutions were engaged in a similar effort with Germans from the Soviet Union. Until the mid-1960s, German resettlement from the Soviet Union could hardly be classified as ethnic at all, because it almost exclusively involved people on whose German citizenship both Germans and Soviets could agree: *Reichsdeutsche* from East Prussia and former *Vertragsumsiedler* who were covered by the 1958 Soviet–West German repatriation agreement.[59] It was based, then, on mutually accepted legal rather than on ethnic ties. During the watershed period, this narrow conception widened to include new groups of ethnic Germans whose German citizenship was either contested or who had no legal ties to Germany and no relatives to justify transborder family reunification. Developments on the ground and the parallel intensified emigration of Soviet Jews to Israel played an important role in this process. In the course of this extension, the hitherto marginal

Russian Germans (*Russlanddeutsche*), who in the 1990s would become almost synonymous with the categories of Aussiedler and Spätaussiedler, entered the horizon of the West German authorities.

Already from the second half of the 1960s, West German institutions involved in the resettlement of Germans from the Soviet Union were considering more proactive approaches to the issue than had previously been embraced. This happened amid increasing mobilization—in a political as well as a spatial sense—among Russian Germans, who, after their wartime deportation, had been confined to special settlements in Siberia and Kazakhstan until 1955. Part of the political mobilization concerned the reestablishment of the former Volga German Autonomous Republic—an issue raised by delegations of Russian Germans to the Kremlin after the 1964 partial rehabilitation decree by the Supreme Soviet.[60] But mobilization also implied the increased willingness of Russian Germans to move both within the Soviet Union and outside it. Between 1966 and 1969, almost 5,000 people were allowed to leave the country for either West or East Germany. Among those going to the German Democratic Republic were several families with no familial ties outside the Soviet Union—something unheard of in West Germany.[61] In this setting, the German embassy in Moscow inquired with the Foreign Office in October 1967 whether Soviet Germans could receive the *vyzov* ("invitation," the equivalent of the Polish *zaproszenie*) required for their exit visa not just from relatives but also from acquaintances or even from a German institution. But rather than referring to the German Democratic Republic, the embassy referred to the example of Israel, whose authorities were allegedly sending institutionalized *vyzovy* to the Soviet Union.[62] The German embassy in Tel Aviv, however, denied this assertion, and so nothing came of this initiative for the time being.[63] Similarly, an alleged case of a Soviet German family with no relatives in West Germany receiving a Soviet exit permit based on an embassy-issued *vyzov* in November 1970 soon turned out to be false alarm, as the mother of the family was a German citizen from East Prussia and was hence eligible for repatriation under the 1958 agreement.[64]

Generally, the responsible institutions responded cautiously to such initiatives to widen the scope of Soviet German Aussiedlung. The Red Cross Tracing Service in particular was reluctant to issue state-sponsored invitations; in its experience, a *vyzov* presupposed actual relatives, and invented relatives would supposedly be of no use to anyone.[65] In an April 1973 report, the Red Cross emphasized that it presently could do nothing to support the emigration attempts by so-called administrative resettlers (*Administrativumsiedler*)—that is, ethnic Germans from Ukraine who had been "resettled" to Germany during the war and "repatriated" to the Soviet Union after the war—and by ethnic Germans without relatives in the Federal Republic of Germany, most of whom were of Volga German origin.[66] Both of these groups were claimed by the Soviet Union as Soviet citizens. The report underlined, however, that not mentioning these groups in the negotiations with the Soviets now would not mean renouncing the later treatment of the topic.[67]

The issue of the emigration of Soviet Germans without relatives in West Germany acquired new urgency because of actual migration trends. In September 1973, the Red Cross reported that it had received, either directly or via the embassy, at least 35,000 such applications. This development was arguably triggered by the successful example of Jewish emigration from the Soviet Union as well as by reports about the "Information" of the Polish government.[68] The increase in applications corresponded with a rise in the number of people allowed to leave: 4,493 Soviet German immigrants were registered in West Germany in 1973 alone, the highest number since 1959.[69]

Amid this trend, the Foreign Office, the German diplomatic missions in the Soviet Union, and the Federal Interior Ministry intensified their deliberations behind the scenes about how to enable Soviet Germans without relatives in the West to leave the Soviet Union. The Foreign Office took reports by the Leningrad consulate general and the Moscow embassy about Soviet Germans who had contacted them to receive an official certification as an opportunity to once again push for the introduction of such state-sponsored invitations.[70] Rising application and emigration numbers could be indicative of the Soviet authorities' willingness to let ethnic Germans of all categories emigrate for "higher political motives" (*aus übergeordneten politischen Gründen*). Since any complication in the takeover procedure caused by the German side could be extremely harmful for the overall resettlement process, the Foreign Office argued that the embassy in Moscow should be authorized to issue certifications stating that applicants would be accepted into the FRG if they received an exit permit from the Soviet Union.

In its response to the Foreign Office's request, the BMI rejected the proposal to turn the Moscow embassy into a preliminary gatekeeper for Soviet Germans, calling it "impossible" as well as "unnecessary."[71] The D1 procedure could process the cases, since it had been created to assess the eligibility of a person for resettlement independently of the actual possibility to emigrate. The resulting immigration permit should also satisfy the Soviet authorities. But, as the Foreign Office pointed out, the situation was not that clear-cut. The ethnic Germans who wanted to emigrate could not enter the German embassy unless they already held a Soviet exit permit. It was not possible to send them the D1 forms, because answering some of the questions on the form could cause the applicants trouble with the Soviet authorities. Neither could people submit their applications directly at the BVA, nor did they have relatives to do this for them. And the embassy was unable to help with this issue, because it usually did not possess the necessary documentation.[72]

Based on these considerations, the Foreign Office suggested a different, simplified procedure. Rather than drafting a new D1 form as in the Polish case, the questionnaires that the embassy had already sent in the past to potential emigrants should be used as the basis for the examination of the cases by the BVA. Soon after, in late November 1973, the first such questionnaire was returned to the embassy in Moscow, which forwarded it to the Foreign Office.[73] The questionnaire had been completed by Eduard Jakowlewitsch A., born in the Omsk region in 1932 and now head of a family with six children living in Alamedin in the Kirgiz Soviet Socialist Republic. From questions five through eight ("When did you come to Germany?" "What was your last place of residence in Germany?" "When and where did you receive German citizenship?" "Number of the citizenship certificate") and number eleven ("When did you come to the Soviet Union?"), it is clear that the questionnaire targeted the so-called *Reichsdeutschen* as well as *Vertragsumsiedler* and *Administrativumsiedler*—that is, people who had either been born on German territory or had at least had some kind of legal connection with the country through resettlement before and during the war. Eduard Jakowlewitsch A., on the other hand, could only respond that he had never been to or lived in Germany, and that he had never received German citizenship. To question number eleven he replied truthfully: "I was born here." And the response to question 16 about relatives outside the Soviet Union could only be: "Outside the USSR we have no relatives."

Since it appeared that the information requested in the old questionnaire would not be sufficient for the Interior Ministry and the Federal Administration Office to assess the eligibility of candidates under section 6 BVFG, the BVA then suggested a new, extended questionnaire which was discussed and approved in a meeting with the Interior Ministry and the Foreign Office.[74] It included additional questions about the applicant's passport nationality, places of residence since 1937, and active and passive knowledge of the German language as well as a similar set of questions about the applicant's parents and spouse. These questions, which were supposed to provide more substantial clues about the German ethnicity of applicants, had previously been suggested by the Moscow embassy and the Leningrad consulate.[75] The embassy had pointed to the relevance of the *natsional'nost'* item registered in the Soviet internal passport. The consulate had moreover suggested specific questions that would help assess an applicant's Germanness: "In which German area of settlement in the

Soviet Union have you lived (Volga Republic, Ukraine, etc.)? When and for how long have you lived there? Do you understand the German language? Do you speak German? Can you write in German?"[76] The public endeavor to emigrate from the Soviet Union would also have to be considered a *Bekenntnis*.

In the transition from the old to the new questionnaire, the changed conception of Soviet-German emigration becomes evident. Like the developments in the Polish case, the new questionnaire demonstrated how the strict adherence to the principle of family reunification, which previously governed the application process, was overcome, thus considerably expanding the scope of potential migrants. But the expansion went much further than this. Until this time, the embassy had not asked about the nationality stated in applicant's Soviet passports. This question was omitted for the simple reason that previously the applicants were expected to be German citizens, either by birth or by naturalization. The 1974 questionnaire shows that this conception had changed. The related remark by the Leningrad consulate general that this extension would concern "several hundred thousand persons" reveals that there was some awareness of the potential consequences for immigration. While the new questionnaire still contained questions about possible stays in Germany, German citizenship, and relatives or acquaintances in the FRG, it was intentionally designed to also accommodate the requirements of section 6 BVFG (i.e., German *Volkszugehörigkeit*). And this was to be judged on the basis of passport nationality, language, and preferably also descent from a particular region of the country that was typically considered a German area of settlement (even though the question was eventually not included in the questionnaire).

A new type of Soviet German was thus emerging before the eyes of the West German administration: someone with a particular geographical descent and particular cultural traits, but also with a particular ascribed nationality. These issues became more salient with the internal recognition procedure in the 1980s, when several actors, including the Landsmannschaft of Germans from Russia, institutionalized this stereotypical image of the Russian German that would leave its imprint on the recognition practice of the Federal Administration Office in the 1990s. But similar to other instances, such as the generational extension discussed previously, the groundwork was laid at the external gate.

ISRAEL: BRINGING IN THE GRANDCHILDREN

The framework for co-ethnic immigration to Israel changed around the same time as it had in West Germany, but in a less protracted and yet more fundamental way. The common point was the extension of the existing arrangement because of a domestic challenge to the status quo, and in anticipation of continued and enhanced immigration due to the changing international environment. Yet the nature of the domestic challenge and the ensuing discussions were completely different in each case. In Germany, the challenge had been against the system of ethnic priority immigration per se, or at least against insufficient controls. Subsequent discussions happened in closed forums away from the public eye. In Israel, the challenge—the Supreme Court ruling in favor of a secular definition of Jewishness in the much publicized Shalit case—had no direct link to immigration, but rather was directed against the common population registration practice by criteria of religious law—that is, matrilineal descent. This challenge was discussed in public and tied into larger discourses of national identity. Consequently, the main cleavage in the contestation of the Israeli extension was not between generous external and cautious internal authorities but between secular nationalists and religious puritans—a recurrent pattern in years to follow.

In contrast to the German case, legislation—the Law of Return—was actually changed in Israel. With the amendment the government tried to accommodate both the domestic and the external factors. The introduction of the restrictive religious definition of Jewishness into the Law of Return was meant to placate the furious religious establishment. The simultaneous extension of legal privileges to non-Jews under this law was triggered by the (soon to be fulfilled) expectation of enhanced Soviet-Jewish immigration, which would supposedly include many mixed families. Unlike the cautious extension by one postwar generation implemented by the Germans, the 1970 amendment to the Law of Return extended the right to Aliyah to two generations of descendants of Jews at any point in time, regardless of whether they were Jewish according to religious law. This radically enlarged the pool of potential immigrants while creating a curious species that matched the "derived German" with an inherited *Bekenntnis*: the "derived Jew," a figure destined to become Israeli without being Jewish.

The following discussion first reconstructs how the Shalit case and the resulting coalition crisis triggered the amendment to the Law of Return; then it analyzes the creation of the amendment and the related debates in the Knesset. The debates revolved around three main issues: mixed marriages and conversion, generational extension, and the law's new definitions of the terms *Jew* and *convert*. Transcending the theoretical discussions and implications of the amendment, the final section examines the implications of the simultaneously restrictive and expansive amendment in administrative practice.

THE SHALIT CASE AND ITS AFTERMATH

The immediate trigger for the 1970 amendment of the Law of Return and the Population Registry Law was a case not related to immigration but to the Population Registry only. Its repercussions for the immigration regime resulted from the close link between Aliyah and registration, which were institutionally connected and both revolved around the notion and definition of the term *Jew*. The Shalit case raised a well-known controversial question that had been dormant for some years: How should a child born of a Jewish father and a non-Jewish mother be registered? According to religious law (halacha), such a child should be considered non-Jewish. Whether this was the only possible registration or whether the child could be registered as Jewish by parental declaration was one of the points of contention in the 1958 "Who is a Jew" debate discussed in chapter 1. A majority of the "Sages of Israel" consulted at that time opined that the halachic criterion—maternal descent—should be decisive. In 1960, Interior Minister Chaim-Moshe Shapira of the National Religious Party (NRP) introduced this criterion into the registration guidelines. In 1968, Benjamin Shalit, an Israeli-born navy officer married to a non-Jewish Scottish woman, Anne Geddes, challenged this arrangement by requesting that his children, Oren and Galia, be registered as Jewish by ethnicity (*leom*), despite their non-Jewish mother. When the registrar refused to do so, the matter went to court.

The Shalit case generated heated public debate both before and after the Supreme Court ruling.[77] It touched on some of the most salient issues in the definition of Israeli Jewishness. In particular, it struggled with whether, in the Jewish state, a person could be Jewish by ethnic affiliation while not meeting the religious criterion of having been born to a Jewish mother. This amounted to questioning the extent to which Jewish religion and nationality could be separated at all. In the Israeli context, by extension, this question also had direct repercussions for the gatekeeper question: Who had the right to define who belonged to the Jewish people and was consequently entitled to Israeli citizenship?

A panel of nine judges (the maximum number) was appointed to rule on Shalit's request. To avoid a controversial ruling, the judges suggested that the government cancel the item *Leom* from the Population Registry altogether.[78] When the government refused, it provided two main reasons that Justice Minister Yaakov Shimshon Shapira stated in the Knesset.[79] The first reason was taken directly from Ben-Gurion's letter to the "Sages of Israel" in 1958 and had to do with security concerns and specifically the fear of infiltrators.[80] The second motive was highly symbolic: Responding to an article by Ben-Gurion (by then elder statesman and member of Knesset) in the daily newspaper *Maariv* on February 6, 1970, Shapira dramatically declared that the Jews of Israel were still—and would be for a long time, if not forever—part of the Jewish people as a whole. Half of world Jewry—2.5 million in Israel and another four million in the Soviet Union and Eastern Europe—had their Jewish nationality (*leumiut yehudit*) registered on their ID card: "Those who suggest we erase it from our ID cards will divide us from them; no Israeli government can allow itself to propose such a deed to the Knesset."[81] Prime Minister Golda Meir made a similar statement, suggesting that canceling this item would "create among the Jewish people the impression that they are separate, and we are Hebrew, Canaanites, Jebusites, I don't know what else—but not Jews. They are Jews but we are not."[82] An isolated attempt to have the item *Leom* erased from the Population Registry by means of legislation, led by Knesset members (of the right-wing Free Center) Shmuel Tamir and Eliezer Shostak, remained unsuccessful.[83]

With the exit option ruled out, the judges handed down their verdict on January 23, 1970.[84] By a slim 5–4 majority, the judges vindicated Shalit's request to have his children registered as Jewish. However, the majority judges refused to give an opinion about whether the children were actually Jewish and thus denied any gatekeeper function of their own.[85] Instead, the majority opinion argued that the registrar had to register the children as Jewish if the parents declared their Jewishness in good faith. It was not up to the registrar to judge the correctness of the statement; his function was merely to gather data for the Population Registry, the contents of which did not constitute a prima facie proof of their truth.[86] This reliance on bona fide declarations contravened the existing 1960 registration guidelines and the firm viewpoint of the religious camp that registration without the halachic test was unacceptable. Consequently, the National Religious Party threatened its resignation from the ruling national unity government on January 25.[87]

THE 1970 AMENDMENT TO THE LAW OF RETURN

The government proposal to amend the Law of Return was an attempt to save the national unity government that encompassed the Labor Alignment, the Revisionist Gahal of Menachem Begin, the Independent Liberal Party, and the National Religious Party, and thus straddled the most salient left-right and secular-religious cleavages. On February 3, the government decided in a 13–3 majority (with one abstention) to submit an amendment proposal to the

Knesset that had been developed by the government ministers and the Ministerial Legislation Committee. It suggested adding a section 4A titled "Partner and Children" to the Law of Return. It read as follows: "The rights of a Jew according to this law, the Citizenship Law of 1952, and any law establishing provisions for an Oleh will also be given to his child and to his spouse, and also to the child's spouse and child, except for a convert from Judaism (*yehudi-mumar*) among them." A proposed section 4B defined the notion of Jew according to this law as follows: "For the purpose of this law, a 'Jew' is someone who was born to a Jewish mother or who converted, and who does not belong to another religion." In addition, the second part of the proposed law amended the Population Registry Law. It stated that the definition of section 4B of the Law of Return should also apply to the Population Registry Law and that no one should be registered as Jewish by *Leom* or religion if other registrations or documents indicate that he or she is not Jewish.[88]

Since they addressed different domestic and international inputs, sections 4A and 4B pulled in diametrically opposed directions. Section 4B and the derived amendment to the Population Registry were restrictive in their intention. As a reaction to the Shalit verdict, which had endorsed the bona fide declaration of Jewishness for registration purposes, they introduced the narrower halachic criterion into both the Law of Return and the Population Registry Law. In contrast, section 4A was expansive. It extended the rights awarded to these narrowly defined Jews to their non-Jewish family members, who were expected to arrive from the Soviet Union in large numbers. The contradiction was not lost on contemporary observers. Moshe Sneh of Maki, the Communist Party of Israel, denounced the amendment as "totally contradictory" and "absurd."[89] Yet it represented a "package deal" compromise between Labor and the NRP that was trying to accommodate contradicting religious and national prerogatives.[90]

In fact, before this draft reached the Knesset floor, it had already undergone some significant changes since the first proposal by Interior Minister Shapira of the NRP on January 27. Shapira had tried to fully assert halachic primacy over the definition of who is a Jew. To do so, he had proposed a definition according to which "a 'Jew' for the purpose of legislation is someone whose mother is Jewish and who does not belong to another religion, or who converted *according to the halacha*."[91] After a first round of deliberations among the ministers, the words "according to the halacha" were removed. The legal counselor (*yoetz mishpati*) to the government, Meir Shamgar, explicitly announced that, in this law, the notion of conversion encompassed any conversion, also Orthodox and Reform, thereby opening up another contentious field of discussion that will be examined below.[92] The same government meeting introduced an original version of section 4A, which restricted the extension of Oleh's rights to the non-Jewish partner and child only.[93] The Ministerial Legislation Committee unanimously decided to also include the spouse and child of the child.[94] In the version that was finally endorsed by the Knesset, the grandchild's spouse was included as well. For non-Jewish family members, the government hoped to convince the chief rabbinate to facilitate and speed up the conversion process to Judaism for them.[95]

The respective debate in the Knesset took place in a first reading on February 9 and 10, 1970, and in a second and third reading on March 10. The heated discussions pitted variations of secular nationalism, religious nationalism, and religious orthodoxy against one another. The next section reconstructs the different positions that were embraced by the multiple political actors in the Knesset discussion about the two contradictory parts of the amendment. The reconstruction focuses on the debates surrounding three issues: the anticipated arrival of mixed families and the resulting question of conversion; the extension of co-ethnic status to derived Jews; and the definition of a Jew according to the law, which, to a great extent, revolved around the question of what constituted a valid conversion. The analysis of these discussions reveals the motivations, intentions, and expectations of the Israeli lawmakers, who in 1970 debated an amendment that would dramatically change their country in the 1990s.

Mixed Marriages and Conversion

Justice Minister Yaakov Shimshon Shapira was tasked with justifying the law proposal to the Knesset. He traced the current situation back to the 1958 "Who is a Jew" controversy and the issues that had arisen at the time: whether the subjective declaration of being Jewish was acceptable and the more general problem of mixed marriages. Shapira justified the introduction of section 4B with the need to have a definition of who was to be considered a Jew in the law. In contrast, he stated that section 4A was the answer to the question of mixed families: they could only be "saved" for Judaism if they were permitted to come to Israel and become part of Jewish society. At the same time, he still supported the idea that they should convert to Judaism.

On the second day of the debate, Prime Minister Golda Meir spoke out in defense of her justice minister, who she felt had been unjustly attacked. Her statement directly addressed the contradiction between the proposed sections. She explicitly defended these incongruities as necessary compromises in light of competing political priorities after the Shalit ruling. She described her reaction to the ruling as follows:

> On the morning the Justice Minister called to tell me that we have a ruling, I thought of two things: first of all that this might be interpreted in the diaspora as a permit from Israel for mixed marriages; and secondly, I thought about the Russian Jews, especially about them, but also about mixed families from the West who want to make Aliyah. I hope they will come to Israel. Here I will not need to worry if their children will be Jewish. It is true, we were looking for ways . . . to find a solution for both problems together.[96]

The prime minister thus felt she had to reconcile two concerns. The first concern was that the Shalit ruling and the extension of the right to return to non-Jewish family members could be understood as an official endorsement of mixed marriages in the diaspora. The viewpoint that mixed marriages were a "disaster" (*ason*) for the Jewish people was not restricted to ultra-Orthodox Knesset members like Yitzhak Meir Levin of Agudat Yisrael.[97] Golda Meir, too, identified them as a threat to Jewish existence in the world.[98] The introduction in section 4B of matrilineal descent into the Law of Return was meant to quell these concerns as it sent this message to Jewish men all over the world: if you want your offspring to be Jewish, you must not intermarry.

At the same time, consideration was given to the expected great Aliyah from the Soviet Union that would extend beyond the rare cases of family reunification to that point—an expectation already familiar from the German case.[99] This expectation was fueled by the ever more visible nationalist mobilization among Soviet Jewry in the late 1960s and especially after the Six-Day War, which found its expression in a growing movement in various cities of the Soviet Union that demanded emigration to Israel in public letters and petitions.[100] This movement had been successful in obtaining a limited number of emigration permits, and the Israelis expected more. The Knesset members assumed that there would be large numbers of mixed and assimilated families among them and that these new arrivals would have to be accommodated somehow. Under current legislation, such families had a problem that Prime Minister Meir summed up as follows: "When a family [came] to Israel, if [only] the husband was Jewish, he came through the open gate, the main gate; and his wife and children did not come with an equal status. The same family did not come with an equal status. We now propose to change this situation."[101]

Among secular and religious nationalists alike, the necessity for finding a solution for these families was beyond doubt. This time, ultra-Orthodox Yitzhak Meir Levin was alone with his contention that there was no point in changing the "image and the essence" of the people to accommodate a so far completely "imaginary" Aliyah.[102] Justice Minister Shapira seemed to have no doubt that this Aliyah would materialize: "What will be when the Great Aliyah comes? The answer is: then we will solve all the problems. And so, we need to begin solving problems. I say: section 4A that we add to the Law of Return solves the question that concerns us in the European, Western, and American diasporas, and also in the Soviet diaspora."[103]

The inclusion of non-Jewish family members was based on the argument that it would "save" mixed families from assimilation in the diaspora and help them merge into the Jewish people in Israel. This idea was put forward by secularist centrists, such as Justice Minister Shapira; secular leftists, such as Yaakov Chazan of Mapam; and religious nationalists, such as Yisrael Shlomo Ben-Meir of the NRP. The latter couched this justification in religious terms as the fulfillment of the *mitzvah* (commandment) of bringing "the sons back to their borders, . . . and those who were severed, were ejected from the Jewish people, by coming back to Israel will find the way to return to the bosom of their fathers, will become part of the Jewish people according to the definition, will convert, will turn into a part of us, and will also increase our force (*kochenu*) in the Land."[104]

According to this logic, the fear of encouraging mixed marriages and of introducing foreign elements into the Jewish people was less important than the "salvation" of those Jews who had been severed from the Jewish people through mixed marriage. Put differently, the focus of the law was more on the Jewish family member than on the non-Jewish family members. The latter were simply expected to blend in. In the words of Israeli historian Yfaat Weiss, "The 1970 amendment to the Law of Return was aimed not at 'non-Jews,' but at Jews, and specifically and unmistakably at the specific situation of Soviet Jewry."[105]

That the non-Jewish family members of these Jews would have to convert to blend in was beyond doubt for a religious person like Ben-Meir, but it was also the preferred solution for a secularist like Yaakov Shimshon Shapira.[106] The opponents of such an imperative to convert decried the "religious coercion" inherent in it. This was the viewpoint adopted, for example, by Knesset member Meir Vilner of the New Communist List (*Rakach*).[107] Another critic, Shoshana Arbeli-Almozlino of the Labor Alignment, emphasized the gendered nature of this "forced conversion," which, due to the matrilineal definition of Jewishness, would only affect women. Yet she mainly took issue with the demanding Orthodox conversion practices, which she described as "demeaning." Facilitated conversion by liberal rabbis she saw as less problematic.[108] For Yaakov Chazan, on the other hand, Aliyah itself constituted "the most genuine conversion"—an approach that somewhat paralleled the notion adopted around the same time by the German administration that Aussiedlung to Germany constituted a *Bekenntnis* to German *Volkstum*.[109]

The reproach of religious coercion was fiercely rejected by Menachem Begin, of the Revisionist Gahal and at the time, minister without portfolio. In his words: "We do not force anything. The man (*ish*) does not want to convert—so he should not convert. He will not be part of the Jewish people. He does not want to be registered as a member of the Jewish nation (*ben ha-umah ha-yehudit*)—he will not be registered."[110] In the context of his speech, this "live and let live" approach made sense: previously he had described Israel as a "free and democratic" state that recognized the equality of all its citizens irrespective of their *Leom* or their religion. Based on this assumption, and leaving aside the importance of Jewishness for personal status law, conversion or not to Judaism could only be a minor issue. Nonetheless, Begin also supported the idea of the facilitated conversion of non-Jewish family members.

Generational Extension and the Creation of Derived Jews

Between the first and second reading of the amendment in the Knesset, another change was introduced to section 4A that would have important long-term consequences but hardly raised an eyebrow at the time. The Knesset legislation committee added a subsection b, which stated: "It shall be immaterial whether or not a Jew by whose right a privilege under subsection a) is claimed is still alive and whether or not he has immigrated to Israel." This change radically altered the nature of this amendment from a mere mixed family extension to a generational extension that went far beyond simultaneous developments in Germany. Whereas the previous version served the purpose of granting equal status to mixed families that immigrated together, this new version opened a whole new possibility: now the halachically non-Jewish (grand)child of a Jew had the right to come to Israel by his or her own right, derived, of course, from the Jewishness of the (grand)father but without his presence.

More than the original wording of section 4A (without subsections), this updated version, which was eventually endorsed by the Knesset, signaled a departure from the original spirit of the 1950 Law of Return, which, in the words of historian Yfaat Weiss, had been "framed as a law of repatriation for Jews and for Jews only."[111] Yet judging from the Knesset discussion, the implications of this seemingly minor addition to the amendment were lost on most of the discussants. In an earlier meeting of the Legislation Committee, Meir Avizohar of

Ben-Gurion's National List seemed to comprehend the potential ramifications but then dismissed his own concerns:

> What are we doing? We are expanding the scope so greatly that even I, who favor expansion, am beginning to hesitate, because all of us are thinking of the immigration of Jews coming to Israel because they are Jews, but not of the immigration of people who will want to come in order to enjoy certain economic benefits which the state gives to immigrants, and in order to put this into practice will go looking for some distant Jewish origins. [Yet] I do not at the moment see a problem of migrants, particularly in light of the war situation that we are currently experiencing.[112]

One would have to agree then with Yfaat Weiss's assessment that, "in 1970, it is safe to say, there was no obvious reason to assume that anyone not connected with Jews and Jewishness through family ties would choose to migrate to Israel for purely utilitarian reasons."[113]

Similarly, concerns about the demographic battle with the Arabs in the greater "Land of Israel," which acquired prominence during the great Soviet Aliyah of the late 1980s, were also largely absent from the discussion, despite occasional remarks like the one by Ben-Meir above about "our force in the land" and Shmuel Tamir's wish for a "large and numerous people" (*am gadol ve-rav*).[114] At the time, merely three years after the occupation of the West Bank and Gaza, the specter of being outnumbered within the confines of former Mandate Palestine was hardly on the agenda, because it was by no means clear that these territories would remain under long-term Israeli control.[115] By the late 1980s, when the right-wing Shamir government contemplated annexing the occupied territories, this threat appeared much more urgent.

It thus appears that neither the reasons for nor the potential consequences of this amendment were thoroughly thought through by the lawmakers at the time. When Yisrael Shlomo Ben-Meir introduced the new subsection on behalf of the Legislation Committee on March 10, 1970, he accompanied it with a harmless anecdote of an English girl born from a mixed marriage whose Jewish father opposed her conversion to Judaism and her Aliyah to Israel. With the new subsection, she would be able to make Aliyah to Israel without having to rely on her renegade father.[116]

In a similar vein, during the first reading, Yaakov Shimshon Shapira told a story that might have played a role in the inclusion of this subsection in the first place. He recounted the case of the son of a deceased Jewish father and a Ukrainian mother who identified as Jewish, went to the Great Synagogue in Moscow, and used to go to the Israeli embassy. According to Shapira, this young man, though not Jewish, should still have the right to come to Israel and become a citizen. And although absorbing such "Ukrainian families" might create problems, the justice minister argued that the first solution to these problems would be that they come to Israel by right and not by an act of grace.[117] The concern raised by Avizohar in the committee did not surface in the plenary discussion, not even when Avizohar himself spoke. The only factions that suggested canceling section 4A altogether were the ultra-Orthodox parties Agudat Yisrael and Poalei Agudat Yisrael. Yet their proposal was unsuccessful, and section 4A was endorsed by the Knesset as it had been suggested by the Legislation Committee.

With this amendment, the Law of Return approached the German conception of "parental *Bekenntnis*." In the German case, this construction of derived entitlement was deemed necessary, because, by definition, a German *Volkszugehöriger* had to have been of age by 1945. As described above, attempts by the administration to move this deadline forward in time were not successful. Therefore, anyone who was too young to have been an expellee in 1945 could be included in the law only by extension and with reference to the parent. The recognition as German was thus based not on the Germanness of the applicant but on that of the ancestor—it was a "derived Germanness."

In Israel, there was no such fixed deadline—a Jew could always acquire the right to come to Israel as a Jew by the mere fact of being Jewish, however defined. According to religious law, a person born to a Jewish mother or who converted to Judaism was a Jew by her or his own right. Subsection b of section 4A introduced a kind of derived Jewishness akin to the German model. In religious law, a Jewish man could not transmit his Jewishness to his offspring if his wife was not Jewish. But under the new Law of Return, he could pass on his right to come to Israel as a Jew, even in his absence and posthumously. Without a fixed deadline, this derived right could be claimed by any person at any point in time who was able to prove he or she had a Jewish grandparent. This amendment dramatically widened the scope of the Law of Return.

Who Is a Jew? Who Is a Convert?

In addition to the apparent improbability of non-Jewish mass immigration to the struggling Israel of 1970, the lack of attention to section 4A—and, in particular, its subsection b—might also have been due to the fact that in the second and third reading of the amendment law, section 4B—the definition of the term *Jew* according to matrilineal descent—and the conversion proviso took center stage. Even more than section 4A, this topic pitted secular and religious members of Knesset against each other, which raised the intensity of the debate. There were two main aspects to the debate of the definition of the term *Jew*: Should there be a definition of the term at all, and a definition taken from religious law in addition? And which conversion was to be considered valid in order to recognize someone as Jewish?

The first point was of concern to the more ardent secularists among the Knesset members. Proposals to cancel or replace the halachic definition of the term *Jew* from the amendment came from Meir Avizohar (National List), Uri Avneri (Haolam Hazeh—Koach Hadash), Reuven Arazi (Labour Alignment), Moshe Sneh (Maki), Eliezer Shostak (Free Center), and Gideon Hausner (Independent Liberal Party).[118] Their alternative suggestions differed. Avizohar preferred no definition at all, since it might exclude people from the law who considered themselves Jewish; also, it was unnecessary in his opinion, since past immigration waves had been accommodated without a legal definition of the term. Avneri just wanted a simple bona fide declaration. Arazi and Sneh supported that proposal, too; alternatively they advocated parental descent from either side, not just through the mother. Shostak argued that it was not up to a secular body like the Knesset—particularly in the presence of a communist member like Meir Vilner and a communist and non-Jewish member like Tawfik Toubi—to decide on matters of halacha; hence, he preferred no definition.[119] Hausner, who had been the chief prosecutor at the Eichmann trial, made perhaps the most interesting suggestion: he proposed a definition according to which a Jew would be someone declaring his Jewishness in good faith, and who was held to be Jewish by his surroundings to vouch for his Jewishness. The proposal bore a resemblance to the German definition of *Volkszugehörigkeit* through public self-identification that could be perceived by others. However, none of these alternative proposals were accepted by the Knesset majority.

The second question was new to the debate surrounding the Shalit case and the amendment.[120] It concerned the formulation chosen in the law proposal that a Jew could also be someone who converted, without specifying the type of conversion. As noted earlier, the restriction to halachic conversion had been removed from Interior Minister Chaim-Moshe Shapira's original proposal. The issue had already been raised by the ultra-Orthodox parties during the first reading but had not caused much discussion. This changed in the session on March 10. In his introduction on behalf of the Legislation Committee, Yisrael Shlomo Ben-Meir of the NRP tried to brush over the issue by saying that there was "nothing to add" to the issue of conversion.

Menachem Porush of Agudat Yisrael begged to differ. He slammed the government's decision to consciously avoid reference to halacha in the conversion proviso and hence to explicitly acknowledge the validity of Reform and Conservative conversions. This was unacceptable, he argued, because Reform conversion required no circumcision (*brit milah*), no ritual bath (*mikveh*), and so on. After a verbal rampage against the dangers of Reform Judaism as a bridgehead for religious and national assimilation, he successfully drew the attention of his colleagues by throwing a Reform prayer book on the ground.

This dramatic gesture caused outrage among the following speakers and was followed by Porush's halfhearted (due to his insistence on calling Reform Jews "heretics") apology at the end of the session. But it underscored the importance that the ultra-Orthodox camp—in this case both Agudat Yisrael and Poalei Agudat Yisrael—attributed to the issue of the validity of non-Orthodox conversions. For actual immigration this issue was not particularly relevant, as Meir Avizohar pointed out when he noted that the number of Reform converts planning to make Aliyah was in fact low and hardly justified such a fuss.[121]

Yet, as in the 1958 debate, the issue at stake was the status quo agreement and the place of the religious camp in the Israeli political system and, in the matter of recognizing Reform and Conservative conversions, of the exclusive gatekeeping function of the Orthodox rabbinate in particular. A statement by Avraham Verdiger of Poalei Agudat Yisrael during the third reading is telling in this regard:

> Now the Reform comes and knocks at our doors—in Israel—in a place where there is no need for it and no place for it, and nobody here wants it because it has no support among the people here, but now it may gain official recognition by the government and the Knesset.
>
> [Interjection] Don't you want Reform Olim?
>
> I want Olim who are Jews, *and a Reform Jew is also a Jew, but whoever converted according to Reform conversion is not a Jew* and will remain gentile forever.[122]

Knesset member Shalom Cohen of Haolam Hazeh scornfully dismissed this last remark as "fantastic casuistry" (*pilpul fantasti*), but in fact it reinforced an important point. The question at stake for the Orthodox was their exclusive control over entry to the Jewish people that they were unwilling to share with other streams of Judaism, be they Reform or Conservative. The matter was different for people who already were Jews by birth.

Among some secularists, the heated atmosphere created by this fundamental argument triggered the fear of a "theocratic state." Those fears were based on an overestimation of the importance of the halachically inspired definition of Jewishness in section 4B and, correspondingly, an underestimation of the impact of section 4A. Uri Avneri's assessment of the expected effect of section 4B is indicative of this fear: "Where will we go with the approach suggested to us by the government, which Member of Knesset Porush even rejects because it is not radical enough for him? We have lost six million Jews. We have lost one third of the Jewish people. Will we today reject those who want to come to us because they are not kosher according to halacha? They want to come and live with us, they want to build our state, they want to serve in our army, are we going to reject them?"[123]

Avneri obviously did not see how sections 4B and 4A dialectically complemented each other: rather than rejecting people as "unkosher" according to section 4B, the amended law would enable many more of those who Avneri described to enter Israel under section 4A. Menachem Porush, on the other hand, had a better understanding of this dialectic relationship: "If this law is accepted, there will be two kinds of Jews: Jews according to the Law of Return and the Population Registry Law, and Jews according to Marriage and Divorce Law" (since Marriage and Divorce Law was under the control of the Orthodox Rabbinate and thus halachic).[124] Porush thus pinpointed an important aspect of the amendment: it would allow people—potentially considerable numbers of people—to come to Israel as Olim, but they would not be recognized as Jews by the rabbinic authorities. His conclusion was, of course, diametrically opposed to Avneri's. Whereas Avneri wanted to do away with the religious definition in section 4B, Porush wanted to do away with the extension to non-Jews in section 4A. In the end, neither of them got their way, and Israel officially opened its gates to people who were not Jewish by religious definition.

IMPLEMENTING THE AMENDMENT IN PRACTICE

The amendment to the Law of Return and the Population Registry Law was ultimately endorsed with a solid 51–14 vote (with nine abstentions) and went into force on March 19, 1970. It created new challenges for the practitioners in Israel's Aliyah and Registration offices by creating new legal categories of eligible people and by introducing new criteria for the assessment of old categories. According to the definition introduced by section 4B, to be eligible to make Aliyah to Israel as a Jew, a person had to be born of a Jewish mother or had to be a convert, and could not be a member of another religion. Despite this amendment to the law, the category of Jewish Oleh did not seem to create any doubts among the practitioners, except about the validity of conversions abroad. Other than that, this was familiar terrain. Section 4A, however, effectively extended this right to two new categories of people: family members and offspring of a Jew who made Aliyah in the company of their Jewish ancestor and those who made Aliyah without the presence of a Jewish ancestor but derived their right to return from the ancestor's Jewishness, provided they were not apostates from Judaism. Candidates for these new categories had to be identified somehow in practice.

To find practical solutions to these challenges, representatives of the Interior Ministry, the Foreign Office, the Ministry of Absorption, and the police convened shortly after the new law went into effect. While judging the amendment to be "mostly clear," they identified a fundamental question that arose when implementing the law abroad, at the external gate: How could facts be assessed to avoid the "infiltration of non-Jewish elements" trying to use the new legal provisions for non-Jews?[125]

The practitioners had a good grasp of the difference between non-Jewish Olim who came in the company of their Jewish family member and derived Jews who claimed entry to Israel by reference to an absent or deceased Jewish ancestor under subsection b of section 4A. With the former category, the treatment was to remain the same as it had been before. Although the document does not explicate what this meant, it may be assumed that it simply implied a personal declaration of Jewishness by the Jewish family member, as will be explained below.

Derived Jews were another matter. Deputy Interior Minister Yosef Goldschmidt (NRP) warned that they "will be difficult as regards their integration in the State of Israel and it will be necessary to act with particular caution towards them, and each case of doubt of this kind should be forwarded to the main office for decision."[126]For administrative purposes, derived Jews were subdivided into two categories: those from the Western world and Eastern Europeans. Those from the West were supposed to prove their Jewish "origin" (*motza*) by submitting documents as evidence. In cases where there was objectively no possibility for them to provide such documentation, they were required to provide a declaration. For Eastern Europeans, the suggested procedure was described and justified as follows:

> Generally the Jewish origin [of the applicant] cannot be checked because the [emigration] request is submitted to the authorities there and not to our missions (even though this also has a positive side, since it can be assumed that the authorities there will only permit people of Jewish origin to exit the country). It is clear that a certain risk needs to be accepted, and it is only

> for the sake of not harming Aliyah from these countries that we need to be content with the person's declaration of his Jewishness if he has no other proof at his disposal. If it transpires at a transit station (like Vienna) that the declaration was false, the Oleh visa will be cancelled.[127]

According to the familiar pattern of the normalization-contestation nexus, the absence of external pressure brought about stricter controls—in this case, the requirement of documentation from Western immigrants to prove their Jewish origin. This way, their origin was supposed to be objectivized, while a subjective declaration was only exceptionally acceptable. For Eastern Europeans, exit restrictions and Cold War pressures prompted a more lenient treatment, which included accepting subjective declarations of Jewishness. Unfortunately, the minutes of the meeting do not specify exactly how the falseness of such a declaration could be established once a migrant reached Vienna. But the possibility of canceling the Oleh visa and thus refusing to take in the migrant in question seems to have been added merely as a last safety valve. Whether this action was actually ever taken is unknown.

The key to the lack of concern about this issue can be found in the phrase in parentheses in the above quote. Much like Foreign Minister Walter Scheel in Germany, the Aliyah officials obviously considered the restrictive exit practice of the state socialist authorities a valid preselection, at least to some extent. The remaining doubts were quelled with the panacea for all problems of identification at the external gate: the personal declaration of Jewishness. In fact, in the same meeting, it was suggested to include a section in the request form for the Oleh visa or the Oleh certificate where the petitioner had to declare that she or he was Jewish and had not changed religion by her or his own will. By the same token, it was to be clarified that the awarding of privileges under the Law of Return did not guarantee registration as Jewish in the population registry. Quite in contrast to the supposed emphasis on objective Jewishness introduced by the Law of Return, the practice envisaged here was satisfied with subjective declarations—not necessarily of Jewishness but of descent from a Jewish ancestor. This underscores the importance of looking beyond the letter of the law and into the bureaucratic practices, which reveal a picture significantly different from the theoretical aspirations of the law and its creators.

What about actual Jews, who could immigrate by their own right? Although the records of the meetings in 1970 do not explicitly answer this question, the protocol of a meeting between Aliyah and Registration Officials and border guards from Lod Airport and the Port of Haifa from early 1973 provides an answer.[128] The context of this meeting was a peculiar one: the Supreme Court had just ruled that the "Black Hebrews," a group of African American immigrants who had come to Israel in 1969 and claimed citizenship under the Law of Return as Jews, were not to be considered Jewish.[129] In light of this ruling, Yehudit Hivner of the Interior Ministry Aliyah and Registration Branch, issued the following instruction to the border guards: "Until now there was an unwritten rule that the Jewishness of a person will not be checked if he declared it himself. But . . . the court ruling determines that the right of a person to be registered as an Oleh is a privilege the veracity of which we can check. We also need to check the veracity of the declaration of someone who comes as a family member in accordance with the Law of Return amendment and claims Oleh rights."[130] In other words, thus far, and despite all assertions about the objective test rather than subjective bona fide declaration being decisive for recognition under the Law of Return, the implementation of the law in practice hinged on subjective declarations that were generally taken at face value.

The Aliyah and Registration Branch tried to improve this practice by requesting that the consulate where the applicant filed the request attach a copy of the request to the passport. The consulate was also instructed to note in the passport under which section of the law the person was issued an entry visa. Consular representations abroad had been instructed to that effect, but to Hivner's regret they did not all follow this instruction. Regardless, it remains unclear from the available material whether the consulates had additional information at their disposal that could objectivize the Jewishness of the applicant, and what that information would be.

A letter that Hivner forwarded to the local Aliyah and registration offices in February 1973 provides some insight into the practices at the internal gate—when people were already in the country applying for Oleh status. In this letter, Hivner admonished the officials to implement stricter controls and gave detailed instructions in this regard. Responding to the question of one head of office who had asked for her definition of the required "meticulous examination" of cases, Hivner explained that the examination should be done by "*certified* document examiners" (emphasis in the original). She critically remarked that "the mistaken opinion has taken root among the heads of office that whoever claims that the Law of Return applies to him has to be believed." While admitting that it was difficult to establish a general pattern for how to ascertain the credibility of a declaration, she suggested a general rule of thumb: "Do not make simple cases difficult, and do not simplify doubtful cases." Her examples are striking and describe how—ideally—a clerk should recognize a (non-)Jew:

> When a man who comes to the country as a visitor is called Christian, and his father's name is also Christian, and in his request to extend his visit he does not write anything in the section *Leom*, then claims that he is a Jew

> and that the Law of Return applies to him—we may be suspicious and ask for evidence.
>
> On the other hand, a man who is called Moshe Levy, who has come to Israel to study Talmud and the history of the Jewish people in university, and who has always written in his request that he is Jewish, is exempt from further investigations.[131]

The difficulty of applying these examples in practice suggests that in the actual bureaucratic assessment of who was a Jew, those on the front line were simply expected to know whether someone was Jewish. This amounted to the administrative adaptation of the intuition-based "Silbergian" test of Jewishness introduced in chapter 3, which hinged on the idea that Jews know best who is a Jew. Somewhat ironically, though, the examples were not wisely chosen: according to the relevant standard of matrilineal descent, the father's name should be all but irrelevant. Moreover, these rather stereotypical examples do not indicate how a civil servant would be able to tell a Jew from a non-Jew in more complicated cases or—perhaps even worse—how to identify someone who claimed to be not Jewish but descended from a Jewish ancestor. It is also not clear what the "certified document inspectors" could do to clarify cases. Even according to Hivner, this was largely up to each individual investigator. Other documents in the same file suggest that any typical Jewish document (such as a *ketubah*, a traditional prenuptial agreement) could be used to satisfy the candidate's Jewishness or Jewish ancestry.[132] This practice reaffirmed the persistent linkage between Jewish religion and nationality: the easiest way to be registered as Jewish under a secular law was by providing a religious certificate.

Strikingly, the documentation of the Aliyah and Registration Branch of the Interior Ministry about the implementation of the Law of Return contains no reference to the possibility of using Soviet documents—in particular, the internal passport with its registration of the holder's *natsional'nost'*—as evidence. This is surprising given that the retention of the *Leom* entry in Israeli ID cards had been justified with reference to the parallel registration of Jewish nationality in the documents of Soviet Jews, and given that the amendment to the law was justified by the need to accommodate these very Soviet Jews. This is also how Deputy Interior Minister Yosef Goldschmidt introduced the issue to the heads of the district offices.[133] This absence points to a certain unease in approaching these documents. Early in the first reading of the law in the Knesset, Menachem Begin had tried to quell such concerns by untypically defending the Soviet regime against the reproach of stigmatizing Jews with this entry, the way the Nazis had done with the infamous "J." The recognition of the Jewish nationality by the Bolsheviks, Begin asserted in front of the Knesset plenary, had been an achievement at the time, and was the basis on which the Soviet Union recognized the State of Israel: as the *evreiskoe gosudarstvo*, the Jewish state.[134]

Others in the Knesset worried even more. Gideon Hausner, for example, disliked the idea that applicants might be constrained to use their Soviet passport entry as evidence, given that it was this very entry that had caused their persecution. However, he also understood the difficulty that Soviet Jews might have in proving their own or their ancestors' Jewishness with religious documentation, which is why he preferred a bona fide declaration.[135] Reuven Arazi had another concern: he estimated that only 25 to 30 percent of all Soviet Jews were registered as *evrei* on their IDs, which limited the evidentiary value of these documents.

For lack of explicit evidence, it would be mere conjecture to claim that it was because of these concerns that Soviet documentation was not mentioned by the practitioners as possible evidence for Jewishness. In principle, this documentation should have been welcome. As Menachem Begin forcefully elaborated in his speech, Israel and the Soviet Union shared the fundamental perception of the Jews being a people in the national sense. From that point of view, a passport entry as Jewish should have been reliable proof of either Jewishness (by matrilineal descent) or Jewish origin. Arazi's concern was pertinent, though: many people with Jewish ancestry would not be registered as being of Jewish *natsional'nost'*. Put differently, passport nationality could be used as sufficient but not as necessary evidence for entitlement to Aliyah. In such a situation, subjective declaration remained the only feasible option to reliably identify a Jew. And as long as one could rely on the exit control of the Soviet authorities, the chance of attracting non-Jewish "infiltrators" was slim. Once the Soviet gates opened in the late 1980s, this situation changed completely.

Designating the period analyzed in this chapter as a watershed and the claim that the developments of this watershed period laid the foundation for mass immigration in the late 1980s and early 1990s is, of course, a product of hindsight. Yet how aware were actors at the time of the implications of the extensions implemented, which in retrospect turned out to open the gates for millions of immigrants? It would appear that, although the potential ramifications were quite well understood, there was no grand scheme on either side to catalyze this kind of development. The expectation of increased migration underlying the extensions was not—and, at that point in time, could not be—an expectation of millions of migrants. It was triggered by an annual increase of a few thousand migrants, and the sources do not reveal a general anticipation that these few thousands could turn into hundreds of thousands or even millions at any time in the immediate future. To be sure, the West German consulate general in Leningrad showed remarkable far-sightedness when it noted that the extension of Aussiedlung to encompass Soviet Germans without relatives in Germany would affect hundreds of thousands of people—as it actually did some 15 years later. But even in the context of détente, a mass emigration of that size did not appear realistic at the time. In Israel, Knesset member Meir Avizohar fully understood that the Law of Return amendment could potentially attract economic immigrants with only remote Jewish links. However, he did not see it as a likely prospect. In the mid-1970s, the future collapse of the Eastern Bloc and the Soviet Union was not on the horizon, inevitable as it may seem to some people in retrospect. In this sense, co-ethnic immigration policy was a matter not of long-term plans but of muddling through on a short-term basis with practical solutions.

One of these practical solutions was to extend the scope of the co-ethnic migration regimes by including descendants (or "derived" Germans and Jews) in the definition of a co-ethnic migrant. This broader definition was meant to accommodate cases that were already occurring and were bound to occur more often. Nonetheless, in both Germany and Israel, it implied an important change in the definition of co-ethnicity that transcended the original narrower definitions of Aussiedler and Olim. Contrary to the common use of the terms *ethnic* and *descent-based* as interchangeable, it was in fact only here that descent became important—not in a primordial sense but as the genealogical connection to a person with a particular legally defined ethnic identity. But again, this identity was not (or not only) based on primordial origin but on other criteria: public self-identification, language, and culture in the German case and religion in the Jewish Israeli case.

Corresponding to the German conception of *Bekenntnis* as an essentially social construct of visible self-identification with the German nation (in the guise of *deutsches Volkstum*), the "inheritable *Bekenntnis*," too, was not conceived as the quasi-genetic inheritance of inalterable traits by descent but as a specific socially transmitted connection of the postwar generation to the experience of war and expulsion. In the Israeli case, it would be wrong to generally identify Jews with people of Jewish descent or origin. According to the halachic definition, which in 1970 became part of Israeli state law, a person born of a Jewish mother is a Jew. The offspring included in the Law of Return in section 4A were defined not as Jewish but as descended from a Jew. In both Germany and Israel, this meant that people were henceforth not just accepted for what they were—or professed to be—but for who their ancestors were.

A crucial difference between the cases persisted, of course. The German conception remained predicated on a circumscribed group of people, ethnic Germans who had remained in Eastern Europe in 1945. Only the first generation of their descendants was supposed to be able to claim entry to Germany as Aussiedler. Deriving *Volkszugehörigkeit* from the generation of grandparents was only permitted counting backward from the first generation born after the war. Ideas circulating in the administration to abandon the fixed deadline of 1945 and allow for a presentist *Bekenntnis* never came to fruition. The one-time inheritable *Bekenntnis* was the restrictive solution to the question of inclusion. In Israel, on the other hand, descent could be claimed from any Jew, anytime, anywhere, down to two generations. That this arrangement consciously mirrored the Nuremberg Laws has to be considered a myth that has no basis in the sources analyzed here. It did, however, enlarge the scope of Israeli Aliyah infinitely more than in the German case. But for the time being, the extensions to descendants brought about a partial convergence of the historical trajectories of co-ethnic immigration to West Germany and Israel, which were originally disparate in their scope and fundamental conception.

NOTES

1. MVFK BW, Vermerk Abt. XIII, July 24, 1962, HStAS EA12/201, Az. 2266, No. 114.
2. For a full account, see HStAS EA12/201, Az. 2266, No. 145.
3. IM BW, Hauptabteilung Vertriebene, Flüchtlinge und Kriegsgeschädigte, January 17, 1967, HStAS EA 12/201, Az. 2266, No. 155.
4. See Ergebnisvermerk der konstituierenden Sitzung vom 16.2.1971, BArch, B136/6469.
5. Staatssekretär im AA, Dr. Frank an Staatssekretär im BKA, Bahr, September 21, 1970, BArch, B136/6469.
6. Dr. Kurt Wagner, Deutsches Rotes Kreuz (DRK) an Dr. Per Fischer, BKA, June 17, 1973, BArch, B136/6469.
7. Aliyah from Morocco, CZA S6/10382.
8. "Total Immigration to Israel by Select Country per Year (1948–Present)," Jewish Virtual Library, American-Israeli Cooperative Enterprise, https://www.jewishvirtuallibrary.org/total-immigration-to-israel-by-country-per-year.
9. Armborst, *Ablösung von der Sowjetunion*, 101.
10. Hacohen, "Olim and Aliyah," 311. Ro'i, "Surfacing of the Jewish Movement"; Cantorovich and Cantorovich, "Impact of the Holocaust." For a profound discussion of Jewish national mobilization in the Soviet Union, see also Armborst, *Ablösung von der Sowjetunion*.

11. BMI an BVA, July 19, 1968, BArch, B 106/28627.

12. BMI an BSMI, December 28, 1965, HStAS EA 12/201, Az. 2250, No. 311.

13. BMI an BSMI, June 3, 1966, HStAS EA 12/201, Az. 2250, No. 311.

14. BMI an die Innenminister der Länder, April 13, 1967, HStAS EA 12/201, Az. 2250, No. 327.

15. IM Schleswig-Holstein an das BMI, nachrichtlich an BMVt und die Innenminister der Länder, July 17, 1967, HStAS EA 12/201, Az. 2250, No. 327.

16. IM Nordrhein-Westfalen (NRW) an BMI, nachrichtlich an BMVt und die Innenminister der Länder, July 1, 1967; BSMI an BMI und die Innenminister der Länder, August 30, 1967—both in HStAS EA 12/201, Az. 2250, No. 327.

17. Besprechung der Ausländerreferenten des Bundes und der Länder in Goslar, April 19–20, 1967, HStAS EA 12/201, Az. 2250, No. 327.

18. BSMI an BMI und die Innenminister der Länder, August 30, 1967, HStAS EA 12/201, Az. 2250, No. 327.

19. Besprechung der Ausländerreferenten Unna-Massen, August 27–28, 1967, HStAS EA 12/201, Az. 2250, No. 327.

20. They had first suggested this in a letter to the Federal Expellee Ministry on December 29, 1966. BArch, B106/39937.

21. BMVt to BMI, January 24, 1967, B106/39937.

22. Entwurf einer Stellungnahme von Baden-Württemberg, July 17, 1967, HStAS EA12/201, Az. 2250, No. 327.

23. BMI an BVA, July 19, 1968, BArch B 106/28627.

24. BSMI an BMI und die Innenminister der Länder, March 8, 1968, HStAS EA 12/201, Az. 2250, No. 338.

25. BVerwG VIII C 92.75, November 10, 1976, *BVerwGE* 51, 298.

26. Joppke, *Selecting by Origin*, 186.

27. Otto, "Aussiedler und Aussiedler-Politik," 49.

28. The draft of the first paper and the related discussion at the Argeflü meeting in Malente-Gremsmühlen, September 18–19, 1975, are documented in HStAS EA 2/811, Az. 2572, No. 12. For the second paper, see Entwurf eines Runderlasses, HStAS EA 2/811, Az. 2572, No. 5. It was discussed at the Argeflü meeting in Öhringen, April 1–2, 1976. HStAS EA 2/811, Az. 2558, No. 1, and Az. 2572, No. 3. Preceding discussions are documented in Argeflü-Rechtsausschuss, Waldbröl, September 19–20, 1974, HStAS EA 2/811, Az. 2572, No. 35, item 2.

29. Argeflü-Rechtsausschuss, Waldbröl, September 19–20, 1974, HStAS EA 2/811, Az. 2572, No. 35, item 2.

30. Ministerium für Arbeit, Gesundheit und Soziales (MAGS) NRW an den Vorsitzenden des Rechtsausschusses, Dengler, August 31, 1976, HStAS EA 12/201, Az. 2572, No. 4.

31. Argeflü-Rechtsausschuss, Bremerhaven, November 24–25, 1977, HStAS EA 2/811, Az. 2558.

32. BVerwG VIII C 92.75, November 10, 1976, *BVerwGE* 51, 298.

33. The final text of these guidelines is reprinted in Liesner, *Aussiedler*, 78–91. A previous draft can be found in HStAS EA 2/811, Az. 2572, No. 20. For the discussions, see Argeflü-Rechtsausschuss, Tegernsee, October 11–12, 1979, HStAS EA 2/811, Az. 2558, No. 18.

34. Argeflü-Rechtsausschuss, Lübeck, May 5–6, 1983, HStAS EA 2/811, Az. 2558, No. 36.

35. Argeflü-Rechtsausschuss, Bremen, May 10–11, 1984, HStAS EA 2/811, Az. 2558, No. 44.

36. Ilarionova, "Zhelaniia i vozmozhnosti," 376–380. See also Foth, "Sowjetdeutsche im Spannungsfeld," 48–49.

37. "(Spät-)Aussiedler und ihre Angehörigen. Zeitreihe 1950–2017," https://www.bva.bund.de/SharedDocs/Downloads/DE/Buerger/Migration-Integration/Spaetaussiedler/Statistik/Zeitreihe_1950_2017.pdf?__blob=publicationFile&v=5.

38. Stola, *Kraj bez wyjścia*, 234.

39. BMI an die Innenminister der Länder, April 13, 1967, HStA Stuttgart EA 12/201, Az. 2250, No. 327.

40. About this procedure and the numerical estimates, see Ergebnisniederschrift der Besprechung am 19. Januar 1971 über die Übernahme von Deutschen in die Bundesrepublik Deutschland aufgrund der Information der Regierung der Volksrepublik Polen, BArch, B 106/39942.

41. Ibid.

42. Ibid.; BMI an die Herren Innenminister (-senatoren) der Länder, December 23, 1970, BArch B 106/39942.

43. See the handwritten minutes of the meeting on January 19, 1971, BArch B 106/39942.

44. Note by Dr. Stöve from the BMI, May 1971, BArch, B 106/39942.

45. Der Bundesminister des Auswärtigen an den Bundesminister des Innern, Herrn Hans-Dietrich Genscher, June 9, 1971, BArch, B 106/39942.

46. BMI an BVA, June 25, 1971, BArch, B 106/39942.

47. BVA an den Herrn Bundesminister des Innern, July 1, 1971, BArch, B 106/39942.

48. The main such discussion, which also included the Federal Administration Office, the Red Cross, and the Argeflü, is documented in Ergebnisniederschrift der Besprechung am 16. August 1971, BArch, B 106/39942.

49. Ibid.

50. This form is documented in PAAA B 85 1168.

51. BVA, der Präsident, an den Bundesminister des Innern, January 13, 1972; AA an BMI, Deutsches Rotes Kreuz und DRK-Suchdienst, March 10, 1972, both in BArch, B 106/39942.

52. Stola, *Kraj bez wyjścia*, 237–238.

53. Ibid., 484.

54. BVA an BMI, May 27, 1974, BArch, B 106/39942.

55. Attachment to Der Beauftragte der Bundesregierung für die Verteilung im Grenzdurchgangslager Friedland an den Landkreis Göttingen, Ausländeramt, April 26, 1974, BArch, B 106/39942.

56. Ibid. In the archival documents, he is listed both as Władysław and as Ladislaus.

57. Landkreis Göttingen, Der Oberkreisdirektor, an das BVA, May 9, 1974; BVA an BMI, November 26, 1974, both in BArch, B 106/39942.

58. BMI an AA, March 10, 1975, BArch, B 106/39942; "(Spät-)Aussiedler und ihre Angehörigen. Zeitreihe 1950–2017."

59. Klötzel, *Russlanddeutsche*, 182.

60. About these delegations and the Volga German autonomy movement in general, see Schmaltz, "Reform, 'Rebirth,' and Regret."

61. Hirschler, "Neue 'alte' Heimat DDR," 332–340.

62. Botschaft Moskau an AA, October 20, 1967, PAAA B 85 813.

63. Botschaft Tel Aviv an AA, January 3, 1968, PAAA B 85 813.

64. Botschaft Moskau an AA, November 26, 1970, BArch, B 106/39944; DRK an AA, July 23, 1971, PAAA B 85 812.

65. DRK Suchdienst an AA und BMI, Abtl. Vt, September 21, 1971, BArch, B 106/28650.

66. About the so-called administrative resettlement of ethnic Germans from Ukraine see Fleischhauer, *Das Dritte Reich und die Deutschen in der Sowjetunion*, chap. 7. About their forced repatriation after the war see Eisfeld and Martynenko, "Filtration und operative Erfassung der ethnischen Deutschen."

67. Rückführung und Familienzusammenführung von Deutschen aus der UdSSR (April 1973), Sachstand, BArch, B 106/28650.

68. DRK an AA, September 21, 1973, PAAA B 85 1129. See also Botschaft Moskau an AA, September 10, 1973, ibid. The increased mobilization among Soviet Germans during the early 1970s is also noted by Armborst, *Ablösung von der Sowjetunion*, 278–287.

69. "(Spät-)Aussiedler und ihre Angehörigen. Zeitreihe 1950–2017."

70. AA an BMI, V II 6 und Vt I 2 (mit Durchdruck für das BVA), August 21, 1973. For the reports, see GK Leningrad an AA, July 23, 1973; Botschaft Moskau an AA, July 23, 1973, and August 8, 1973, all in PAAA B 85 1129.

71. BMI an AA, September 5, 1973, BArch, B 106/39944.

72. AA an BMI, November 2, 1973, PAAA B 85 1129.

73. Botschaft Moskau an AA, November 29, 1973, PAAA B 85 1129.

74. BMI an AA, May 24, 1974, BArch, B 106/39944.

75. Botschaft Moskau an AA, January 28, 1974, BArch, B 106/39944.

76. GK Leningrad an AA, February 1, 1974, BArch, B 106/39944.

77. Don-Yehiya, "Religion and National Identity."

78. Ibid., 382.

79. 7th Knesset, Session 37, February 9, 1970, 41–42, ISA 60.0.23.138 (=183/6-כ).

80. Yfaat Weiss has dismissed this argument as irrelevant after the 1967 War and the related consolidation of Israel's borders. See Yfaat Weiss, "Golem and Its Creator," 95.

81. 7th Knesset, Session 37, February 9, 1970, 42.

82. 7th Knesset, Session 38, February 10, 1970, 112, ISA 60.0.23.139 (=183/7-כ).

83. 7th Knesset, Session 50, March 10, 1970, ISA 60.0.23.143 (=183/11-כ).

84. The official English translation of the complete text is in Landau, *Selected Judgments*.

85. Kraines, *Impossible Dilemma*, 49–50.

86. Sapir, "How Should a Court," 24.

87. Don-Yehiya, "Religion and National Identity," 390.

88. Attachment to government decision No. 327, February 3, 1970, ISA 77.0.7.454 (=6943/7-ג).

89. 7th Knesset, Session 50, March 10, 1970, 193.

90. See also Yfaat Weiss, "Golem and Its Creator," 94; Don-Yehiya, "Religion and National Identity," 390.

91. Chaim Moshe Shapira to Government Secretary, January 27, 1970, ISA 77.0.7.454 (=6943/7-ג), emphasis added.

92. Ministerial Legislation Committee, February 2, 1970, ISA 77.0.7.454 (=6943/7-ג).

93. Government Decision 318, January 29, 1970, ISA 77.0.7.454 (=6943/7-ג).

94. Ministerial Legislation Committee, February 2, 1970, ISA 77.0.7.454 (=6943/7-ג).

95. Government Decision 318, January 29, 1970, ISA 77.0.7.454 (=6943/7-ג); Kraines, *Impossible Dilemma*, 54.

96. 7th Knesset, Session 38, February 10, 1970, 113–115.

97. 7th Knesset, Session 37, February 9, 1970, 48–58.

98. 7th Knesset, Session 38, February 10, 1970, 102–105.

99. About the limited extent of Jewish emigration from the Soviet Union during the 1950s and 1960s, see Armborst, *Ablösung von der Sowjetunion*, 100.

100. Ro'i, "Strategy and Tactics;" Armborst, *Ablösung von der Sowjetunion*, esp. 136–162.

101. 7th Knesset, Session 38, February 10, 1970, 116.

102. 7th Knesset, Session 37, February 9, 1970, 53–55.

103. 7th Knesset, Session 38, February 10, 1970, 158–160.

104. 7th Knesset, Session 50, March 10, 1970, 122–123.

105. Yfaat Weiss, "Golem and Its Creator," 99.

106. 7th Knesset, Session 37, February 9, 1970, 46–47.

107. Ibid., 139–140.

108. Ibid., 133–135.

109. Ibid., 107–108.

110. Ibid., 88–90.

111. Yfaat Weiss, "Golem and Its Creator," 93.

112. Avizohar in the Knesset Legislation Committee on February 18, 1970, quoted after Yfaat Weiss, "Golem and Its Creator," 97.

113. Yfaat Weiss, "Golem and Its Creator," 97.

114. This point has been forcefully made by Yfaat Weiss, "Golem and Its Creator," 94. Shmuel Tamir's statement is from 7th Knesset, Session 50, March 10, 1970, 163.

115. Gilbert, *Israel: A History*, 396–400.

116. 7th Knesset, Session 50, March 10, 1970, 127–130.

117. 7th Knesset, Session 38, February 10, 1970, 158–161.

118. All in 7th Knesset, Session 50, March 10, 1970.

119. 7th Knesset, Session 38, February 10, 1970, 48–50.

120. Don-Yehiya, "Religion and National Identity," 392.

121. 7th Knesset, Session 50, March 10, 1970, 173.

122. Ibid., 154–155 (emphasis added).

123. Ibid., 166.

124. Ibid., 147.

125. Minutes of the Meeting at the Interior Ministry, April 5, 1970, ISA 56.0.62.175 (=12050/5-גל). Participants included representatives of the Interior Ministry Aliyah and Registration Branch, Aliyah and Citizenship Department, and Visa Department; a delegate from the Foreign Office Consular Department; the legal advisor to the Ministry of Absorption; and the superintendent of the Police National Headquarters.

126. Minutes of the Meeting of the Heads Office, April 12, 1970, ISA 56.0.62.120 (=12045/3-גל).

127. Minutes of the Meeting at the Interior Ministry, April 5, 1970, ISA 56.0.62.175 (=12050/5-גל).

128. Minutes of the Meeting with border control officers from Lod and Haifa, January 18, 1973, ISA 56.0.62.123 (=12045/6-גל).

129. About the case, see Michaeli, "Another Exodus," 73–74.

130. Meeting Minutes, January 18, 1973, ISA 56.0.62.123 (=12045/6-גל).

131. Head of Department Yehudit Hivner to Heads of Aliyah and Registration Offices, February 4, 1973, ISA 56.0.62.123 (=12045/6-גל).

132. Minutes of the Meeting of Aliyah and Registration Heads of Office at Lod Airport, November 24, 1971, ISA 56.0.62.123 (=12045/6-גל).

133. Meeting Minutes, April 12, 1970, ISA 56.0.62.120 (=12045/3-גל).

134. 7th Knesset, Session 37, February 9, 1970, 77; see also Yfaat Weiss, "Golem and Its Creator," 96.

135. 7th Knesset, Session 50, March 10, 1970, 211.

FIVE

THE SOVIET EXODUS

IN JUNE 1990, HORST WAFFENSCHMIDT, the German federal government's special representative for Aussiedler affairs (*Sonderbeauftragter der Bundesregierung für Aussiedlerfragen*), wrote an open letter to the ethnic Germans living in the Soviet Union. Amid an unprecedented and seemingly unstoppable influx of Aussiedler from that country, which had already brought more than 150,000 newcomers to the Federal Republic during the preceding three years (in addition to more than 400,000 from Poland), Waffenschmidt asked his "dear fellow countrymen" (*liebe Landsleute*) to consider their migration plans very carefully: "To leave your place of residence and to start over elsewhere is a grave decision that should be well considered. That is why I want to give you some information and ask you to consider it while making your decision. The most important aim of the federal government is to improve your living conditions in the Soviet Union.... Before you emigrate you should gather precise information about conditions in the Federal Republic of Germany."[1]

When the Aussiedler stream continued unabated, Waffenschmidt's agency developed a "master plan for Russian Germans" (*Gesamtkonzept Russlanddeutsche*), which sharpened the government's developing restrictive agenda for co-ethnic migration. Published in January 1992, it stated as its first goal: *"As many of the two million Russian Germans as possible should stay in the CIS* [Commonwealth of Independent States]. The gate to Germany remains open, both legally and politically, but there are numerous good reasons to act in such a way that many Russian Germans obtain a perspective for the future for themselves and their children in their current homeland."[2] To create this "perspective for the future," the federal government invested in development projects in German areas of settlement in both Russia and Kazakhstan, which, in Waffenschmidt's Christian-inspired rhetoric, came to be called "islands of hope" (*Inseln der Hoffnung*).[3] Though largely ineffective, these projects are eloquent testimony to the German government's intention to discourage Russian Germans from emigrating without abandoning co-ethnic migration altogether.

Around the same time, Israeli officials invested much effort to ensure that the Jews who were also leaving the Soviet Union in large numbers would come to Israel instead of "dropping out" during their layover in Vienna and moving on to the United States or other Western countries, as many had done in the past and continued to do. Since direct flights from Moscow to Tel Aviv were not yet an option in the late 1980s, the typical means for achieving this aim was to direct the migrants through other transit stations in countries of the Eastern Bloc, where they were not free to go wherever they pleased. Beginning in late 1988, the Israeli government's secret Liaison Bureau (*lishkat ha-kesher,* also known as Nativ or Path) in charge of organizing emigration from the Soviet Union set up such stations in Bucharest, Budapest, and Warsaw, which the Jewish Agency soon took charge of.[4]

Israeli officials who were involved in these events have offered different explanations of how they made Soviet Jews "choose" one of these pathways through Eastern Europe. These explanations range from giving the migrants financial incentives to simply fooling them into believing they had no other choice. Baruch Gur-Gurevitz, head of the Jewish Agency's Soviet Union department between 1989 and 1995, acknowledged the former. According to his account, as of 1989, the Israeli government incentivized Soviet Jews to migrate via Bucharest by refunding their plane tickets, which they had paid for in rubles, at a very favorable exchange rate in US dollars.[5]

In his memoirs and in a related interview with a major Israeli daily, Yasha Kedmi (formerly Kazakov) of the Liaison Bureau proudly proclaimed that he had used the latter tactic. Kedmi maintains that he convinced Soviet Jews who wanted to leave the country that they could obtain an Israeli visa only after 5 p.m.—that is, after the Austrian embassy, which could have given them a transit visa for Vienna, was closed—and only upon presenting a plane ticket to either Bucharest or Budapest for the same night.[6] According to Kedmi, this scam worked because of the Soviet Jews' alleged blind obedience to authority—which, of course, had not stopped them from gaming the system in the past by ignoring their Israeli visas and redirecting their journeys to more attractive destinations at the first possible opportunity.[7] While there is thus good reason to doubt the particulars of Kedmi's story—especially his claim to having single-handedly provided Israel with as many as one million additional immigrants—both his and Gur-Gurevitz's accounts reveal the lengths to which Israeli representatives were willing to go to make sure Soviet migrants came to Israel. This active and even deceitful promotion of Aliyah stands in stark contrast to the cautious approach promoted by Horst Waffenschmidt around the same time.

The contrast between the two countries' master plans for their Soviet co-ethnics is even more pronounced. At the same time that the German government started establishing (futile) projects in German areas of settlement to keep as many people as possible where they were, the Jewish Agency established itself in the former Soviet Union with the opposite aim of attracting more immigrants. According to its strategy, the explicit mission was to "strengthen Jewish identity; provide Jewish education based on the centrality of Israel; develop the Jewish national movement; and encourage Aliyah."[8] For this purpose, emissaries (*shlichim*) were sent to the Soviet Union and later its successor states to implement all kinds of educational programs for children and adults and youth summer camps that were designed to foster identification with Israel and commitment to Aliyah. In a less benign reading of these activities, some contemporary observers accused the emissaries of inflating the dangers of anti-Semitism in Russia while exaggerating the benefits that immigrants could expect in Israel.[9] In fact, even a strongly partisan author, writing on behalf of the Jewish Agency, conceded that "emissaries were confronted with angry accusations of brainwashing and indoctrination" by parents who were unwilling to leave Russia for Israel but were being pushed to do so by their children.[10]

With their diametrically opposed agendas, the schemes and initiatives adopted by German and Israeli institutions capture the contrasting reactions of the two countries to the exodus of their co-ethnics from the Soviet Union and the Eastern Bloc during the years of political and economic transition in the region. This transition period began with Gorbachev's perestroika in the mid-1980s and resulted in the dissolution of the Eastern Bloc and the Soviet Union itself. Within this broader moment of political change, the liberalization and eventual abolition of exit restrictions opened the gates for all who were willing and had the resources to emigrate. Economic breakdown and political instability—both pertinent issues during the transition period—added to the factors pushing potential migrants out of their countries. The result was the largest movement of migrants to the West in the postwar period. Most of these migrants were ethnic Germans and Jews. Germany and Israel received around three million and one million of their co-ethnics, respectively, between the beginning of mass emigration in the late 1980s and when it was phased out in the mid-2000s. But the way these immigration numbers were realized differed greatly: while Aussiedler continued flocking to the FRG despite the government's declared intention to keep them where they were and despite growing bureaucratic hurdles, reduced integration benefits, and rising unemployment in post-unification Germany, Israel had to work hard to make mass Aliyah happen.

The divergent German and Israeli reactions to post-1987 Eastern European mass migration appear to signal a break with the converging trend of the two migration regimes identified in the previous chapter. The simultaneous extension of the regimes' original scope was the result of a changing international context during the watershed period from the mid-1960s to the mid-1970s. In both countries, the beginnings of détente and the concomitant liberalization of emigration regimes in Eastern Europe had raised similar expectations of continued and increased migration. These expectations triggered comparable answers on a national level, which resulted in an initial partial alignment of the originally dissimilar German and Israeli cases.

The convergence of the national trajectories became more pronounced in the mid-1970s due to another powerful factor related to the international system, détente, and the Cold War: the creation of the Conference for Security and Cooperation in Europe (CSCE) and the resulting "Helsinki process" which culminated in the 1975 CSCE Final Act. The provisions of the Third Basket of this Final Act standardized a human rights discourse that provided a common framework to address the issues of both Jewish and German emigration within a more general context that may be described in shorthand as the "freedom of movement."[11] The Third Basket's provisions regarding "human contacts" included facilitations for family members who wanted to meet across borders and a reference to the "reunification of families," which should be dealt with quickly and without excessive costs for the applicants. From the German point of view, these provisions had initially been particularly important to the situation of divided families in the "two Germanies."[12] Yet there were also clear implications for the members of ethnic minorities, who, in most cases, were still officially migrating under family reunification schemes. The Helsinki Accords provided a point of reference for state actors, transnational societal actors, and emigration activists alike to demand increased freedom of movement—be it the German government, the international Soviet Jewry Movement, or Soviet Jews and Germans struggling for their right to emigrate.[13] In this way, pre-perestroika German and Jewish ethnic migrations came to resemble each other due to the common international context in which they occurred. The eventual outcome in the late 1980s and the 1990s—co-ethnic immigration on a massive scale—was even more strikingly similar.

Despite these similarities in an international context, this chapter argues that the post–Cold War divergence was firmly rooted in the logic of preexisting domestic trends. The chapter presents internal political, ideological, institutional, and legal developments in both countries from the mid-1970s—the years after the watershed period—until the migration peak of the early 1990s. Placed in such a long-term perspective, the contrasting initiatives and policy measures sketched at the beginning of this chapter appear as less of a radical break with the past, and instead as the realization of existing ideas and trends under the "right" conditions after the breakdown of the common Cold War framework.

On the level of politics and ideology, the fundamental question addressed in the first chapter returns to the center of attention: To what extent did either country embrace a homeland stance and actively pursue the "return" of its co-ethnic diaspora? Taking a cue from Christian Joppke's identification of ethnic immigration policy with the political right, an additional question arises: Given that both countries witnessed significant political changes during the period under consideration, to what extent was the stance of each country influenced by party politics?[14] It will become clear that beyond both states' ostentatious commitment to open gates for co-ethnics, the level of active commitment to bring these co-ethnics to the country as migrants differed greatly. The basic parameters of this commitment were relatively constant and hardly subject to party political influence.

The institutional discussion examines the gatekeeper struggles in each context—struggles that took place below the surface of the officially prevailing discourse on open gates. In both countries, the definition of who was eligible to pass through the co-ethnic immigration gate and under which conditions remained contested. The specialized gatekeepers—the expellees and the religious establishment respectively—struggled to maintain or enhance their position and their definitional power within the overall framework of the state and in contradistinction to the regular state authorities. Their fundamental concern was similar: to secure the entry of real co-ethnics as they defined them, whether through a particular type of "collective fate of persecution" or through halachic purity. Yet the basic thrusts of their definitional challenges were diametrically opposed. Whereas the German expellees fought even limited restrictions to the co-ethnic immigration regime tooth and nail, the ultra-Orthodox in Israel valued religious purity more than high immigration numbers. Despite partial successes, in the end, neither got their way in the face of mass immigration. In Germany, the restrictively minded state won out against the expansively minded specialized gatekeepers. In Israel, the expansively minded state won out against the restrictively minded specialized gatekeepers.

Returning to the laws of return, this chapter analyzes in detail the conceptually opposed legal reactions of each country toward mass immigration after

Cold War–related immigration restrictions were lifted. While the historical chapter of German Aussiedlung was basically closed with the introduction of the 1992 Law for the Settlement of War Consequences (*Kriegsfolgenbereinigungsgesetz*, or KfbG), Israeli Aliyah and the underlying Law of Return persisted. These outcomes are interpreted in light of the preceding conceptual and legal discussions in the respective migration regimes, revealing a large degree of continuity.

Moreover, the chapter fleshes out the paradoxical nature of these processes of demise and persistence. In Germany, the gradual undoing of the co-ethnic migration regime occurred in conjunction with the increased ethnicization of definitions, and indeed the multiplication of ethnic categories in the form of the "Jewish quota refugee" (*jüdischer Kontingentflüchtling*). In Israel, the persistence of ethnic migration went hand in hand with its conceptual de-ethnicization, as the country received increasing numbers of halachically non-Jewish immigrants who were still entitled to immigration under the 1970 version of the Law of Return.

GERMANY: AUSSIEDLER POLICY BETWEEN THE LEFT AND THE RIGHT

From the mid-1970s until the onset of post-1987 mass migration, there was a steady influx of co-ethnic immigration from Eastern European countries to West Germany. Especially from Poland there was a well-established immigration channel after the conclusion of the Polish-German emigration protocol in 1975, in which the two governments agreed on the emigration of 125,000 ethnic Germans in exchange for a loan worth one billion deutsche marks.[15] As agreed, this number was reached in 1979, but informal emigration continued and increased. In 1981 alone, as many as 50,983 Aussiedler from Poland were registered in West Germany, only about 40 percent of whom held official exit permits.[16] Although numbers dropped over the following years, they remained considerable. The lowest annual figure was 17,455 Aussiedler in 1984, the vast majority of whom had come on tourist visas and stayed.[17] Despite martial law and General Jaruzelski's military dictatorship, Polish-German mobility had almost become an ordinary phenomenon.[18] Similarly, Aussiedler numbers from Romania were almost constantly above 10,000 per year from 1977 onward.[19] This migration took place in exchange for "compensation payments," a practice that had started in the late 1960s and was inspired by the Israeli "ransom" payments for Romanian Jews.[20] In contrast, ethnic German immigration from the Soviet Union reached its high point as early as 1976, when there were 9,704 migrants in one year. Arguably, this relatively high figure was a product of the improved German-Soviet relations that followed the 1970 Treaty of Moscow and the general spirit of détente that prevailed in the early 1970s, culminating in the 1975 Helsinki Accords. However, numbers dipped significantly over the following years, down to just 460 migrants in 1985.[21]

In the domestic political arena, West Germany saw ongoing change at the highest level during this period, with government coalitions swinging from the center-right to the center-left and back. The 1970s were the "social democratic" decade of West German history. A coalition of Willy Brandt's Social Democratic Party of Germany (*Sozialdemokratische Partei Deutschlands*, or SPD) and the Liberal Democrats of the Free Democratic Party (*Freie Demokratische Partei*, or FDP) had taken over the government in 1969 after two decades of rule by the Christian Democratic Union (*Christlich-Demokratische Union*, or CDU), the last three years of which had been in a grand coalition. They stayed in power until the CDU's successful vote of no confidence against Brandt's successor, Helmut Schmidt, in 1982. What followed was a 16-year period of conservative-liberal government under Helmut Kohl, who promised nothing less than a "spiritual and moral turnaround" (*geistig-moralische Wende*), thus signaling a clean break with the reign of the most left-wing government of West German history to that date.

In this polarized political setting, Aussiedlung became more of a public political issue throughout the 1970s and 1980s than it had been in the past, and it became even more so after the onset of mass immigration in the late 1980s. The post-1987 discussions in particular have contributed to the scholarly view that identifies "re-ethnicizing" migration policies—including co-ethnic preferentialism—with the political right, while "de-ethnicizing" policies are considered a trademark of the political left.[22] In West German public discourse at the time, ethnic German immigration was prominently contested by the Social Democratic opposition leader Oskar Lafontaine. In the so-called asylum compromise in 1992, the ruling Christian Democrats and the oppositional Social Democrats struck a deal in which each of them agreed to concessions regarding their supposed respective "pet case": Aussiedler policy for the CDU and the constitutional right to political asylum (Article 16 of the Basic Law) for the SPD.[23] This unbalanced trade-off, which in fact merely reinforced the already progressing process of phasing out Aussiedler immigration while putting an immediate end to the liberal reception of asylum seekers, created the lasting impression that Aussiedlung was a project of the conservative right and was opposed by the political left.[24]

In a historical perspective, this right-left dichotomy is contradicted by plain numbers. All in all, more than half a million German immigrants came to West Germany throughout only 13 years of social-liberal rule under chancellors Brandt and Schmidt—a mere 100,000 less than during the preceding 20 years of conservative government under chancellors Adenauer, Erhard, and Kiesinger.[25] This increased influx was the product of the government's contentious *Ostpolitik*, which was vehemently rejected by the right-wing opposition and particularly by expellee politicians, who resented the de facto renunciation of the formerly German Eastern Territories in the 1970 Warsaw Treaty.[26] Herbert Hupka, member of parliament and head of the Silesian Landsmannschaft—one of the most vocal and influential expellee associations—even defected from the SPD to the CDU on these grounds. And yet, one outcome of the rapprochement with Poland was the 1975 Polish-German emigration protocol. During these years, German emigration from the Soviet Union also reached a historical high point. By continuing the clandestine policy of "buying" ethnic Germans from Romania, the social-liberal government ensured that emigration from there would continue as well.[27]

It was only after Helmut Kohl's ascension to power in 1982 that Aussiedler policy became strongly associated with the conservative right. Already during the 1970s, and in particular in the context of Polish-German negotiations in 1975, the then oppositional CDU had repeatedly attacked the social-liberal government for supposedly not doing enough on behalf of Germans from Poland and for being too soft in their negotiations with their Communist counterparts. Given the actual effectiveness of the government's strategy, these attacks on the government concerning emigration have to be interpreted as part of an "ersatz discourse" embraced by the right after the contentious issue of the Eastern Territories had effectively become obsolete.[28] By the 1980s, the CDU's rhetorical commitment to Aussiedler and Aussiedlung was matched by the Social Democrats' gradual renunciation of the topic.

However, neither development was related to actual migration policies. During the 1980s, Chancellor Kohl embraced the issue of the expulsion of Germans after the Second World War as part of his overall attempt to rehabilitate notions of German nationhood that had become discredited as awareness of German crimes and the Holocaust grew.[29] His *Geschichtspolitik* caused opposition among the political left, who resented the "re-nationalization of the political sphere."[30] Polarization came to a head over the Bitburg affair in 1985, when Kohl and President Reagan commemorated SS men among other fallen soldiers at the Bitburg military cemetery, and during the *Historikerstreit* starting in 1986. In this climate, references to the German "nation" became increasingly unacceptable for the political left, because they smacked of the Nazi past and conservative revisionism. As Daniel Levy has pointed out, Kohl's "politics with history" had no direct connection to Aussiedler immigration. Yet in the polarized public sphere of the late 1980s, the discursive association of ethnic German expellees and the perceived whitewashing of the German past made the center-left renounce any stronger commitment to the issue of ethnic German immigration from the East. For them, such immigration was unacceptable because it was based on a narrative of German suffering. This, in turn, meant that, as conservative politicians increasingly spoke of the "national responsibility" for Germans in the Eastern Bloc, Social Democrats and the recently emerged Green Party dismissed such calls as *Deutschtümelei*.[31] By the time Aussiedler immigration occurred on a massive scale in the late 1980s, both sides were happily oblivious to the fact that the resettlement of Germans from Eastern Europe in West Germany had reached its high point under a Social Democratic government.

Despite the stronger rhetorical commitment of the CDU to the issue of ethnic Germans and the concomitant renunciation of the Aussiedler issue by the SPD, there was no fundamental difference between relevant policies during the social-liberal 1970s and the conservative-liberal 1980s—certainly not in the sense that the CDU generally favored co-ethnic immigration while the SPD generally rejected it. As long as the Cold War persisted, both parties supported the right of ethnic Germans to move freely. Yet as noted at the beginning of this chapter, when the Eastern Bloc opened up and Aussiedler started to flock into Germany in much greater numbers, the CDU government was quick with appeals urging the migrants to carefully consider their immigration decision. These appeals were followed by the introduction of legal changes to stem this tide and, eventually, by the phasing out of ethnic priority immigration—despite public campaigns launched by the same government that tried to convince the public that the arrival of Eastern European Germans was beneficial for the country.[32] As was the case during the contestation of Aussiedlung from Yugoslavia, and in general during the 1960s, rising immigration numbers and the reduced exceptionality of co-ethnic migration triggered a more general anti-immigration reflex that did not halt at ethnic Germans.

A HOMELAND AFTER ALL?

Even during the time between the Helsinki Accords and the mass exodus from Eastern Europe, commitment to free movement did not equal an active homeland stance or the ideological pursuit of diaspora return. As noted above, during the 1950s and 1960s, West German co-ethnic policy remained limited in its scope as Aussiedlung was exclusively conceived of as ethno-humanitarian family reunification. Moreover, before the recognition of the Oder-Neisse border, any return-to-the-homeland ideology toward Aussiedler was precluded by the belief that their rightful place was in the "German East" and not in the Federal Republic. Despite the conceptual extensions analyzed in chapter 4, as well as the Brandt government's de facto recognition of the Oder-Neisse border in 1970, these parameters did not change in essence. Until the onset of Russian-German mass immigration, the notion of return had had no prominent place in the description of Aussiedlung. Rather than claiming that ethnic Germans were returning home, in the 1970s the slogan became canonized that they came to Germany because they wanted "to live as Germans among Germans."

This interpretation of Aussiedler migration had already been coined during the emigration wave from Poland in the late 1950s, and it acquired greater publicity as immigration numbers and public awareness for the phenomenon grew.[33] It was the title, for example, of a 1978 publication by the Federal Agency for Civic Education (*Bundeszentrale für politische Bildung*).[34] In the foreword to this essay collection, Interior Minister Werner Maihofer (FDP) made some programmatic declarations. After claiming the increased immigration numbers as the success of the government's *Ostpolitik*, Maihofer stated: "Aussiedler coming to us today have made use of the human right to decide for themselves in which country, in which type of society, with which language and in which cultural sphere they want to live. *They have given up their Heimat*, their workplace, their familiar environment and often also their friends. They have taken a step into an uncertain future, *only to live as Germans among Germans*."[35] Two elements in this statement stand out: the unequivocal statement that the migrants had given up their *Heimat* (rather than returning to it) and the absence of a territorial reference. The slogan was not "as Germans in Germany" but "as Germans among Germans."

The reason for this nonterritorial formulation has to be sought in the origin of the majority of newcomers at the time of this brochure's publication. Most of them came from Poland and thus from territories that, even after the 1970 Warsaw treaty, were actively claimed by some as part of the German Reich that had never ceased to exist. Avoiding a territorial reference catered to such sensitivities. As Herbert Hupka declared in the same brochure, these Aussiedler from Upper Silesia or Eastern Prussia were not "Germans from Poland" but "Germans who move from Germany to Germany in order to live as free Germans among free Germans."[36]

While the insistence on the continued existence of the German Reich in its 1937 borders was against the spirit of the social-liberal *Ostpolitik*, it was part of the standard repertoire of the expellee associations. As discussed below, Aussiedler immigration was a field in which these associations went to great lengths to make their influence felt. Ideologically, however, their stance somewhat ironically limited the West German state's ability to identify itself as a homeland for Germans from the East that they could return to as long as the majority of these Germans left what was supposedly their rightful German *Heimat*.

The notion of return only acquired relevance in the early 1990s, as the term *Aussiedler* became almost synonymous with "Germans from Russia," who, in many cases, could trace their ancestry back to regions of present-day Germany.[37] It seems quite possible that the "return" vocabulary was in fact first introduced by migrants and migrant activists.[38] A case in point is the Re Patria Association founded by the Russian German émigré Herbert Mickoleit in 1974. Before his emigration, he had coauthored a samizdat publication with the same title.[39] The adaptation of migrant conceptions into official discourses was also hinted at in one of the contributions of the quoted 1978 volume, in which the author attributed the phrase "to live as Germans among Germans" to the Aussiedler themselves, who allegedly stated it as their main motivation to come to the Federal Republic of Germany.[40] It remains open for question whether the slogan was actually adapted from the usage of German immigrants or whether the migrants appropriated it in view of the West German state's expectation that this should be their motivation to relocate (rather than much-shunned "material and economic motivations").[41]

Yet even without a notion of return migration, there were attempts by politicians of the nationalist-conservative right during the 1980s to have Germany assume a stronger homeland stance (understood in Brubaker's sense as a commitment to "co-nationals" across borders) akin to that taken by Israel. In his speech about "the state of the nation" in June 1983, Alfred Dregger, chairman of the CDU group in the Bundestag and prominent representative of the far-right *Stahlhelm* faction, stated that "Israel is the advocate and the homeland of all Jews in distress. The Federal Republic of Germany is the advocate and homeland of all Germans in distress, I emphasize: of all Germans in distress."[42] In a similar vein, expellee politician Herbert Hupka reminded the federal government in November 1984 of its "duty of care (*Obhutspflicht*) for all the Germans."[43] This duty of care was also declared by Chancellor Kohl in a March 1987 government declaration.[44]

The new government's nation-centered discourse thus also included advocacy of a more prominent role for the Federal Republic of Germany as a national center for all Germans. One expression of this stance was the full rehabilitation of the Association for Germans Abroad (*Verein für das Deutschtum im Ausland*, or VDA), the reference to which had in the 1960s still served to quell calls for the extended resettlement of Germans from Eastern Europe beyond humanitarian family reunification. By the early 1980s, the VDA's annual congresses, which took place in the capital city of Bonn, were graced with the patronage of personalities such as President Karl Carstens or the president of the Bundestag Rainer Barzel (both CDU), while government members contributed to the association's publication, *Globus*.[45] Without sharing extreme interpretations of some authors who claim nothing less than a *großdeutsch* and *völkisch* conspiracy of the Foreign Office and the VDA, the rehabilitation of this association is indeed indicative of a strengthened national-ideological component in German Aussiedler policy under the Kohl government.[46]

Despite this increased rhetorical commitment, historian Kerstin Armborst has come to the conclusion that support for ethnic Germans in Eastern Europe—and particularly in the Soviet Union—by the West German government (as well as civil society) remained modest throughout. This is especially evident when compared with the efforts that Israel, the United States, and the international Soviet Jewry movement invested in their promotion of a Soviet Jewish "exodus."[47] German engagement included repeated exhortations of the Soviet side to respect the Helsinki stipulations about family reunification, submitting lists with urgent cases to Soviet representatives and raising the issue in international forums like the CSCE, the European Parliament, and the Council of Europe.[48] These efforts, though by no means negligible, could not match the endeavors of the international Soviet Jewry movement. However, for the time being, their effects (or lack thereof) were the same—at least as far as the Soviet Union is concerned. Emigration numbers of both Germans and Jews from the Soviet Union were exceptionally low during the first half of the 1980s, while the flow of Germans from Poland and Romania remained quite steady.

Once the massive influx of Aussiedler started in 1987, the federal government embraced a somewhat inconsistent position that combined special integration efforts for Aussiedler inside the country with initially mixed signals to those still abroad; and these soon transformed into the "better stay where you are" appeals quoted at the beginning of this chapter. In August 1988, the government endorsed a "special program (*Sonderprogramm*) for the integration of Aussiedler," which included measures for quicker registration, temporary accommodation, language courses, and professional integration.[49] In September of the same year, the parliamentary secretary of state in the Interior Ministry, Horst Waffenschmidt, was appointed to the newly created office of special

Aussiedler representative—a position responsible for coordinating these integration efforts while convincing the increasingly skeptical public about their benefit for society at large.[50] This appointment was not accidental; Waffenschmidt had already shown an interest in issues of Germans abroad in the past, and he had contributed to the VDA's *Globus* magazine.[51]

While Waffenschmidt's affiliation with an association committed to Germans abroad did entail measures that could be defined as a homeland stance and a more inclusive discourse toward transborder ethnic Germans, it did not translate into anything that resembled the return ideology embraced by Israel. In the first edition of his official organ from November 1988, the *Info-Dienst Deutsche Aussiedler*, Waffenschmidt praised the newcomers as being of "great benefit for our society" because of their "large number of children, their rich cultural heritage, and their exemplary religious faith."[52] In an "FAQ list" published in March 1989, he asserted that the Aussiedler were Germans, either by citizenship or by cultural affiliation, who had a constitutional right to be received in the Federal Republic.[53] This statement was a far cry from the past conviction that *Volksdeutsche* without German citizenship had no such legal entitlement. It was indicative of a shift in perception that had taken place, according to which ethnic Germans in Eastern Europe were considered "long distance citizens," as migration scholars Rainer Münz and Rainer Ohliger described them a decade later.[54]

At the same time, however, Waffenschmidt made it clear that the federal government was not pursuing a pro-active policy. Answering FAQ number four, "Why does the federal government make these people come to the Federal Republic of Germany?" he stated: "The federal government does not encourage anyone to come to the Federal Republic of Germany. Neither does it encourage people to stay in their countries of origin (*in den Aussiedlungsgebieten*). Our policy aim is first of all to improve the living conditions of these Germans in their countries of origin, hard as that may be. However, the federal government respects the decision of every German in these countries to come to us. . . . That is why a restriction of Aussiedler reception is out of the question."[55]

Thus, while maintaining the open-door policy of unrestricted Aussiedler immigration, the German government did not engage in active pro-immigration propaganda—quite in contrast to what will be seen in the Israeli case. Waffenschmidt still stressed in March 1989 that the government would respect "the decision of every German . . . to come to us," but his June 1990 open letter to the "dear fellow countrymen" quoted earlier was already more explicit in its attempt to influence that decision. By that time, the Law for the Reception of Aussiedler (*Aussiedleraufnahmegesetz*, or AAG) was about to be put into force.

Responding to the complaints of the Länder concerned about the uncontrolled influx of newcomers from Poland, the law closed the internal gate and left an official written procedure at the external gate as the only alternative way into the country. In line with Waffenschmidt's call to prospective Aussiedler to think well before leaving, the new procedure gave them more time to ponder their decision while providing the institutions of the migration regime the ability to control the pace of migration through bureaucratic delays. In addition, the request to support the application with documents was meant to ensure stricter controls.[56] Nonetheless, since previously issued "takeover permits" (*Übernahmegenehmigungen*) remained valid, the immigrant stream continued unabated. In 1990 and 1991, 619,000 Aussiedler came to Germany, almost half of them (295,000) from the collapsing Soviet Union.

Against this background, the January 1992 "master plan" for Russian Germans signaled the transition to an unequivocal anti-immigration agenda, which was soon supported by further restrictive legislative measures (discussed in more detail below). If these legal changes were the stick, Waffenschmidt's projected "islands of hope" were the carrot in the attempt to make people stay in their countries of origin. The VDA became an important subcontractor in these projects, but the vast majority of them failed to achieve their aim and even prompted charges of wasting public money.[57] At that point during the early 1990s, the eventually abortive re-creation of the former Volga German Republic that had existed between 1924 and 1941 was also still on the agenda. But despite triumphant declarations by the Interior Ministry that "the federal government's aid measures for Russian Germans begin to show effect—German districts in Russia keep Russian Germans in their current homeland," the exodus from Russia and Kazakhstan to Germany continued to grow.[58] In 1992, 230,489 Aussiedler came to Germany. Of this figure, 195,576 originated from the former Soviet Union—unlike what will be seen in the Israeli case, not because of but despite government efforts.

GATEKEEPER STRUGGLES

Despite the absence of either a return ideology or the active seeking of co-ethnic immigrants, the West German door for Aussiedler of different generations was demonstratively kept open during the 1970s and 1980s, irrespective of the party in power. But as it had been in the preceding two decades, this openness was conditional on the fulfillment of certain criteria by the migrants, which in turn had to be assessed by particular gatekeepers. Under the surface of the professed openness, the 1980s saw intense struggles regarding both the admission criteria and gatekeeping competences. One issue at stake was whether so-called expulsion pressure should be assessed in addition to German *Volkszugehörigkeit*, which questioned the fundamental assumption that every ethnic German in Eastern Europe was by definition a victim of persecution. A second issue was the meaning of German *Volkszugehörigkeit* in the increasingly important Soviet context: Who was—and who was not—a "real" Soviet German? In both instances, the expellee associations and their affiliated institutions (the *Heimatauskunftstellen*) struggled to assert their role as specialized gatekeepers of Aussiedler immigration with some success.

Expulsion Pressure; or, Who Is (Still) an Expellee?

In a March 1977 ruling, the Federal Administrative Court (BVerwG) for the first time considered the possibility that even someone who was a German *Volkszugehöriger* according to section 6 BVFG might not be recognized as an expellee. And once again, the contentious borderline case involved a Jewish candidate. The BVerwG doubted that a Jew from Prague, who had left Czechoslovakia in late 1968 and eventually immigrated to West Germany in 1973, could be considered an expellee. While not doubting the man's Germanness, the judges argued that, in all likelihood, he had not left his home country "as a German"—which, in this case, meant "because of his being a German." They concluded that whenever there was a strong indication that the person in question had left the country for different—in this case, presumably political—reasons, "the causal link between expulsion pressure (*Vertreibungsdruck*) and emigration (*Wohnsitzaufgabe*)" needed to be checked.[59]

In other words, just because Germans from Eastern Europe left their home countries, they would not necessarily be considered expellees. What mattered was the causal link between Germanness and departure. This question of causality affected the younger generations in particular. To what extent could it be assumed that the postwar generations still left their home countries "as Germans," understood in this causal sense? At the November 1981 meeting of the Argeflü, the coordinating body of the Länder refugee administrations, it was suggested that "expulsion pressure" could still be generally assumed for the second postwar generation (despite the reservations about this generation's inclusion in the definition of Aussiedler discussed in the previous chapter), but not for the third generation.[60] In effect, this would have meant the creation of a last generation of Aussiedler at this point. The discussion surrounding the

Argeflü's attempt to develop guidelines for the examination of this causality, starting in 1983, consequently turned into a fierce battleground about the future of German Aussiedlung from the East. The Federation of Expellees (*Bund der Vertriebenen*) and its chairman, Dr. Herbert Czaja, stand out as having gone to great lengths to avoid the implementation of these guidelines, which they perceived as a threat to continuous ethnic priority immigration.

The new guidelines were supposed to harmonize the diverging administrative practices of the Länder refugee administrations regarding expulsion pressure.[61] In view of some overly zealous offices, which took to questioning emigration motives in every individual case rather than just doubtful ones, the draft for new guidelines started with the observation that, according to the BVerwG, expulsion pressure was generally assumed to be the cause for the emigration of ethnic Germans from their home countries. Individual persecution did not have to be proved by the applicant. Following the administrative judges' reasoning, the individual motives for emigration were to be checked only if there were "clear indications" (*eindeutige Anhaltspunkte*) that emigration had been caused by factors unrelated to expulsion (*vertreibungsfremde Gründe*). These indications included:

- legal persecution because of criminal acts;
- political problems unrelated to the applicant's Germanness (an application for asylum could be a clue for this);
- marriage to a person in the West without having displayed any prior will to emigrate;
- full integration into the society of the home country—for example, through an outstanding professional or political position;
- previous travels to the West if the applicant had already had the possibility to emigrate; and
- an obvious lack of consciousness concerning German citizenship or ethnicity at the time of emigration.

If there were multiple emigration motives, those related to expulsion had to be of "substantial importance" in bringing about the decision to emigrate. If the person had wanted to emigrate in any case, unrelated motives that triggered the emigration decision did not rule out recognition as an expellee.[62] These guidelines were agreed on in March 1983. Before the vote, it was established that the indications listed here were merely examples and not an exhaustive list. At the same time, it was pointed out that all of these points were clues to initiate an examination of the emigration motives, but they did not rule out recognition as an expellee.[63]

The Argeflü repeatedly stressed the importance of expulsion pressure as an administrative tool to properly include the second generation of Aussiedler born after the war in the BVFG.[64] Since this inclusion was bound to cause considerable additional expenditure, a corrective was needed to prevent any kind of abuse. In other words, if the authorities were generally to assume that expulsion pressure still caused the second generation born after the war to leave, they needed the ability to refute this assumption in cases where it was obviously untrue. As the head of judicial committee of the Argeflü correctly pointed out, the incorporation of this generation already went beyond the principles established by the Federal Administrative Court, and it was only sustainable if there was a safety valve—the possibility to refute expulsion pressure.[65] This view was supported by the Federal Interior Ministry, which justified introducing the notion of expulsion pressure as "a necessary attempt to update the BVFG, which so far has not been done by the legislature." Any change to the law was to be avoided if it affected the expellee status in any way.[66] A similar argument was later made by the project group instituted by the Argeflü in 1984, which was tasked with suggesting amendments to the BVFG. There, it was argued that Aussiedler could be recognized as expellees even down to the third postwar generation. The concept of expulsion pressure was to prevent unfair decisions.[67]

The aim of the administration in passing the expulsion pressure guidelines was hence twofold. First, the idea was to get back in line those regional offices that had started checking the emigration motives of every expellee card applicant. In this sense, the guidelines were a defensive, pro-Aussiedler measure that tried to control and reverse restrictive trends in the administration. Second, the exceptional possibility to assess the emigration motives of Aussiedler had a restrictive tendency in that it allowed for the exclusion of some ethnic Germans from being recognized as expellees. The justification given, however, was expansive: Only with a safety valve like this would the inclusion of the second postwar generation be possible at all. Otherwise, the fear of abuse loomed large. In effect, this meant that only by excluding some could many others be included.

As soon as they became known, the expulsion pressure guidelines met with the fierce resistance of expellee representatives. First and foremost among these was Herbert Czaja, head of the *Bund der Vertriebenen* and member of the Bundestag for the city of Stuttgart. In repeated letters to the Baden-Württemberg Interior Ministry and other ministries, he aggressively promoted his case against any kind of restriction. Czaja's strategy was to gain the support of CDU-governed federal states, especially Baden-Württemberg, where he was well connected.[68] In particular, Czaja feared that the status of the Aussiedler as expellees might be affected. These fears were based on an episode in 1977, when the social-liberal government had tried to introduce a special Aussiedler card to replace the expellee card. The initiative had been welcomed by the Polish government, which did not like seeing its former citizens still being labeled as expellees despite the fact that they were allowed to emigrate under an official agreement.[69] Though the government had changed in the meantime and Czaja's own party, the CDU, had taken over, he still suspected the malicious influence of bureaucrats who had served under the former government.[70]

Czaja invoked a mix of legal, political, and historical arguments to support his criticism. His main legal argument was that the BVerwG could not decide on questions of status, because basic rights (such as freedom of settlement) were affected. Only the constitutional court was permitted to do this.[71] In general, the BVerwG decisions were binding only for individual cases judged, not for the administrative practice as a whole.[72] Czaja further argued that the notion of expulsion pressure had no basis whatsoever in the BVFG. The Aussiedler provision requested only that people left their home countries "as Germans," which left no leeway for questioning causality.[73]

In the political realm, the centerpiece of Czaja's argument was that there was no peace treaty and the "German question" was still open, which is why the status of Germans from the East should not be touched.[74] He took issue with the stipulation of the guidelines stating that missed opportunities to emigrate in the past could now be held against the applicant as an indication of lacking expulsion pressure. This contradicted the repeated claims of the expellee lobby for a *Recht auf Heimat*.[75] His main historical argument was that the situation of the Germans in communist countries had not changed since the Second World War. The youth were still forcibly being assimilated. The passing of time (*Zeitablauf*) alone was not enough to remedy this condition, and it was certainly not a justification to introduce any restriction on Aussiedler recognition.[76]

Czaja's interventions succeeded in breaking up the unified position taken by the Länder, some of which chose not to implement the expulsion pressure guidelines.[77] Because this position contravened the aim of harmonizing administrative practices, in the course of 1983 and 1984 the Argeflü produced two new drafts that were supposed to be acceptable for everyone. Neither of these drafts included substantial changes to the original version, merely reducing the catalog of possible clues against expulsion pressure and introducing the so-called theory of relevance (*Relevanztheorie*) to weigh emigration motives.[78] As Dr. Nowak from the Interior Ministry in Stuttgart remarked after the circulation of the second draft, it was slightly better than the first one, "but other than that it copies verbatim the Argeflü draft. What is all of this fuss about?"[79]

Probably to his dismay, the "fuss" that Nowak bemoaned continued unabated in 1985. In January, the judicial committee of the Argeflü entered another round of discussions about the expulsion pressure guidelines and produced, not surprisingly, a new draft.[80] It defined Aussiedler as the latecomers (*Nachzügler*) of the general expulsion of the Germans who still suffered from the consequences of this expulsion in their homelands, which had been largely stripped of Germans. This "solitarization" (*Vereinsamung*) was identified with expulsion pressure. The original phrase, "It cannot be ignored any longer that conditions have changed in the expulsion areas" was changed on initiative of Baden-Württemberg and Bavaria. They believed that this formulation might cause annoyance, obviously thinking of Czaja's dogma that, in fact, nothing had changed in the communist countries. The sentence was eventually merged with the one immediately following and read: "It cannot be ignored anymore that the consequences of the general expulsion measures are increasingly eclipsed by other political processes and by other political and personal ideas and destinies of the people concerned. This is especially true for the members of the second and subsequent generations born after the war."[81]

Based on this assumption, the second paragraph of the draft suggested that the motives for emigration of the generation that had experienced the general expulsion (*Erlebnisgeneration*) and the first postwar generation should be checked only in exceptional cases. For members of the second and subsequent generations, the causality between the events of the Second World War and emigration would generally have to be examined. This latter proposal met resistance because of its differential treatment of generations. Instead, it was reformulated as follows: "This causal link is also assumed for members of the second postwar generation, provided that they leave their homeland together with a member of the *Erlebnisgeneration* or the first postwar generation."[82] The question of what to do with members of this generation if they came on their own was dodged, because it was arguably not a pressing issue yet. The third paragraph contained the enumeration of possible clues for checking expulsion pressure, already known from the former drafts, which was eventually removed on Bavarian initiative. With two abstentions, the draft was accepted by the judicial committee of the Argeflü.

Anyone who had believed that Czaja would be appeased now was disappointed. Before the latest draft had become known to him, he had already sent an angry letter to the Federal Interior Ministry. Questioning the government's respect for the separation of powers, he insinuated that the Interior Ministry had inspired the administrative jurisdiction that now served as the basis for the expulsion pressure guidelines.[83] After receiving the guidelines from Nowak in

Stuttgart, Czaja replied with a scathing critique, spiked with insults against bureaucrats whom he suspected of looking for something to do and therefore creating such guidelines.[84] Whereas in past drafts Czaja had criticized the enumeration of possible clues as a potential incitement for the responsible authorities to question cases that should not be questioned, he was not happy with this new, "clueless" version either. This time he claimed that the guidelines were opaque, ambiguous, and allowed for all kinds of interpretations. He condemned the draft as a "hotchpotch of undefined terms and legal terms far removed from real life" and renewed his demand that legal experts in the field should be heard.[85]

Once again, Czaja's lobbying was effective: the January 1985 draft had existed for barely half a year when the Federal Interior Ministry developed a new proposal for guidelines.[86] The new proposal contained no reference to changed conditions in the countries of origin. Instead it echoed Czaja's position that, fundamentally, nothing had changed. It is quite revealing that these guidelines enumerated facts that were *not* suitable for starting an investigation about emigration motives, including:

- lack of attempts to emigrate, as well as missed opportunities for emigration in the past (since the aim was not to make people emigrate but to keep them in their homelands);
- marriage to a German living in the Federal Republic, unless it was the only reason for emigrating;
- a professional career within reasonable limits; and
- being a member of a generation born after the war, since expulsion pressure affected all Germans alike.

What remained as possible clues were:

- an elevated professional or political position;
- the negation of German *Volkstum*;
- criminal persecution in the Eastern Bloc; and
- an application for asylum in the West.

In general, no examination of emigration motives was to take place. In the exceptional case that an examination did occur, the authorities needed to positively prove that the Aussiedler had not emigrated because of expulsion pressure. German *Volkszugehörigkeit* would have to be assessed in any case. After further discussions, this version of the expulsion pressure guidelines was approved by the social ministers' conference and implemented by both the federation and the Länder.[87]

In the end, Czaja's insistence partly paid off. Although he had not been able to prevent the expulsion pressure guidelines altogether, he stated that he could live with their final version if it was implemented generously.[88] And indeed, he had reason to be content. His aggressive lobbying with the conservative ministries had broken up the initial consensus of the federation and the Länder. Compared with the initial version drafted in 1983, the guidelines had been watered down considerably. As a consequence, many of the initially suggested reasons to check expulsion pressure had been turned into reasons not to check expulsion pressure. To an extent, of course, this was more of a symbolic victory. As it was stated time and again by the Argeflü, the aim had never been to generally tighten the recognition practice. Instead, the idea behind the guidelines had been to systematize the diverging and increasingly restrictive practices of some of the local authorities in the Länder as well as to create a safety valve against abuse that would facilitate the inclusion of the younger generations of Aussiedler. In this respect, the final guidelines did not substantially differ from the initial draft.

But Czaja had imposed a crucial argument on the BMI and the Argeflü: Despite 40 years having passed since the end of the war, nothing had changed in the communist East. Germans were still generally repressed, and therefore expulsion pressure was still presumed for all the generations of Germans in the East. And of course, the "German question" was still open. Czaja's insistence on these issues must be understood in the context of the time. In 1985, the Association of Expellees from Silesia (*Landsmannschaft Schlesien*) had caused a great deal of controversy with its (in)famous motto: "40 years since the expulsion—Silesia remains ours" (*40 Jahre Vertreibung—Schlesien bleibt unser*). Czaja's insistence on the unaltered conditions in the expulsion areas was a continuation of the "Schlesier-Motto" with other means. The basic message in each case was that nothing had changed.

Especially in the context of Aussiedler migration, this was a purely defensive reaction. In fact, a lot had changed, and the administration was quite aware of it. As early as 1982, the judicial committee of the Argeflü had considered the possibility of introducing some geographic differentiation in the definition of the expulsion area.[89] The freedom of movement from Yugoslavia and the lack of German Aussiedlung from Hungary despite relative freedom to do so were perceived as indications of a lack of expulsion pressure. The suggestion to generally examine the emigration motives of Aussiedler who came to Germany from these countries was dismissed at the time. But the perception of change was clear—and even more so in 1986, when the winds of change began to whistle through Europe. The fact that more than 22,000 Germans were able to emigrate from post–martial law Poland in 1985, most of them on tourist visas for West Germany, was another indication of the degree of relative openness that had been established by that time.[90] The fiction of persisting expulsion pressure was becoming increasingly difficult to sustain. That is why Herbert Czaja went to such lengths to impose his static view of history on the refugee administration—a view that became impossible to uphold once the gates of the Eastern Bloc opened and the state socialist systems collapsed.

Collective Fate: Who Is a Russian German?

If the discussions surrounding expulsion pressure were a follow-up to the generational extension of the 1970s, the debate about the ethnic profile of Russian Germans was a consequence of the conceptual extension of Aussiedlung to Soviet Germans without German citizenship. Under the surface of the unaltered general legal definition of who was a German *Volkszugehöriger*, the criteria used to identify a German from the Soviet Union had been undergoing a process of change since the initially exclusive focus on the repatriation of German citizens had been overcome. During the 1970s, an image began to emerge of a typical applicant with German passport nationality and a particular region of origin. In the 1980s, this image became canonized and enriched by another element: the "collective fate" of the German *Volksgruppe*. This happened through the interplay of the Landsmannschaft-affiliated *Heimatauskunftstelle* for the Soviet Union and the Foreign Office, and in contradistinction to another Soviet national minority: the Jews.

The question of whether Jews ("people of the Mosaic faith") could be recognized as German *Volkszugehörige* had already been a salient issue in the 1960s (as was discussed in chapter 3). Starting in the 1970s, these Jewish immigrants to Germany had mainly come from the Soviet Union, both as part of the larger drop-out phenomenon (see below) and as emigrants from Israel.[91] Many of them attempted to obtain an expellee card, often successfully. Allegations of fraud and ensuing criminal investigations in the city of Offenbach (Hesse) had prompted calls for a more systematic recognition procedure. The outcome of this contestation were the 1980 "ethnicity guidelines," which, thanks to the persistent action of a sympathetic land like Hesse and of Jewish organizations, came a long way in accommodating Jewish applicants.

According to the guidelines, neither a Zionist past nor emigration to Israel would reduce an applicant's chances. More significantly, the import of the opinions of the *Heimatauskunftstellen* was officially reduced. Based on their view of inter-ethnic relations during the interwar period, these had frequently deemed Jewish applicants to be non-German. The underlying logic of sidelining the *Heimatauskunftstellen* was that the exclusion of Jews in the past (e.g., from *volksdeutsche* institutions or from registration as a German) should not be repeated in the present. In effect, this meant that just because a Jewish person was not perceived as German in the anti-Semitic climate of the interwar period, this should not mean that he or she could not be defined by contemporaries as a German *Volkszugehöriger*. The power to define who was to be considered a German *Volkszugehöriger* was firmly placed in the hands of the present-day German authorities.

This generous and inclusive definition was rolled back beginning in the mid-1980s. The Foreign Office took the initiative in this regard in late 1985, triggered by the (re)discovery of the Soviet nationality nomenclature, which fixed every person's *natsional'nost'* in the internal passport.[92] The German embassy in Moscow had reported that this passport nationality was unalterable, unequivocal, and strictly adhered to by the Soviet authorities, which would allow only Germans to emigrate to Germany, while Jews had to go to Israel.[93] The implication was that whoever came to Germany via Israel (or with an exit visa to Israel) could not be German.

The Foreign Office further based its new position on a 13-page document produced by the *Heimatauskunftstelle* (HASt) for the Soviet Union.[94] This document suggested examining the birth certificates of children, in which the *natsional'nost'* of the parents was noted. The HASt then compared the histories of the German and Jewish minorities in the Soviet Union. The author of the document told the story of the discrimination of the German minority, the deportation of the Volga Germans to Siberia and Kazakhstan in 1941, their suffering in the *trudarmiia* ("labor army"), and their release from collective banishment only in 1955. The Jews, he claimed by contrast, had never been persecuted as a group by the Soviets. While the HASt showed sympathy for the Jews' present-day wish to emigrate, it did not see itself in a position to certify their German descent and *Bekenntnis*. The author was absolutely certain that there had been no Germans of the Mosaic faith in the Soviet Union—Soviet Germans were all Lutheran, Catholic, Baptist, or Mennonite. Also, there had been no German-speaking Jews in the Soviet Union: Jews spoke Yiddish, Hebrew, or Russian, while Germans spoke Swabian and Hessian dialects. The conclusion seemed crystal clear: "The Germans have always publicly declared their German *Volkstum* and have been registered as Germans in their documents. . . . The Jews have always declared their Jewish *Volkstum*. They have been registered as Jews in their documents. They do not possess a *Bekenntnis* to German *Volkstum*."[95]

The essentialist conclusion merits attention: The Germans have declared their German *Volkstum,* while the Jews have declared their Jewish *Volkstum.* The HASt obviously knew in advance who was supposed to belong to each group. It developed something that may be described as a collective biography for each minority. For the Soviet Germans, it corresponded to the narrative of suffering developed in publications such as *Volk auf dem Weg,* the journal of the Russian-German Landsmannschaft explicitly quoted in the text. A life story that did not correspond to this ideal narrative could, by definition, not be Soviet German. Consequently, the individual applicant under consideration in the document—Jakob G. from St. Petersburg, Jewish by religion, a Red Army officer during the Second World War, and a resident of Leningrad after 1946—was declared not to be German since his biography did not match this pattern.

The point here is not to question the validity of the Landsmannschaft historical narrative. The basic parameters of this story—the deportation of the Germans from the Volga region in 1941, their banishment alongside Black Sea German resettlers to Kazakhstan and Siberia until 1955, and their predominant adherence to certain religious denominations—are well established by historiography and ethnography and capture the experience of many Germans from the Soviet Union.[96] The point is that this narrative became canonized to an extent that the individual performance of Germanness due to other criteria became very difficult—and cost someone like Jakob G. his recognition as an expellee. This standard narrative also ignored the fact that non-Jewish Soviet Germans could also have life trajectories that did not conform to the basic parameters. An example encountered during the research undertaken for this book is Katharina T., who was born in 1941 in Mukachevo (Mukacheve/Munkács) of Carpatho-Ukraine—a formerly Hungarian region that belonged to Czechoslovakia during the interwar period, was occupied by Hungary from 1938 to 1944, and became part of the Soviet Union only in 1945. At no point was she, or her family, subjected to deportation, *trudarmiia,* or any of the characteristic experiences of the stereotypical "Russian German."[97] This illustrates that even within the group of those designated as German in the Soviet Union, there were significant experiences that are insufficiently captured by the notion of collective fate.

But even those who did not share the collective Volga German experience of suffering supposedly had one thing in common with the deportees of 1941: the mentioned passport registration as "German" (*nemets*). Jews, on the other hand, were registered as "Jews" (*evrei*)—not only according to the *Heimatauskunftstelle* Soviet Union but increasingly also according to those who tried to sift Jews from non-Jews among the Olim to Israel, as will be discussed below. Based on this assumption, the Argeflü decided at its meeting in Nuremberg in 1987 that section 2.5.7 of the ethnicity guidelines, which stipulated that emigration to Israel was not an indication against German *Volkstum,* should be considered null and void. An applicant whose documents stated that he or she (or his or her parents) were Jewish or who had left the Soviet Union with an emigration permit for Israel could only be considered a German *Volkszugehöriger* if he or she had managed to dispel all doubts. As a rule, however, Jewish *natsional'nost'* and emigration to Israel precluded recognition as German. In general, official certificates were to be ordered from the Soviet Union for every applicant whose fate did not correspond to the typical fate of the Soviet Germans.[98]

It would be unfair to highlight that this decision about the mutual exclusivity of Germanness and Jewishness should have been made in Nuremberg of all places. But apart from being polemic, it would also be misleading. The Nuremberg guidelines were not about racial exclusivity. Instead, they represented the double surrender by the German expellee bureaucracy of its defining power. First, *Volkszugehörigkeit* in the sense of the German expellee law came to be identified with the *natsional'nost'* recorded in the Soviet internal passport. According to this logic, the question of who is a German was no longer answered by the German authorities but rather by the Soviet authorities that had issued the passport. Even before the amendment was passed, the Hesse Social Ministry criticized this aspect, but to no avail.[99] Second, the historical narrative of the HASt Soviet Union, which was the narrative of the Landsmannschaft, was fully embraced by the administration and used as an ideal type to fill the notion of German *Volkszugehöriger* from the Soviet Union with content. In the following discussion of the amendment to the Federal Expellee Law in late 1992, it becomes clear that the new definition of German *Volkszugehörigkeit* introduced at this point included certain elements of this narrative, while a different solution was found for Jewish immigrants.

THE LAST AUSSIEDLER GENERATION

With the developments of the early 1990s in place—the closing of the internal gate through the Aussiedler Reception Law and the declaration of wanting to keep potential Aussiedler in their countries of origin—the Federal Republic of Germany had come a long way in reversing the open-door policy that had persisted since withstanding the Bavarian Interior Ministry's attacks in the late 1960s. The Law for the Settlement of War Consequences

(*Kriegsfolgenbereinigungsgesetz*, or KfbG) was the next—and decisive—step in this direction. It amended the Federal Expellee Law in such a way as to phase out Aussiedler immigration in the long run by introducing a final generational limit: anyone born after December 31, 1992, could not become a "late" Aussiedler (*Spätaussiedler*), as newcomers leaving their home country after that date were thereafter officially called (section 4 of the law). From then on, German co-ethnics could no longer reproduce into the future.

In the short run, the idea was first of all to drastically reduce the geographic scope of Aussiedler immigration. Only applicants from the former Soviet Union continued to be admitted automatically based simply on their German *Volkszugehörigkeit* (section 4). Applicants from all other countries had to prove they were still suffering from the consequences of the Second World War and thus from a so-called *Kriegsfolgenschicksal*, which was merely a renamed version of the 1980s expulsion pressure that Herbert Czaja had so vehemently fought against. After the mass exodus of Germans from the Eastern Bloc, the collapse of that same bloc and its dominating power, and the solution of the German question, Czaja's view on history had become unsustainable. As the introduction to the law acknowledged, conditions had changed, and consequently many of the ideas contained in the various drafts of expulsion pressure guidelines entered the new law.[100]

In addition, the new law amended the definition of German *Volkszugehörigkeit* in section 6. As in the case of expulsion pressure/*Kriegsfolgenschicksal*, preexisting ideas from the administration were introduced into the new law. The new section 6 differentiated those who arrived in Germany after January 1, 1993, according to generations, with an evident focus on Russian Germans as the target group:

- someone born before 31 December 1923 (i.e., who had been of age when the Volga Germans were deported in 1941) would be judged by the old standard;
- someone born after this date was a German *Volkszugehöriger* if:
    1. He was descended from a German citizen or a German *Volkszugehöriger*;
    2. His parents, one parent or other relatives had passed confirming characteristics, such as language, upbringing, culture on to him;
    3. He declared himself, up until he left the area of German settlement (*Aussiedlungsgebiete*), to be of German nationality (*Nationalität*), or made a *Bekenntnis* to German *Volkstum* in some other manner or belonged to German nationality according to the law of his country of origin.

> The requirements of Number 2 are seen as fulfilled if the passing on of such confirming characteristics was not possible, or cannot be reasonably expected because of the conditions in the country of origin.
>
> The requirements of Number 3 are seen as fulfilled if the recognition as a German would have endangered life and limb, or would have been connected with grave professional or economic disadvantages, but the general circumstances leave no doubt about the will to belong to the German *Volksgruppe* and no other.[101]

This new section 6 resembled the amendment to section 6 already proposed (but never adopted) by the Federal Interior Ministry in 1966, which also contained separate subsections for different generations. However, the definition given for the subsequent generation was more complex than the 1966 proposal and incorporated ideas that had been developed in the following decades. The 1966 proposal wanted to make the *Bekenntnis* of the parent belonging to the war generation inheritable for the postwar generation—an idea that was embraced by the Federal Administrative Court in 1976 and had since been used by the administration. Here this construct returned in item number one in the guise of "descent from a German citizen or *Volkszugehöriger.*" The drafters of the law obviously understood this as upgrading previously facultative descent (one of the possible confirming characteristics) to a mandatory objective criterion, as descent was deleted from the objective criteria listed under item two. However, the provisional guidelines to the new law explicitly stated that the ancestor's *Volkszugehörigkeit* should in turn be judged by section 6—and this necessarily required a *Bekenntnis.*[102] This provision was thus a differently phrased version of the mandatory parental *Bekenntnis* that had been used since 1976.

Numbers two and three picked up conceptions that had not been part of official guidelines but had been envisioned in the past. Much like the Argeflü had unsuccessfully proposed in the mid-1970s, the present-day *Bekenntnis* of the applicant was now taken into consideration as well as the objective criteria to support it. The crucial difference lay in the fact that the Argeflü had then suggested to use either the parental or the present-day *Bekenntnis,* thus choosing an inclusive solution. The new section 6, however, demanded that the applicant have both. This made it harder for applicants to be recognized, especially given that the temporary guidelines for implementation explicitly stated that demanding such a *Bekenntnis* from applicants who had grown up in the former Soviet Union was perfectly reasonable.[103]

The federal chairman of the Association of Germans from Russia, Alois Reiss, criticized the KfbG in a meeting in February 1993 as "a terrible law (*schlimmes Gesetz*), but we have been able to prevent the worst."[104] "The worst," from the point of view of the Landsmannschaft, would have been a serious enforcement of the language requirement (which, in fact, happened after 1996). Landsmannschaft lobbying had achieved the addition to item two, which essentially rendered the requirement moot. It was justified with explicit reference to "the difficulties that Russian Germans were facing after the end of the war due to deportation from their original area of settlement and their dispersion across the republics of the former USSR."[105] Still, a Russian-German author like Johann Warkentin was furious and desperate that language should be so important to identify a German after years of linguistic assimilation in Russia that never resulted in full acceptance because of the "passport stigma": "And despite the moral outrage / no one cares about my passport anymore / they want to hear me talk in German, not in Russian! / There my good Russian was for the birds / What was written in the passport was the measure of all things / How could I not be upset about this?"[106]

What such criticism missed was the fact that the KfbG was largely tailored to accommodate Russian German candidates. The 1923 cut-off date was chosen with regard to the oft-quoted 1941 deportation of the Volga Germans; the belonging "to German nationality according to the law of his country of origin" was a clear reference to the Soviet passport system. The passport entry hence continued to be the measure at least of some things for a little longer. This changed in 1996, when the mandatory language test turned language into a condition sine qua non for recognition as a German Aussiedler.

DEMISE BY ETHNICIZATION

The *Kriegsfolgenbereinigungsgesetz* fixed another principle in the law that had made its appearance during the 1980s: the restriction of Aussiedler immigration by ethnic circumscription of the criteria. This mechanism is one of the central paradoxes of Aussiedler migration: its demise, which Christian Joppke has correctly characterized for the time after the opening of the Iron Curtain, went hand in hand with an increasingly "ethnicized" approach to the immigration procedure.[107] A reduction of the number of immigrants could only be achieved by introducing stricter selection criteria—in this case, higher standards as to who could be considered German. To reduce co-ethnic immigration, the screening turned more ethnic. As will be seen in the Israeli case, the reverse was also true: to attract more co-ethnic immigrants, the ethnic threshold in the selection practice had to be lower.

One aspect of ethnicization was the increased emphasis on language—especially after 1996, when mandatory language tests were introduced. These tests proved to be efficient as a means of restricting immigration. Between 1996 and 2008, the Federal Administration Office implemented more than 320,000 language tests; 52 percent of the examinees were successful and 48 percent did not exhibit enough knowledge of German to pass.[108] While language per se is, strictly speaking, not an ethnic criterion—after all, languages can be learned by anyone—it became one because of the way the language criterion was framed in the law and the resulting testing practice by the Federal Administration Office. According to the KfbG, knowledge of the German language had to be the result of "family mediation" (*familiäre Vermittlung*) to count toward recognition as German. Rather than testing proficiency in standard German, the simple language test therefore preferably tried to assess knowledge—however imperfect—of typical Russian-German dialects as a strong indication of "family mediation."[109] If one failed the test, it could not be taken again, since the idea was not to encourage candidates to acquire some short-term knowledge of German. Instead, this test was looking for "authentic" Russian Germanness, and speaking a dialect was considered a part of this authenticity.[110]

Another ethnicizing development involved candidates who based their claim to Aussiedler status on the registration of their ancestor(s) in the Deutsche Volksliste (DVL) in Poland during the war. According to long-standing administrative practice, such candidates had generally been recognized as German citizens by virtue of this registration, which gave them automatic entitlement to Aussiedler status. This practice was questioned in the late 1980s, when growing numbers of applicants from Poland based their claim on such a registration.[111] Since many communities were struggling with the massive influx of newcomers from Poland who needed to be accommodated, the administration started looking for ways to reject candidates. Questioning the legal implications of a DVL registration was one obvious starting point. Parts of the refugee administration unilaterally stopped recognizing the validity of these naturalizations, making it conditional of the fulfillment of the *Volkszugehörigkeit* criteria of section 6. With the introduction of the *Kriegsfolgenbereinigungsgesetz*, this practice became part of the federal guidelines for the implementation of the law.[112] But, in fact, the question of the extent to which a DVL registration justified the assumption that the ancestor had become a German citizen or could at least be considered a German *Volkszugehöriger* had already been the object of controversial discussions since the Polish immigration wave of the 1970s. These discussions contained a recurring paradox: to exclude people registered in the

DVL or their ancestors from present-day recognition as Aussiedler, one needed to be more ethnically selective than the Nazis themselves. This was demise by ethnicization taken to the extreme.

The DVL had been created by the Nazi authorities in occupied Poland in October 1939. It was composed of four categories: The first two categories (DVL 1 and DVL 2) were defined to contain German activists from the interwar period (*Bekenntnisdeutsche* or *Volksdeutsche*) and people who had maintained German language and culture without being politically active (*Stammesdeutsche* or *Deutschstämmige*). They immediately received German citizenship. The third category (DVL 3) supposedly contained Germans with strong ties to Polish *Volkstum* (*Eingedeutschte*), as well as the nationally undefined inhabitants of Upper Silesia (*Zwischenschicht* or *schwebendes Volkstum*, as they were called in *völkisch* parlance). They received German citizenship until revoked (*auf Widerruf*). The fourth category (DVL 4) were allegedly of German descent but considered themselves Poles (*Renegaten* or *Rückgedeutschte*). They were candidates for German citizenship until revoked.[113] The 1955 First Law for the Settlement of Citizenship Issues had validated these naturalizations, which meant that whoever had been on the *Volksliste* and had not explicitly refuted German citizenship afterward was still considered a German citizen by the West German state and was hence entitled to enter the country.

However, the wording of section 1 of the citizenship settlement law was ambiguous, because it affirmed the German citizenship "of German *Volkszugehörige*" who had been subject to naturalization. If this was not taken as a tautology (i.e., whoever was naturalized by the Nazi authorities was a German *Volkszugehöriger* by definition), this sentence could be interpreted to mean that German citizenship acquired via *Volksliste* was only valid after the war if the person in question was also German according to section 6 BVFG, to be assessed by the refugee administration of the FRG. The question that arose for the administration was whether everyone who had been registered in the *Volksliste* had also been a German *Volkszugehöriger*. Did registration in these lists mean just that? Or, alternatively, did such registration constitute at least a *Bekenntnis* to German *Volkstum*? These questions were anything but negligible. Nor were they unique. In the parallel case of former members of the Heimatbund of Lower Styria in German-occupied Slovenia, similar questions arose but remained unresolved because of the low number of cases in which people, usually Slovenian guest workers, actually claimed German citizenship in this way.[114] The *Volksliste* in Poland, on the other hand, provided an entry ticket to West Germany for large numbers of Polish citizens, which is why it remained a contentious issue for more than 15 years, until the guidelines unequivocally answered all these questions in the negative.

The paradoxical nature of *Volksliste* discussions could already be discerned in related debates of the refugee administration in the 1970s. Probably triggered by the increasing influx of Aussiedler from Poland, the Argeflü discussed the legal implications of a DVL registration in February 1976. A discussion paper of the Federal Equalization Office (*Bundesausgleichsamt*, or BAA) stated that in principle, people in categories one, two, and three had received German citizenship. The question of their *Volkszugehörigkeit* should therefore be irrelevant. However, in case of doubt, categories one and two should be considered German *Volkszugehörige*. Concerning the third category, the paper suggested differentiating between "Germans with Polish ties" (*Deutsche mit Bindungen zum Polentum*), who could be considered German *Volkszugehörige* in the present, and "ethnically undetermined Slavic speakers" (*völkisch nicht klar zuzuordnende Slawischsprecher*), who could not, for lack of objective criteria. People registered in category four could not generally be considered German *Volkszugehörige*, and their registration in the *Volksliste* should not be taken as evidence in their favor. The reason given for this opinion was quite remarkable: "Their registration has to be seen against the backdrop of the balance of power and the *Volkstumspolitik* of the Third Reich at the time. As is well known, German *Volkszugehörigkeit* was granted quite generously. Given the definitions provided for the single categories, the division of the population of the annexed Eastern Territories into four categories can only mean that members of category 4 were generally assimilated into Polish culture (*polnisch assimiliert*)."[115]

The statement of the BAA captures one of the basic paradoxes that the recognition of Nazi naturalizations brought with it. On the one hand, the attempt was made here to take away some of the defining power of the Nazi list—not everybody registered by the Nazis as German at the time would have to be considered German by present-day authorities. On the other hand, it implied being ethnically more selective than the apparently so generous Nazis, differentiating between Germans with Polish ties and autochthonous Slavs—as if such a distinction could be made that simply. At the same time, though, the classification of the Nazi authorities was, to an extent, taken at face value, since a registration in category four implied assimilation into Polish *Volkstum*, just like the authorities had defined it at the time. In reality, this ex post selection was not taken to the extreme implied in the 1976 Argeflü decision. According to another decision in 1978, members of DVL 3 were not further differentiated into Germans and Slavs; rather, they were generally considered to have retained their German citizenship unless they had explicitly rejected it.[116]

This generous practice came under challenge when the massive outflow of Aussiedler from Poland started in the late 1980s. For the Länder, who had to accommodate this unprecedented number of immigrants, denying the validity of DVL 3 naturalizations was the only way to exclude people from recognition as Aussiedler who otherwise, as German citizens, could not be excluded. Again, in effect, this implied being ethnically more selective than the Nazis: Slavs who were German enough to be included in the *Volksliste* and receive conditional citizenship during the Second World War were not German enough to be recognized as German *Volkszugehörige* in the late 1980s. In the contemporary perception, the initiative to restrict recognition based on a DVL registration came from Social Democratic Länder authorities in late 1989.[117] But in fact, the original initiative had already come from CDU-governed Baden-Württemberg in December 1987, when the Interior Ministry instructed its subordinate authorities to investigate the *Volkszugehörigkeit* of DVL 3 candidates.[118] However, the Stuttgart ministry limited its restrictive intention by instructing the lower authorities to take the registration in the *Volksliste* as an indication in favor of an applicant's German *Volkszugehörigkeit*. This view was supported by an administrative court in Düsseldorf in a March 1989 ruling.[119]

The Federal Interior Ministry opposed this restrictive trend and claimed that the citizenship obtained through DVL 3 was still valid.[120] Even so, the refugee administrations of the Länder insisted. At its meeting in Göttingen in October 1989, the Argeflü judicial committee accepted Baden-Württemberg's suggestion and decided that the German *Volkszugehörigkeit* of DVL 3 members should generally be checked.[121] The confrontation between the Länder and the federation came to a head in the following months. In a meeting of the citizenship authorities of the Länder and the federation, the former tried to convince the latter of the necessity of this examination. The practice of the Federal Administration Office in Friedland of generally recognizing the German citizenship of DVL 3 members was considered too generous. The representatives of the federation, on the other hand, argued with the moral obligation of the German state toward those Aussiedler who had served in the Wehrmacht. They nevertheless agreed to reconsider the Friedland guidelines.[122]

The final push to end the generous recognition practice came from an initiative of SPD-governed federal states spearheaded by the city of Hamburg. In a letter to Interior Minister Wolfgang Schäuble in December 1989, the interior senator of Hamburg, Werner Hackmann, claimed that the federation was not acting fast enough on the DVL problem. The number of Aussiedler was too high and put an enormous strain on Länder and communities.[123] As of February 1990, Hamburg unilaterally changed its recognition practice and asked for anyone on a tourist visa not to be sent to Hamburg, because they might be sent back to their home countries after their visa had expired.[124] Given these acts of disobedience, the BMI eventually gave in and in April 1990 instructed the BVA to check the German *Volkszugehörigkeit* of DVL 3 members as requested by the Länder.[125] With the introduction of the July 1990 Aussiedler Reception Law, which made the written takeover procedure compulsory and thus abolished the uncontrolled influx of tourists-turned-Aussiedler, the confrontation was resolved. In fact, the idea for this closure of the internal gate was generated in the context of the Länder-Bund controversy over DVL 3 citizenship and *Volkszugehörigkeit*: Hackmann had already suggested in December 1989 making the recognition as Aussiedler dependent on passing the written procedure.[126] Berlin, too, had suggested in February to make the D1 procedure the sole reception procedure (*Aufnahmeverfahren*). The AAG fulfilled these wishes.

From a practical viewpoint, restricting Aussiedler recognition with regard to the *Volksliste* was a success, because it gave communities and Länder the option to reject the applications of people who otherwise would have been German citizens with full legal entitlements. Moreover, this meant finally transcending the classificatory scheme of the Nazis introduced in the *Volksliste* and thus ending a highly problematic practice. But this break with the past came at the cost of being more ethnically restrictive than the Nazi authorities had been, since German *Volkszugehörige* who had been registered in the *Volksliste* did retain their claim to German citizenship, while non-German *Volkszugehörige* did not. As long as the larger system of reference remained predicated on ethnicity as a selection criterion, such paradoxes could not be avoided.

CONTAGIOUS ETHNICIZATION: THE INVENTION OF THE JEWISH QUOTA REFUGEE

An additional aspect of the paradoxical nature of post–Cold War ethnic immigration to Germany is evident in the way Jewish immigrants from the Soviet Union were included beginning in 1990 by using an additional ethnically coded category: the Jewish "quota refugee" (*Kontingentflüchtling*). As discussed above, Jewish immigration was not an entirely new phenomenon. Between 1955 and 1985, some 40,000 Jewish immigrants came to West Germany, and from the 1970s on, increasing numbers of them were from the Soviet Union. Whereas in the past there had been the—however contested—possibility for those immigrants to find recognition as German Aussiedler, this option was curtailed after 1987. But the issue persisted. In 1990, the continuous trickle of Soviet Jews coming to Germany started to turn into a stream. Initially, this new migration movement was directed to East Berlin, after the GDR government had decided to grant asylum to Soviet Jews threatened by persecution.[127] With unification, these migrants became a concern for the federal authorities. While there were initial considerations to continue the traditional practice of treating the issue according to expellee law, a different solution was eventually chosen.[128] Soviet Jews who had entered the country on a tourist visa after June 1, 1990, were retroactively recognized as quota refugees—a legal category that had previously been used for the Vietnamese boat people.[129] In operation as of November 10, 1991, a new formal immigration procedure included the filing of an application at a German embassy in the former Soviet Union, its processing by the Federal Administration Office (*Bundesverwaltungsamt*) and the Länder, and the embassy's eventual granting of an entry permit to the successful applicant.[130] From this point on, Jews would have to prove to the German bureaucracy that they were Jewish rather than German in order to be accepted. From 1991 until 2004, 219,604 immigrants came to Germany through this new procedure.[131]

The ethnicization in immigration policy thus turned out to be contagious. In addition to the ethnically German Aussiedler, a second ethnic immigration category was developed. As the administration raised the ethnic threshold for attaining German status, it became harder for Jewish immigrants to fulfill the criteria. This process had already begun with the Nuremberg guidelines of 1987. The quota refugee system took this beginning separation of German and Jewish immigrants to the next level by introducing a wholly separate Jewish immigration category. The only feature distinguishing Russian Jewish immigrants from the mostly "Russified" German Aussiedler from Kazakhstan and Siberia who were immigrating to Germany at the same time was their a priori definition as German or Jewish by origin, based on the primordial Soviet nationality nomenclature and an idealized collective biography of Russian German suffering. The demise of ethnic selectivity resulted not in the loosening of the legal category of ethnic Germanness but in a process of "nuclear fission" that produced an additional ethnic category.[132]

Although the German authorities changed the legal definition of German *Volkszugehörigkeit* and its administrative implementation several times in the 1990s, they refrained from providing their own official definition of who was a Jew. In effect, this defining power again devolved to the Soviet authorities that had issued the prospective immigrants' papers. According to instructions by the Foreign Office to the German embassies, applicants with "Jewish" *natsional'nost'* in their documents or descendants of at least one parent with such a registration should be eligible for immigration as quota refugees.[133]

This went beyond the narrower halachic definition of a Jew as someone born of a Jewish mother or who had converted to Orthodox Judaism, but it was more restrictive than the Israeli Law of Return, which also extended eligibility to persons with a Jewish grandparent.[134] Since the Jewish communities in Germany adhered to the halachic definition, many of the newcomers were excluded from official membership in the communities.[135] This is why, in 2001, the immigration commission headed by former minister Rita Süssmuth suggested the introduction of the halachic criterion into immigration policy.[136] In doing so, the commission followed a *Zentralrat* recommendation.[137] This suggestion was not implemented at the time. As the sociologist and Jewish community activist Irene Runge pointed out, "immigration according to halacha" would have been something that not even the Orthodox in Israel had ever been able to impose.[138] As discussed later in this chapter, this was not for lack of trying.

ISRAEL: ALIYAH POLICY BETWEEN THE LEFT AND THE RIGHT

While co-ethnic immigration to the Federal Republic of Germany was generally high during the 1970s and 1980s, the same cannot be said for Israel. This difference occurred despite the fact that Israel was open to Jewish immigration from anywhere in the world. Despite economic difficulties and growing unemployment, West Germany was still an economic powerhouse in Western Europe and an attractive destination for co-ethnics who had the option of going there. Israel, on the other hand, was facing conditions of perpetual insecurity as well as increasing economic difficulties and high inflation, especially in the 1980s. Instead of attracting large-scale Aliyah, Israel had to cope with increasing *Yeridah* (emigration, literally "descent").[139]

To be sure, emigration had already troubled the country in the 1950s and 1960s. But at that time, it was counterbalanced by repeated waves of mass immigration from places such as Morocco, Romania, and Poland. Aliyah numbers during the 1970s and 1980s, by contrast, were significantly below the levels of the preceding decades. According to official statistics, 329,938 Olim came to Israel between 1971 and 1980 compared with 385,898 between 1961 and 1970. Between 1981 and 1989, the year before Soviet Aliyah took off, only 133,405 new Olim came to Israel, making the 1980s the decade with the lowest Aliyah levels in the history of the state.[140] Immigration from Western countries remained limited throughout this period. Immigration from the Soviet Union was high during the first half of the 1970s, but virtually ran dry afterward due to Soviet emigration restrictions. As discussed below, many Soviet émigrés who could have come to Israel chose the United States or other countries instead. Aliyah from Romania (in exchange for "ransom" payments) continued throughout the period under study, but at a decreasing rate as the pool of Romanian Jews was depleted. The other principal sources of Jewish migrants to Israel were countries in political and economic crisis, such as Argentina and Iran.

As in West Germany, the 1970s and 1980s brought significant change to the political history of Israel. In a reversal of the West German situation, initially this meant the replacement of a long-term left-wing government by the right-wing opposition. The 1977 election saw the end of Labor rule after almost three decades and the triumphant victory of Menachem Begin's Likud party, which had been created as a union of several right-wing parties under the leadership of Begin's Herut in 1973.[141] From 1977 to 1981, the Likud governed in a coalition with the National Religious Party (NRP)—Labor's long-term ally—and ultra-Orthodox Agudat Yisrael as well as initially the short-lived centrist Democratic Movement for Change (Dash).[142] This coalition was extended by the Mizrachi Tami party and Moshe Dayan's Telem in 1981—an arrangement that lasted until the 1984 Knesset election.[143]

From 1984 to 1988, Israel was governed by a national unity government consisting of Likud and Labor (with their respective leaders Yitzhak Shamir and Shimon Peres alternately holding the position of prime minister); the NRP; Agudat Yisrael; the newly founded ultra-Orthodox Mizrachi party Shas; ultra-Orthodox Morasha (in the government until 1986); secular-liberal Shinui; and the right-wing Ometz party, which later merged with Likud.[144] After the 1988 elections, the national unity government was made up of Likud, Labor, the NRP, Shas, Agudat Yisrael, and ultra-Orthodox Degel Ha-Torah, and it was led by Likud's Yitzhak Shamir.[145] After Labor left the government in 1990, the Likud governed in a purely right-wing-religious coalition that included the previous coalition members and several other smaller right-wing parties.[146] In 1992, Labor under Yitzhak Rabin took over once again, this time in a more clearly left-wing alliance with secularist Meretz, as well as ultra-Orthodox Shas, tolerated by the Arab Democratic Party and Communist Hadash.

Similar to the German case, political change did not substantially affect co-ethnic immigration policy. Within the mainstream of Zionist parties, both the left and the right were committed to the immigration of Jews to Israel. The differences that did exist concerned the increasing identification of the religious parties with the political right and the resulting overlap between left-right and secular-religious cleavages. As will be seen, the religious parties were in favor of a halachic and thus more restrictive definition of the term *Jew* in the Law of Return, and they found support for this among the basically secular Likud. This support, however, was never unanimous, which is why all respective initiatives failed.

At the same time, the left-wing secular parties remained committed to a broader definition that would allow for a maximum of openness toward new Olim. In this sense, the political left was even more committed to large-scale Aliyah than the political right—an inversion of the German situation, where the Social Democratic left was moving away from its former pro-Aussiedlung stance and increasingly distanced itself from co-ethnic immigration. Yet within the ethnic framework of Jewish immigration, the secular leftists were indeed the liberals promoting a more open—less ethnic—definition of ethnicity. But the Likud and other secular nationalists forgot their puritan concerns very quickly once the mass immigration of both Jews and (halachic) non-Jews from the Soviet Union started in the late 1980s, given that this new immigration was giving the country a helpful demographic boost after a decade with low immigration and increased emigration rates. The general lines of Aliyah policy also remained constant after 1992, when the government shifted back to a left-wing coalition. Within the Zionist consensus, the left-right cleavage had no bearing on the stance toward Jewish immigration—quite unlike the secular-religious cleavage, which is discussed in more detail below.

AGAINST ALL ODDS: ISRAEL'S HOMELAND POLITICS

Irrespective of the government and in contrast to Germany's reserved position on co-ethnic immigration, Israel remained the committed national homeland that it had been since abandoning the policy of selective Aliyah during the 1960s. The nation's Aliyah policy was predicated on the active pursuit of bringing Jewish immigrants to Israel. The consensus across the political spectrum—save for the ultra-Orthodox fringe and the conspicuously silent Arab politicians—about the necessity and desirability of Aliyah in general and from the Soviet Union in particular had become very clear in the 1970 Knesset debates. Many of the post-1970 efforts to bring in new immigrants focused on Soviet Jews, many of whom, during that period, had the opportunity to leave their country for the first time.

These efforts were carried out by two well-established institutions: the semi-official Jewish Agency and Nativ, the secret "Liaison Bureau" created in 1952 and directly responsible to the prime minister's office.[147] These organizations were not able to operate inside the Soviet Union, but they had offices running in Vienna, which, during the 1970s and 1980s, was the first transit station for the emigrants outside the Eastern Bloc. Nativ has also been identified by some scholars as having been instrumental in fostering civil society engagement for

Soviet Jewry (the so-called Soviet Jewry movement), particularly in the United States.[148] And indeed, Soviet Olim did arrive in Israel in significant numbers throughout the 1970s—official statistics state 156,318 for 1971–1980, almost half of the total number of immigrants during that period. However, this wave of migration almost ceased in the 1980s due to Soviet emigration restrictions.[149]

But even during the 1970s, a trend emerged that threatened to ruin the high hopes placed in Soviet Aliyah: the so-called drop-out phenomenon, or *Neshirah* in Hebrew. In principle, it was nothing new that Jewish migrants did not go to Israel; the phenomenon was discussed in chapter 3 regarding Romanian emigrants in the 1960s. In addition, significant numbers of North African Jews chose Francophone countries such as France or Canada over Israel.[150] The vexing issue for Israel concerning Soviet Jews was that, in most cases, the Soviet Union granted them exit visas specifically for Israel, but as soon as the migrants reached the transit station in Vienna, they redirected their journey to their preferred destinations. Most of them chose the United States, which received them as refugees; others went to Canada, Australia, New Zealand, Latin America, and also to West Germany.[151] The Hebrew Immigrant Aid Organization (HIAS) assisted them on these alternative migration trajectories, much to the annoyance of Israel. Those supporting the drop-outs stressed their "freedom of choice."[152] Israel, by contrast, believed that those with affidavits sent from Israel should be sent to Israel only, and it accused the HIAS and the American Joint Distribution Committee of encouraging migrants to drop out.[153] From the Israeli point of view, there could be no such thing as a Jewish refugee, because Israel would provide all Jews with citizenship at any time.[154]

Experience had thus taught the Israeli state that Aliyah did not happen by itself. This became especially obvious when the Soviet Union opened its gates in 1987. In contrast to Germany, which was receiving astonishing numbers of immigrants from Poland and the Soviet Union beginning that year, Israel saw only a modest increase in Olim numbers. The reason was *Neshirah*. In 1987, of 8,155 émigrés, only 2,072 ended up in Israel, while 6,083 chose other destinations. In 1988, only 2,173 chose the Jewish state, while 16,788 dropped out.[155] Given that a strategic absorption plan developed in 1986 had calculated 50,000 Olim per year, this ratio was disappointing to say the least.[156] Israel felt compelled to act.

In the struggle against *Neshirah*, the closing of the US gates for Soviet Jewish refugee immigration in particular had been a long-standing Israeli request.[157] This finally happened in October 1989. From then on, Soviet Jews who wanted to migrate to the United States had to apply for a visa at the US embassy in Moscow, ruling out the possibility of applying for refugee status at US embassies in other European countries. This made *Neshirah* practically impossible, especially because drop-outs were no longer to receive aid from HIAS or the American Joint Distribution Committee.[158] In addition, the US government introduced a quota for 50,000 Soviet refugees per year, giving priority to some 30,000 people awaiting their US visa in Rome or Vienna, and another 41,600 whose applications were pending in Moscow (most of them not Jews, but Armenians).[159] In effect, this meant that no new refugee applications could be successful for almost one and a half years, thus turning Israel into the main destination for Soviet Jewish emigrants by default.

Even so, it would appear that Israeli influence was not directly responsible for bringing about this change in 1989, though not for lack of trying. According to Baruch Gur-Gurevitz, Prime Minister Yitzhak Shamir's interventions to that effect with President George H. W. Bush and Secretary of State James Baker were not crowned with success.[160] Instead, Gur-Gurevitz attributes the eventual change in US government policy to US concerns about the rising number of drop-outs and the expectation of even more Soviet immigrants once the gates of the Soviet Union opened.[161] Previous such plans to stop receiving Soviet-Jewish refugees in the United States had been resisted by American Jewish organizations, which had embraced the "freedom of choice" approach. By 1989, they were ready to compromise on this issue because of the rising cost of maintaining the overcrowded Ladispoli camp for drop-outs near Rome and the cost of integrating them once they arrived in the United States, given that the government was not willing to pay for all the newcomers.[162] Fred A. Lazin argues that, "in contrast to the 1970s, the American Jewish establishment in 1989 was more willing to support the Israeli demand that Soviet Jews be resettled in Israel. Many felt Israel needed them and that Israel provided a better opportunity for them to remain Jewish and be part of the Jewish people."[163]

Israel took further proactive measures to make sure Soviet Jewish émigrés would actually arrive in Israel. It introduced the alternative transit stations inside the Eastern Bloc that are described earlier, where migrants would be unable to drop out. The idea to use Romania as a transit country had already been suggested in the 1970s but was dismissed at the time due to Romanian opposition. Yet in 1987 Ceauşescu agreed to the renewed Israeli initiative, and in November 1988 the Bucharest transit station officially opened. As a result, 10,787 Soviet Jews made Aliyah via Romania in 1989, 43,020 in 1990, and 40,032 in 1991.[164]

During the second half of 1989, Soviet Jews also started transiting in Budapest, and beginning in February 1990, Malev, the Hungarian state airline, operated flights from Moscow, Leningrad, and Kiev to Israel via Budapest.[165] The Hungarian transit station was even busier than the Romanian one: in 1990 alone, 101,107 people came to Israel via Hungary, and another 51,223 came in

1991.[166] Warsaw also became a point of transit in early 1990.[167] After the introduction of direct flights from the Soviet Union in late 1991, the transit stations fell out of use and were closed down.[168] In their place, the Jewish Agency began to operate exit stations in the (by then former) Soviet Union that had the task to facilitate transportation, process cargo, provide information on travel arrangements, and offer orientation for life in Israel.[169]

With the combination of the United States closing its gates and Israel redirecting migrants through countries that did not allow *Neshirah*, the migration tide turned decisively. In 1989, the number of Olim to Israel increased significantly to 12,117—though it was still less than the 58,888 Jews that went to other countries.[170] As of 1990, Israel experienced the most significant influx of Olim since the days of mass Aliyah in 1950, receiving more than 330,000 Soviet immigrants in 1990–1991 alone, compared with some 85,000 who chose other destinations.[171]

By then, Germany was also slowly emerging as a major destination for Soviet-Jewish immigrants. As mentioned earlier, this phenomenon was not completely new, but, as a result of the new German policy of receiving Soviet Jews as quota refugees, its numerical dimensions in the 1990s transcended past developments by far. Between 1990 and 1993, 16,597 (former) Soviet citizens came to Germany on a Jewish ticket. From the mid-1990s, their number was consistently above 15,000 per year, which turned Germany into a serious challenger of the Israeli monopoly on Jewish immigration.[172] For the time being, though, Israel had established itself as the main destination for Soviet Jews and their families.

Even so, awareness persisted among Israeli officials that these immigrants did not all come of their own accord, which is why the master plan for the Soviet Union mentioned earlier was developed under the coordination of Baruch Gur-Gurevitz, and emissaries were sent to the country to convince Soviet Jews to move to Israel. As immigration numbers dropped back below 100,000 in 1992, programs to encourage Aliyah implemented by the Jewish Agency became particularly relevant. The constant immigration numbers over the following years speak to their success. Until the end of the decade, the number of arrivals was consistently between 50,000 and 70,000 every year except 1998.[173]

Ironically, Israel had to struggle to keep immigration at that level, while Germany received up to four times as many co-ethnic immigrants until the mid-1990s, despite attempts to curb immigration and keep Russian Germans in their home regions. Even after the introduction of the language test in 1996, absolute Aussiedler numbers remained above the level of Olim numbers to Israel.[174] Apart from the fact that, according to the 1989 Soviet census, there were only 1.4 million self-declared Jews in the Soviet Union compared with about two million Germans, these numbers suggest that ideological and political commitment to co-ethnic immigration and the active recruitment of migrants did not necessarily translate into larger immigrant numbers. At the same time, the fact that so many Russian Germans and their families continued to migrate to Germany does not mean that Germany actively sought their immigration. Instead, it indicates that co-ethnic migration is still "normal" migration in the sense that economic pull factors are crucial—and in this regard Germany had much more to offer than Israel, despite reduced Aussiedler benefits and rampant unemployment. The growing number of Jewish immigrants to Germany spoke to that fact, too.

RELIGIOUS-SECULAR GATEKEEPER STRUGGLES

Although the necessity of Aliyah was uncontested in 1970s and 1980s Israel, the definitions of who was eligible for it were not. On repeated occasions during these decades, a growing coalition of religious and right-wing parties tried to restrict the recognition of converts to Judaism under the Law of Return to those who had converted according to halacha. While past "Who is a Jew?" controversies (both in 1958 and in 1970) had been about secular-religious relations and the position of the religious subsystem within the Israeli political system, the "Who is a convert?" debate activated an additional inner-religious cleavage: Orthodox Judaism was intent on asserting its primacy over other streams, be they Reform or Conservative.

For Aliyah, the debate over the definition of a convert was of little practical importance, because the number of Reform converts trying to immigrate to Israel was minute.[175] Yet despite the minor numerical importance of the phenomenon, the discussions were of interest for Aliyah, because they raised an important question by implication: Who is in charge of protecting the immigration gate? Beyond the traditional attempts by the religious institutions to wield influence by imposing certain religious definitions on secular law, the issue also obtained an institutional aspect in the 1980s, which is explored further in this section. As new and large immigration waves from the Soviet Union and Ethiopia began to materialize, the institutional gatekeeping role of the religious subsystem gained practical significance—with strikingly different outcomes in each case.

The Conversion Debate

The focus of the "Who is a Jew?" debates during the 1970s and 1980s was the issue of adding the phrase "according to halacha" to the conversion proviso of section 4B of the Law of Return—a demand that the ultra-Orthodox parties had already made during the amendment debates in 1970. Such proposals were submitted by ultra-Orthodox Knesset members Shlomo Lorincz (Agudat Yisrael) and Kalman Kahana (Poalei Agudat Yisrael) in 1972 (when it was overwhelmingly defeated by a 57–19 vote with eight abstentions) and in 1976 (when it was defeated 39–25).[176] In 1983, Lorincz tried again, this time supported by fellow Agudat Yisrael Knesset members Rabbi Shmuel Halpert, Menachem Porush, and Avraham Yosef Shapira (Kahana had dropped out of politics by then).[177] A parallel amendment proposal to the same effect was submitted by Chaim Druckman of the National Religious Party, which was supported by Interior Minister Yosef Burg from the same party. Speeches against the proposals were delivered by two prominent secularists—Amnon Rubinstein (Shinui) and Yair Tzaban (Labor Alignment)—who framed their opposition in terms of the division of state and religion (Rubinstein) and the fear of a widening rift between secular and religious Jews (Tzaban). The two bills were voted on together and were defeated in a 58–50 vote. This was a much narrower margin than in the past, but it pointed to a pattern that would be repeated in the following years: despite the government coalition with the NRP and Agudat Yisrael, not all Likud Knesset members supported the halachic amendment. Otherwise, the vote should have been successful, given that the coalition held 63 of 120 Knesset seats.

By 1985, the group of politicians that was sponsoring the renewed attempt to introduce halachic conversion into the Law of Return had grown significantly. Shlomo Lorincz was no longer a member of the Knesset, but others continued the struggle. The bill was sponsored by a broad coalition of the right represented by Avner-Chai Shaki and David Danino (both NRP), Avraham Yosef Shapira (Agudat Yisrael), Rafael Pinchasi (Shas), Gershon Shafat and Eliezer Waldman (both from Tehiya, a right-wing nationalist party associated with the settler movement), and the Likud Knesset members Yigal Cohen, Roni Milo, Ovadiah Eli, Dov Shilansky, and Benny Shalita (who withdrew during the session). Significantly, ultra-Orthodox (Agudat Yisrael and Shas), national-religious (NRP and, to an extent, Tehiya), and nonreligious (Likud) parties were represented here, and all of them except Tehiya were part of the government coalition. The Knesset, which was perfectly divided between right-wing and religious, and left-wing and secular parties, voted against the bill 62–51. All the leftist-secular camp except for Rabbi Menachem Cohen of the Labor Alignment voted against it, whereas the Likud counted four defectors who also voted against the bill, one abstention, and four absences (in addition to the absence of "outlaw" ultranationalist Meir Kahane).[178]

During the same Knesset period, the issue returned to the parliament floor in July 1987, this time in the form of three separate halachic proposals (one proposal was made by three Knesset members from the NRP, the ultra-Orthodox Morasha, and Likud; one by a lone Likudnik; and one by a lone Shas deputy); one counterproposal was made by the ardently secularist Movement for Civil Rights and Peace (Ratz) group of veteran Knesset member Shulamit Aloni. The results of the vote were almost exactly the same as in 1985, and the bills came to naught, as did a subsequent attempt in June 1988.[179]

Yet it is worthwhile to take a closer look at the 1987 debate for two reasons. First, one of the proposed amendments, submitted by David Magen of Likud, went beyond anything that had been demanded so far. While the—by then almost ritualized—request was to add the phrase "according to halacha" to the Law of Return conversion proviso, Magen had a more far-reaching idea. He suggested the following definition: "A Jew is who was born to a Jewish mother and does not belong to another religion, *or who was declared Jewish by the Chief Rabbinate of Israel.*"[180] This proposal amounted to nothing less than turning the chief rabbinate into the official gatekeeper of Aliyah, and, not surprisingly, it provoked strong reactions from the secular camp. Interestingly, Magen thought of his proposal as a kind of compromise solution that would be acceptable also to those who objected to the explicit inclusion of halacha in the law. He was mistaken in his belief. A second reason for a closer look at this debate is that, when it took place in July 1987, Soviet mass Aliyah reappeared as a realistic scenario on the horizon and entered the debate as a topic, despite the fact that the issue of conversion itself had no bearing whatsoever on Soviet Jewry.

Introducing her secularist counterproposal, Shulamit Aloni openly challenged the religious pretenses to being gatekeepers of the nation. She began with the observation that conversion was a matter of religious ritual, not of a civil law, and hence the Knesset should have no business with it. She further pointed out that the chief rabbinate was responsible only for matters of personal status, not for immigration and citizenship. Any step taken in that direction would be another step on the way to turning Israel from a *medinat chok* (literally "state of law," the literal Hebrew translation of the German *Rechtsstaat*) into a *medinat halachah* (a halachic state). Aloni compared the Law of Return to other repatriation laws in Germany, Finland, and post-imperial Britain, which centered on the granting of citizenship to repatriates but had no religious implications, as an explicitly halachic Law of Return would have. She suggested an inclusive definition of Jewishness: "For the purposes of this law, he is entitled to Israeli citizenship who is Jewish according to his consciousness and declares it in good faith and links his fate to the fate of the Jewish people, one of his parents is Jewish, including adoptive parents, he who is registered in a Jewish community or who is registered in his country of origin in official documents as Jewish, and also he who was converted by the Chief Rabbi (*mara daatra*) [of the respective country of origin] and is not of another religion."[181] With this catchall definition, Aloni hoped to include Russian, Ethiopian, European, and all the other Jews who might want to make Aliyah without yielding any defining power to the religious camp in Israel.

Chaika Grossman of the leftist-Zionist Mapam had no alternative definition of Jewishness to offer but spoke in favor of removing the NRP-Shas-Likud proposal from the agenda. In her speech, the impending Soviet Aliyah loomed large. Grossman pointed to the problems these immigrants would face if things in Israel went according to halacha and insinuated that at least part of the rampant dropout phenomenon was caused by proposals such as this one. Grossman directed a dramatic appeal against the religious parties and the political right:

> We cannot speak with two voices: One voice that demands the right for Jews to leave and come to Israel and unite with their people; and a second voice that makes proposals such as this one. You act against your own convictions by driving Israel into a dead end, and we might not be able to realize Zionism the way we want it to be realized, in essence by ingathering the exiles. What you are proposing is against the ingathering of the exiles, it means to divide the people. I am telling you, you are playing with fire. Don't play with fire.[182]

Grossman's linking of the conversion bill to Russian Aliyah was not exactly to the point: Orthodox versus Reform Judaism was a purely Israeli-American issue. However, her general point about Israel's "two voices" and the problems that a greater influence of the halacha on Aliyah policy toward Russian Jews might cause was farsighted, as will be seen below.

Chaim Druckman of NRP gave a scathing response to these reproaches: Aloni's proposed law, he thundered, helped assimilation (*hitbolelut*), and assimilation threatened Judaism with extinction (*kilayon*).[183] He accused Aloni of lying about the religious camp's position toward Aliyah and of being "eaten up by hatred for Israel." Druckman claimed that the religious camp welcomed Russian and Ethiopian Olim with open arms: "Who takes care of the Olim from Russia? Religious Jews take care of the Olim from Russia. Religious Jews opened their doors for the Jews from Ethiopia. In general, the Aliyah in its majority is religious Aliyah."[184]

This last point underscores an important aspect of the Israeli situation: while the left-right division of the political spectrum was irrelevant for determining a party's stance toward Aliyah, the secular-religious cleavage was much more salient.

Aliyah as such was perceived as a state priority across the Zionist party spectrum, with a secular leftist like Grossman and a right-wing religious-nationalist settler like Chaim Druckman rhetorically competing for the greatest commitment to Jewish immigration. The difference lay in the anticipated scope of eligible people. While secularists like Aloni and Grossman spoke in favor of inclusive definitions of Jewishness that would enable maximum Aliyah, Druckman added an important qualification: the perceived religiousness of the immigrants. As a rhetorical device, this was good enough to reconcile the restrictive thrust of halachic law proposals with the simultaneous endorsement of large-scale immigration. In practice, however, the fact that many of the Russian newcomers were neither religious nor—in many instances—Jewish according to halachic standards, put strains on the supposedly welcoming stance of the religious parties.

The New Russian Aliyah

When the Great Russian Aliyah got under way in 1990, the 1970 Law of Return and its definitions were unchanged—despite all the attempts by the religious camp and parts of the nonreligious right to impose halachic restrictions and despite the pivotal role the religious parties seemed to hold after the inconclusive November 1988 elections, which eventually resulted in another Likud-Labor unity government.[185] But the religious parties did assume a significant role in the gatekeeping of the new Russian Aliyah. After the Labor Party pulled out of the coalition government in early 1990, the country was governed by the right-wing-religious coalition of the Likud under the premiership of Yitzhak Shamir. In this government, religious parties held three ministries important for Aliyah and its absorption: the Interior Ministry under Arieh Deri of Shas, the Absorption Ministry led by Deri's fellow Shas member Yitzhak Chaim Peretz, and the Education Ministry under Zevulun Hammer of the NRP.[186] The latter two were of supreme importance for the reception and treatment of immigrants in Israel, and the Interior Ministry also had an institutionalized gatekeeping function as the interior minister was in charge of implementing the Law of Return.[187]

This political constellation resulted in a rift between the internal and external recognition procedures at the same time that Germany had merged its immigration gate and externalized it to better control the immigrant influx. In Israel, the internal gate was now in the hands of an ultra-Orthodox party, while the external gate was operated by the Jewish Agency and the Israeli consular authorities. These different actors applied different standards in immigration control. According to Clive Jones, who wrote what remains to this day the most comprehensive account of the political and institutional side of Soviet Jewish Aliyah, the Jewish Agency required prospective Soviet immigrants to prove their Jewishness by submitting documents such as birth and marriage certificates as well as internal passports. Only then would they receive a visa for Israel. Once there, however, Deri's Interior Ministry officials would often not accept many of these documents as sufficient proof of Jewish identity. In Jones's words, "while cases of forged documents did arise, it appeared that the halachic interpretation of immigrant status exercised undue influence over the absorption process. For some Soviet migrants, the withdrawal of Jewish identity had the most serious ramification: the denial of full Israeli citizenship and attendant civil rights."[188]

Jones further mentions that Deri "used his office to question openly the character of the immigrants and declared that the new Olim should provide additional proof of Jewish identity."[189] According to Jones, this was part of a more general Orthodox challenge to this new Soviet Aliyah that was also carried by the absorption minister, Yitzhak Chaim Peretz. Jones argues that Peretz tried to counteract the potential of the predominantly European and secular immigrants to diminish the political influence of Oriental and Orthodox communities in Israel, both of which were represented by Shas. Through his office he therefore challenged "the Jewish character of Soviet Aliyah, and the secularism that dominated the immigrant perceptions of the Jewish state."[190] During a visit to Moscow in November 1990, Peretz went so far as to call the Law of Return "a bad law because it allows large numbers of non-Jews to come to Israel," estimating their percentage to be 40 percent.[191]

Here, then, Israel was indeed speaking with the two voices that Chaika Grossman had warned against in July 1987. Moreover, it transpired that the religious parties' welcoming stance toward the newcomers was conditional, as Chaim Druckman's reference to their purported religiousness had insinuated. However, Druckman was correct to point out that religious institutions were the ones that received the new immigrants well, if only to counter the effects of a predominantly secular immigration. According to Clive Jones, the religious parties consciously tried to keep nonreligious organizations out of the absorption process, both during its initial stage and when it came to housing (no settlement in kibbutzim) and education (strong religious emphasis in the language schools, the *ulpanim*).[192]

Meanwhile, the screening and recognition practice of the secular authorities at the external gate was evolving as well. Once Israel had reestablished diplomatic relations with the Soviet Union in October 1991 (and after the latter's dissolution with the successor states joint in the Commonwealth of Independent States), consular guidelines for the treatment of Aliyah candidates from the

Commonwealth of Independent States were released.[193] These guidelines reflect the experience that the Israeli authorities had made with (post-)Soviet Aliyah up to that point. In general, a prospective immigrant would be accepted only after an interview, in which the consul could assess the candidate's earnest will to settle in Israel—memories of *Neshirah* and *Yeridah* were still fresh—and could establish whether there were possible reservations under section 2B of the Law of Return (health issues, criminal past) that remained. In addition, candidates were required to submit a host of original documents considered pertinent for eligibility, such as passports and birth, marriage, and death certificates. In the absence of such original documents, or in case of doubt, the consul was supposed to check for the following information: the name of the candidate, the name of his or her parents, possible relatives in Israel, and so on. However, no "certifications of Jewishness" from local communities or religious authorities would be accepted as evidence, nor would declarations to that effect by former Soviet citizens or "conversion certificates" from local rabbis (except for Pinhas Goldschmidt in Moscow, on verification). Fake documents would be stamped as such, and the rejected application would be sent to Israel. If the consul was convinced that the candidate was eligible despite having forged documents, then only the forged document would be stamped invalid, and the request would be granted.

The Aliyah request with a detailed report by the consul, the necessary documents, and the consul's opinion would be forwarded to the Consular Department of the Foreign Ministry, which could either grant the request or send it to the Interior Ministry for decision. In each case, the consul was supposed to note on the Aliyah questionnaire the section of the Law of Return under which the candidate was eligible (4B if the candidate had a Jewish mother, 4A if she or he derived entitlement from a family member). If there were doubts about the mother's Jewishness but not about the candidate's eligibility in general, he or she would receive a permit under section 4A, with the option to submit more documents once in Israel to prove the mother's Jewishness after all. In case of rejection, appeal was possible. True to the law, people who were born to a Jewish mother but had changed their religion would generally not be accepted; children of converts, on the other hand, could invoke descent from their Jewish grandparents.

Interestingly, the guidelines also list several acceptable passport entries to prove Jewishness, in addition to the usual *evrei* (which was so obvious that it was not even mentioned in the document):[194]

- Tat [Persian-speaking mountain Jew]
- Gorskii Evreii [mountain Jew]
- Krymchak [Jew from Crimea]

- Karai [adherent of Karaite Judaism from Crimea]
- Lakhlukh [Kurdish Jew]
- "Iranian Jew" or Yehada—descendent of Mashadi converts (a small group lives in Turkmenistan, mainly in the city of Yoloten)
- "Assyrian"—usually a designation for Christians to distinguish them from Muslim Kurds, needs to be checked closely.

These guidelines create the impression of a thorough and bureaucratized screening process adapted to local conditions. The list of Soviet variants of Jewish subnationalities speaks to the expert knowledge that the Israeli authorities invested. As to the emphasis on original documents and the warning against forgeries, it can only be guessed at this point that this was a reaction to the skepticism encountered by the internal gatekeeper at the Interior Ministry, who, in case of doubt, could be consulted by the consular authorities as well. At the same time, the fact that requests for Aliyah might be granted despite exposed forged documents seems to suggest a certain admission of the exercise's futility by the consular authorities. Asking people to prove by original documents something as blurry as Jewish descent down to the third generation in an atheist state with hardly any community structures was virtually an invitation to submit forgeries, and the authors of the guidelines seemed to know it.

All these safeguards could not change the simple fact that large numbers of non-Jews (as defined by halacha) were perfectly eligible to make Aliyah to Israel under the Law of Return without having to forge anything. This was precisely what Yitzchak Peretz had meant when he spoke of the Law of Return as a "bad law." The halacha simply played no role in the screening process of (post-)Soviet Jews, and neither the religious parties nor the chief rabbinate could change this fact. This matter was quite different for Ethiopian Jewry.

The Ethiopian Aliyah

Gatekeeping for Ethiopian Aliyah, which was happening in parallel to the Soviet exodus, was a different story altogether compared with Soviet Aliyah.[195] For the "Beta Israel" or "Falashas," as Ethiopian Jews were called, the defining power of the rabbinate and the religious establishment had been quite explicit from early on, arguably for lack of interest among the secular state authorities. In contrast to the position toward Soviet Jewry, the Israeli governments during the first decades of statehood made no effort to encourage Ethiopian-Jewish immigration. In 1954, Prime Minister Moshe Sharett explicitly rejected the idea of bringing the Falashas to Israel:

> I think it is clear that the Aliyah of Falasha Jews to Israel means creating a racial problem (*beayah gizit*) within the society (*yishuv*). There are those who claim that already now we have discrimination against Yemenite and Moroccan Jews. I deny this, here we can say it is not a racial problem, but rather an ethnic problem (*beayah adatit*), but the Aliyah of black Jews (*yehudim shchorim*) to Israel can result in much harsher problems. . . . There can be the usual cultural assistance, but it must be clear that their future is in Ethiopia and not in the State of Israel.[196]

Given this racialized view of Ethiopian Jewry, it is not surprising that the secular Israeli institutions took no initiative to include the Falashas, whose Jewishness was doubted by Orthodox Judaism, in the Law of Return. It was the Sephardic Chief Rabbi Ovadiah Yosef—later the spiritual leader of Shas—who in 1973 declared the Beta Israel to be "Jews, descendants of Jewish tribes who moved south," basing his judgment on the opinions of rabbinic authorities who saw them as the descendants of the biblical tribe of Dan.[197] Yosef further urged: "The Falashas are Jews whom we must save from assimilation and whose immigration to Israel is to be hastened, to educate them in the spirit of our holy Torah and engage them in the rebuilding of our Holy Land."[198] It was only after this rabbinical clearance that an interministerial committee decided in March 1975 to include the Falashas in the Law of Return. From 1984, they were unconditionally registered as Jewish in their ID cards, whereas before then, they were required to undergo a ceremonial conversion. This adjustment arrived just before the first major airlifts of Ethiopian Jews to Israel during "Operation Moses" and "Operation Queen of Sheba" in 1984–1985.[199] The next comparable operation was "Operation Solomon" in 1991, which brought some 14,500 Ethiopian Jews to Israel.

Among the newcomers in 1991 were the "Falashmura"—former Ethiopian Jews who had converted to Christianity—whom the chief rabbinate had requested to be brought to Israel as well, despite state hesitations.[200] The government tasked a committee with examining the Falashmura's claim to Aliyah under the Law of Return. The committee was headed by government secretary and later Supreme Court judge Elyakim Rubinstein. The committee concluded that the Falashmura were descendants of apostates and were therefore not eligible for immigration under the Law of Return. However, they could be returned to Judaism by a "task force" of rabbis and *qessoch* (Beta Israel priests, *qes* in the singular). Yet due to the restrictions of conversion on Ethiopian soil, this was not a realistic option before emigration.[201] A similar approach was upheld by a committee under Absorption Minister Yair Tzaban of Mapam in 1992, who was a decided secularist. Falashmura were taken in, however, under family reunification schemes as well as by virtue of ancestral right in case of descent from one Jewish grandparent, which in turn would be certified by a *qes*.[202] According to guidelines by a rabbinical committee appointed by the chief rabbinate in 1993, they should be treated as Jews and brought to Israel under the Law of Return, though under the condition of a full conversion.[203]

In effect, and in stark contrast to Russian Aliyah, for both the original Falasha immigration and the Falashmura, the secular Israeli authorities claimed no defining power whatsoever and devolved it completely to the chief rabbinate, even when the heads of the responsible committees were secularists such as Rubinstein or Tzaban. Clearly, different cases allowed different gatekeepers, but the reasons behind this decision are unclear. One plausible explanation would be the obvious lack of interest in this particular group of immigrants, which characterized Israeli state policy since day one. The state simply had no incentive to claim definitional authority over this group of people.

But another explanation is conceivable is well: the state's lack of know-how. Whereas the consular bureaucracy was perfectly capable of framing Soviet Jews' eligibility with documents containing the familiar language of Eastern European ethno-nationalism spiked with some acquired ethnographic knowledge, this was not the case with the bewildering and foreign terrain of Ethiopian tribes and traditions. In view of this foreignness, not even intuition-based recognition seemed promising: officials could hardly be expected to recognize a Falasha when they saw one. Therefore, it might have appeared safer to state bureaucrats to let the rabbinic authorities do the work, who, in case of doubt about collective definitions, could always fall back on the unassailable authority of great rabbis of the past. On the level of individual recognition, including the *qessoch* in the process added a significant element of local knowledge—after all, who would know better who is an Ethiopian Jew than an Ethiopian Jewish priest?

RESILIENCE BY DE-ETHNICIZATION

Unlike Germany, Israel implemented no change to the legal status quo of co-ethnic immigration in the early 1990s. In contrast to Aussiedlung, whose demise was effectively sealed with the introduction of the 1993

Kriegsfolgenbereinigungsgesetz, Aliyah remained untouched, and the Law of Return in its 1970 version remained firmly in place, despite a host of "liberal" as well as "restrictive" challenges that Christian Joppke has analyzed.[204] Co-ethnic immigration to Israel survived the postwar period, but at the cost of its substantial de-ethnicization, which had been precisely the target of the religious camp's restrictive challenge.

In this process, the meaning of Aliyah changed from the immigration of Jews strictly speaking to something much bigger: an immigration regime for Jews in the halachic sense as well as for people of Jewish descent and all their respective family members. Russian Aliyah at that scale was possible only by lowering the ethnic threshold to be passed. Even though the dimensions that the phenomenon would later acquire were not anticipated when the 1970 amendment was voted on, the principle had already been understood. It was affirmed in the early 1990s, when its effects became visible.[205] By then, the arrival of so many "non-Arab" immigrants (to borrow Ian Lustick's term) turned out to be of crucial importance in the virtual demographic battle with Palestinian Arabs within the framework of Eretz Israel—that is, Mandate Palestine west of the River Jordan.[206] In 1970, the West Bank and the Gaza Strip had been under occupation for barely three years. By the time the Great Russian Aliyah began, more than 20 years had passed since the Six-Day-War and the annexation of the Occupied Territories was being discussed by the Shamir government.[207] This made these non-Jewish immigrants acceptable even to those religious right-wingers who shortly before had been supportive of the religious parties' quest to introduce halachic definitions into the law.[208]

A fictitious case developed by Uri Gordon of the Jewish Agency captures the de-ethnicization implied in the 1970 Law of Return, applied to the realities of the 1990s. In his thought experiment, the two children and five grandchildren of a hypothetical deceased Jewish communist, Meir Levi, and his non-Jewish wife made Aliyah together with their non-Jewish spouses, bringing Levi's non-Jewish wife with them. This way, 15 non-Jews (by halachic criteria) would have legally entered the Jewish state under the Law of Return, which, once upon a time, had ceremoniously codified the right of "every *Jew*" to immigrate to Israel.[209]

Although this example was both hypothetical and extreme (yet fully within the realm of the possible), available statistics show that, until 1995, 85,000 new immigrants were registered as either "without religious classification" (66,000) or "Christian" (19,000)—amounting to roughly 14 percent of the entire post-Soviet immigration until then.[210] In January 2000, the number of non-Jewish Soviet immigrants had risen to some 200,000, thus making up almost one-quarter of the entire new immigrant population.[211] Beginning in 2000, non-Jewish immigrants outnumbered Jewish immigrants among the new arrivals, raising the overall number to 310,000 until 2007, which is equivalent to no less than 4 percent of the overall Israeli population.[212]

Yet it is important to stress that the distinction of Israeli de-ethnicized and German ethnicized approaches to co-ethnic immigration is conceptual and does not correspond to sociological or ethnographic facts. In effect, the different regimes produced similar outcomes, as both countries received large numbers of Russian-speaking immigrants—some of them with co-ethnic status in their own right, some of them as accompanying family, some of them as descendants of real co-ethnics, and some of them with a different ethnic status (the Jewish quota refugees in Germany). Significantly different consequences resulted from being assigned to one or the other status group. In Germany, these differences were far less important than they were in Israel, although the ratio between German and non-German Aussiedler was much lower much earlier than the ratio of Jews to non-Jews in Israel. In 1993, some 75 percent of the newcomers were Germans, but this ratio dropped to 50 percent as early as 1996, and by 2004, it had dropped below 25 percent after several years of almost linear decline.[213] Non-German family members received different social benefits than Spätaussiedler; quota refugees received yet different benefits and had no automatic entitlement to citizenship. But none of these differences in status acquired the salience of the corresponding differentiation between Jews and non-Jews in Israel.

The supreme importance of the Jewish/non-Jewish distinction is a consequence of the peculiarities of the Israeli secular-religious status quo and the related religious control over matters of personal status. For instance, those who were eligible under the Law of Return to make Aliyah but are not halachically Jewish are not entitled to marry a Jew inside Israel, for civil marriage does not exist.[214] Given their integration into mainstream Jewish society in Israel and the absence of sociological differences between them, the new immigrants who are legally Jewish, and most veteran secular Israelis, this problem is anything but theoretical and continues to haunt the Israeli public and the Olim.[215]

In fact, the differential status of non-Jews in mainstream Israeli-Jewish society literally haunts some immigrants to the grave. Due to the long-time Orthodox monopoly over cemeteries and burial, "the [former Soviet Union] immigration, as in the case of marriage, has turned burial into a critical problem that, unlike marriage, could not be delayed or solved outside the country."[216] The issue of burial in Orthodox-controlled cemeteries is particularly sensitive with regard to non-Jewish immigrants who are killed during their military service. An example was the case of 23-year-old Tanya Lansky in late 2010.

Lansky, who was born to a non-Jewish mother and served as a prison guard as part of her mandatory service, died in the line of duty during the wildfires in the Mount Carmel National Park near Haifa in December 2010, while on a mission to rescue prisoners from Damon prison located inside the park. Because of her gentile mother, the rabbinate refused to allow Lansky to be buried in the Jewish section of Ashkelon's military cemetery.[217] In 2013, the deceased soldier Yevgeny Tolochko was not honored as the last soldier to have died before Memorial Day, because he was buried in a section of Mount Herzl military cemetery reserved for soldiers with uncertain Jewish credentials.[218] Still in 2017, the case of non-Jewish soldier Viacheslav Gargai caused considerable resentment among the secular public. While the Tolochko incident had led to non-Jewish soldiers being buried in the same cemetery as their Jewish comrades, Gargai was placed in a grave at a distance from the adjacent Jewish grave, following Orthodox burial practices.[219] With future war casualties likely to include more cases like these, the issue will remain salient.[220]

Beyond the problems the halachically non-Jewish immigrants face in Israel, their immigration has had a significant effect on the meaning of Jewishness in Israeli society. It has brought about a further de facto separation of Jewishness and Israeliness. The "non-Jewish Jews" that the sociologist Asher Cohen has extensively written about are not Jewish by religious or any other standards but are clearly Israeli in a national sense as they pass the mainstream Israeli-Jewish educational institutions, speak Hebrew, and join the Israel Defense Forces.[221] In a long-term perspective, Major Shalit is getting de facto what he wanted to have acknowledged de jure in the late 1960s: a secular, nationally defined Hebrew-Israeliness. Even though this is still not recognized on paper, it is a reality that can hardly be ignored. Predicting whether this sociological fact will eventually give rise to an official recognition of Israeliness decoupled from Jewishness is, of course, not within the purview of the historian.

NOTES

1. "Informationen für Deutsche in der Sowjetunion," *Info-Dienst Deutsche Aussiedler* (*IDDA*) No. 13, June 1990. For immigration numbers, see "(Spät-)-Aussiedler und ihre Angehörigen. Zeitreihe 1950–2017," https://www.bva.bund.de/SharedDocs/Downloads/DE/Buerger/Migration-Integration/Spaetaus-siedler/Statistik/Zeitreihe_1950_2017.pdf?__blob=publicationFile&v=5.
2. "Gesamtkonzept Russlanddeutsche," *IDDA* No. 32, January 1992 (emphasis in the original).
3. See, for example, *IDDA* No. 49, January 1994.

4. Arbel, *Riding the Wave,* 42–43, 47–48.

5. Gur-Gurevitz, *Open Gates,* 94–95.

6. Kedmi maintained this in Ronen Bergman, "The Russian Maneuver," *7 Yamim* (weekend edition of *Yediot Aharonot*), April 15, 2011, 40; and Kedmi, *Hopeless Wars.*

7. Bergman, "Russian Maneuver," 42.

8. Gur-Gurevitz, *Open Gates,* 75; Arbel, *Riding the Wave,* 70.

9. Jones, *Soviet-Jewish Aliyah,* 121.

10. Arbel, *Riding the Wave,* 95.

11. On the change of the international system in the wake of Helsinki, see Thomas, *Helsinki Effect;* Snyder, *Human Rights Activism;* Bange and Niedhardt, *Helsinki 1975.* On the establishment of a global human rights discourse, see also Moyn, *Last Utopia.*

12. Hakkarainen, *State of Peace,* 233–238.

13. Numerous examples can be found in Armborst, *Ablösung von der Sowjetunion,* e.g., 163, 284, and at various points in chap. 8. Specifically for the Soviet Jewish case, see Fainberg, "Friends Abroad," esp. 397. See also the somewhat more cautious assessment of the interaction between national and human rights movements by Ro'i and Rubenstein, "Human Rights and National Rights."

14. Joppke, *Selecting by Origin,* 242–243.

15. Ministerialdirigent Meyer-Landrut an die Botschaft in Warschau, August 5, 1975, in *Akten zur Auswärtigen Politik der Bundesrepublik Deutschland* (*AAPD*) 1975, Vol. 2, Doc. 244; Stola, *Kraj bez wyjścia,* 244.

16. Stola, *Kraj bez wyjścia,* 480, 484–485.

17. Ibid.

18. About the various legal and illegal movements of Polish citizens (Aussiedler and others) to Western Europe during the 1980s, see Stola, *Kraj bez wyjścia,* chap. 12. See also Pallaske, *Migrationen aus Polen.*

19. "(Spät-)Aussiedler und ihre Angehörigen."

20. Aufzeichnung des Staatssekretärs van Well, January 16, 1978, in *AAPD,* 1978, Vol. 1, Doc. 11. See also Ioanid, *Ransom of the Jews,* 141–146. A comprehensive account of Transylvanian Saxon migration from Romania to West Germany is given by Weber et al., *Emigration der Siebenbürger Sachsen;* for Banat Swabians, see Sebaux, *(Post)colonisation—(Post)migration.*

21. For a detailed account of Soviet German migration and its relation to Soviet-West German relations, see Foth, "Sowjetdeutsche im Spannungsfeld." For numbers, see "(Spät-)Aussiedler und ihre Angehörigen."

22. Joppke, *Selecting by Origin,* 242–243.

23. Levy, "Remembering the Nation," 174–176.

24. For an analysis of the Aussiedlung dimension of the asylum compromise and the bad deal that the Social Democrats struck, see Panagiotidis, "Kein fairer Tausch."

25. "(Spät-)Aussiedler und ihre Angehörigen."

26. About expellees and *Ostpolitik*, see Ahonen, *After the Expulsion*.

27. Baier and Meinhardt, *Kauf von Freiheit*.

28. For an analysis of the 1975 debates and the notion of *Ersatzdiskurs*, see Thumann, "Aussiedlerzuwanderung."

29. Levy, "Remembering the Nation," 110–124.

30. Ibid., 112.

31. Regarding this charge, see Levy, "Remembering the Nation," 163. Levy furthermore documents the denouncing of ethno-cultural references and expellee politics as *Deutschtümelei* already in the 1970s (100) as well as the association of ethnic Germandom and Nazism (94–96).

32. Ibid., 137–141.

33. See von Koenigswald, "Das dritte Problem," 15.

34. Ludwig, *Als Deutsche unter Deutschen leben*.

35. Maihofer, "Starthilfe leisten!," 11 (emphasis added).

36. Hupka, "Die Aussiedler," 58.

37. For example, Bade, "Aussiedler—Rückwanderer über Generationen hinweg." Other examples of the use of the "returning home" motif in a scholarly context are Troen and Bade, *Returning Home*, and Rock and Wolff, *Coming Home to Germany*.

38. Already during the interwar period, Russian-German activists in Germany had developed a discourse on Germany as the "historical homeland" of Germans from Russia, to which they could return. Through personal and organizational continuities, this discourse also carried into the postwar period. See Panagiotidis, "Zwischen Wahlheimat und Urheimat."

39. Armborst, *Ablösung von der Sowjetunion*, 389.

40. Krajczyk, "Ankunft in Friedland," 31.

41. The publication repeatedly stresses that "material and economic motivations" are secondary. See esp. Kudlich, "In der alten Heimat ohne Freiheit."

42. Bundestag, 10th period, 16th session, June 23, 1983, 1013.

43. Bundestag, 10th period, 98th session, November 8, 1984, 7073.

44. Klötzel, *Russlanddeutsche*, 287.

45. von Goldendach and Minow, *"Deutschtum erwache!,"* 363ff. About the 1983 annual congress, see *Globus* 15, no. 4 (1983). The congress did not take place due to a fire in the designated venue.

46. This conspiratorial argument is advanced by Goldendach and Minow, *"Deutschtum erwache!"*

47. Armborst, *Ablösung von der Sowjetunion*, 390, 419.

48. Ibid., 384.

49. *IDDA* No. 1, November 1988.

50. About rising hostility among the West German population toward Aussiedler, see, for example, Christian Wernicke, "Erst gerufen, dann verachtet," *Die Zeit*, June 30, 1989.

51. Horst Waffenschmidt, "Aufgabe aller Deutschen. Zur Weitergabe des Kulturerbes," *Globus* 16, no. 5 (1984): 7. He wrote, among other things, that "the historical development of the German East, its cultural heritage and its spiritual potency (*geistige Wirksamkeit*) are part of our history; therefore it is a national task to keep and foster the spiritual link to the territories in the East and their culture."

52. *IDDA* No. 1, November 1988.

53. *IDDA* No. 3, March 1989.

54. Münz and Ohliger, "Long Distance Citizens."

55. *IDDA* No. 3, March 1989.

56. "Merkblatt zum Aufnahmeverfahren für Aussiedler," *IDDA* No. 16, September 1990.

57. "Steuerbund zeigt Ministerium an: Verschwendete Kanther-Behörde Finanzhilfen für Russlanddeutsche?" *Die Welt*, July 13, 1998. A largely uncritical description of these programs is provided by Roesler, *Russlanddeutsche Identitäten*, chap. 3.

58. *IDDA* No. 33, March 1992.

59. BVerwG VIII C 58.76, March 16, 1977, *BVerwGE* 52, 167.

60. Argeflü-Rechtsausschuss, Saarbrücken, November 12, 1981, HStAS EA 2/811, Az. 2558, No. 28.

61. Arbeitsgruppe des Argeflü-Rechtsausschusses, Aschaffenburg, December 2–3, 1982, HStAS EA 2/811, Az. 2558, No. 35, and Arbeitsgruppe des Argeflü-Rechtsausschusses, Oberreifenberg, July 11–13, 1983, ibid., No. 39.

62. Arbeitsgruppe des Argeflü-Rechtsausschusses, Bonn, March 21–22, 1983, HStAS EA 2/811, Az. 2558, No. 38.

63. Argeflü-Rechtsausschuss, Lübeck, May 5–6, 1983, HStAS EA 2/811, Az. 2558, No. 36.

64. Arbeitsgruppe des Argeflü-Rechtsausschusses, Oberreifenberg, July 11–13, 1983, HStAS EA 2/811, Az. 2558, No. 39.

65. Argeflü-Rechtsausschuss, Worms, September 29–30, 1983, HStAS EA 2/811, Az. 2558, No. 37.

66. Ibid.

67. Tagung der Projektgruppe der Argeflü in Wiesbaden, June 28–29, 1984, HStAS EA 2/811, Az. 2558, No. 42.

68. Aktenvermerk Dr. Nowak, July 7, 1983, HStAS EA 2/811, Az. 2558, No. 39, item 3.

69. Related discussions are documented in HStAS EA 2/811, Az. 2570-4, No. 5, as well as in PAAA B85 1326.

70. Dr. Czaja an Ministerialdirigent Stemmler im IM BW, August 10, 1983, HStAS EA 2/811, Az. 2570-4, No. 13, item 12.

71. Ibid.

72. Czaja an den Leitenden Ministerialrat für Soziales, Gesundheit und Umwelt, Herrn W. Franken, Mainz, March 29, 1984, HStAS EA 2/811, Az. 2570-4, No. 13, item 35.

73. Ibid., and Vermerk von Dr. Czaja, March 8, 1984, HStAS EA 2/811, Az. 2570-4, No. 13, item 32.

74. Czaja an Stemmler, August 10, 1983, HStAS EA 2/811, Az. 2570-4, No. 13, item 12.

75. Dr. Czaja an Stemmler, October 26, 1983, HStAS EA 2/811, Az. 2570-4, No. 13, item 20.

76. Ibid., and Dr. Czaja an Stemmler, August 10, 1983, HStAS EA 2/811, Az. 2570-4, No. 13, item 12.

77. CDU/CSU-Fraktion des Bundestags, Gruppe der Vertriebenen- und Flüchtlingsabgeordneten an Dr. Czaja, September 21, 1983, HStAS EA 2/811, Az. 2570-4, No. 13, item 15; Argeflü-Rechtsausschuss, Worms, September 29–30, 1983, HStAS EA 2/811, Az. 2558, No. 37.

78. MAGS NRW and die Landesflüchtlingsverwaltungen, das Bundesinnenministerium und das Bundesausgleichsamt, December 21, 1983, EA 2/811, Az. 2570-4, No. 13, item 28.

79. Dr. Nowak an Stemmler, November 7, 1984, HStAS EA 2/811, Az. 2570-4, No. 27, item 12.

80. Argeflü-Rechtsausschuss, Karlsruhe, January 24–25, 1985, HStAS EA 2/811, Az. 2558, No. 45.

81. Ibid.

82. Ibid.

83. Czaja an Ministerialrat Gassner, BMI, February 27, 1985, HStAS EA 2/811, Az. 2570-4, No. 27, item 21.

84. "Gegen die Ablehnung der Anerkennung von Vertriebenen (Aussiedlern) wegen Überwiegens von 'vertreibungsfremder [*sic*] Ausreisegründe'," von Dr. Herbert Czaja, HStAS EA 2/811, Az. 2570-4, No. 27, item 25.

85. Ibid.

86. "Überlegungen zur Anwendung des § 1 Abs. 2 No. 3 BVFG" nach dem Stand vom 15. Juli 1985, HStAS EA 2/811, Az. 2570-4, No. 27, item 31.

87. Vermerk Dr. Stemmler, June 24, 1986, HStAS EA 2/811, Az. 2570-4, No. 27, item 57; circulation to the regional councils (*Regierungspräsidien*) ibid., items 58–60. The final version can also be found in Liesner, *Aussiedler*, 97–107.

88. Czaja an Nowak, July 16, 1986, HStAS EA 2/811, Az. 2570-4, No. 27, item 65.

89. Argeflü-Rechtsausschuss, Münster, September 28–29, 1982, HStAS EA 2/811, Az. 2558, No. 34.

90. Stola, *Kraj bez wyjścia*, 480, 484–485.

91. For this and the following, see Panagiotidis, "Oberkreisdirektor Decides," esp. 520–529.

92. The fact that the Foreign Office came up with this revelation only in 1985 indicates short institutional memory. As noted in chapter 4, the embassy in Moscow had suggested using passport nationality as a criterion to identify ethnic Germans already in early 1974. By the mid-1980s, Soviet nationality policy attracted greater attention and became the object of scholarly interest. See, for example, Karklins, *Ethnic Relations*. For a German-language example see Mark, *Völker der Sowjetunion*.

93. AA an BMI, Ref. VtK I 5, January 8, 1985, HStAS EA 2/811, AZ 2570-4, No. 8, item 8, attachment 1.

94. AA an BMI, Ref. VtK I 5, December 17, 1985, HStAS EA 2/811, AZ 2570-4, No. 8, item 8, attachment 2.

95. Ibid.

96. See most comprehensively Mukhina, *Germans of the Soviet Union*.

97. Interview with Family T., Korbach, April 15, 2008.

98. Argeflü-Rechtsausschuss, Nürnberg, March 19–20, 1987, HStAS EA 2/811, AZ 2558, No. 52.

99. See the intervention by Hesse (and also North Rhine Westphalia) in Argeflü-Rechtsausschuss, Berlin, October 2–3, 1986, HStAS EA 2/811, AZ 2558, No. 51. See also the letter by Prof. Dr. Dr. Kraus from the Hesse Social Ministry to the Bundesausgleichsamt, January 19, 1987, HStAS EA 2/811, AZ 2570-4, No. 8, item 22.

100. In addition to differentiating between the countries of the expulsion area and including expulsion pressure in the guise of *Kriegsfolgenschicksal*, the legislature promoted the "elevated political or professional position" from a clue to check expulsion pressure to an official "criterion for exclusion" (*Ausschlusstatbestand*) from recognition as a Spätaussiedler, alongside "violation of principles of humanity and rule of law" (*Verstoß gegen die Grundsätze der Menschlichkeit und Rechtsstaatlichkeit*) and "considerable support of the system" (*erhebliches Vorschubleisten des Systems*).

101. Partially quoted after Klekowski von Koppenfels, "Decline of Privilege," 111, and Silagi, *Vertreibung und Staatsangehörigkeit*, 131. The non-gender-neutral language is kept from the original text of the law.

102. Thus the provisional guidelines, published in *IDDA* No. 41, May 1993.

103. *IDDA* No. 41, May 1993, 20.

104. "Das Kriegsfolgenbereinigungsgesetz ist ein 'schlimmes' Gesetz, aber wir haben das Allerschlimmste verhindern können," *Volk auf dem Weg* (*VadW*) 44, no. 4 (1993): 5.

105. Quote from *IDDA* No. 38, January 1993, 18. For the lobbying and consultation, see "Mitarbeitertagung der Landsmannschaft um die neue Vertriebenen-Gesetzgebung," *VadW* 43, no. 10 (1992): 5, and "Vorstellungen der Landsmannschaft wurden berücksichtigt," *VadW* 44, no. 1 (1993): 6.

106. Johann Warkentin, "Verkehrte Welt," *VadW* 45, no. 5 (1994): 8.

107. Joppke, *Selecting by Origin*.

108. Hensen, "Geschichte," 57.

109. Interview in the Federal Administration Office, Cologne, August 26, 2009.

110. When asked whether the reproach of "state-supported cheating" (Joppke, *Selecting by Origin*, 213) was pertinent, a representative of the Federal Administration Office insisted that it was possible to tell the difference between "language class German" and "family-mediated German" and pointed precisely to the aspect of dialect (Interview, August 26, 2009). Similar statements from officials in the Friedland transit camp are reported by Wallem, "Spätaussiedleraufnahme," 146.

111. "Das schafft böses Blut," *Spiegel* No. 52, December 25, 1989.

112. *IDDA* No. 38, January 1993, 17. "Persons who were registered in one of the categories 1 to 3 of the German *Volksliste* in the annexed Eastern Territories (*in den eingegliederten Ostgebieten*) have only effectively become German citizens if they were German *Volkszugehörige* the very latest at the point in time specified by section 6 BVFG. It cannot be assumed that persons who were registered in category 3 of the German *Volksliste* have necessarily received German citizenship until revoked (*deutsche Staatsangehörigkeit auf Widerruf*) as German *Volkszugehörige*. Registration itself does not constitute sufficient evidence for German *Volkszugehörigkeit*. This is only the case if all criteria of section 6 BVFG are fulfilled."

113. A concise overview of the history of the *Deutsche Volksliste* in occupied Poland is provided by Wolf, "Deutsche Volksliste." Regarding the alternative terminology for each category, see also Otto, "Aussiedler und Aussiedler-Politik," 33–34.

114. The related discussions within the Argeflü from the late 1970s and early 1980s are documented in HStAS EA 2/811, Az. 2558, No. 23. Further material pertaining to the implications for German-Yugoslav relations in the late 1960s can be found in PAAA B 85 938.

115. Vorlage Bundesausgleichsamt, HStAS EA 2/811, Az. 2572, No. 1, item 2.

116. Argeflü-Rechtsausschuss, Oppenheim, June 8–9, 1978, HStAS EA 2/811, Az. 2558, No. 13.

117. "Das schafft böses Blut," *Spiegel* No. 52, December 25, 1989; "Schwebendes Volkstum," *Spiegel* No. 3, January 15, 1990.

118. IM BW an die RPs, December 4, 1987, HStAS EA 2/811, Az. 2572, No. 50, item 12.

119. Urteil VG Düsseldorf, 6 K 4947/87, March 9, 1989, HStAS EA 2/811, Az. 2572, No. 50, item 1.

120. BMI an Czaja, June 29, 1989, HStAS EA 2/811, Az. 2572, No. 50, item 5.

121. Argeflü-Rechtsausschuss, Göttingen, October 19–20, 1989, HStAS EA 2/811, Az. 2572, No. 50, item 7.

122. Hackmann an Schäuble, December 18, 1989, HStAS EA 2/811, Az. 2572, No. 50, item 17.

123. Ibid. Also IM Schleswig Holstein an BMI, February 7, 1990; Staatsverwaltung für Inneres Berlin an BMI, February 13, 1990, HStAS EA 2/811, Az. 2572, No. 50, items 16 and 19.

124. Innensenator Hamburg, February 5, 1990, HStAS EA 2/811, Az. 2572, No. 50, item 18.

125. IM Schleswig-Holstein an Bundesinnenminister Schäuble, May 30, 1990, HStAS EA 2/811, Az. 2572, No. 50, item 22.

126. Hackmann an Schäuble, December 18, 1989, HStAS EA 2/811, Az. 2572, No. 50, item 17.

127. Dietz, "German and Jewish Migration," 639.

128. "Verbales Versteckspiel um sowjetische Juden: DDR-Ausländerbeauftragte Almuth Berger empört über Bonner Einreisestopp," *Süddeutsche Zeitung*, September 14, 1990; "Quote für Juden aus der UdSSR: Stuttgart denkt an Kontingente auch für Aussiedler," *Die Welt*, December 5, 1990 (both in ACDP 23/2).

129. Dietz, "German and Jewish Migration," 639.

130. Ibid.

131. Haug, "Jüdische Zuwanderer."

132. The idea of "nuclear fission" corresponds to Ranabir Samaddar's notion of the "molecular" logic of ethnic partition. See Samaddar, "Introduction," 5–6.

133. Haug, "Jüdische Zuwanderer," 8; Becker, *Ankommen in Deutschland*, 55.

134. Yinan Cohen and Kogan, "Jewish Immigration," 252.

135. This growing discrepancy becomes clearly visible in Dietz, Lebok, and Polian, "Jewish Emigration," 37, table 4. According to these statistics, in 1994, 8,811 people came to Germany as Jewish quota refugees, but only 5,521 (62.6%) were registered as Jews by the communities. In 1997, only 7,092 of 19,437 quota refugees (36.5%) were recognized as halachically Jewish.

136. "Zuwanderung gestalten—Integration fördern: Bericht der unabhängigen Kommission Zuwanderung. Zusammenfassung," 11, http://www.fluechtlingsrat.org/download/berkommzusfas.pdf.

137. Runge, "Einwanderung nach der Halacha," 1031.

138. Ibid.

139. Sobel, *Migrants from the Promised Land.*

140. Calculated from "Total Immigration to Israel per Year (1948–Present)," Jewish Virtual Library, American-Israeli Cooperative Enterprise, https://www.jewishvirtuallibrary.org/total-immigration-to-israel-by-year.

141. About the 1977 election, see Arian, *Elections in Israel, 1977.*

142. Government 18, June 20, 1997–August 5, 1981, http://www.knesset.gov.il/govt/eng/GovtByNumber_eng.asp?govt=18.

143. Government 19, August 5, 1981–October 10, 1983, http://www.knesset.gov.il/govt/eng/GovtByNumber_eng.asp?govt=19.

144. Government 21, September 13, 1984–October 20, 1986, http://www.knesset.gov.il/govt/eng/GovtByNumber_eng.asp?govt=21.

145. Government 23, December 22, 1988–June 11, 1990, http://www.knesset.gov.il/govt/eng/GovtByNumber_eng.asp?govt=23; see also Arian and Shamir, *The Elections in Israel, 1988.*

146. Government 24, June 11, 1990–July 13, 1992, http://www.knesset.gov.il/govt/eng/GovtByNumber_eng.asp?govt=24.

147. About Nativ, see Hägel and Peretz, "States and Transnational Actors," 476.

148. The crucial role of Nativ in triggering this movement is independently claimed by Hägel and Peretz, "States and Transnational Actors," and Lazin, *Struggle for Soviet Jewry.*

149. Calculated from "Total Immigration to Israel by Select Country by Year (1948–Present)," Jewish Virtual Library, https://www.jewishvirtuallibrary.org/total-immigration-to-israel-by-country-per-year.

150. See, for instance, Yolande Cohen, "Migrations of Moroccan Jews"; Shepard, *Invention of Decolonization,* chap. 6.

151. See the contemporary account by Jacobson, "Soviet Jewry," 83. He does not explicitly list Germany, just "Western Europe." See also Lazin, *Struggle for Soviet Jewry,* 80–88, and Jones, *Soviet-Jewish Aliyah,* 28–35.

152. For example, Jacobson, "Soviet Jewry," 85. Jacobson was the executive vice president of HIAS, New York.

153. Ibid., 87. The debate between freedom of choice and Israeli's national interest is reconstructed in detail by Lazin, *Struggle for Soviet Jewry,* chaps. 3, 4.

154. Gur-Gurevitz, *Open Gates,* 23, 26.

155. Lazin, *Struggle for Soviet Jewry,* 310.

156. Jones, *Soviet-Jewish Aliyah,* 75.

157. The reasons why this request failed until 1989 are elaborated by Lazin, *Struggle for Soviet Jewry.*

158. Lazin, "Refugee Resettlement," 13.

159. Ibid., 11, 13.

160. Gur-Gurevitz, *Open Gates,* 23; Lazin, "Refugee Resettlement," 9, mentions earlier such initiatives by Shamir in 1987.

161. Gur-Gurevitz, *Open Gates,* 23.

162. Ibid., 27; Lazin, "Refugee Resettlement," 12.

163. Lazin, "Refugee Resettlement," 12.

164. Gur-Gurevitz, *Open Gates,* 114.

165. Ibid., 101.

166. Ibid., 113.

167. Ibid., 104.

168. Arbel, *Riding the Wave*, 99, 102.

169. Ibid., 108.

170. Lazin, *Struggle for Soviet Jewry*, 310.

171. Ibid.

172. Dietz, Lebok, and Polian, "Jewish Emigration," 35.

173. "Total Immigration to Israel by Select Country by Year," Jewish Virtual Library.

174. "(Spät-)Aussiedler und ihre Angehörigen."

175. The cases that did occur obtained their fair share of publicity. One example is that of Suzy Miller, an American Reform convert whose registration as a Jew was denied by the Shas-directed Interior Ministry in 1986 but had her registration enforced by the Supreme Court. See Richmond, "Israel's Law of Return," 112–113.

176. 7th Knesset, Session 328, July 12, 1972, ISA 60.0.23.274 (=1951/11-כ); 8th Knesset, Session 361, December 22, 1976, ISA 60.0.24.262 (=230/5-כ).

177. 10th Knesset, Session 190, March 21, 1983, ISA 60.0.25.204 (=267/6-כ).

178. 11th Knesset, Session 46, January 16, 1985, ISA 60.0.25.299 (=277/1-כ).

179. 11th Knesset, Session 340, July 8, 1987, ISA 60.0.27.239 (=296/9-כ); see also Dan Izenberg, "Who Is a Jew over the Years," *Jerusalem Post*, July 25, 1989.

180. 11th Knesset, Session 340, July 8, 1987, 35 (emphasis added).

181. Ibid., 45.

182. Ibid., 58.

183. Ibid., 64–67.

184. Ibid., 66.

185. Government 23, December 22, 1988–June 11, 1990, https://knesset.gov.il/govt/eng/GovtByNumber_eng.asp?govt=23.

186. Government 24, June 11, 1990–July 13, 1992, http://www.knesset.gov.il/govt/eng/GovtByNumber_eng.asp?govt=24.

187. Jones, *Soviet-Jewish Aliyah*, 133.

188. Ibid., 134, with reference to an interview with Marina Heifetz, a Soviet immigrant lawyer working with the Olim for Ratz (Meretz), Tel Aviv, June 24, 1993.

189. Ibid., 135.

190. Ibid., 134.

191. Ibid., 135.

192. Ibid., 136–137.

193. The document, published in Corinaldi, *Enigma of Jewish Identity*, 245–254, is undated, but the reference to the "former Soviet Union" in the text indicates that it was drafted after the dissolution of the Soviet Union in late 1991.

Since Corinaldi claims to have received the document in 1994 (179), it was most likely created in 1992 or 1993.

194. Ibid. Information in brackets has been supplied; information in parentheses is contained in the original source.

195. For a comprehensive anthropological study of Ethiopian Olim in Israel, see Anteby-Yemini, *Juifs éthiopiens*.

196. Coordination Committee Minutes, June 28, 1954, ISA 43.0.6.2089 (=5383/16-ג).

197. Corinaldi, *Jewish Identity*, 111, and appendix IV.

198. Ibid., 112.

199. Ibid, 112. This did not help them with their problems of personal status, which persisted due to rabbinical doubts about their possible origin from non-halachic converts as well as their marriage and divorce rites.

200. Ibid., 133.

201. Ibid., 133–134.

202. Ibid., 135–136.

203. Ibid., 137–138.

204. Joppke, *Selecting by Origin*, 191–204.

205. Scholars studying post-1990 immigration agree that the magnitude of the phenomenon was an unintended rather than a deliberate consequence of the 1970 amendment. See Asher Cohen and Susser, "Jews and Others," 56; Lustick, "Israel as a Non-Arab State," 422; Yfaat Weiss, "Golem and Its Creator."

206. Lustick, "Israel as a Non-Arab State."

207. The demographic, territorial, and ideological discussions surrounding Soviet-Jewish Aliyah are analyzed by Jones, *Soviet-Jewish Aliyah*, chap. 3.

208. Lustick, "Israel as a Non-Arab State," 426.

209. Quoted ibid., 423.

210. Numbers are taken from Asher Cohen and Susser, "Jews and Others," 59, and Dietz, Lebok, and Polian, "Jewish Emigration," 35.

211. Asher Cohen and Susser, "Jews and Others," 60 (200,000 calculated from the difference between "Jews" and "Extended Jewish Population"). Total immigrant numbers are taken from Dietz, Lebok, and Polian, "Jewish Emigration," 35.

212. Asher Cohen and Susser, "Jews and Others," 59, 61.

213. Hensen, "Geschichte," 57. As Hensen, president of the Federal Administrative Office from 1995 to 2010, points out, this shift was largely due to the different incentive structure created by the language test introduced in 1996, since family members were originally not required to past this test. Since 2005, they, too, must prove basic knowledge of the German language.

214. On this issue and countervailing secularizing trends see Ben Porat, *Between State and Synagogue*, chap. 3.

215. Yair Ettinger, "Religious Services Ministry Bans Alternative Wedding Ceremonies Performed by Tzohar Rabbis," *Haaretz*, November 8, 2011; "Israel's Rabbinate Must Be Stripped of Its Powers," *Haaretz*, October 24, 2011.

216. Ben Porat, *Between State and Synagogue*, 110.

217. Leonard Fein, "Who by Fire?" *Jewish Daily Forward*, December 6, 2010; Shmulik Hadad, "'Our Heart Is Torn': Fire Victim Laid to Rest," *Ynet*, December 5, 2010.

218. Gili Cohen, "Family of Fallen Soldier: Jewish Status Shouldn't Have Mattered in Memorial Ceremony," *Haaretz*, April 13, 2013.

219. Liza Rozovsky, "Brothers in Arms – but Not to the Grave," *Haaretz*, January 24, 2017.

220. On secularizing trends in private burial practices see Ben Porat, *Between State and Synagogue*, chap. 4.

221. Asher Cohen and Susser, "Jews and Others;" Asher Cohen, *Non-Jewish Jews*.

CONCLUSION

The Rise and Demise of Co-Ethnic Immigration

TODAY, IN BOTH GERMANY AND Israel, co-ethnic immigration has almost reached the point of completion. Despite a continuous trickle of newcomers, German Aussiedlung from Eastern Europe has effectively come to an end. The legal definition of Spätaussiedler does not apply to anyone born after January 1, 1993. Those born before this date may still be eligible, but they face more stringent legal requirements than the ones in place before the 1990s—for example, the compulsory language test introduced in 1996.[1] Since 1993, applicants who are not from the former Soviet Union have had to prove that their German ethnicity puts them at a disadvantage in their home country. As a consequence, the annual number of Spätaussiedler who come to Germany has been decreasing since the second half of the 1990s. Although this figure was consistently above 200,000 between 1988 and 1995 (reaching almost 400,000 in 1990), in 2000 it dropped below 100,000 for the first time since 1987. By 2012, only 1,817 newcomers were registered, 98 percent of whom were from the former Soviet Union.[2] After the language test requirements were relaxed in 2013, numbers rose again and reached 7,059 in 2017—an impressive increase in terms of percentage but a modest number compared with the late 1980s and the first half of the 1990s.[3] In theory, of course, Aussiedlung could continue well into the twenty-first century. Provided the Federal Expellee Law remains in place in its current form, a person born in the former Soviet Union on December 31, 1992, could still claim Spätaussiedler status to retire in Germany in 2060. In reality, however, co-ethnic migration is all but over.

That numerical decline might not be surprising in the German case, since it is consistent with the intention of the German legislation that amended the legal framework for immigration, the Law for the Settlement of War Consequences

(*Kriegsfolgenbereinigungsgesetz*), which was adopted in late 1992. Additionally, though, despite the post–Cold War resilience of the Law of Return, with its open call to the Jews of the world to gather in Israel, the days of Aliyah as it existed in the past are over, and Israel has recognized this. After 1990 and 1991, which saw the arrival of some 375,000 new Olim, more than 330,000 of whom came from the Soviet Union, throughout the 1990s Aliyah numbers were relatively constant, remaining between 60,000 and 80,000 per year. In the wake of the Second Intifada, these numbers steadily declined, reaching a low of 13,701 new immigrants in 2008—the lowest number since 1986. Since then, Aliyah has been increasing slowly, with some 27,000 new arrivals per year between 2015 and 2017.[4] Thus, there was a return to the level of the early 2000s, but arrivals remain far below the rates of the 1990s.

In part, these changing migration patterns are a function of shifts in global Jewish demography. When it was founded in 1948, Israel was home to only about 6 percent of all Jews in the world, while a third still lived in Europe—mainly Eastern Europe and the Soviet Union—and another 10 percent in Asia and Africa.[5] Nowadays the two largest Jewish population centers by far are Israel and North America. In 2016, 44 percent of world Jewry lived in Israel, and 42 percent lived in North America, mainly in the United States.[6]

Over six decades of statehood, the *Kibbutz Galuyot* has achieved much. In the 1950s and 1960s, the age-old communities in the Arab world were resettled in Israel almost in their entirety. Most of the Jews from Ethiopia—who, like the Arab-Jewish diaspora, had been there from time immemorial—were relocated to Israel during the 1980s and 1990s. During the post-perestroika mass exodus, most Russian Jews who wanted to leave Russia and the other Soviet successor states did so. As a consequence, there are few potential Olim left outside North America: 77 percent of the estimated 16.5 million potential immigrants under the Law of Return (that is, both Jews and people with Jewish ancestry) living outside the State of Israel resided in North America in 2016.[7] Organizations such as Nefesh b'Nefesh operate in the United States and target the American middle-class immigrants whom Israel has been longing for since day one. Other American Jews come to Israel for religious reasons and make the streets of holy cities such as Jerusalem or Safed (Tzfat) look like those of Williamsburg or Monsey. Even so, not even the most committed Zionist would expect millions of American Jews to relocate to Israel today. And despite press reports about increased Jewish emigration from Western Europe and especially France because of rising Arab-Muslim anti-Semitism, a mass Aliyah of French Jewry does not seem a likely prospect in the near future.[8]

Against this background, the Jewish Agency, traditionally the Israeli state's subcontractor in charge of promoting immigration to Israel, has changed its focus from immigrant recruitment to creating "Jewish identity through education."[9] With this focus, which may be interpreted as a twenty-first-century version of Zionist *Gegenwartsarbeit*, the agency aims to bring the Jewish diaspora culturally closer to Israel rather than making it physically move there.[10] Nevertheless, the Law of Return is most likely to remain in place because of its symbolic value and because there is really no reason to change it in light of the post-Aliyah reality. If the aim of Israeli policy in the early 1990s was to bring in "non-Arabs" to win the demographic battle in "Greater Eretz Israel," as Ian Lustick has claimed, Aliyah has done what it could.[11] More should not be expected—not least because natural reproduction rates of the Jewish population in Israel are higher than in the diaspora.

Is the history of co-ethnic immigration to both countries thus a case of "intended consequences," as Christian Joppke has argued?[12] To an extent, yes. The original purposes of Aussiedlung and Aliyah were the reunification of divided expellee families from Eastern Europe in the German case and the ingathering of the diaspora to build a new nation in the Israeli case. Both of these aims have largely been achieved. By passing the *Kriegsfolgenbereinigungsgesetz*, Germany essentially put an end to the postwar conception of Aussiedlung as an immediate response to the consequences of expulsion. In all countries except the former Soviet Union, the consequences of the war are thus officially in the past. Israel has established itself as a nation-state with a solid Jewish majority, which represents almost half of world Jewry. Most of the historical diaspora from Eastern Europe and Arab countries has been gathered in the Jewish state.

At the same time, the present-day situation is an unintended consequence of past policies. Although it never pursued a *Kibbutz Galuyot* of its own, Germany has essentially completed the ingathering of its East European diaspora within its borders west of the Oder-Neisse line. With the main exception of some 600,000 self-identified Germans remaining in the former Soviet Union (of whom only about one-seventh consider German their native language), the centuries-old presence of Germans and German speakers in Eastern and Southeastern Europe is essentially a thing of the past.[13] Israel, despite its explicit ingathering agenda and the Zionist tradition of negating the diaspora, has come to acknowledge the legitimate existence of Jews in other countries, despite occasional calls on European Jews to escape rising anti-Semitism by moving to the Jewish state.[14] By trying to emotionally tie a diaspora permanently residing abroad to Israel, the country's policy comes to resemble that of countries such as Greece, which engages in diaspora politics among Greeks and people with Greek ancestry abroad but without aiming for large-scale "return."[15]

There were thus no straight lines leading from the original intentions to their outcomes, because the ideologies and concepts of co-ethnic migration were fluid and subject to historical change. As I have demonstrated in this book, the historical trajectories of Germany and Israel diverged initially but, over time, partially converged—particularly during and after the watershed period of the mid-1960s to the mid-1970s. During that key period, the co-ethnic immigration regimes of both countries underwent significant transformations in terms of their conceptions, policies, and institutions. Those transformations laid the groundwork for mass immigration to both countries in the late 1980s and the 1990s. Once mass migration actually happened, the two countries' pathways diverged once again.

The German co-ethnic immigration regime originated from the institutions of the postwar ethnic refugee state, which were designed to accommodate German refugees and expellees. As the first step in opening these arrangements to the future, the 1949 Basic Law and the 1953 Federal Expellee Law extended this co-ethnic asylum and the associated welfare benefits to German citizens and ethnic Germans who remained in Eastern Europe after the war and who managed to relocate to West Germany to join relatives already living in the Federal Republic. Triggered by domestic challenges in the wake of changing migration patterns related to international developments, this still-limited scope was extended during the watershed period to include the first generation of descendants of the original target group as well as ethnic Germans without a family connection to Germany. Aussiedlung thus became a more encompassing co-ethnic immigration regime than before, and it resembled the Israeli model as it had evolved at that point.

In its original form, the Israeli migration regime was intent on bringing Jews to Israel to build the Jewish nation-state. After four years of unrestricted immigration between 1948 and 1951, during the 1950s and the first half of the 1960s, it embraced a selective immigration regime to be able to choose those Jews from among the potential immigrants who were fit to build the nation. This policy of selectivity implied a utilitarian logic of immigrant selection that had no equivalent in the West German Aussiedler regime. It was abandoned during the 1960s. The 1970 Law of Return amendment—itself a consequence of a domestic challenge represented by the Shalit case coupled with the expectation of increased future immigration from the Soviet Union—then extended Aliyah privileges to halachically non-Jewish descendants of Jews down to the generation of grandchildren. As a result, by the mid-1970s, both West Germany and Israel possessed co-ethnic immigration regimes that were nonselective regarding immigrant ability. They embraced not just co-ethnics in the original narrow sense but also their descendants, and they accepted co-ethnic immigrants because of their ethnicity and not solely for humanitarian motives related to family reunification.

Despite this process of convergence, this book reveals that significant ideological differences persisted between the two nations' approaches to immigration over the four and a half decades under examination. The notion of return, which was the ideological background to Jewish Aliyah to Israel, was absent from the German discourse for most of this time. West Germany could not conceive of Aussiedler migration as return because of its equally ideological position that these people were leaving the place where they rightfully belonged, their *Heimat*—which, for the numerically dominant Aussiedler from Poland, was supposedly still German territory. This position also limited the active pursuit of co-ethnic immigration, which would have de facto negated the right to the *Heimat* that the expellee associations held dear. In fact, even the proclaimed open door for co-ethnics was not open unconditionally: Unlike German citizens, ethnic Germans without German citizenship had no guaranteed right to enter the country. Until they actually resettled in the FRG, they were treated as foreigners for all intents and purposes. Applicants for Aussiedlung from Yugoslavia, who were rejected during the 1950s and 1960s in increasing numbers, experienced this unforthcoming attitude firsthand.

Israel, by contrast, actively and openly claimed the role of homeland for the Jewish people in both its Declaration of Independence and the Law of Return. It sent emissaries around the world to recruit Jewish immigrants, whom it wanted and needed. Yet, at least during the first 15 years of statehood, this ideologically motivated commitment to the ingathering of the diaspora had its limits. Those limits were a result of nation-building imperatives. Although the Law of Return stated that "every Jew has the right to immigrate to this country (*laalot artzah*)," this statement was significantly qualified by a series of medical and social selection guidelines adopted between 1949 and 1963. Israeli policy makers justified the obvious contradiction with reference to the difference between *laalot*—to actively make Aliyah—and *lehaalot*—to be brought to Israel. Olim coming of their own accord would supposedly never be turned down. Nevertheless, medical and social selection was tightened to the point that, in 1963, unwelcome Olim who reached Israel's borders faced the real possibility that they might be rejected.

The restrictive potential inherent in both regimes became apparent when co-ethnic immigration did not cross the fault lines of the international conflicts—the Cold War or the Israeli-Arab conflict—that normally affected these cases. While West Germany and Israel erected few obstacles for migrations that crossed the Iron Curtain or those that were classified as rescue Aliyah from hostile Arab states, the open doors came under much closer scrutiny once migrations were free and predictable—as was the case in Yugoslavia and colonial North Africa.

These case studies have also revealed that, in the absence of exceptional circumstances, co-ethnic immigration could become the object of more general contestation. During the 1950s and 1960s, related debates remained within the arcane realm of state administration. Contestation became public only in the context of migrations in the 1980s and 1990s. But irrespective of publicity, the normalization-contestation nexus was generally valid, with two intervening factors. In both cases, the challenges were led by institutions with a general preference for immigration control. In the face of normalization, they extended their restrictive stance to the normally privileged case of co-ethnic immigration, which, in the Israeli case, was the only kind of immigration during the period under examination. Prioritizing certain groups of migrants over others could in turn cause the same state and the same institutions to react in different ways to changes in the normality and freedom of migrations—hence, the quick and generous Israeli reaction to "Gomulka's Aliyah" from Poland in 1956, which contrasted with the slow response to the closing of the Moroccan emigration gates that same year.

International developments were not only important for activating restrictive policies but also decisive in triggering the extensions and convergences of the watershed period. In the late 1960s, West Germany kept its contested co-ethnic gate open and even extended it in view of the beginning rapprochement with Poland and the apparent cracks in the Iron Curtain. Similarly, Israel amended the Law of Return in 1970 to include non-Jewish family members and descendants, because it expected that Soviet-Jewish immigration would increase as a result of détente. The process of convergence under international influence became even more pronounced with the 1975 Helsinki Accords and the common human rights language of freedom of movement they provided to address the issue of German and Jewish co-ethnic migrations—which, after large-scale Jewish migrations from Arab lands ended, were predominantly East–West migrations.

Meanwhile, under the surface of similar East–West migrations in the Cold War context, national differences continued to matter. The generational extension of German Aussiedlung occurred with restraint among the courts and authorities responsible for extending it. The refugee administration initially limited this extension to one postwar generation but somewhat reluctantly included the second postwar generation as well. At the same time, the postwar expulsion and the years 1944–1945 remained as a fixed deadline: entitlement to Aussiedlung could only be derived from ancestors who had been alive at the end of the war. In this sense, Germany never made the transition from expulsion-related co-ethnic asylum to an Israeli-style co-ethnic immigration regime with no temporal restrictions and fixed deadlines. In keeping with this global approach to Aliyah, Israel's two-generation extension of the 1970 amendment to the Law of Return took place with reference to a moving line in time. Any person with a Jewish ancestor in up to two generations in the past could claim entitlement to Aliyah. The scope of this extension was significantly wider and reached indefinitely into the future.

When the Cold War framework disappeared, the two states' reactions to the new conditions diverged. Germany was quick to implement restrictive measures to reduce and regulate the mass influx of ethnic Germans from Eastern Europe and the Soviet Union starting from the late 1980s. Israel made massive efforts to channel Jewish emigrants from the Soviet Union toward Israel and to actively encourage those still willing to stay in the (former) Soviet Union to make Aliyah. That divergence was the result of national differences that had been pushed to the background since the 1970s but never disappeared.

Contrary to the impression that the end of the Cold War marked a rupture, both countries, in fact, maintained a significant degree of continuity in their policies. In Israel, this continuity was obvious, given that the Law of Return remained unchanged. But the legal changes introduced in Germany in the face of the mass Aussiedler influx in the late 1980s and early 1990s, too, were much less of a rupture than one might expect. The 1992 *Kriegsfolgenbereinigungsgesetz*, which marked the end of the Aussiedler migration regime as it had existed since the 1950s, incorporated many ideas that had been under discussion in the administration over the preceding decade and a half. With the end of the Cold War and the concomitant end of the fiction that nothing had changed in the Eastern Bloc, legislation finally implemented these ideas.

Yet because the overall framework in both cases was still predicated on ethnicity, both restriction and expansion were accompanied by a paradox. To reduce and eventually phase out Aussiedler immigration, Germany raised the ethnic threshold that candidates had to pass. This, in turn, triggered the creation of a new ethnic immigration category: the Jewish quota refugee, which allowed the country to accommodate the simultaneous arrival of Jews from the Soviet Union. Reducing and eventually ending co-ethnic migration thus implied further ethnicizing of immigration control. Israel, by contrast, was not much concerned about the "pure" Jewishness of incoming candidates, because it wanted mass immigration from the former Soviet Union to continue. Continuing and enhancing co-ethnic migration thus implied the de-ethnicization of selection criteria.

ETHNICITY IN THEORY AND PRACTICE

The post–Cold War shifts in selection criteria direct us to the core issue examined in this book: the selection practices of the gatekeeping institutions (the "bouncers") of each country when carrying out their task of ethnic screening and the drawing of boundaries around the respective nations. Embracing a praxeological, comparative, and transnational approach to the study of migration regimes, I have demonstrated that these practices were not unilateral acts of definition but part of a multilevel, transnational politics of identification involving state representatives, experts, civil society actors, and the migrants themselves. Studying these negotiations over official belonging provided insight into the theoretical and practical content of the respective ethnic codes used to regulate co-ethnic immigration and the implications of this form of immigration for conceptions of ethnicity and citizenship.

On the theoretical plane, the analysis of definitions of belonging revealed different levels of complexity in each case. The German definition of who is a German emerged as particularly complex and grounded in specific historical circumstances. It was multiply coded in that a German Aussiedler had to be an expellee (defined as someone who left his or her home in Eastern Europe in the context of the events of the Second World War) *and* a German *Volkszugehöriger.* The latter concept in turn comprised a subjective component (*Bekenntnis*) and an objective one (the "confirming characteristics" of language, descent, upbringing, and culture). Even though the link between Aussiedlung and the events of the Second World War was not part of the screening process, it tied the very concept of ethnicity to a specific point in time. The definition of *Volkszugehörigkeit* remained rooted in a particular historical context: the multi-ethnic space of Central and Eastern Europe during the interwar period and the war years. This context was never transcended, as the *Bekenntnis* had to have occurred before the end of the war. The question "When is a German?" was thus always answered in the past.

In contrast, the Jewish-Israeli definition of the term *Jew,* while contested, was simple in its essence and transcended time. The definition of a Jew as someone born of a Jewish mother or converted to Judaism, which was codified in administrative guidelines in 1960 and in the Law of Return in 1970, was as simple as it was circular—what, after all, made the mother Jewish? In any event, it did not depend on historical context: a person could be a Jew anytime.

These different levels of theoretical complexity had significant implications for the practice of co-ethnic immigration control. Beyond the question of whether subjective or objective criteria were decisive for establishing ethnic belonging, in practice the main issue was how much objective information the authorities required for the assessment. The German definition, with its apparently strong subjective *Bekenntnis* component, depended in fact quite heavily on objective clues. At the first point of control, the external gate, immigration application forms asked for a series of specific details that would allow the deciding authority to assess whether the candidate had a "typically German" life story. This objectivizing tendency became even more pronounced with the introduction of the written procedure in 1990.

Israeli forms, by contrast, requested far less information of this type. The one decisive criterion that indicated whether someone was Jewish by nationality was religion—but early forms did not consistently solicit even this basic piece of information from applicants. Even after the supposedly objective halachic criterion of maternal descent was adopted, ethnic recognition of Aliyah candidates remained largely a matter of bona fide declarations by the immigrants and the intuition of the responsible official. This rather loose practice met with internal criticism in the 1970s, and officials were urged to make more use of "typical" documents, which were usually of a religious nature. However, paper-based controls using greater amounts of information and documents seem to have become the rule only during the (post-)Soviet Aliyah of the 1990s.

At the second point of immigration control, the internal gate, the difference between German and Israeli procedures became even more pronounced. As the court cases analyzed in chapter 3 have shown, German courts reached their judgments about the validity of a person's claim to German *Volkszugehörigkeit* on the basis of extensive information, which the judges processed according to two different, but not mutually exclusive, models: a performative model in which a coherent German life story was constructed out of the biographical facts provided and Germanness was thus performed; and a declarative model, in which this coherent narrative had to be decisively complemented with proof of an explicit past declaration of Germanness made in an official context.

In contrast, the analysis of the Israeli Brother Daniel case has revealed that Jewishness could not be performed. The Israeli Supreme Court judges denied Brother Daniel's claim that he was a Jew despite abundant evidence for his national commitment and identification. He failed to meet the one make-or-break criterion of Jewishness—religion—which the majority of the judges deemed indispensable and which was determined based on the opinion of a somewhat vaguely defined "man in the street." According to Justice Moshe Silberg, this man in the street could not accept a Catholic monk as a Jew. The intuition-based model thus moved co-ethnic recognition into the realm of intuition, much as it was in fact practiced in administrative reality.

Another finding of this book is that the specific content that the category of ethnicity acquired in each instance hinged decisively on the gatekeeper in charge of providing and applying definitions. In both Germany and Israel, particular institutions strove to assert their influence over the internal gate that marked the (not only) symbolic entrance to the nation. In Germany, those were the expellee associations, which played a semi-institutionalized role in the screening process through the *Heimatauskunftstellen*. They provided the narratives that described the collective fate of certain German minorities, be they from Yugoslavia or from the Soviet Union. These narratives, which became more influential over the years, tended to exclude people who did not match this ideal type, whether they were Yugoslav-German partisans or Romanian and Soviet Jews and irrespective of their linguistic skills and cultural affiliation. The Russian German Landsmannschaft narrative of deportation, *trudarmiia*, and suffering eventually became the foundation for the *Spätaussiedler* and *Volkszugehörigkeit* definitions of the revised Federal Expellee Law in 1992.

In Israel, it was the religious establishment within the political system that repeatedly tried to assert its definitional power over Jewish belonging. In the "Who is a Jew?" controversies of 1958 and 1970, they did so successfully. They failed, however, to exclude non-Orthodox converts from Aliyah. Also, religious reservations regarding the halachic quality of Soviet Aliyah did not have major consequences, given the priority that this immigration had for the state. It was only in the relatively less important case of Ethiopian Aliyah that the secular state institutions left the defining power up to religious institutions. Whether this happened because of a lack of interest or a lack of know-how remains open to further investigation.

Yet the defining power of gatekeeping institutions was never absolute; ethnic screening was a dynamic and relational process that played out between different states and different time levels. The way the receiving state's institutions defined the concept of a migrant's ethnicity necessarily interacted with the definition provided by the country of origin. In the case of triangular migrants who moved from Eastern Europe to West Germany via Israel, the German definition also interacted with the Jewish-Israeli definition. Ideally, ethnicity was a matter of consensus: as long as the definitions and classifications in the country of origin and the country of destination were in agreement, ethnic recognition was a straightforward process.

In ambiguous cases, the process became quite complicated. The German cases described in chapter 3 illustrate this very clearly. The same person could be classified as Jewish in the country of origin and be granted an emigration permit as such; subsequently, he or she could be received as Jewish in Israel and then claim recognition as German in Germany. In each case, the problem was defining precisely what *Jewish* meant. If understood in a national sense, it became incompatible with German *Volkszugehörigkeit* under German law. If understood as a religious confession, it was deemed neutral by the German authorities. However, this alleged neutrality resulted in further discrimination, because it neglected the fact that being a Jew by religion or origin had been anything but neutral in the anti-Semitic reality of the interwar period, which was the decisive system of reference. This could result in someone not being recognized as German after the war simply because he or she had not been recognized as such before the war—at the time due to a particular interpretation of the Jews as a separate national minority in the best case or a separate race in the worst case. The German refugee administration made sustained efforts in the late 1970s to avoid such ex post facto discrimination and created ethnicity guidelines that were very accommodating in this regard. However, the problem remained.

The relational aspect became particularly relevant with the system of ethnonational classification used in the Soviet Union. As more and more migrants originated from that country, both Germany and Israel had to deal with the question of what a *natsional'nost'* entry as German, Jewish, or something else meant for co-ethnic recognition. Again, the most problematic issue related to Jews who applied for German status. In their case, the lure of the supposedly objective Soviet documentation of ethnicity in personal documents proved too strong for the German refugee administration. By excluding from recognition as German applicants whose Soviet documents identified them as *evrei*, the German authorities effectively surrendered their power to define who is a German to their Soviet counterparts. A passport entry as *nemets*, in turn, counted as *Bekenntnis* but was never fully identified with German *Volkszugehörigkeit* as such, because it provided no clues about the required confirming characteristics—in particular, knowledge of the German language.

In Israel, the different religious and secular concepts of Jewishness and Jewish descent used in the Law of Return had various degrees of compatibility with Soviet classifications. The Soviet *natsional'nost'* entry *evrei* could not satisfy the criteria of Jewishness under the halachically inspired section 4B of the post-1970 Law of Return, because the Soviet definition did not presuppose matrilineal descent. Yet such an entry could at least reliably indicate patrilineal or matrilineal descent from a Jew, which entitled the candidate to Aliyah under section 4A of the amended Law of Return. This latter section thus spoke the same secular ethno-national language as the Soviet documents and eventually enabled the immigration of significant numbers of "non-Jewish Jews" from the former Soviet Union.

ETHNICITY AS DECLARATION, PERFORMANCE, INTUITION, AND CONSENSUS

This book's praxeological approach to ethnic screening also shed light on the way migration regime actors combined certain criteria and markers to produce co-ethnic belonging. Contrary to the idea that such belonging was based mainly on ascriptive ethno-cultural characteristics of descent and culture, I have shown that the notion of German *Volkszugehörigkeit* was fundamentally based on the concept of self-avowal or *Bekenntnis*. In principle it was thus a "Renanian" notion: a German *Volkszugehöriger* was someone who had voted yes in the daily plebiscite for German *Volkstum* up to 1945. Yet this vote was not free, because it had to have been accepted by others in the past and had to be acceptable to experts in the present. In practice, a *Bekenntnis*—and its antithesis, the *Gegenbekenntnis*—could mean different things in different circumstances and was subject to change over time. For Germans from Yugoslavia, the Federal Administration Office believed that a *Bekenntnis* was reliably indicated by the use of the German language in the family. This, however, could be canceled out by pro-partisan engagement during the Second World War. Before 1959, intermarriage with a non-German was also generally taken as a *Gegenbekenntnis*. Here, then, a mixture of linguistic, political, and ethnic (i.e., in terms of endogamy within the ethnic group) motives determined who was recognized as German and who was not. As explained in chapter 3, Valentina Colien could perform her *Bekenntnis* by attributing declarative character to everyday actions—a construction that, in the 1980 ethnicity guidelines, appeared in the guise of "conclusive behavior" that could indicate *Bekenntnis*. For Josef Floris, it should have been explicitly declared in an official context, which came to be seen by the administration as the most reliable method to assess *Bekenntnis* when the life story was ambiguous.

Volkszugehörigkeit was thus not simply based on ascriptive criteria of descent or culture. Descent was insufficient for Yugoslav citizens whose parents were deemed German by the German authorities but who lived in mixed marriages and did not use the German language in their family. Culture, in turn, was insufficient for Jewish applicants who undoubtedly belonged to the German "cultural and linguistic sphere" but did not possess a *Bekenntnis*. For Yugoslav German partisans, their anti-Nazi (and thus anti-German) engagement voided the presence of both of these criteria. Here, *Volkszugehörigkeit* became a highly political concept. It could also turn into a *völkisch* notion if interpreted that way by officials who rejected a Jewish candidate with reference to the view that, in interwar Europe, everyone belonged to a naturally assigned *Volksgruppe*. *Volkszugehörigkeit* was also a historical notion when it came to be identified with a particular fate that a member of a certain German minority had to have suffered. It was not a notion primarily defined by race and blood, as overly zealous critics maintained. On the contrary, when *Volkszugehörigkeit* was constructed as inheritable within the family, it explicitly turned into a social construct. With its emphasis on self-identification, it was a plebiscitary notion, but like many compulsory plebiscites, it was not especially democratic, because it forced binary options on ambiguous life stories.

What, in turn, was Jewishness in the context of co-ethnic immigration to Israel? In theoretical terms, Christian Joppke's verdict that it was an "irremediably religious condition" stands.[16] Being of the Jewish religion was the one sufficient condition that qualified a candidate as an Oleh. Abandoning the Jewish religion was the one condition that surely disqualified a candidate, even if she or he was clearly of Jewish descent, as Brother Daniel found out in court. Yet an important qualification needs to be made: It was irremediable not because remedies were not offered but because they were not taken up. Both in the 1970 amendment debate and in later years, alternative suggestions were put on the table. Gideon Hausner's proposal in 1970 to have a candidate's bona fide declaration confirmed by his or her surroundings could have been an interesting model to consider (chapter 4). Similarly, Shulamit Aloni's all-encompassing definition (which, however, also excluded converts from Judaism) was on the Knesset floor in 1987 but remained on paper (chapter 5). In no case was the political constellation conducive to change since the religious establishment remained firmly in place as the main provider of symbolic identity.

But here, too, examination of the actual recognition practices was illuminating. It emerges that religious criteria were not always relevant for co-ethnic recognition, as subjective bona fide declarations remained important into the 1970s, and possibly also afterward. The decision about whether they were credible remained up to the discretion of the examiner, who, in the absence of clear guidelines, had to rely on intuition: Moshe Levy was likely to be accepted; Christian, the son of Christian, raised serious doubts. Cases lying between these constructed opposite ideal types remained murky. Ideally, of course, the administration hoped to have candidates bring a *teudat kashrut* ("kosher certificate") from a rabbi or a religious document such as a *ketubah* in order to prove their origins in the Jewish religious community. However, Eastern European Jews often did not possess such documentation, in which case the authorities simply accepted the fact that someone had left the country of origin with a visa for Israel as sufficient proof of Jewishness. Defining power was thus yielded to the authorities of the country of origin. This was also the case when Soviet nationality registrations were taken as indicative of Jewishness or at least of Jewish descent. A Jew for the purposes of immigration was thus someone who claimed to be a Jew and who was believed to be a Jew by the examining official and/or the authorities of the country of origin. Here, too, ethnicity was a matter of consensus.

In fact, the secular Israeli state authorities—unlike their religious counterparts—were quite flexible when it came to reaching this consensus. Since Jewishness meant different things in different contexts, they readily adapted their own definition to these contexts. Within a (post-)Soviet framework, Jews were defined by ethno-nationality rather than religion—the Israeli state easily adjusted to this familiar language and drew up extensive guidelines on how to interpret the related evidence. In the Ethiopian context, Jews were defined by a particular type of Jewish religious rite—the Israeli state gladly left the definitional and decision-making power up to religious authorities. Thus, despite the supposedly timeless and context-transcending definition of Jewishness by halacha as it was partially adopted for the Law of Return, in practice Jewishness remained an elusive and context-specific concept that required flexible answers by a state that was intent on ingathering Jews.

CHANGING THE CENTER FROM THE MARGINS

As co-ethnic migration brought the definitions of belonging that were valid in the diaspora to the national center, traditional notions of a homogeneous national society in both countries began to shift. In Germany, the immigration of large numbers of people who had been regarded as German in their countries of origin, self-identified as German, and were treated as German by the state but in many instances did not speak any German caused (and continues to cause) irritation. But this irritation may be interpreted as having contributed to normalizing diversity within German society, because it broke down the traditional dichotomy of "Germans" and "foreigners." Aussiedler, in a sense, were both. Their identification as German challenged the close link between the German language and German identity. At the same time, majority society's perception of these Germans as foreign highlighted the advanced Germanization of permanently settled but nonnaturalized labor migrants and their descendants, who, until the 1990s, were still labeled *Ausländer* (aliens), which also challenged German descent as a necessary criterion for German identity. In the new millennium, all these people are subsumed under the large label of "people with migrant background" (*Menschen mit Migrationshintergrund*), a category that by 2016 comprised 22.5 percent of the population residing in Germany.[17] Though criticized for its ascriptive character and its supposed stigmatization of people, this concept represents a significant step forward from a time when *Deutsche* and *Ausländer* were mutually exclusive categories.[18]

In Israel, post-Soviet Olim have contributed to overcoming traditional notions of Israeli society as a melting pot in which immigrants would simply shed their languages and cultures of origin and blend into the new Hebrew nation.[19] While this alleged societal homogeneity has arguably always been a fiction, the massive immigration of Russian-speaking immigrants has made linguistic diversity more visible on a national scale, firmly establishing the Russian language in the Israeli public sphere—be it on shop signs, ATMs, or official government websites. The growing number of "sociologically converted" non-Jewish-origin Israelis speaking both Hebrew and Russian has contributed and continues to contribute to the development of a secular notion of Hebrew Israeliness. Contrary to traditional fears that such processes of secularization and Israelization would disconnect Israel from global Jewry, Israelis are becoming part of a new global Jewish diaspora that is defined less than it ever has been by religion and is one in which both Hebrew and Russian are typical Jewish languages.[20]

The migrations examined in this book have also led to something of a reentanglement of Germany and Israel, Germans and Jews. While Jews have been constantly immigrating to Germany throughout the postwar decades, it was Russian-Jewish immigration since 1990 that led to the creation of what historian Dmitrij Belkin has called "German Jewry Two" (*Deutsches Judentum Zwei*)—a new German Jewry that consciously chose Germany as its new home, living in the country with a much higher degree of normalcy than the postwar Jewish community living on the proverbial "packed suitcases" ever could.[21] The "impossible homeland" has turned into a "possible homeland."[22] This does not imply the "renaissance" of German-Jewish life of yore—Belkin calls this scenario both "impossible and undesirable."[23] The result is instead a self-consciously transnational and multilingual community of people who, like Belkin himself, might in many instances have merely immigrated on a "Jewish ticket" but then "became Jewish"—some in a substantial religious sense, some as a consciously secular self-positioning, some in a "light kosher" version—while also claiming an active role in the creation of a new German society.[24] This transnational new German Jewry, then, is the somewhat ironic outcome of an ethnicized migration regime that for decades would accept Jews only if they could prove they were German before taking them in as Jews.

Meanwhile, Germany, and in particular Berlin, has become the destination of Israeli immigrants—some of them also of Russian origin—who contribute to the mosaic of German society.[25] Unlike immigrants from Israel in the 1950s, the majority of whom were returning survivors of "German Jewry One," these predominantly young people are undoubtedly Israeli, though in many cases descendants of past emigrants from Germany.[26] It would be misleading to suggest that history has come full circle with their migration to Germany, even if they travel on a German passport claimed with reference to their *Yekke* ancestors.[27] Rather, it opens up a new chapter, in which the violently disentangled German and Jewish collectivities may start to re-entangle as equals.

While Israeli migration to Germany is still not perceived as normal in political and public discourse on either side, one may agree with anthropologists Hadas Cohen and Dani Kranz that "Israelis in Berlin are perhaps not all that different from other migrants."[28] As their ethnographic fieldwork has shown, the emigrants are increasingly unapologetic about their *Yeridah* from Israel, choosing a diasporic existence without feeling they are in exile, aware of the fraught past but living in the present while reconnecting with both Ashkenazi and Mizrachi roots in a multicultural city. As anti-Semitic incidents involving Arab-origin youngsters show, the story of Israelis and other Jews in Berlin and Germany is not a story of perfect harmony either. But it is a new story that "lies beyond the past and could perhaps be explicated only in the future from the ways in which this community will develop a home for itself in this charged locality."[29]

The co-ethnic migration regimes examined in this book were responses to a particular historical situation—postwar migrations of ethnic disentanglement. In a homogenizing international order where members of ethnic groups were allocated to "their" nation-states, they served the purpose of channeling and managing the resulting migration flows. That historical period is over. The migratory challenges both Germany and Israel are facing in the twenty-first century are different, and regimes predicated on ethnicity as their criterion of admission are not a suitable response. Nevertheless, both countries' past experiences with co-ethnic migration since the Second World War hold potential lessons for present and future movements of people. On various occasions during these seven decades, the migration regimes of both countries proved remarkably capable of processing and integrating large numbers of immigrants in short periods of time. In the 1950s, Israel still found it necessary to make the unrestricted and unselected influx of immigrants manageable by introducing utilitarian selection criteria into the regime's selection code. As the state consolidated, this type of selectivity disappeared from the migration regime. Israel received the post-1987 Soviet exodus without sorting the candidates by age, ability, or qualification. So, too, Germany received Aussiedler and Spätaussiedler without any utilitarian restrictions and, until 1992, also without numerical quotas. In both cases, the integration of these substantial numbers of immigrants was nevertheless largely successful, not least because of the generosity of their reception, which included immediately granting them citizenship as well as elaborate integration schemes that provided language classes and financial subsidies. Like any social process, the absorption of millions of immigrants within a few years did entail difficulty and conflict—and yet, from the perspective of a quarter century later, it has worked. If nothing else, the conclusion of studying several decades of co-ethnic migration might be that—contrary to the intuition of many present-day pundits and policy makers—generosity, not restrictiveness, may be the key to successful migration management.

NOTES

1. Klekowski von Koppenfels, "Decline of Privilege," 112–113.
2. "(Spät-)Aussiedler und ihre Angehörigen. Zeitreihe 1950–2017," https://www.bva.bund.de/SharedDocs/Downloads/DE/Buerger/Migration-Integration/Spaetaussiedler/Statistik/Zeitreihe_1950_2017.pdf?__blob=publicationFile&v=5.
3. Ibid.
4. "Immigration to Israel: Total Immigration, by Country per Year (1948–Present)," Jewish Virtual Library, American-Israeli Cooperative Enterprise, https://www.jewishvirtuallibrary.org/total-immigration-to-israel-by-country-per-year, and "Total Immigration to Israel by Year (1948–Present)," Jewish Virtual Library, https://www.jewishvirtuallibrary.org/total-immigration-to-israel-by-year.
5. Calculated from DellaPergola, "Some Fundamentals"; and "Demographics of Israel: Jewish & Non-Jewish Population of Israel/Palestine (1517–Present)," Jewish Virtual Library, American-Israeli Cooperative Enterprise, http://www.jewishvirtuallibrary.org/jsource/Society_&_Culture/israel_palestine_pop.html.

6. DellaPergola, "World Jewish Population, 2016," 16.

7. Ibid., 20.

8. George Arnett, "Is There Really a Jewish Exodus from Western Europe?" *The Guardian*, February 5, 2015, http://www.theguardian.com/news/datablog/2015/feb/05/is-there-really-a-jewish-exodus-from-western-europe. See also Gil Yaron, "Jüdische Fluchtwelle—Lieber Raketenhagel als Leben in Frankreich," *Spiegel Online*, March 21, 2012, http://www.spiegel.de/politik/ausland/immer-mehr-juden-fliehen-aus-frankreich-nach-israel-a-822369.html.

9. Raphael Ahren, "With Jewish Agency Out, Zionist Groups Get into Promoting Aliyah," *Haaretz*, May 27, 2011, https://www.haaretz.com/1.5016860.

10. I owe the *Gegenwartsarbeit* analogy to Frank Wolff (Osnabrück).

11. Lustick, "Israel as a Non-Arab State."

12. Joppke, *Selecting by Origin*, 218.

13. Vserossijskaja perepis' naselenija 2010 g. Natsional'nyi sostav naseleniia Rossiiskoi Federatsii, http://demoscope.ru/weekly/ssp/rus_nac_10.php; "Itogi natsional'noi perepisi naseleniia Respubliki Kazakhstan 2009 goda." Analiticheskij otchet. Astana 2011, 21–22, http://www.stat.gov.kz/getImg?id=WC16200032648.

14. Peter Beaumont, "Leaders Reject Netanyahu Calls for Jewish Mass Migration to Israel," *The Guardian*, February 16, 2015, https://www.theguardian.com/world/2015/feb/16/leaders-criticise-netanyahu-calls-jewish-mass-migration-israel.

15. Article 108 of the Greek constitution postulates that "The State must take care for emigrant Greeks and for the maintenance of their ties with the Fatherland." Hellenic Parliament, *The Constitution of Greece: As Revised by the Parliamentary Resolution of May 27th 2008 of the VIIIth Revisionary Parliament*, 2008, https://www.hellenicparliament.gr/UserFiles/f3c70a23-7696-49db-9148-f24dce6a27c8/001-156%20aggliko.pdf. The official body in charge of this task is the World Council of Hellenes Abroad, http://www.sae.gr.

16. Joppke, *Selecting by Origin*, 165.

17. Bevölkerung und Erwerbstätigkeit: Bevölkerung mit Migrationshintergrund—Ergebnisse des Mikrozensus 2016, Statistisches Bundesamt (Destatis), Fachserie 1, Reihe 2.2, https://www.destatis.de/DE/Publikationen/Thematisch/Bevoelkerung/MigrationIntegration/Migrationshintergrund2010220167004.pdf?__blob=publicationFile.

18. For such criticisms, see, for instance, "Name, Date of Birth, Migration Background: Of All the Ways European Countries Classify Ethnicity, Germany's May Be the Worst," *The Economist*, May 26, 2016, https://www.economist.com/europe/2016/05/26/name-date-of-birth-migration-background; Ferda Ataman, "Schafft den Migrationshintergrund ab," *Spiegel Online*, June 2, 2018, http://www.spiegel.de/kultur/gesellschaft/schafft-den-migrationshintergrund-ab-kolumne-von-ferda-ataman-a-1210654.html.

19. In his classic study of immigrant absorption in 1950s Israel, Shmuel Noah Eisenstadt already noted the pluralization of Israeli society due to mass immigration. At the time, he interpreted this phenomenon as a deviation from the allegedly homogenous model of absorption in the Yishuv. See Eisenstadt, *Absorption of Immigrants*.

20. Cathryn J. Prince, "Is Russian the New Yiddish?" *The Times of Israel*, April 7, 2017, https://www.timesofisrael.com/is-russian-the-new-yiddish. On new diasporic forms of Jewishness, see, for instance, Kranz, "Forget Israel." On the global Israeli diaspora see Gold, *Israeli Diaspora*.

21. Belkin, "Mögliche Heimat."

22. On the notion of Germany as an "impossible homeland" for Jews after the Second World War, see Kauders, *Unmögliche Heimat*.

23. Belkin, "Mögliche Heimat," 25.

24. Belkin, *Germanija*; Kranz, "Forget Israel"; Gromova, *Generation "koscher light."*

25. Kranz, "Forget Israel"; Hadas Cohen and Kranz, "Israeli Jews."

26. Panagiotidis, "Policy for the Future"; Hadas Cohen and Kranz, "Israeli Jews."

27. On the reclaiming of German passports among the present-day generation of mainly Israeli and American Jews, see Swarthout, "Revoked and Restored."

28. Hadas Cohen and Kranz, "Israeli Jews," 336.

29. Ibid.

BIBLIOGRAPHY

ARCHIVES

Archiv für Christlich-Demokratische Politik, Sankt Augustin (ACDP)
Bundesarchiv, Koblenz (BArch)
Bundestagsarchiv, Berlin
Central Zionist Archives, Jerusalem (CZA)
Hauptstaatsarchiv Stuttgart (HStAS)
Israel State Archives, Jerusalem (ISA)
International Tracing Service Digital Archive, Bad Arolsen (ITSDA)
Politisches Archiv des Auswärtigen Amts, Berlin (PAAA)
Stadtarchiv Mannheim

PUBLISHED SOURCES

Akten zur Auswärtigen Politik der Bundesrepublik Deutschland (AAPD)
Entscheidungen des Bundesverfassungsgerichts (BVerfGE)
Entscheidungen des Bundesverwaltungsgerichts (BVerwGE)

NEWSPAPERS

Der Donauschwabe
Globus
Info-Dienst Deutsche Aussiedler (IDDA)
Volk auf dem Weg (VadW)

INTERVIEWS

Family T., Korbach, April 15, 2008
Federal Administration Office, Cologne, August 26, 2009

BOOKS AND ARTICLES

Abramov, S. Zalman. *Perpetual Dilemma: Jewish Religion in the Jewish State*. Rutherford, NJ: Fairleigh Dickinson University Press, 1976.

Ackermann-Gemeinde, ed. *Hans Schütz—Helfer und Wegweiser in schwerer Zeit: Gewerkschaftler, Sozialpolitiker, Jungaktivist, Vertriebenenpolitiker, Europapolitiker.* Munich: Ackermann-Gemeinde, 1982.

Ahonen, Pertti. *After the Expulsion: West Germany and Eastern Europe, 1945–1990*. Oxford: Oxford University Press, 2003.

Ahonen, Pertti, Gustavo Corni, Jerzy Kochanowski, Rainer Schulze, Tamás Stark, and Barbara Stelzl-Marx. *People on the Move: Forced Population Movements in Europe in the Second World War and Its Aftermath*. Oxford: Berg, 2008.

Akcam, Taner. *A Shameful Act: The Armenian Genocide and the Question of Turkish Responsibility*. New York: Metropolitan Books, 2006.

Aktürk, Sener. *Regimes of Ethnicity and Nationhood in Germany, Russia, and Turkey*. Cambridge: Cambridge University Press, 2012.

Alroey, Gur. *Immigrants: Jewish Immigration to Palestine in the Early Twentieth Century*. [In Hebrew.] Jerusalem: Yad Ben-Zvi, 2004.

Alter, Peter, Claus-Ekkehard Bärsch, and Peter Berghoff, eds. *Die Konstruktion der Nation gegen die Juden*. Munich: Wilhelm Fink, 1999.

Aly, Götz. *"Endlösung": Völkerverschiebung und der Mord an den europäischen Juden*. Frankfurt a.M.: Fischer Taschenbuch, 1995.

Ancel, Jean. "Chernovtsy." In *Encyclopedia of the Holocaust*. Vol. 1, *A–D*, edited by Israel Gutman, 287–288. New York: Macmillan, 1990.

———. *The History of the Holocaust in Romania*. Lincoln: University of Nebraska Press, 2011.

———. "'The New Jewish Invasion'—The Return of Survivors from Transnistria." In Bankier, *The Jews Are Coming Back*, 231–256.

Anteby-Yemini, Lisa. *Les juifs éthiopiens en Israël. Les paradoxes du paradis*. Paris: CNRS Éditions, 2004.

Arad, Yitzhak. *The Holocaust in the Soviet Union*. Lincoln: University of Nebraska Press, 2009.

Arbeits- und Sozialminister des Landes Nordrhein-Westfalen, ed. *Das Dritte Problem. Betrachtungen zur Aufnahme der Spätaussiedler aus dem Osten*. 2nd ed. Troisdorf, Germany: Der Wegweiser, 1958.

Arbel, Andrea S. *Riding the Wave: The Jewish Agency's Role in the Mass Aliyah of Soviet and Ethiopian Jewry to Israel, 1987–1995*. Hewlett, NY: Gefen, 2001.

Arian, Asher, ed. *The Elections in Israel, 1977*. Jerusalem: Jerusalem Academic Press, 1980.

Arian, Asher, and Michal Shamir, eds. *The Elections in Israel, 1988*. Boulder, CO: Westview, 1990.

Armborst, Kerstin. *Ablösung von der Sowjetunion: Die Emigrationsbewegung der Juden und Deutschen vor 1987*. Münster, Germany: LIT, 2001.

Arnon, Yishai. "Immigration and Absorption Policy 1954–1956: Implementation and Outcome." [In Hebrew.] In Hacohen, *Ingathering of Exiles*, 317–341.

Bade, Klaus J. "Aussiedler—Rückwanderer über Generationen hinweg." In *Neue Heimat im Westen: Vertriebene, Flüchtlinge, Aussiedler*, edited by Klaus J. Bade, 128–149. Münster, Germany: Westfälischer Heimatbund, 1990.

Bade, Klaus J., Pieter C. Emmer, Leo Lucassen, and Jochen Oltmer, eds. *The Encyclopedia of European Migration and Minorities: From the Seventeenth Century to the Present*. Cambridge: Cambridge University Press, 2013.

Baier, Hannelore, and Ernst Meinhardt, eds. *Kauf von Freiheit. Heinz-Günther Hüsch im Interview mit Hannelore Baier und Ernst Meinhardt*. Hermannstadt, Romania: Honterus, 2013.

Bange, Oliver, and Gottfried Niedhardt, eds. *Helsinki 1975 and the Transformation of Europe*. New York: Berghahn Books, 2008.

Bankier, David, ed. *The Jews Are Coming Back: The Return of the Jews to Their Countries of Origin after WWII*. Jerusalem: Yad Vashem, 2005.

Barkai, Avraham. *"Wehr Dich!" Der Centralverein deutscher Staatsbürger jüdischen Glaubens (C.V.) 1893–1938*. Munich: Beck, 2002.

Bauer, Yehuda. *Flight and Rescue: Brichah*. New York: Random House, 1970.

Becker, Franziska. *Ankommen in Deutschland. Einwanderungspolitik als biographische Erfahrung im Migrationsprozess russischer Juden*. Berlin: Reimer, 2001.

Beer, Mathias. *Flucht und Vertreibung der Deutschen: Voraussetzungen, Verlauf, Folgen*. Munich: Beck, 2011.

———. "Flüchtlinge—Ausgewiesene—Neubürger—Heimatvertriebene. Flüchtlingspolitik und Flüchtlingsintegration in Deutschland nach 1945, begriffsgeschichtlich betrachtet." In *Migration und Integration. Aufnahme und Eingliederung im historischen Wandel*, edited by Mathias Beer, Martin Kintzinger, and Marita Krauss, 145–167. Stuttgart: Steiner, 1997.

Belkin, Dmitrij. *Germanija: Wie ich in Deutschland jüdisch und erwachsen wurde*. Frankfurt a.M.: Campus, 2016.

———. "Mögliche Heimat: Deutsches Judentum Zwei." In *Ausgerechnet Deutschland! Jüdisch-russische Einwanderung in die Bundesrepublik. Begleitpublikation zur Ausstellung im Jüdischen Museum Frankfurt*, edited by Dmitrij Belkin and Raphael Gross, 25–29. Berlin: Nicolai, 2010.

Ben Ariye, Reut. "The Immigration (Aliya) Policy in the Immigration Department of the Jewish Agency Managed by Yitzhak Rephael between 1948–1953." [In Hebrew.] MA thesis, University of Haifa, 2009.

Ben Porat, Guy. *Between State and Synagogue: The Secularization of Contemporary Israel*. Cambridge: Cambridge University Press, 2013.

Benz, Wolfgang. "Zweifache Opfer Nationalsozialistischer Bevölkerungspolitik: Die Zwangsmigration von Volksdeutschen." In *Zwangsmigrationen im mittleren und östlichen Europa: Völkerrecht—Konzeptionen—Praxis,* edited by Ralph Melville, Jiří Pešek, and Claus Scharf, 247–258. Mainz, Germany: Philipp von Zabern, 2007.

Bergen, Doris L. "The Nazi Concept of 'Volksdeutsche' and the Exacerbation of Anti-Semitism in Eastern Europe, 1939–45." *Journal of Contemporary History* 29, no. 4 (October 1994): 569–582.

Berlinghoff, Marcel. "Transnationale, Internationale oder Nationale Migrationspolitik? Der deutsche Anwerbestopp von 1973." In *Migration und Integration: Akzeptanz und Widerstand im transnationalen Nationalstaat,* edited by Sandra Kostner, 109–132. Berlin: LIT, 2016.

Best, Renate. "Juden und Judenbilder in der gesellschaftlichen Konstruktion einer deutschen Nation (1781–1804)." In Haupt and Langewiesche, *Nation und Religion,* 170–214.

Bethke, Carl. "'Erweckung' und Distanz: Aspekte der Nazifizierung der 'Volksdeutschen' in Slawonien 1935–1940." In *Der Einfluss von Faschismus und Nationalsozialismus auf Minderheiten in Ostmittel- und Südosteuropa,* edited by Mariana Hausleitner, 183–217. Munich: IKGS, 2006.

———. "Von der 'Umsiedlung' zur 'Aussiedlung': Zur destruktiven Dynamik 'ethnischer Flurbereinigung' am Beispiel der Deutschen in Bosnien und Kroatien 1941–1948." In *Vom Faschismus zum Stalinismus: Deutsche und andere Minderheiten in Ostmittel- und Südosteuropa 1941–1953,* edited by Mariana Hausleitner, 23–39. Munich: IKGS, 2008.

Biale, David. *Not in the Heavens: The Tradition of Jewish Secular Thought.* Princeton, NJ: Princeton University Press, 2011.

Bloxham, Donald. "The Great Unweaving: The Removal of Peoples in Europe, 1875–1949." In *Removing Peoples: Forced Removal in the Modern World,* edited by Richard Bessel and Claudia B. Haake, 167–207. Oxford: Oxford University Press, 2009.

Borutta, Manuel, and Jan C. Jansen, eds. *Vertriebene und Pieds Noirs in Postwar Germany and France: Comparative Perspectives.* Basingstoke, UK: Palgrave Macmillan, 2016.

Braham, Randolph L. *The Politics of Genocide: The Holocaust in Hungary.* New York: Columbia University Press, 1981.

Brenner, Michael. "Religion, Nation oder Stamm: zum Wandel der Selbstdefinition unter deutschen Juden." In: Haupt and Langewiesche, *Nation und Religion,* 587–601.

Brix, Emil. *Die Umgangssprachen in Altösterreich zwischen Agitation und Assimilation: Die Sprachenstatistik in den zisleithanischen Volkszählungen 1880 bis 1910.* Vienna: Böhlau, 1982.

Broszat, Martin. "Von der Kulturnation zur Volksgruppe: Die nationale Stellung der Juden in der Bukowina." *Historische Zeitschrift* 200, no. 3 (June 1965): 572–605.

Brubaker, Rogers. *Citizenship and Nationhood in France and Germany*. Cambridge, MA: Harvard University Press, 1992.

———. "The Manichean Myth: Rethinking the Distinction between 'Civic' and 'Ethnic' Nationalism." In *Nation and National Identity: The European Experience in Perspective*, edited by Hanspeter Kriesi, Klaus Armingeon, Hannes Siegrist, and Andreas Wimmer, 55–71. Chur, Switzerland: Rüegger, 1999.

———. "Migrations of Ethnic Unmixing in the New Europe." *International Migration Review* 32, no. 4 (Winter 1998): 1047–1065.

———. *Nationalism Reframed: Nationhood and the National Question in the New Europe*. Cambridge: Cambridge University Press, 1996.

———. "Religion and Nationalism: Four Approaches." *Nations and Nationalism* 18, no. 1 (January 2012): 2–20.

Brubaker, Rogers, and Jaeeun Kim. "Transborder Membership Politics in Germany and Korea." *Archives européennes de sociologie/European Journal of Sociology* 52, no. 1 (April 2011): 21–75.

Brunner, José, and Iris Nachum. "'Vor dem Gesetz steht ein Türhüter': Wie und warum israelische Antragsteller ihre Zugehörigkeit zum deutschen Sprach- und Kulturkreis beweisen mussten." In *Die Praxis der Wiedergutmachung: Geschichte, Erfahrung und Wirkung in Deutschland und Israel*, edited by Norbert Frei, José Brunner, and Constantin Goschler, 387–424. Göttingen, Germany: Wallstein, 2009.

Bryant, Chad. "Either German or Czech: Fixing Nationality in Bohemia and Moravia, 1939–1946." *Slavic Review* 61, no. 4 (Winter 2002): 683–706.

Burleigh, Michael. *Germany Turns Eastwards: A Study of Ostforschung in the Third Reich*. Cambridge: Cambridge University Press, 1988.

Cantorovich, Irena, and Nati Cantorovich. "The Impact of the Holocaust and the State of Israel on Soviet Jewish Identity." In Ro'i, *Jewish Movement*, 119–136.

Čapková, Kateřina. *Czechs, Germans, Jews? National Identity and the Jews of Bohemia*. New York: Berghahn Books, 2012.

Chetrit, Sami Shalom. *The Mizrahi Struggle in Israel: Between Oppression and Liberation, Identification and Alternative, 1948–2003*. [In Hebrew.] Tel Aviv: Am Oved, 2004.

Chu, Winson. *The German Minority in Interwar Poland*. Cambridge: Cambridge University Press, 2012.

Clark, Bruce. *Twice a Stranger: How Mass Expulsion Forged Modern Greece and Turkey*. London: Granta, 2006.

Cohen, Asher. *Non-Jewish Jews: Jewish-Israeli Identity and the Challenge of Expanding the Jewish Nation*. [In Hebrew.] Jerusalem: Shalom Hartman Institute, 2006.

Cohen, Asher, and Bernard Susser. "Jews and Others: Non-Jewish Jews in Israel." *Israel Affairs* 15, no. 1 (January 2009): 52–65.

Cohen, Gerard D. *In War's Wake: Europe's Displaced Persons in the Postwar Order.* Oxford: Oxford University Press, 2012.

Cohen, Hadas, and Dani Kranz. "Israeli Jews in the New Berlin: From Shoah Memories to Middle Eastern Encounters." In *Cultural Topographies of the New Berlin,* edited by Karin Bauer and Jennifer Ruth Hosek, 322–346. New York: Berghahn Books, 2017.

Cohen, Yinan, and Irena Kogan. "Jewish Immigration from the Former Soviet Union to Germany and Israel in the 1990s." *Leo Baeck Institute Year Book* 50, no. 1 (January 2005): 249–265.

Cohen, Yolande. "The Migrations of Moroccan Jews to Montreal: Memory, (Oral) History and Historical Narrative." *Journal of Modern Jewish Studies* 10, no. 2 (July 2011): 245–260.

Corinaldi, Michael. *The Enigma of Jewish Identity: The Law of Return—Theory and Practice.* [In Hebrew.] Jerusalem: Nevo, 2001.

———. *Jewish Identity: The Case of Ethiopian Jewry.* Jerusalem: Magnes Press, 1998.

Davidovitch, Nadav, and Shifra Shvarts. "Health and Zionist Ideology: Medical Selection of Jewish European Immigrants to Palestine." In *Facing Illness in Troubled Times: Health in Europe in the Interwar Years 1918–1939,* edited by Iris Borowy, 409–424. Frankfurt a.M.: Peter Lang, 2005.

Davidovitch, Nadav, and Rakefet Zalashik. "Medical Borders: Historical, Political, and Cultural Analyses." *Science in Context* 19, no. 3 (September 2006): 309–316.

DellaPergola, Sandro. "The Global Context of Migration to Israel." In *Still Moving: Recent Jewish Migration in Comparative Perspective,* edited by Daniel J. Elazar and Morton Weinfeld, 13–59. New Brunswick, NJ: Transaction, 2000.

———. "Some Fundamentals of Jewish Demographic History." In *Papers in Jewish Demography 1997,* edited by Sandro DellaPergola and Judith Even, 11–33. Jerusalem: The Hebrew University, 2001.

———. "World Jewish Population, 2016." In *The American Jewish Year Book* 116 (2016), edited by Arnold Dashefsky and Ira M. Sheskin, 253–332, as found at the Berman Jewish Data Bank: https://www.jewishdatabank.org/databank/search-results?search=world+jewish+population.

Demshuk, Andrew. *The Lost German East: Forced Migration and the Politics of Memory, 1945–1970.* Cambridge: Cambridge University Press, 2012.

———. "What Was the 'Right to the Heimat'? West German Expellees and the Many Meanings of Heimkehr." *Central European History* 45, no. 3 (September 2012): 523–556.

Deutsches Rotes Kreuz, Generalsekretariat. *60 Jahre Suchdienst.* Berlin: Deutsches Rotes Kreuz, 2005.

Dietz, Barbara. "*Aussiedler/Spätaussiedler* in Germany since 1950." In Bade et al., *Encyclopedia of European Migration,* 245–250.

———. "German and Jewish Migration from the Former Soviet Union to Germany: Background, Trends, and Implications." *Journal of Ethnic and Migration Studies* 26, no. 4 (October 2000): 635–652.

Dietz, Barbara, Uwe Lebok, and Pavel Polian. "The Jewish Emigration from the Former Soviet Union to Germany." *International Migration* 40, no. 2 (June 2002): 29–48.

Diner, Dan. "Im Zeichen des Banns." In *Juden in Deutschland, von 1945 bis zur Gegenwart*, edited by Michael Brenner, 15–66. Munich: Beck, 2012.

Don-Yehiya, Eliezer. "Religion and National Identity in the Law: The Shalit Affair and the 'Who Is a Jew' Controversy." [In Hebrew.] In Zameret and Yablonka, *The Third Decade*, 379–400.

Dumbrava, Costica. *Nationality, Citizenship and Ethno-Cultural Belonging: Preferential Membership Policies in Europe*. Basingstoke, UK: Palgrave Macmillan, 2014.

Edelheit, Abraham J. *The Yishuv in the Shadow of the Holocaust: Zionist Politics and Rescue Aliya, 1933–1939*. Boulder, CO: Westview, 1996.

Eisenstadt, Shmuel Noah. *The Absorption of Immigrants: A Comparative Study Based Mainly on the Jewish Community in Palestine and the State of Israel*. London: Routledge & Kegan Paul, 1954.

Eisfeld, Alfred, Guido Hausmann, and Dietmar Neutatz, eds. *Besetzt, interniert, deportiert: Der Erste Weltkrieg und die deutsche, jüdische, polnische und ukrainische Zivilbevölkerung im östlichen Europa*. Essen, Germany: Klartext, 2013.

Eisfeld, Alfred, and Vladimir Martynenko. "Filtration und operative Erfassung der ethnischen Deutschen in der Ukraine durch die Organe des Inneren und der Staatssicherheit während des Zweiten Weltkrieges und in der Nachkriegszeit." *Nordost-Archiv* 21 (2012): 104–181.

Elam, Yigal. *Judaism as Status Quo: The 1958 Who Is a Jew Controversy in the Light It Shed on Relations between Religious and Secular Circles in the State of Israel*. [In Hebrew.] Tel Aviv: Am Oved, 2000.

Eley, Geoff, and Jan Palmowski, eds. *Citizenship and National Identity in Twentieth-Century Germany*. Stanford, CA: Stanford University Press, 2008.

Fahrmeir. Andreas. "Law and Practice: Problems in Researching the History of Migration Controls." In *Migration Control in the North Atlantic World: The Evolution of State Practices in Europe and the United States from the French Revolution to the Inter-War Period*, edited by Andreas Fahrmeir, Olivier Faron, and Patrick Weil, 301–315. New York: Berghahn Books, 2003.

Fainberg, Sarah. "Friends Abroad: How the Western Campaign for Soviet Jews Influenced Activists in the Soviet Union." In Ro'i, *Jewish Movement*, 392–418.

Fairchild, Amy L. "The Rise and Fall of the Medical Gaze: The Political Economy of Immigrant Medical Inspection in Modern America." *Science in Context* 19, no. 3 (September 2006): 337–356.

Falk, Raphael. "The Settlement of Israel as a Eugenic Enterprise." [In Hebrew.] *Alpayim* 23 (2002): 179–198.

Fisher, Netanel. "Who Is a Jew in Israel?" In *Who Is a Jew? Reflection on History, Religion, and Culture,* edited by Leonard J. Greenspon, 127–138. West Lafayette, IN: Purdue University Press, 2014.

Fisher, Netanel, and Avi Shilon. "Integrating Non-Jewish Immigrants and the Formation of Israel's Ethnic–Civic Nationhood: From Ben Gurion to the Present." *Middle Eastern Studies* 53, no. 2 (2017): 166–182.

Fleischhauer, Ingeborg. *Das Dritte Reich und die Deutschen in der Sowjetunion.* Stuttgart: Deutsche Verlags-Anstalt, 1983.

Foth, Rolf-Barnim. "Die Sowjetdeutschen im Spannungsfeld von Innen- und Außenpolitik der UdSSR und der Bundesrepublik Deutschland." Dissertation, Free University of Berlin, 1996.

Frank, Matthew. "Reconstructing the Nation-State: Population Transfer in Central and Eastern Europe, 1944–8." In Reinisch and White, *Disentanglement of Populations,* 27–47.

Fulbrook, Mary. "Germany for the Germans? Citizenship and Nationality in a Divided Nation." In *Citizenship, Nationality, and Migration in Europe,* edited by Mary Fulbrook and David Cesarani, 88–105. New York: Routledge, 1996.

Gatrell, Peter. *The Making of the Modern Refugee.* Oxford: Oxford University Press, 2013.

———. "Trajectories of Population Displacement in the Aftermaths of Two World Wars." In Reinisch and White, *Disentanglement of Populations,* 3–26.

Gelber, Yoav. "Difficulties and Changes in the Zionist Attitude to Aliyah." [In Hebrew.] In Hacohen, *Ingathering of Exiles,* 249–282.

Gerlach, Christian. *Kalkulierte Morde: Die deutsche Wirtschafts- und Vernichtungspolitik in Weißrußland 1941 bis 1944.* Hamburg: Hamburger Edition, 1999.

Gilbert, Martin. *In Ishmael's House: A History of Jews in Muslim Lands.* New Haven, CT: Yale University Press, 2010.

———. *Israel: A History.* London: Black Swan, 1998.

Glass, Hildrun. *Zerbrochene Nachbarschaft. Das deutsch-jüdische Verhältnis in Rumänien (1918–1938).* Munich: Oldenbourg, 1996.

Goeke, Pascal. "Yugoslav Labor Migrants in Western, Central, and Northern Europe since the End of World War II." In Bade et al., *Encyclopedia of European Migration,* 745–747.

Gold, Hugo. *Geschichte der Juden in der Bukovina.* 2 vols. Tel Aviv: Olamenu, 1958 (vol. 1) and 1962 (vol. 2).

Gold, Steven J. *The Israeli Diaspora.* London: Routledge, 2002.

Goldendach, Walter von, and Hans-Rüdiger Minow. *"Deutschtum erwache!" Aus dem Innenleben des staatlichen Pangermanismus.* Berlin: Dietz, 1994.

Gregor, Neil, Nils Roemer, and Mark Roseman, eds. *German History from the Margins.* Bloomington: Indiana University Press, 2006.

Grill, Tobias, ed. *Jews and Germans in Eastern Europe: Shared and Comparative Histories.* Berlin: De Gruyter Oldenbourg, 2018.

Gromova, Alina. *Generation "koscher light": Urbane Räume und Praxen junger russischsprachiger Juden in Berlin*. Bielefeld: transcript, 2013.

Grossmann, Atina. *Jews, Germans, and Allies: Close Encounters in Occupied Germany*, Princeton, NJ: Princeton University Press, 2007.

Gur-Gurevitz, Baruch. *Open Gates: The Inside Story of Mass Aliya from the Soviet Union and Its Successor States*. [In Hebrew.] Jerusalem: Jewish Agency for Israel, 1996.

Hacohen, Dvora. "Ben-Gurion and the Second World War: Plans for Mass Immigration to Palestine." *Studies in Contemporary Jewry: An Annual* 7 (1991): 247–268.

———. *Immigrants in Turmoil: Mass Immigration to Israel and Its Repercussions in the 1950s and After*. Syracuse, NY: Syracuse University Press, 2003.

———. "Immigration Policy in the First Decade of Statehood: The Attempts to Restrict Immigration and Their Outcome." [In Hebrew.] In Hacohen, *Ingathering of Exiles*, 285–316.

———, ed. *Ingathering of Exiles: Aliyah to the Land of Israel—Myth and Reality*. [In Hebrew.] Jerusalem: Zalman Shazar Center for Jewish History, 1998.

———. "The Law of Return as an Embodiment of the Link between Israel and the Jews of the Diaspora." *Journal of Israeli History* 19, no. 1 (Spring 1998): 61–89.

———. "Mass Aliyah or Selective Aliyah? The Discussions of the Government and the Jewish Agency in the 1950s." In *Proceedings of the Eleventh World Congress of Jewish Studies. Division B: The History of the Jewish People*. Vol. 2, *Modern Times*, 357–360. [In Hebrew.] Jerusalem: World Union of Jewish Studies, 1993.

———. "Olim and Aliyah." [In Hebrew.] In Zameret and Yablonka, *The Third Decade*, 303-318.

Hägel, Peter, and Pauline Peretz. "States and Transnational Actors: Who's Influencing Whom? A Case Study in Jewish Diaspora Politics during the Cold War." *European Journal of International Relations* 11, no. 4 (December 2005): 467–493.

Hakkarainen, Petri. *A State of Peace in Europe: West Germany and the CSCE, 1966–1975*. New York: Berghahn Books, 2011.

Halamish, Aviva. *A Dual Race against Time: Zionist Immigration Policy in the 1930s*. [In Hebrew.] Jerusalem: Yad Ben-Zvi, 2006.

Haug, Sonja. "Jüdische Zuwanderer in Deutschland: Ein Überblick über den Stand der Forschung." Working Papers 3/2005. Bundesamt für Migration und Flüchtlinge, Nuremberg. http://www.bamf.de/SharedDocs/Anlagen/DE/Publikationen/WorkingPapers/wp03-juedische-zuwanderer.pdf?__blob=publicationFile.

Haupt, Heinz-Gerhard, and Dieter Langewiesche, eds. *Nation und Religion in der deutschen Geschichte*. Frankfurt a.M.: Campus, 2001.

Heinemann, Isabel. *"Rasse, Siedlung, deutsches Blut". Das Rasse- und Siedlungshauptamt der SS und die rassenpolitische Neuordnung Europas*. Göttingen, Germany: Wallstein, 2003.

Helman, Anat. *Becoming Israeli: National Ideals and Everyday Life in the 1950s.* Waltham, MA: Brandeis University Press, 2014.

Hensen, Jürgen. "Zur Geschichte der Aussiedler- und Spätaussiedleraufnahme." In *Aussiedler- und Minderheitenpolitik in Deutschland: Bilanz und Perspektiven,* edited by Christoph Bergner and Matthias Weber, 47–61. Munich: Oldenbourg, 2009.

Herbert, Ulrich. *A History of Foreign Labor in Germany, 1880–1980.* Ann Arbor: University of Michigan Press, 1990.

Hilberg, Raul. *The Destruction of the European Jews.* Chicago: Quadrangle Books, 1961.

Hirsch, Francine. *Empire of Nations: Ethnographic Knowledge and the Making of the Soviet Union.* Ithaca, NY: Cornell University Press, 2005.

Hirschler, Nicole. "Neue 'alte' Heimat DDR. 'Repatriierung' und Familienzusammenführung von Personen deutscher Herkunft aus der UdSSR in die DDR: Konzeptionen und ihre Umsetzung im innen- und außenpolitischen Spannungsfeld." Dissertation, University of Osnabrück, 2002.

Hirschon, Renée, ed. *Crossing the Aegean: An Appraisal of the 1923 Compulsory Population Exchange between Greece and Turkey.* New York: Berghahn Books, 2006.

Hoerder, Dirk, Jan Lucassen, and Leo Lucassen. "Terminologies and Concepts of Migration Research." In Bade et al., *Encyclopedia of European Migration and Minorities,* xxv–xxxix.

Hoffmann, Werner. *Gesetz zur Regelung von Fragen der Staatsangehörigkeit vom 22. Februar 1955.* Erläutert von Dr. jur. Werner Hoffmann. Stuttgart: Kohlhammer, 1955.

———. *Kurzer Grundriss des deutschen Staatsangehörigkeitsrechts.* Frankfurt a.M.: Metzner, 1959.

Hogwood, Patricia. "Citizenship Controversies in Germany: The Twin Legacy of *Völkisch* Nationalism and the *Alleinvertretungsanspruch.*" *German Politics* 9, no. 3 (December 2000): 125–144.

HOK—50 Jahre Kirchlicher Suchdienst: die Heimatortskarteien der kirchlichen Wohlfahrtsverbände. Munich: Kirchlicher Suchdienst, 1996.

Holz, Klaus. *Nationaler Antisemitismus: Wissenssoziologie einer Weltanschauung.* Hamburg: Hamburger Edition, 2001.

Hupka, Herbert. "Die Aussiedler—eine geistige Herausforderung." In Ludwig, *Als Deutsche unter Deutschen leben,* 58–60.

Iglicka, Krystyna. "Are They Fellow Countrymen or Not? The Migration of Ethnic Poles from Kazakhstan to Poland." *International Migration Review* 32, no. 4 (Winter 1998): 995–1014.

Ilarionova, T. S. "Zhelaniia i vozmozhnosti: problema vyezda nemtsev iz SSSR v kontekste poslevoennykh sovetsko-zapadnogermanskikh otnoshenii (1955–1964)." In *Migratsionnye protsessy sredi rossiiskikh nemtsev: istoricheskii aspekt.*

Materialy mezhdunarodnoi nauchnoi konferentsii, edited by Arkadij German and Igor' Pleve, 367–384. Moscow: Gotika, 1998.

Immig, Nicole. *Zwischen Partizipation und Emigration: Muslime in Griechenland 1878–1897*. Wiesbaden, Germany: Harrasowitz, 2015.

Ioanid, Radu. *The Ransom of the Jews: The Story of the Extraordinary Secret Bargain between Romania and Israel*. Chicago: Dee, 2005.

Jacobson, Gaynor I. "Soviet Jewry: Perspectives on the 'Dropout' Issue." *Journal of Jewish Communal Service* 55, no. 1 (September 1978): 83–89.

Janjetovic, Zoran. *Between Hitler and Tito: The Disappearance of the Vojvodina Germans*. 2nd ed. Belgrade: Privately printed, 2005.

Jones, Clive. *Soviet-Jewish Aliyah, 1989–1992: Impact and Implications for Israel and the Middle East*. London: Cass, 1996.

Joppke, Christian. *Selecting by Origin: Ethnic Migration in the Liberal State*. Cambridge, MA: Harvard University Press, 2005.

Joppke, Christian, and Zeev Rosenhek. "Contesting Ethnic Immigration: Germany and Israel Compared." *Archives européennes de sociologie/European Journal of Sociology* 43, no. 3 (December 2002): 301–335.

Judson, Pieter M. "Nationalism in the Era of the Nation State, 1870–1945." In *The Oxford Handbook of Modern German History*, edited by Helmut Walser Smith, 499–526. Oxford: Oxford University Press, 2011.

———. "When Is a Diaspora Not a Diaspora? Rethinking Nation-Centered Narratives about Germans in Habsburg East Central Europe." In O'Donnell et al., *The Heimat Abroad*, 219–247.

Kaelble, Hartmut. "Die interdisziplinären Debatten über Vergleich und Transfer." In *Vergleich und Transfer: Komparatistik in den Sozial-, Geschichts- und Kulturwissenschaften*, edited by Hartmut Kaelble and Jürgen Schriewer, 469–495. Frankfurt a.M.: Campus, 2003.

Kann, Robert A. *Das Nationalitätenproblem der Habsburgermonarchie*. Vol. 2, *Ideen und Pläne zur Reichsreform*. Graz, Austria: Böhlau, 1964.

Kaplan, Eran, and Derek J. Penslar, eds. *The Origins of Israel, 1882–1948: A Documentary History*. Madison: University of Wisconsin Press, 2011.

Karklins, Rasma. *Ethnic Relations in the Soviet Union: The Perspective from Below*. Boston: Allen & Unwin, 1986.

Karsh, Ephraim. *Palestine Betrayed*. New Haven, CT: Yale University Press, 2010.

Kauders, Anthony D. *Unmögliche Heimat: eine deutsch-jüdische Geschichte der Bundesrepublik*. Munich: Deutsche Verlags-Anstalt, 2007.

Kedmi, Yakov (Yasha). *Hopeless Wars*. [In Hebrew.] Tel Aviv: Matar, 2011.

Khalidi, Walid. "Plan Dalet: The Zionist Master Plan for the Conquest of Palestine." *Middle East Forum* 37, no. 9 (November 1961): 22–28.

Khazzoom, Aziza. "Did the Israeli State Engineer Segregation? On the Placement of Jewish Immigrants in Development Towns in the 1950s." *Social Forces* 84, no. 1 (September 2005): 115–134.

———. "The Great Chain of Orientalism: Jewish Identity, Stigma Management, and Ethnic Exclusion in Israel." *American Sociological Review* 68, no. 4 (August 2003): 481–510.

Klekowski von Koppenfels, Amanda. "The Decline of Privilege: The Legal Background to the Migration of Ethnic Germans." In Rock and Wolff, *Coming Home to Germany*, 102–118.

Klötzel, Lydia. *Die Russlanddeutschen zwischen Autonomie und Auswanderung: die Geschicke einer nationalen Minderheit vor dem Hintergrund des wechselhaften deutsch-sowjetischen/russischen Verhältnisses*. Münster, Germany: LIT, 1999.

Klusmeyer, Douglas B., and Demetrios G. Papademetriou. *Immigration Policy in the Federal Republic of Germany: Negotiating Membership and Remaking the Nation*. New York: Berghahn Books, 2009.

Kochanowski, Jerzy, and Maike Sach, eds. *Die "Volksdeutschen" in Polen, Frankreich, Ungarn und der Tschechoslowakei. Mythos und Realität*. Osnabrück, Germany: fibre, 2006.

Kocka, Jürgen, and Heinz-Gerhard Haupt. "Comparison and Beyond: Traditions, Scope, and Perspectives of Comparative History." In *Comparative and Transnational History: Central European Approaches and New Perspectives*, edited by Jürgen Kocka and Heinz-Gerhard Haupt, 1–30. New York: Berghahn Books, 2009.

Koenigswald, Harald von. "Das dritte Problem." In *Das dritte Problem. Betrachtungen zur Aufnahme der Spätaussiedler aus dem Osten*, 2nd ed., edited by Arbeits- und Sozialminister des Landes Nordrhein-Westfalen, 5–15. Troisdorf, Germany: Der Wegweiser, 1958.

Kraines, Oscar. *The Impossible Dilemma: Who Is a Jew in the State of Israel?* New York: Bloch, 1976.

Krajczyk, Franz. "Ankunft in Friedland: Erste Kontakte im Bundesgebiet." In Ludwig, *Als Deutsche unter Deutschen leben*, 29–32.

Kranz, Dani. "Forget Israel—The Future Is in Berlin! Local Jews, Russian Immigrants, and Israeli Jews in Berlin and across Germany." *Shofar: An Interdisciplinary Journal of Jewish Studies* 34, no. 4 (Summer 2016): 5–28.

Krauss, Marita. "Jewish Remigration: An Overview of an Emerging Discipline." *Leo Baeck Institute Year Book* 49, no. 1 (January 2004): 107–119.

Kudlich, Jörg. "In der alten Heimat ohne Freiheit: Materielle Motive spielen nur eine untergeordnete Rolle." In Ludwig, *Als Deutsche unter Deutschen leben*, 35–40.

Kühnrich, Heinz, and Franz-Karl Hitze. *Deutsche bei Titos Partisanen 1941–1945: Kriegsschicksale auf dem Balkan in Augenzeugenberichten und Dokumenten*. Schkeuditz, Germany: GNN, 1997.

Landau, Asher Felix, ed. *Selected Judgments of the Supreme Court of Israel*. Special Volume. Jerusalem: Ministry of Justice, 1971.

Laqueur, Walter. *A History of Zionism*. New York: Schocken Books, 2003.

Laskier, Michael. *Israel and Jewish Immigration from North Africa, 1948–1970*. [In Hebrew.] Sdeh Boker, Israel: Ben-Gurion Institute, 2006.

———. *North African Jewry in the Twentieth Century: The Jews of Morocco, Tunisia, and Algeria*. New York: New York University Press, 1994.

Lazin, Fred A. "Refugee Resettlement and 'Freedom of Choice': The Case of Soviet Jewry." Backgrounder. Washington, DC: Center for Immigration Studies, June 2005. http://www.cis.org/sites/cis.org/files/articles/2005/back705.pdf.

———. *The Struggle for Soviet Jewry in American Politics: Israel versus the American Jewish Establishment*. Lanham, MD: Lexington Books, 2005.

Leibler, Anat, and Daniel Breslau. "The Uncounted: Citizenship and Exclusion in the Israeli Census of 1948." *Ethnic and Racial Studies* 28, no. 5 (September 2005): 880–902.

Lenhard, Philipp. *Volk oder Religion? Die Entstehung moderner jüdischer Ethnizität in Frankreich und Deutschland 1782–1848*. Göttingen, Germany: Vandenhoeck & Ruprecht, 2014.

Levy, Daniel. "Introduction: Changing Configurations of German and Israeli Immigration Regimes—A Comparative Perspective." In Levy and Weiss, *Challenging Ethnic Citizenship*, 1–12.

———. "Remembering the Nation: Ethnic Germans and the Transformation of National Identity in the Federal Republic of Germany." PhD dissertation, Columbia University, 1999.

Levy, Daniel, and Yfaat Weiss, eds. *Challenging Ethnic Citizenship: German and Israeli Perspectives on Immigration*. New York: Berghahn Books, 2002.

Liebich, André, and Rainer Bauböck, eds. "Is There (Still) an East-West Divide in the Conception of Citizenship in Europe?" RSCAS Working Paper 2010/19. Florence: European University Institute. http://hdl.handle.net/1814/13587.

Liesner, Ernst. *Aussiedler: Die Voraussetzungen für die Anerkennung als Vertriebener*. Herford, Germany: Maximilian-Verlag, 1988.

Lissak, Moshe. "The Demographic-Social Revolution in Israel in the 1950s: The Absorption of the Great Aliyah." *Journal of Israel History* 22, no. 2 (Autumn 2003): 1–31.

Litvin, Baruch, and Sidney B. Hoenig, eds. *Jewish Identity: Modern Responsa and Opinions on the Registration of Children of Mixed Marriages*. New York: Feldheim, 1965.

Lohr, Eric. *Nationalizing the Russian Empire: The Campaign against Enemy Aliens during World War I*. Cambridge, MA: Harvard University Press, 2003.

Lucassen, Leo. "A Brave New World: The Left, Social Engineering, and Eugenics in Twentieth-Century Europe." *International Review of Social History* 55, no. 2 (August 2010): 265–296.

Ludwig, Egon, ed. *Als Deutsche unter Deutschen leben: Eingliederung der Aussiedler*. Bonn: Bundeszentrale für politische Bildung, 1978.

Lumans, Valdis O. *Himmler's Auxiliaries: The Volksdeutsche Mittelstelle and the German National Minorities of Europe, 1933–1945*. Chapel Hill: University of North Carolina Press, 1993.

Lustick, Ian S. "Israel as a Non-Arab State: The Political Implications of Mass Immigration of Non-Jews." *Middle East Journal* 53, no. 3 (Summer 1999): 417–433.

Maihofer, Werner. "Starthilfe leisten!" In Ludwig, *Als Deutsche unter Deutschen leben*, 11.

Malka, Haim. "Selection in Immigration of Moroccan Jews in 1948–1956." [In Hebrew.] MA thesis, University of Haifa, 1997.

———. *The Selection: Selection and Discrimination in the Immigration and Absorption of Jews from Morocco and North Africa in the Years 1948–1956*. [In Hebrew.] Privately printed, 1998.

Manley, Rebecca. *To the Tashkent Station: Evacuation and Survival in the Soviet Union at War*. Ithaca, NY: Cornell University Press, 2009.

Manz, Stefan. *Constructing a German Diaspora: The "Greater German Empire", 1871–1914*. New York: Routledge, 2014.

Mark, Rudolf. *Die Völker der Sowjetunion: ein Lexikon*. Opladen, Germany: Westdeutscher Verlag, 1989.

Martin, Terry. *The Affirmative Action Empire: Nations and Nationalism in the Soviet Union, 1923–1939*. Ithaca, NY: Cornell University Press, 2001.

Marzano, Arturo. "Relief and Rehabilitation of Jewish DPs after the Shoah: The *Hachsharot* in Italy (1945–48)." *Journal of Modern Jewish Studies* 18 (January 2019). https://doi.org/10.1080/14725886.2018.1559555.

Mattes, Monika. *"Gastarbeiterinnen" in der Bundesrepublik: Anwerbepolitik, Migration und Geschlecht in den 50er bis 70er Jahren*. Frankfurt a.M.: Campus, 2005.

Mazower, Mark. "Minorities and the League of Nations in Interwar Europe." *Daedalus* 126, no. 2 (Spring 1997): 47–63.

Mendel, Meron. "The Policy for the Past in West Germany and Israel: The Case of Jewish Remigration." *Leo Baeck Institute Year Book* 49, no. 1 (January 2004): 121–136.

Messerschmidt, Rolf. "Die Flüchtlingsfrage als Verwaltungsproblem im Nachkriegsdeutschland. Das Phänomen der klientenorientierten Flüchtlingssonderverwaltung in Ost und West." In *Vertriebene in Deutschland: Interdisziplinäre Ergebnisse und Forschungsperspektiven*, edited by Dierk Hoffmann, Marita Krauss, and Michael Schwartz, 167–186. Munich: Oldenbourg, 2000.

Michaeli, Ethan. "Another Exodus: The Hebrew Israelites from Chicago to Dimona." In *Black Zion: African American Religious Encounters with Judaism*, edited by Yvonne Patricia Chireau and Nathaniel Deutsch, 73–87. New York: Oxford University Press, 2000.

Mor, Sagit. "'Tell My Sister to Come and Get Me Out of Here'—A Reading of Ableism and Orientalism in Israel's Immigration Policy (the First Decade)." *Disability Studies Quarterly* 27, no. 4 (2007). http://dsq-sds.org/article/view/43/43.

Morris, Benny. *The Birth of the Palestinian Refugee Problem, 1947–1949*. Cambridge: Cambridge University Press, 1987.

———. *The Birth of the Palestinian Refugee Problem Revisited*. Cambridge: Cambridge University Press, 2004.

———. *1948: A History of the First Arab-Israeli War*. New Haven, CT: Yale University Press, 2008.

Moyn, Samuel. *The Last Utopia: Human Rights in History*. Cambridge, MA: Belknap Press of Harvard University Press, 2012.

Mukhina, Irina. *The Germans of the Soviet Union*. London: Routledge, 2007.

Müller, Filip. *Sonderbehandlung. Drei Jahre in den Krematorien und Gaskammern von Auschwitz*. Munich: Steinhausen, 1979.

Münz, Rainer, and Rainer Ohliger. "Diasporas and Ethnic Migrants in Twentieth-Century Europe: A Comparative Perspective." In *Diasporas and Ethnic Migrants: Germany, Israel, and the Post-Soviet Successor States in Comparative Perspective*, edited by Rainer Münz and Rainer Ohliger, 2–17. London: Cass, 2003.

———. "Long Distance Citizens: Ethnic Germans and Their Immigration to Germany." In *Paths to Inclusion: The Integration of Migrants in the United States and Germany*, edited by Peter H. Schuck and Rainer Münz, 155–210. New York: Berghahn Books, 1998.

Nachum, Iris. "Reconstructing Life after the Holocaust: The Lastenausgleichsgesetz and the Jewish Struggle for Compensation." *Leo Baeck Institute Year Book* 58, no. 1 (January 2013): 53–67.

Naimark, Norman. *Fires of Hatred: Ethnic Cleansing in Twentieth-Century Europe*. Cambridge, MA: Harvard University Press, 2001.

Nathans, Eli. *The Politics of Citizenship in Germany: Ethnicity, Utility and Nationalism*. Oxford: Berg, 2004.

O'Donnell, Krista, Renate Bridenthal, and Nancy Reagin, eds. *The Heimat Abroad: The Boundaries of Germanness*. Ann Arbor: University of Michigan Press, 2005.

Oltmer, Jochen. "Einführung: Europäische Migrationsverhältnisse und Migrationsregime in der Neuzeit." *Geschichte und Gesellschaft* 35, no. 1 (January–March 2009): 5–27.

———. "Einleitung: Staat im Prozess der Aushandlung von Migration." In *Handbuch Staat und Migration in Deutschland seit dem 17. Jahrhundert*, edited by Jochen Oltmer, 1–42. Berlin: De Gruyter Oldenbourg, 2015.

———. *Migration und Politik in der Weimarer Republik*. Göttingen, Germany: Vandenhoeck & Ruprecht, 2005.

Oltmer, Jochen, Axel Kreienbrink, and Carlos Sanz Díaz, eds. *Das "Gastarbeiter"-System. Arbeitsmigration und ihre Folgen in der Bundesrepublik Deutschland und Westeuropa*. Munich: Oldenbourg, 2012.

Otto, Karl A. "Aussiedler und Aussiedler-Politik im Spannungsfeld von Menschenrechten und Kaltem Krieg: Historische, politisch-moralische und rechtliche Aspekte der Aussiedler-Politik." In *Westwärts-Heimwärts?—Aussiedlerpolitik zwischen 'Deutschtümelei' und 'Verfassungsauftrag'*, edited by Karl A. Otto, 11–68. Bielefeld, Germany: AJZ, 1990.

Oz-Salzberger, Fania, and Eli M. Salzberger. "The Hidden German Sources of the Israel Supreme Court." *Tel Aviv University Studies in Law* 15 (2000): 79–121.

Pallaske, Christoph. *Migrationen aus Polen in die Bundesrepublik Deutschland in den 1980er und 1990er Jahren: Migrationsverläufe und Eingliederungsprozesse in sozialgeschichtlicher Perspektive*. Münster, Germany: Waxmann, 2002.

Panagiotidis, Jannis. "Kein fairer Tausch. Zur Bedeutung der Reform der Aussiedlerpolitik im Kontext des Asylkompromisses." In *20 Jahre Asylkompromiss. Bilanz und Perspektiven*, edited by Stefan Luft and Peter Schimany, 105–126. Bielefeld, Germany: transcript, 2014.

———. "The Oberkreisdirektor Decides Who Is a German: Jewish Immigration, German Bureaucracy, and the Negotiation of National Belonging, 1953–1990." *Geschichte und Gesellschaft* 38, no. 3 (July–September 2012): 503–533.

———. "A Policy for the Future: German-Jewish Remigrants, Their Children, and the Politics of Israeli Nation-Building." *Leo Baeck Institute Year Book* 60, no. 1 (January 2015): 191–206.

———. "Utilitaristische und ethnodemographische Überlegungen zur Migration ethnischer Deutscher aus Polen in beide deutsche Staaten (1949–1989)." In *Demographischer Wandel in Polen, Deutschland und Europa. Geschichte, Verflechtungen und neue Forschungsperspektiven*, edited by Tim Buchen, Dagmar Jajeśnikak-Quast, Mark Keck-Szajbel, and Katharina K. Kowalski, 19–38. Berlin: epubli, 2014.

———. "What Is the Germans' Fatherland? The GDR and the Resettlement of Ethnic Germans from Socialist Countries (1949–1989)." *East European Politics and Societies and Cultures* 29, no. 1 (February 2015): 120–146.

———. "Zwischen Wahlheimat und Urheimat: Multiple russlanddeutsche Heimatdiskurse nach dem Zweiten Weltkrieg." *Spiegelungen* 12, no. 2 (2017): 11–22.

Pappé, Ilan. *The Ethnic Cleansing of Palestine*. Oxford: Oneworld, 2006.

Parlamentarischer Rat: Verhandlungen des Hauptausschusses. Bonn, 1948/1949.

Patt, Avinoam J. "Stateless Citizens of Israel: Jewish Displaced Persons and Zionism in Post-War Germany." In Reinisch and White, *Disentanglement of Populations*, 162–182.

———. *Finding Home and Homeland: Jewish Youth and Zionism in the Aftermath of the Holocaust*. Detroit: Wayne State University Press, 2009.

Peach, Ceri. "Postwar Migration to Europe: Reflux, Influx, Refuge." *Social Science Quarterly* 78, no. 2 (June 1997): 269–283.

Pfundtner, Raimund. *Spätaussiedler—Tragödie: Ursachen, Folgen, Perspektiven*. Hannover: Fackelträger, 1979.

Picard, Avi. "The Beginning of Selective Immigration in the 1950s." [In Hebrew.] *Iyunim Bitkumat Yisrael* 9 (1999): 338–394.

———. *Cut to Measure: Israel's Policies Regarding the Aliyah of North African Jews, 1951–1956*. [In Hebrew.] Kiryat Sdeh Boker, Israel: Ben-Gurion Research Institute for the Study of Israel and Zionism, 2013.

———. "Immigration, Health, and Social Control: Medical Aspects of the Policy Governing Aliyah from Morocco and Tunisia, 1951–54." *Journal of Israeli History* 22, no. 2 (Autumn 2003): 32–60.

———. "The Reluctant Soldiers of Israel's Settlement Project: The Ship to Village Plan in the Mid-1950s." *Middle Eastern Studies* 49, no. 1 (January 2013): 29–46.

Polonsky, Antony. *The Jews in Poland and Russia*. Vol. 3, *1914–2008*. Oxford: Littman Library of Jewish Civilization, 2012.

Portmann, Michael. *Die kommunistische Revolution in der Vojvodina 1944–1952: Politik, Gesellschaft, Wirtschaft, Kultur*. Vienna: Verlag der Österreichischen Akademie der Wissenschaften, 2008.

Presner, Todd Samuel. *Muscular Judaism: The Jewish Body and the Politics of Regeneration*. London: Routledge, 2007.

Rabinovich, Itamar, and Jehuda Reinharz, eds. *Israel in the Middle East: Documents and Readings on Society, Politics, and Foreign Relations, Pre-1948 to the Present*. Waltham, MA: Brandeis University Press, 2008.

Rahden, Till van. "Germans of the Jewish *Stamm*: Visions of Community between Nationalism and Particularism, 1850 to 1933." In Gregor et al., *German History from the Margins*, 27–46.

Rass, Christoph, and Frank Wolff. "What Is in a Migration Regime? Genealogical Approach and Methodological Proposal." In *Was ist ein Migrationsregime? What Is a Migration Regime?* edited by Andreas Pott, Christoph Rass, and Frank Wolff, 19–64. Wiesbaden, Germany: Springer, 2018.

Rauschenberger, Katharina, and Werner Renz, eds. *Henry Ormond—Anwalt der Opfer. Plädoyers in NS-Prozessen*. Frankfurt a.M.: Campus, 2015.

Reichhardt, Sven. "Praxeologische Geschichtswissenschaft. Eine Diskussionsanregung." *Sozial.Geschichte* 22, no. 3 (2007): 43–65.

Reichling, Gerhard. *Die deutschen Vertriebenen in Zahlen*. Teil 1, *Umsiedler, Verschleppte, Vertriebene, Aussiedler, 1940–1985*. Bonn: Kulturstiftung der Deutschen Vertriebenen, 1986.

Reich-Ranicki, Marcel. *The Author of Himself: The Life of Marcel Reich-Ranicki*. London: Weidenfeld & Nicolson, 2001.

Reinisch, Jessica. "Introduction." In Reinisch and White, *Disentanglement of Populations*, xiv–xxiv.

Reinisch, Jessica, and Elizabeth White, eds. *The Disentanglement of Populations: Migration, Expulsion and Displacement in Post-War Europe, 1944–9*. Basingstoke, UK: Palgrave Macmillan, 2011.

Renan, Ernest. "What Is a Nation?" In *Becoming National: A Reader,* edited by Geoff Eley and Ronald Grigor Suny, 42–55. New York: Oxford University Press, 1996.

Richmond, Nancy Caren. "Israel's Law of Return: Analysis of Its Evolution and Present Application." *Dickinson Journal of International Law* 12 (1993–1994): 95–133.

Riecken, Andrea. *Migration und Gesundheitspolitik. Flüchtlinge und Vertriebene in Niedersachsen, 1945–1953.* Göttingen, Germany: V&R Unipress, 2006.

Robinson, Shira. *Citizen Strangers: Palestinians and the Birth of Israel's Liberal Settler State.* Stanford, CA: Stanford University Press, 2013.

Rock, David, and Stefan Wolff, eds. *Coming Home to Germany? The Integration of Ethnic Germans from Central and Eastern Europe in the Federal Republic.* New York: Berghahn Books, 2002.

Rodriguez, Julia. "Inoculating against Barbarism? State Medicine and Immigrant Policy in Turn-of-the-Century Argentina." *Science in Context* 19, no. 3 (September 2006): 357–380.

Roesler, Karsten. *Russlanddeutsche Identitäten zwischen Herkunft und Ankunft. Eine Studie zur Förderungs- und Integrationspolitik des Bundes.* Frankfurt a.M.: Peter Lang, 2003.

Rogge, Heinrich. "Eingliederung und Vertreibung im Spiegel des Rechts." In *Die Vertriebenen in Westdeutschland. Ihre Eingliederung und ihr Einfluß auf Gesellschaft, Wirtschaft, Politik und Geistesleben,* Vol. 1, edited by Eugen Lemberg and Friedrich Edding, 174–245. Kiel, Germany: Hirt, 1959.

Ro'i, Yaacov, ed. *The Jewish Movement in the Soviet Union.* Baltimore: Woodrow Wilson Center Press, 2012.

———. "Strategy and Tactics." In Ro'i, *Jewish Movement,* 46–95.

———. "The Surfacing of the Jewish Movement." In Ro'i, *Jewish Movement,* 15–45.

Ro'i, Yaacov, and Joshua Rubenstein. "Human Rights and National Rights: The Interaction of the Jewish Movement with Other Dissident Groups." In Ro'i, *Jewish Movement,* 198–224.

Rozin, Orit. *A Home for All Jews: Citizenship, Rights, and National Identity in the New Israeli State.* Waltham, MA: Brandeis University Press, 2016.

———. "Negotiating the Right to Exit the Country in 1950s Israel: Voice, Loyalty, and Citizenship." *Journal of Israeli History* 30, no. 1 (March 2011): 1–22.

Runge, Irene. "Einwanderung nach der Halacha?" *Blätter für deutsche und internationale Politik* no. 9 (September 2001): 1031–1034.

Ruppin, Arthur. "The Selection of the Fittest." In Kaplan and Penslar, *Origins of Israel,* 94–102.

Saal, Yuliya von. *KSZE-Prozess und Perestroika in der Sowjetunion: Demokratisierung, Werteumbruch und Auflösung 1985–1991.* Munich: Oldenbourg, 2014.

Sachar, Howard. *A History of Israel: From the Rise of Zionism to Our Time*. 3rd ed. New York: Knopf, 2010.

Salzborn, Samuel. *Ethnisierung der Politik: Theorie und Geschichte des Volksgruppenrechts in Europa*. Frankfurt a.M.: Campus, 2005.

Samaddar, Ranabir. "Introduction: The Infamous Event." In *Partitions: Reshaping States and Minds*, edited by Stefano Bianchini, Sanjay Chaturvedi, Rada Iveković, and Ranabir Sammadar, 1–10. London: Cass, 2005.

Sammartino, Annemarie. "After Brubaker: Citizenship in Modern Germany, 1848 to Today." *German History* 27, no. 4 (October 2009): 583–599.

———. *The Impossible Border: Germany and the East, 1914–1922*. Ithaca, NY: Cornell University Press, 2010.

Sapir, Gideon. "How Should a Court Deal with a Primary Question That the Legislature Seeks to Avoid? The Israeli Controversy over Who Is a Jew as an Illustration." bepress Legal Series Working Paper 988. February 22, 2006. http://law.bepress.com/expresso/eps/988.

Schechtman, Joseph B. *On Wings of Eagles: The Plight, Exodus, and Homecoming of Oriental Jewry*. New York: Yoseloff, 1961.

Schießl, Sascha. "Im Niemandsland. Die 'Operation Link' und der Beginn der Aussiedleraufnahme in der Bundesrepublik Deutschland." *Jahrbuch des Bundesinstituts für Kultur und Geschichte der Deutschen im östlichen Europa* 24 (2016): 309–334.

———. *"Das Tor zur Freiheit". Kriegsfolgen, Erinnerungspolitik und humanitärer Anspruch im Lager Friedland (1945–1970)*. Göttingen, Germany: Wallstein, 2016.

Schmaltz, Eric J. "Reform, 'Rebirth,' and Regret: The Early Autonomy Movement of Ethnic Germans in the USSR, 1955–1989." PhD dissertation, University of Nebraska, 2002.

Schnurr, Joseph. "Die Aussiedler aus dem sowjetischen Bereich." In *Die Aussiedler in der Bundesrepublik Deutschland, Ergebnisbericht*. Vol. 1, *Herkunft, Ausreise, Aufnahme*, edited by Wilhelm Arnold, 57–101. Vienna: Braumüller, 1980.

Schulin, Ernst. "Doppel-Nationalität? Die Integration der Juden in die deutsche Kulturnation und die neue Konstruktion der jüdischen Geschichte." In Alter et al., *Konstruktion der Nation*, 243–259.

Schulte, Christoph, ed. *Deutschtum und Judentum. Ein Disput unter Juden aus Deutschland*. Stuttgart: Reclam, 1992.

Schweid, Eliezer. "The Rejection of the Diaspora in Zionist Thought: Two Approaches." *Studies in Zionism* 5, no. 1 (1984): 43–70.

Sebaux, Gwénola. *(Post)colonisation—(Post)migration: ces Allemands entre Allemagne et Roumanie. Carrefours d'empires*. Paris: Le Manuscrit, 2015.

Seeler, Hans-Joachim. *Die Staatsangehörigkeit der Volksdeutschen*. Frankfurt a.M.: Metzner, 1960.

Segev, Tom. *1949: The First Israelis*. New York: Henry Holt, 1998.

Senders, Stefan, "*Jus Sanguinis* or *Jus Mimesis*? Rethinking 'Ethnic German' Repatriation." In Rock and Wolff, *Coming Home to Germany*, 87–101.

Service, Hugo. *Germans to Poles: Communism, Nationalism and Ethnic Cleansing after the Second World War*. Cambridge: Cambridge University Press, 2013.

———. "Upper Silesia in the Age of the Ethnically Homogeneous State." In *Creating Nationality in Central Europe, 1880–1950: Modernity, Violence and (Be)longing in Upper Silesia*, edited by James Bjork, Tomasz Kamusella, Tim Wilson, and Anna Novikov, 185–209. London: Routledge, 2016.

Sha'ari, David. "Die jüdische Gemeinde von Czernowitz." In *Czernowitz: Die Geschichte einer ungewöhnlichen Stadt*, edited by Harald Heppner, 103–127. Cologne: Böhlau, 2000.

Shepard, Todd. *The Invention of Decolonization: The Algerian War and the Remaking of France*. Ithaca, NY: Cornell University Press, 2006.

Shephard, Ben. *The Long Road Home: The Aftermath of the Second World War*. New York: Knopf, 2010.

Shilo, Margalit. "The Immigration Policy of the Zionist Institutions 1882–1914." *Middle Eastern Studies* 30, no. 3 (July 1994): 597–617.

———. "Mass Immigration or Selective Immigration? The Zionist Policy (1882–1914)." [In Hebrew.] In Hacohen, *Ingathering of Exiles*, 107–130.

Shonick, Kaja. "Politics, Culture, and Economics: Reassessing the West German Guest Worker Agreement with Yugoslavia." *Journal of Contemporary History* 44, no. 4 (October 2009): 719–736.

Silagi, Michael. *Vertreibung und Staatsangehörigkeit*. Bonn: Kulturstiftung der deutschen Vertriebenen, 1999.

Silber, Marcos. "Foreigners or Co-nationals? Israel, Poland, and Polish Jewry (1948–1967)." *Journal of Israeli History* 29, no. 2 (September 2010): 213–232.

Sinanoglou, Penny. "British Plans for the Partition of Palestine, 1929–1938." *Historical Journal* 52, no. 1 (March 2009): 131–152.

Smith, Andrea L., ed. *Europe's Invisible Migrants*. Amsterdam: Amsterdam University Press, 2003.

Smith, Jeremy. *Red Nations: The Nationalities Experience in and after the USSR*. Cambridge: Cambridge University Press, 2013.

Snyder, Sarah B. *Human Rights Activism and the End of the Cold War: A Transnational History of the Helsinki Network*. Cambridge: Cambridge University Press, 2011.

Sobel, Zvi. *Migrants from the Promised Land*. New Brunswick, NJ: Transaction Books, 1986.

State of Israel, the Supreme Court. *Judgment: High Court Application of Oswald Rufeisen v. The Minister of the Interior*. Jerusalem: Ministry of Justice, 1963.

Steinert, Johannes-Dieter. *Migration und Politik: Westdeutschland, Europa, Übersee, 1945–1961*. Osnabrück, Germany: Secolo, 1995.

Steinhart, Eric C. *The Holocaust and the Germanization of Ukraine*. Cambridge: Cambridge University Press, 2015.

Sternberg, Jan-Philipp. *Auswanderungsland Bundesrepublik: Denkmuster und Debatten in Politik und Medien 1945–2010*. Paderborn, Germany: Schöningh, 2012.

Stjepanovic, Dejan. "Claimed Co-ethnics and Kin-State Citizenship in Southeastern Europe." *Ethnopolitics: Formerly Global Review of Ethnopolitics* 14, no. 2 (2015): 140–158.

Stola, Dariusz. *Kraj bez wyjścia? Migracje z Polski 1949–1989*. Warsaw: Instytut Pamięci Narodowej, 2010.

———. "Opening a Non-exit State: The Passport Policy of Communist Poland, 1949–1980." *East European Politics and Societies and Cultures* 29, no. 1 (February 2015): 96–119.

Straßmann, Walter, Josef Rösler, and Helmut Krüzner. *Bundesvertriebenengesetz. Gesetz über die Angelegenheiten der Vertriebenen und Flüchtlinge. Kommentar*. 2nd ed. Munich: Beck, 1958.

Strauss, Herbert. "Jewish Emigration from Germany: Nazi Policies and Jewish Responses." *Leo Baeck Institute Yearbook* 25, no. 1 (January 1980): 313–361; 26, no. 1 (January 1981): 343–409.

Strippel, Andreas. *NS-Volkstumspolitik und die Neuordnung Europas. Rassenpolitische Selektion der Einwandererzentralstelle des Chefs der Sicherheitspolizei und des SD (1939–1945)*. Paderborn, Germany: Schöningh, 2011.

Swanson, John C. *Tangible Belonging: Negotiating Germanness in Twentieth-Century Hungary*. Pittsburgh: University of Pittsburgh Press, 2017.

Swarthout, Donna. "Revoked and Restored: Facts and Figures." In *A Place They Called Home: Reclaiming Citizenship. Stories of a New Jewish Return to Germany*, edited by Donna Swarthout, 193–203. Berlin: Berlinica, 2019.

Tec, Nechama. *In the Lion's Den: The Life of Oswald Rufeisen*. New York: Oxford University Press, 1990.

Ther, Philipp. *Deutsche und polnische Vertriebene: Gesellschaft und Vertriebenenpolitik in der SBZ/DDR und in Polen 1945–1956*. Göttingen, Germany: Vandenhoeck & Ruprecht, 1997.

———. *Die Dunkle Seite der Nationalstaaten: "Ethnische Säuberungen" im modernen Europa*. Göttingen, Germany: Vandenhoeck & Ruprecht, 2011.

Ther, Philipp, and Ana Siljak, eds. *Redrawing Nations: Ethnic Cleansing in East-Central Europe, 1944–1948*. Lanham, MD: Rowman & Littlefield, 2001.

Thomas, Daniel C. *The Helsinki Effect: International Norms, Human Rights, and the Demise of Communism*. Princeton, NJ: Princeton University Press, 2001.

Thränhardt, Dietrich. "European Migrations from East to West: Present Patterns and Future Directions." *New Community* 22, no. 2 (April 1996): 227–242.

Thumann, Anja. "Aussiedlerzuwanderung im parlamentarischen Diskurs—eine Analyse der Bundestagsdebatten über die deutsch-polnischen Vereinbarungen vom 9. Oktober 1975." MA thesis, University of Osnabrück, 2015.

Tinguy, Anne De, and Magdalena Hadjiisky. "Repatriation of Persons Following the Political Changes in Central and Eastern Europe." Strasbourg, France: Council of Europe, 1997.

Torpey, John. *The Invention of the Passport: Surveillance, Citizenship and the State.* Cambridge: Cambridge University Press, 2000.

Toumarkine, Alexandre. *Les Migrations des Populations Musulmanes Balkaniques en Anatolie, 1876–1913.* Istanbul: Isis, 1995.

Troen, S. Ilan, and Klaus J. Bade, eds. *Returning Home: Immigration and Absorption into Their Homelands of Germans and Jews from the Former Soviet Union.* Beer Sheva, Israel: Hubert H. Humphrey Institute for Social Ecology, 1994.

Tsur, Yaron. "Carnival Fears: Moroccan Immigrants and the Ethnic Problem in the Young State of Israel." *Journal of Israeli History* 18, no. 1 (Spring 1997): 73–103.

———. "The Ethnic Problem in the Jewish Agency's Discussions at the End of the Mass Immigration Era." [In Hebrew.] *Israel* 2 (2002): 81–106.

Ulitskaya, Ludmila. *Daniel Stein, Interpreter: A Novel.* New York: Overlook, 2012.

Urban, Thomas. *Deutsche in Polen. Geschichte und Gegenwart einer Minderheit.* 3rd ed. Munich: Beck, 1994.

Veidlinger, Jeffrey. "One Doesn't Make Out Much with Furs in Palestine: The Migration of Jewish Displaced Persons, 1945–7." *East European Jewish Affairs* 44, no. 2–3 (2014): 241–252.

Vogel, Walter. *Westdeutschland 1945–1950. Der Aufbau von Verfassungs- und Verwaltungseinrichtungen über den Ländern der drei westlichen Besatzungszonen.* Vol. 3, *Einzelne Verwaltungszweige: Finanzen, Post und Verkehr, Arbeit und Soziales, Flüchtlinge, Suchdienst und Kriegsgefangene, Justiz, Inneres.* Boppard, Germany: Boldt, 1983.

Volkov, Shulamit. *Antisemitismus als kultureller Code: zehn Essays.* 2nd ed. Munich: Beck, 2000.

Voutira, Eftihia. *The "Right to Return" and the Meaning of "Home": A Post-Soviet Greek Diaspora Becoming European?* Münster, Germany: LIT, 2011.

Wahrhaftig, Zerach. *A Constitution for Israel—State and Religion.* [In Hebrew.] Jerusalem: Mesilot, 1988.

Wallem, Gesine. "Spätaussiedleraufnahme als Aushandlungsprozess: Die Interaktion zwischen staatlichen Verwaltungsakteuren und Migrant_innen aus ethnographischer Perspektive." In *"Jenseits der Volksgruppe": Neue Perspektiven auf die Russlanddeutschen zwischen Russland, Deutschland und Amerika,* edited by Victor Dönninghaus, Jannis Panagiotidis, and Hans-Christian Petersen, 137–154. Berlin: De Gruyter Oldenbourg, 2018.

Walser Smith, Helmut. *The Continuities of German History: Nation, Religion, and Race across the Long Nineteenth Century.* Cambridge: Cambridge University Press, 2008.

———. *German Nationalism and Religious Conflict: Culture, Ideology, Politics, 1870–1914.* Princeton, NJ: Princeton University Press, 1995.

———, ed. *Protestants, Catholics and Jews in Germany, 1800–1914.* Oxford: Berg, 2001.

Weber, Georg et al. *Emigration der Siebenbürger Sachsen: Studien zu Ost-West-Wanderungen im 20. Jahrhundert*. Wiesbaden, Germany: Westdeutscher Verlag, 2003.

Wehler, Hans-Ulrich. *Nationalitätenpolitik in Jugoslawien. Die deutsche Minderheit 1918–1978*. Göttingen, Germany: Vandenhoeck & Ruprecht, 1980.

Weindling, Paul. "'Belsenitis': Liberating Belsen, Its Hospitals, UNRRA, and Selection for Re-emigration, 1945–1948." *Science in Context* 19, no. 3 (September 2006): 401–418.

Weiss, Karin. "Between Integration and Exclusion: Jewish Immigrants from the Former Soviet Union in Germany." In *United and Divided: Germany since 1990*, edited by Mike Dennis and Eva Kolinsky, 176–194. New York: Berghahn Books, 2004.

Weiss, Meira. *The Chosen Body: The Politics of the Body in Israeli Society*. Stanford, CA: Stanford University Press, 2002.

Weiss, Yfaat. *A Confiscated Memory: Wadi Salib and Haifa's Lost Heritage*. New York: Columbia University Press, 2011.

———. "The Golem and Its Creator, or How the Jewish Nation-State Became Multiethnic." In Levy and Weiss, *Challenging Ethnic Citizenship*, 82–104.

Weitz, Eric D. "Self-Determination: How a German Enlightenment Idea Became the Slogan of National Liberation and a Human Right." *American Historical Review* 120 (April 2015): 462–496.

Welskopp, Thomas. "Die Dualität von Struktur und Handeln: Anthony Giddens' Strukturierungstheorie als 'praxeologischer' Ansatz in der Geschichtswissenschaft." In *Struktur und Ereignis*, edited by Andreas Suter and Manfred Hettling, 99–119. Göttingen, Germany: Vandenhoeck & Ruprecht, 2001.

Werber, Clemens, Günter Bode, and Werner Ehrenforth. *Bundesvertriebenengesetz: Gesetz über die Angelegenheiten der Vertriebenen und Flüchtlinge. Textausgabe mit erläuternden Beiträgen unter besonderer Berücksichtigung der Flüchtlingssiedlung, der steuerlichen Bestimmungen und der Schuldenregelung*. Stuttgart: Kohlhammer, 1953.

———. *Bundesvertriebenengesetz: Gesetz über die Angelegenheiten der Vertriebenen und Flüchtlinge. Mit Nebengesetzen und Durchführungsbestimmungen*. Stuttgart: Kohlhammer, 1954.

Wolf, Gerhard. "Deutsche Volksliste." In *Handbuch der völkischen Wissenschaften*, edited by Ingo Haar and Michael Fahlbusch, 129–135. Munich: K. G. Saur, 2008.

———. *Ideologie und Herrschaftsrationalität: Nationalsozialistische Germanisierungspolitik in Polen*. Hamburg: Hamburger Edition, 2012.

Wolff, Frank. *Die Mauergesellschaft: Kalter Krieg, Menschenrechte und die deutsch-deutsche Migration 1961–1989*. Berlin: Suhrkamp, 2019.

Wörsdörfer, Rolf. "Transnationale Aspekte italienischer und deutscher Besatzungsherrschaft in Slowenien 1941–1945." In *Die "Achse" im Krieg: Politik, Ideologie und Kriegführung 1939–1945*, edited by Lutz Klinkhammer, Amedeo Osti Guerrazzi, and Thomas Schlemmer, 340–367. Paderborn, Germany: Schöningh, 2010.

Zahra, Tara. *The Great Departure: Mass Migration from Eastern Europe and the Making of the Free World*. New York: W. W. Norton, 2016.

———. "Imagined Non-Communities: National Indifference as a Category of Analysis." *Slavic Review* 69, no. 1 (Spring 2010): 93–119.

———. *Kidnapped Souls: National Indifference and the Battle for Children in the Bohemian Lands, 1900–1948*. Ithaca, NY: Cornell University Press, 2008.

———. *The Lost Children: Reconstructing Europe's Families after World War II*. Cambridge, MA: Harvard University Press, 2011.

Zameret, Zvi, and Hanna Yablonka, eds. *The Third Decade, 5728–5738 [1968–1978]*. Jerusalem: Yad Ben-Zvi, 2008.

Zolberg, Aristide. *A Nation by Design: Immigration Policy in the Fashioning of America*. Cambridge, MA: Harvard University Press, 2006.

INDEX

Pages in italics signify photos.

JANNIS PANAGIOTIDIS is Junior Professor of Migration and Integration of Russian Germans at the Osnabrück University Institute for Migration Research and Intercultural Studies (IMIS). He is editor (with Victor Dönninghaus and Hans-Christian Petersen) of *"Jenseits der Volksgruppe": Neue Perspektiven auf die Russlanddeutschen zwischen Russland, Deutschland und Amerika.*

www.ingramcontent.com/pod-product-compliance
Lightning Source LLC
Chambersburg PA
CBHW032341280326
41935CB00008B/413

* 9 7 8 0 2 5 3 0 4 3 6 2 7 *